THE DYNAMICS OF RELIGIOUS REFORM IN NORTHERN EUROPE, 1780-1920
THE CHURCHES

In memory of Nigel Yates

THE DYNAMICS OF RELIGIOUS REFORM IN CHURCH, STATE AND SOCIETY
IN NORTHERN EUROPE, 1780-1920

Editors-in-chief: Joris van Eijnatten and Nigel Yates †

Before the last quarter of the eighteenth century there was a generally clear and remarkably uniform pattern of church-state relationships across Europe, which had emerged from the religious conflicts of the sixteenth and seventeenth centuries. In the course of the 'long' nineteenth century this firm alliance between political and religious establishments broke down all over Europe. A substantial degree of religious pluralism developed everywhere, requiring church and state to accommodate change. Defining religious reform as 'the conscious pursuit of renewal with the aim of adapting organised religion to the changing relations between church, state and society', this series examines the reforms initiated by the organised religions of Northern Europe between c.1780 and c.1920. There has been an assumption that it was the change in the church-state relationship that was largely responsible for the ecclesiastical reform movement of the nineteenth century, and that it was the state that was the principal agent of change, with the national churches seen as resisting changes that had to be forced upon them. Recent research across Europe has shown that in some parts of Europe ecclesiastical reform was initiated by the churches; and that there were times and places when it was the state rather than the church that was hostile to alterations in the status quo. This series explores this process of change from different angles, looking particularly at its impact on the question of religious reform, in England, Ireland, Scotland, Wales, Belgium, the Netherlands, Germany, Denmark, Sweden and Norway.

Board members: Jan De Maeyer (KADOC-K.U.Leuven), Joris van Eijnatten (Utrecht University), Andreas Gestrich (German Historical Institute, London), Anders Jarlert (Lund University), James Kennedy (University of Amsterdam), Liselotte Malmgart (Aarhus University), Peter Jan Margry (Meertens Institute Amsterdam), Keith Robbins (Emeritus Vice-Chancellor, University of Wales, Lampeter), Nigel Yates† (University of Wales, Lampeter), Paula Yates (University of Wales, Trinity St David).

Financial assistance for the research programme on 'The Dynamics of Religious Reform in Northern Europe, 1780-1920' is gratefully acknowledged from the Netherlands Organisation for Scientific Research (NWO), University of Wales, Trinity St David (formerly University of Wales, Lampeter) and the Documentation and Research Centre for Religion, Culture and Society at K.U.Leuven (KADOC).

THE DYNAMICS OF RELIGIOUS REFORM IN NORTHERN EUROPE
|| 1780-1920

LEUVEN UNIVERSITY PRESS

EDITED BY JORIS VAN EIJNATTEN & PAULA YATES

THE
CHURCHES

The series 'The Dynamics of Religious Reform in Northern Europe, 1780-1920' is a sub-series of the 'KADOC Studies on Religion, Culture and Society', published under the supervision of the KADOC Editorial Board:

Urs Altermatt, *Université de Fribourg*
Jan Art, *Universiteit Gent*
Jaak Billiet, *Katholieke Universiteit Leuven*
Jan De Maeyer, *Katholieke Universiteit Leuven - KADOC*
Jean-Dominique Durand, *Université Lyon 3*
Emmanuel Gerard, *Katholieke Universiteit Leuven - KADOC*
James C. Kennedy, *Universiteit van Amsterdam*
Mathijs Lamberigts, *Katholieke Universiteit Leuven*
Emiel Lamberts, *Katholieke Universiteit Leuven*
Jean-Michel Leniaud, *École pratique des hautes études, Sorbonne, Paris*
Patrick Pasture, *Katholieke Universiteit Leuven*
Andrew Saint, *University of Cambridge*
Liliane Voyé, *Université Catholique de Louvain*

© 2010
Leuven University Press / Presses universitaires de Louvain / Universitaire Pers Leuven
Minderbroedersstraat 4 bus 5602, B-3000 Leuven (Belgium)

All rights reserved. Except in those cases expressly determined by law, no part of this publication may be multiplied, saved in an automated data file or made public in any way whatsoever without the express prior written consent of the publishers.

ISBN 978 90 5867 826 3
D/2010/1869/33
NUR: 694

Contents

Introduction — 7
Joris van Eijnatten & Paula Yates

Bibliography — 27

The United Kingdom of Great Britain & Ireland — 29

Internal Church Reform 1780-1850. Establishment under Fire — 31
Nigel Yates †

The Oxford Movement and the Legacy of Anglican Evangelicalism — 53
Peter Nockles

Internal Church Reform 1850-1920. An Age of Innovation in Ecclesiastical Reform — 67
Frances Knight

Bibliography — 95

The Low Countries — 99

Church Reform and Modernity in Belgium — 101
Jan Art, Jan De Maeyer, Ward De Pril & Leo Kenis

Contested Unity. Church, Nation and Reform in the Netherlands — 123
Joris van Eijnatten

Bibliography — 153

Germany 157

Internal Church Reform in Catholic Germany 159
Claus Arnold

The Protestant Churches in Germany and Ecclesiastical Reform 185
Klaus Fitschen

Bibliography 215

The Nordic Countries 227

Church, State and Reform in Denmark 229
Jes Fabricius Møller

Self-Reform and Swedish Christianity 247
Erik Sidenvall

The Limits of Ecclesiastical Reform in Norway 261
Øyvind Norderval, Dag Thorkildsen & Hallgeir Elstad

Bibliography 277

Index 280

Map of Northern Europe c.1870 285

Authors 286

Colophon 288

Introduction

Joris van Eijnatten & Paula Yates

"Reform is the conscious pursuit of renewal with the aim of adapting organised religion to the changing relations between church, state and society." The definition of reform used by this series seems quite straightforward, and all contributors to this volume have judged it to be relevant to the various national contexts they have examined. But every age is, of course, an age of reform. The conscious pursuit of change is not limited to Norway or Prussia or Ireland, nor did it occur only between 1780 and 1920. Clearly, this volume is not the first to apply the concept of 'reform' to religious history, let alone history in general. Judging only by the Anglophone literature, however, it would seem that 'reform', as both idea and practice, applies to some ages more than others. Apparently, popular 'ages of reform' were the sixteenth, eighteenth and nineteenth centuries. The reason why is fairly obvious, since these are, respectively, the ages of Reformation, Enlightenment, and constitutional change.[1] On the other hand, the fact that such periods of reform are demarcated in various ways demonstrates the universality of the phenomenon. Ages of religious reform in some cases span the fifteenth and seventeenth centuries, in others the thirteenth and sixteenth.[2] The 'long' nineteenth century fares no better. If we look only at the British case, some would have the age of reform begin in 1780 and end in 1850, while others suggest 1850-1890.[3] Frances Knight in her contribution to this volume offers a brief account of the prominence in British history writing of the concept of 'reform', arguing that it should be extended to the

---

[1] Some examples are Jensen, *Reformation Europe*; Beales, *Enlightenment and Reform in Eighteenth-Century Europe*; Turner, *British Politics in an Age of Reform*.
[2] Louthan, *Conciliation and Confession*; Ozment, *The Age of Reform*.
[3] Contrast Rich, *The Age of Nationalism and Reform 1850-1890* with Burns and Innes, eds., *Rethinking the Age of Reform: Britain 1780-1850*.

period after 1850, despite the fact that the later period has gone down in the annals as an 'age of religious decline'. She identifies the period as one of "extraordinary energy and innovation", setting the stage for religion in its modern context.

Is reform, then, distinctive for religious life during the 'long' century between 1780 and 1920? As far as 'internal church reform' is concerned, the pursuit of reform within the church, by the church and for the church, which is the subject of this volume, the answer is, yes. Two aspects stand out. Firstly, as Part I in this series shows, the legal and constitutional changes in the period 1780-1920 had a profound effect on religious organisations. The latter were themselves sometimes involved in the process that led to new laws and regulations being imposed specifically on the churches themselves (such as church constitutions) or, more generally, on society at large (such as freedom of worship). But whether or not they were implicated in government-sponsored reforms 'from without', they were in all cases bound to respond to the directives issued by the state, and sometimes did so in ways the state had not anticipated. Secondly, churches and religious organisations had their own dynamics of reform, spilling over from the eighteenth century into the nineteenth. Churches naturally responded to their environment, which changed rapidly: in many regions an older agricultural system based on subsistence broke up, the market economy developed everywhere, the French Revolution and the Napoleonic era provoked national crises all over Europe, Enlightenment and liberalism called for freedom and equality, technological change offered hitherto undreamt-of opportunities for mobility and contact, and so on. Interestingly, between 1780 and 1920 the term reform was often associated with such concepts as 'revival', 'renaissance' and even 'restoration'.

It is important to understand the complex meanings these words could take on. The religiously-minded frequently regarded reform as rebirth, a return to a period before their world was corrupted by Protestantism, Enlightenment, Pietism, ultramontanism or simply 'modernity' - but they saw rebirth as a renewal, which therefore involved 'reform' pursued consciously. For Protestants, reform more often than not suggested a return to the Reformation, that is, a revival of the 'true' spirit of Christendom. For Catholics the term 'reform' was no less filled with historical associations, since the Roman Catholic Church had a lengthy tradition of 'internal' reform, often prompted from below by religious orders; the long nineteenth century was a time in which these traditions were invented or reinvented. In the (Anglican)[4] Oxford Movement, reform at times even signified a thorough reformation, if not outright rejection, of the Reformation itself. 'Reform' may be an English word but there is no indication that the concept it implies is applicable only to Britain. Dutch Protestants were not unique in attributing different meanings and values to words like *hervorming* ('reform' or 'reformation') and *gereformeerd* ('reformed'). Such terms often simultaneously implied institutional, administrative, intellectual, and, last but not least, religious change. This series builds

---

[4] 'Anglican' in this case refers to the established Church of England, Wales and Ireland but its meaning also includes reference to any of the Episcopal churches worldwide which belong to the Anglican communion.

Introduction

on the insight that the 'long nineteenth century as an age of religious reform' is a proposition valid for Northern Europe.[5]

Internal church reform refers to reforms engendered within churches and other organisations or movements that saw 'religion' as their core business. Internal reform was inspired in part by eighteenth-century ideas on, and blueprints for, reform, whether 'Enlightened' or not. Around 1780, responding to the changes in politics and society brought on by a rapidly declining *ancien régime*, those who had long wanted to initiate reforms were able finally to get down to practicalities. Meanwhile, as we suggested above, the legal and constitutional reforms instigated or enforced by the state allowed (or provoked) churches and religious organisations to further develop reformist programmes. By 1920, many such programmes had been realised. This is not to say that churches stopped reforming. Far from it: but the main issues surrounding church-state relations had now been settled and religious organisations enjoyed greater autonomy than before, if not *de jure* than certainly *de facto*. Attempting to bind large parts of the population to their ideals (reform in the long nineteenth century was pursued partly through the unprecedented mobilisation of believers), they felt they had successfully absorbed the impact of change and weathered the storm of doubt. The effects of the First World War and the rise of the welfare state posed altogether different challenges.

Internal church reform is a relevant topic even in those countries where the church was bound closely to the state. Denmark is a case in point. 'The parish priest as civil servant' is a well-known theme in Danish church history. Could reforms originating at grassroots level really be expected in a nation where 'the church's project' was always 'the state's project', where clergymen were local representatives of state power as well as spiritual advisors?[6] Under such circumstances, the question which of the two - the church or the state - was responsible for which reforms may well be the wrong one to ask. The presence at the local level of a clergy actively concerned with welfare and education probably did much to keep the population content and mediate state power through a decentralised society. In return, the church enjoyed the administrative, financial and moral support of the state. Yet even in Denmark and other Lutheran societies in which church and state were two sides of the coin, or, for that matter, in the Church of England, reform 'from below' occurred, with or without the retrospective blessings of the state.

The extent to which church and state mutually influenced each other in matters concerning ecclesiastical reform, and how and why they did so, are questions that have never been examined from a comparative perspective. This brings us to the general instructions with which the contributors to this volume went to work. They were asked to focus on churches and semi-independent or independent organisations in which leaders, both clerical and lay, on various levels, experimented with institutional

---

[5] See, for example, Saunders, *Russia in the Age of Reaction and Reform*.

[6] Jespersen, *History of Denmark*, 91-96.

and intellectual reform, in order to ensure the continuity of their tradition in a rapidly changing world. The contributors collaborating on the volume were requested to test the hypothesis that developments in church-state relationships in Northern Europe between 1780 and 1920 had a substantial impact on reformist ideas, projects and movements within the churches; and, conversely, that the dynamics of internal ecclesiastical reform prompted the state to react in various ways, through direct intervention or by adapting its policies and/or promulgating laws. The authors were specifically asked to address the following five themes:
1. Church organisation (including administrative and financial reform, church orders, the restoration of the Roman Catholic organisation wherever it was lacking, and monastic orders).
2. The education and professionalization of the clergy and other issues concerning pastoral leadership.
3. Separatism and reunion.
4. Theology and doctrine.
5. Mission and outreach, including such topics as lay-led organisations, 'secularisation', and use of media.

Inevitably, the themes were discussed differently, and to different degrees, by the various authors. It is apparent that some themes are more relevant to some national contexts than to others, while not all countries have produced equal amounts of research on each of the various themes. Belgium is in many ways an interesting case, since its Catholicism was, as it were, more 'Romance' than other brands, and therefore unique among the countries discussed here and literally beyond compare; on the other hand, as Keith Robbins' introduction to Part I has made clear, it is part and parcel of Northern Europe in general and the Low Countries in particular. Because the authors were free to structure their accounts as they saw fit, the chapters and subchapters vary in style and approach. Some authors preferred to cover a single confession (Roman Catholicism in Germany, for example), or a specific period (say, the British Isles between 1780 and 1850). Some chapters are thematic, some chronological, some a combination of both. But in spite of these differences, this volume shows how processes of church reform were actively pursued, in one way or another by the churches in each country.

All texts were written in, or translated into, English. However, if words are relatively easy to translate, this does not apply to the layers of meanings that were (and in many cases still are) attached to many of those words. Equally, some English words are not necessarily understood by those who are able to read English but do so from different backgrounds and within different contexts. Take, for example, the concept of a 'people residing within a certain state and sharing a common identity', which is as relevant a concept to internal church reform as it is to legal, liturgical or educational reform. In the long nineteenth century, the most relevant word signifying that concept was 'nation'. But here the problems begin, because other languages may use linguistically related or unrelated words which, in either case may have similar or significantly different connotations. In the countries under consideration here, nation occurs as *natie* and *Nation* but also as *Volk*, *volk* and *folk*. For nineteenth-century men and women, of course, these and other words referring to the people had complex meanings. 'Nation' is a relatively simple example; difficulties multiply if we look at derivatives and combinations. The Danish *folkelig* may be literally translated as 'popular' (though even that word has significantly changed its meaning in modern English), but its many primary and secondary resonances are lost on non-Danish ears. Thus, the revivalist and educationist Grundtvig (on whom more below) coined the term *folklighed*, which in Denmark would have also included in its meaning "popular democracy, folksiness, simplicity, unassuming warmth and ease and so on!"[7] The term seems to border on the Dutch notion of *gezelligheid*, which means something like sociability combined with cosiness. But *gezelligheid* lacks the 'national' connotation implied in the root *folk*. Similarly, *Volkskirche* in German corresponds more or less with *Folkekirke* in Danish and *volkskerk* in Dutch. None of these are exact synonyms of 'popular church' or 'national church' in English. In Britain it would have been more common to simply use the names 'Church of England' or 'Church of Scotland', taking for granted the national, popular, historical and traditional meanings they imply.

For this reason the original names of historical institutions, groups, movements, organisations or other phenomena have been used in the various chapters. A few more examples will show why this is useful and in some cases necessary. What the British recognised as 'awakening' or 'revival' was called *Erweckung* in Germany, *vækkelse* in Denmark, *väckelse* in Sweden, and *opwekking* in the Netherlands. This is pretty straightforward. But what to do with 'Evangelicals', or the now less widely used 'Puritans', in Britain? To avoid a Babel of confusion, this volume accepts that these words in many cases correspond to varieties of 'Pietists' on the continent. The assumption here is that 'Pietism' refers to those who stressed 'heart-felt' religion and who valued a fully internalised faith, and acted accordingly by associating with fellow believers, spurning the more formal institutional structures, and so on. The German term *Pietismus* is an established expression, and the same applies to its Scandinavian versions. In Dutch, however, the word *pietisme* until a few decades ago referred exclusively to the Lutheran phenomenon, whether German or Scandinavian. Many nineteenth-century Dutch Reformed preferred the word *gereformeerd*, which to them signified the true orthodoxy that took seriously its tradition (which reached back to the Synod of Dordt and beyond that to the Reformation) and its mission (to reform or, in more radical cases, re-establish what was seen, unhistorically, as the 'national' church). The 'proper' Dutch word for Pietism, in so far as there is one, is *bevindelijk gereformeerd*, meaning those orthodox Calvinists who stress the experience of the heart (*bevindelijk* means 'experiential'). But then again, experiential faith was valued by continental Pietists and Evangelicals alike, even though the former were predominantly Lutheran by confession (even if Moravians claimed to be interconfessional) and the latter

---

[7] Jespersen, *History of Denmark*, 108.

stood in the Reformed tradition but could be either Arminian (Wesleyan Methodists in England and Ireland) or Calvinist (Calvinistic Methodists in Wales).

In Denmark, the term *statskirken* only began to be used after 1830; in the Netherlands, the equivalent, *staatskerk*, was not used at all. In Norway, the Enlightened ideal of the pastor was the *folkelærer* or 'folk teacher'. Among Dutch Protestants, the term *leraar* (literally, 'teacher') had gained currency even before the Enlightenment, as a synonym for the *dominee* ('minister') or *predikant* ('preacher'). Similar problems concerning meanings arise in the context of church administration. In Calvinist churches with a Presbyterian government, the administrative unit at the parish level was the consistory, which in the Netherlands would be called the *kerkenraad* (literally, church council) and in Scotland the 'session'. At the regional level, Dutch Calvinists had a *classis*; at the provincial or national, a synod. The Danish *sognekommune*, established by law in 1841, is practically untranslatable; it means something like 'parish municipality', i.e. a unit of local administration coinciding with a parish.

The concept of home mission is another example. In the British context, home mission is usually contrasted with foreign mission. It is a Protestant term that refers to initiatives to spread the Gospel domestically rather than abroad. Outreach at home is what the various 'home missionary' societies were all about. However, home mission may be similar but it is not identical to the German *Innere Mission*, the Danish *indre mission* or the Norwegian *indremisjonen*, all of which could be translated as 'inner mission'. In Germany *Innere Mission* seems to have been strongly orientated towards solving the 'social question', one of the central issues of the nineteenth century, a problem therefore which all churches needed to deal with (and which will be treated at greater length in a later volume). But the Danish variety of *indre mission* was, quite specifically, a Pietist revival movement, formally established in 1853 as a lay-led enclave within the Lutheran state church. In 1861, the *indre mission* was clericalized, as it were, when the clergyman Vilhelm Beck took control. Since then the movement has to all intents and purposes acted as a reformist lobby group within the established church aiming to revive the spirit and doctrines of 'true', primeval Lutheranism. Clearly, this is not quite the same as 'home mission' in Britain, although, again, there are obvious resemblances.

One last issue should be mentioned by way of introduction. This is the interesting fact that most authors have identified a watershed at or about the year 1850. This means that the 140 years that make up the long nineteenth century show a clear division into two halves of equal length. This elegant partition may seem a little neat but it was not one that was purposely sought after. However, the central position of 1850 (or rather, in most cases, the 1840s, culminating in 1848) is probably due to its traditional stature as the year in which the 'age of revolutions' was brought to a close. The prominence of 1850 seems to suggest that political events were strongly influential in some aspects of internal church reform. Freedom of association was, after all, in many cases made possible by the constitutional reforms that led up to, or took place in, 1848. In some countries, of course, that momentous year was just a blip on the screen of national history. The structure of the Danish and Norwegian state churches only began to be

Introduction

reformed around 1920. In England and Wales there was a watershed but it was marked more by the religious census of 1851 than by political events. This revealed not only that nonconformity was considerable stronger in relation to the established church than anyone, including the nonconformists, had suspected, but also that about half the population attended no place of worship at all. The political and denominational responses to this revelation contributed significantly to developments in the second half of the century.

This second section of the introduction offers a summary of some of the main developments as they have been sketched out in the chapters of this volume. Four themes will be addressed: the role of the laity in church reform, the development of organisations as a symptom of reform, the improvement of the clergy, and the adaptation of theology to the new world that emerged during the long nineteenth century.

Laity

Lay leadership was common in many of the non-established churches, including, in some cases, leadership by women as well as men. By contrast, the institutional influence of 'ordinary' laymen in most established churches was limited at the beginning of our period but had become substantially larger at the end - albeit in many different ways. Presbyterian churches are an interesting case in this respect because they involve lay influence practically by definition. In Scotland and the Netherlands laymen had always participated fully at the level of the consistory (the Scottish 'session'). On the other hand, the consistories had more often than not been dominated by the wealthy and the powerful. The first half of the nineteenth century was no different: in both Scotland and the Netherlands, the local elite were long dominant among the laity. But even then change loomed on the horizon. In Scotland congregations could be sufficiently independent to object to the landowners' choice of minister, in some cases to the point of schism. Interestingly, but not surprisingly, there could be strong resistance to ecclesiastical reform within the church itself. The parish clergy in Germany did not necessarily welcome the prospect of transferring control over local church affairs to a council of elders. However, the real modernisation of the Presbyterian system occurred in the second half of the nineteenth century, step by step in Germany after 1850 (previous attempts in the 1840s had failed) and likewise in the Netherlands after 1867. In Scotland, too, changes occurred gradually as the middle classes began to dominate congregations. Discussions on elective congregations had by then been initiated elsewhere, albeit in different degrees. In Norway, for instance, the debate had begun in the 1850s, as it had in Germany and the Netherlands. In the Norwegian case, questions concerning voting rights were not easily resolved. Should only confirmed believers be allowed to elect parish councils? Or should the right to vote be accorded to all church members? In the end, there was much debate and little reform; not until 1920 was a more democratic system introduced in the Norwegian church.

The increase, perhaps not so much of lay participation but of lay influence, was very much the result of those two currents traditionally labelled 'Enlightenment' and 'Pietism'. The apparent contrast between Enlightenment and revival has been coloured by the rise, in the nineteenth century, of various kinds of orthodoxies (conservative as well as revivalist) and secularisms (both liberal and ant-clerical). But the two currents had much in common. The practical measures proposed by those who adhered to the so-called 'moderate' Enlightenment (a version of Enlightenment, occurring in most countries considered in this volume, that sought to reform rather than abolish religion), regardless of whether they advocated the abolition of slavery or the adaptation of school curricula, were often warmly applauded by revivalists. If the leaders of Pietism and Enlightenment (an English term coined in the middle of the nineteenth century, which contrasts with the eighteenth-century German term *Aufklärung*) differed on pastoral or doctrinal matters, they also had much in common. There is no need to define either phenomenon here. Few scholars would agree on a definition but more importantly, it is not essential to strictly demarcate the boundaries of such notoriously slippery concepts. The important point here is that both Enlightenment and Pietism attached more significance to 'the individual' than mainstream Christianity had done under the *ancien régime*. Since the Reformation (if not earlier), the established churches of Northern Europe had privileged communal confessions over individual insights, public organisations over private associations, and clergymen over laypeople. The Enlightenment now empowered individuals by stressing reason, freedom and equality; Pietism did the same by calling attention to heartfelt beliefs and literal readings of orthodox Bible translations (which were idiosyncratic in the sense that they appealed to a measure of literalism avoided by the mainstream churches). The two currents differed in many respects but they shared an emphasis on the freedom of individual men (and not infrequently women) to judge for themselves. As Jes Fabricius Møller observes, Pietist churches were really very modern: they were communities of choice rather than tradition.

Stressing the fathomless abyss separating the converted from the unconverted, the elect from the reprobate, the saved from the unsaved, the awakened from the dead, Pietists resisted the power of established secular and religious authorities. They undermined the official clergy's monopoly on preaching and they assembled congregations outside the church. Their message was not one any church that valued its relationship with the state, or saw itself as the true guardian of the nation's ethos, was likely to welcome. In some cases the worst fears of the established clergy were realised, for example during the riots in northern Norway in 1847, the unintended result of the Laestadius movement's activities, as described in this volume by Øyvind Norderval, Dag Thorkildsen and Hallgeir Elstad. The Protestant established churches, most of which were dominated by a liberal clergy who subscribed to a moderate Enlightenment, largely opposed the reformist impulse stemming from Pietism and sought the assistance of the state. In the Netherlands in the 1830s, the state used fines and imprisonment to suppress the grass-roots call for religious change. In 1834, the German Old Lutherans, who were orthodox dissenters rather than Pietists in any stricter sense (this again, shows the limitations of words like 'Pietism') were similarly forbidden to worship outside their homes, under penalty of a fine or imprisonment.

Pietist movements were not infrequently led by educated men (Johann Hinrich Wichern in Germany, John Wesley and William Wilberforce in England and Wales, Thomas Chalmers in Scotland, N.F.S. Grundtvig in Denmark, Hendrik de Cock in the Netherlands, Gisle Johnson and Wilhelm Wexels in Norway, are examples). On the other hand, leaders with charisma could find a following even without either education or wealth. Hans Nielsen Hauge in Norway was a farmer, Niels Johansen in Denmark a weaver. Though many of its leaders were educated, it seems clear that revivalism, because of its down to earth language and accessible ideas, appealed also to the poor and uneducated. In some cases differences of language between classes or national groups reinforced this appeal. This was the case in Wales, where the Anglicised clergy of the established church often spoke a different form of Welsh from their congregations or occasionally spoke no Welsh at all. In Norway, Hauge's brand of Pietism made headway particularly among farmers, that of Laestadius mostly among the poverty-stricken Sámi population. In England and Wales, Primitive Methodism retained both its working class congregations and its revivalist ethos, while other nonconformist groups were becoming increasingly middle class and sober. In Germany, too, the Old Lutherans and the *Evangelischer Brüderverein* attracted a mixed following. Pietism was a banner under which believers were able to unite, inside and outside the church. However, the aim of practically all Pietists was not to reorganise the church but to organise individual faith. Large-scale mobilisation took place only in the second half of the period and, indeed, was only possible then. Mobilisation required religious liberties, print technologies and an electorate. These elements appeared only after approximately 1850. From the point of view of the state, mobilisation sometimes occurred in spite of measures to prevent it, as in the case of the *Kulturkampf*. In those 'culture wars', Catholics had been relegated to a second-rate position but gained political clout, as they did in the Netherlands. In the latter country the increase in the number of voters led also to the political as well as the ecclesiastical mobilisation of Protestants. As Joris van Eijnatten shows in his contribution, the emergence of Reformed orthodoxy within the 'national' churches was quite spectacular. A similar point is made by Erik Sidenvall in his contribution on Sweden, where during the 1870s a low-church traditionalist movement led by Paul Petter Waldenström succeeded in gaining ground.

Organisation

Church reforms were often the unavoidable result of mundane developments, including population growth, industrial and commercial expansion, urbanisation, and so on - all of which progressed very unevenly in different countries, and in different parts of these countries. A prosaic statistical fact such as the general rise in population during the long nineteenth century often meant a nightmare to church administrators, simply because the increase in souls was not everywhere accompanied by a concomitant increase in pastors. But ideas were important in setting the reformist agenda and some clerical leaders had a very clear picture of what needed to be done. In Ireland, Wales and England, as Nigel Yates suggests, church reform was in part a practical response to regional conditions, with bishops taking the initiative, independently but following the best practices of their colleagues. Within the dioceses, reformist measures reflected local needs, of which the bishop presumably was the best judge. But a general pattern emerges: diocesan reform between 1780 and 1850 emphasised such things as clerical residence, the clergy's exemplary conduct, and the necessity to preach and catechise. At the same time, a hierarchical diocesan administration ensured greater efficiency. In England rural deans, which had survived in Wales, were revived in the 1820s and 1830s, as an important administrative layer under the archdeacons.

Elsewhere, different methods were used to implement reforms. The popularity of revivalist movements in Germany and the Nordic nations had much to do with frictions between, on the one hand, the rationalising reforms imposed from above by secular and ecclesiastical authorities (whether separately or in conjunction), and, on the other, religious idealists concerned about the deplorable spiritual plight of local congregations (often including that of the clergy). But this did not mean that their leaders were never interested in institutional reform. Evangelicals in the (established) Church of Scotland pressured the government to do something about the lack of adequate church buildings. They waged battles against private patronage, which could result in unwanted clergymen being thrust upon a parish. The Norwegian Pietist Hauge combined a revivalist agenda with Enlightenment ideas on education and agriculture. Sometimes reforms were initiated as a response by the moderates to what might have been seen as the threat of Pietism. The increasing popularity of psalmody and hymn singing in the Anglican Church was at least partly driven by a recognition that services were dull by comparison with nonconformist groups.

For Protestants, regardless of whether they remained inside, or separated from, the established churches, private or semi-private reformist associations provided the logical environment in which to pursue reform. These organisations offered opportunities to both laymen and clergy seeking opportunities and means which the mainstream churches simply were not able, or did not wish to, afford. The Church of England already had a Society for the Promotion of Christian Knowledge, founded in 1698, and a Society for the Propagation of the Gospel in Foreign Parts, established in 1701. Like the older societies, the new associations spawned between about 1790 and 1820 were largely independent from direct government influence and authority but they were more likely to have strong regional branches where magistrates and local elites provided the main leadership. They proliferated everywhere. In Britain there was a Society for Distributing Religious Tracts (1782), a London Abolition Society (1787), a Church Missionary Society (1799), a British and Foreign Bible Society (1804), and a Wesleyan Methodist Missionary Society (1814). Most of these societies were open to various persuasions, as long as they were Protestant and not too liberal, and most were based on the collaboration of laymen and clergy. In Ireland, for example, Anglicans and Presbyterians worked together in such societies as the Ulster Evangelical Society (1798) and the Hibernian Church Missionary Society (1814). However, and this is the point we want to make in presenting the reader with this list of assorted religious associations: such organisations were not limited to Britain. Idealists on the continent did frequently look upon the British societies as the trendsetters. The *Nederlandsch Zendelinggenootschap* (1798) found a role model in the London Missionary Society (1795), while the British and Foreign Bible Society inspired the *Danske Bibelselskab* (1821).

Religious societies arose everywhere, whether initiated from within or from outside the churches, and after 1850 they continued to flower. Anglican societies proliferated, such as the Church of England Men's Society and the Mothers' Union. By the last quarter of the nineteenth century and the beginning of the twentieth, these societies mostly had thriving parochial units, helping to maintain the worshipping community as well as providing an opportunity for outreach. Klaus Fitschen describes, in his contribution to this volume, what might be called a veritable 'association boom' that occurred in Protestant Germany, especially, though not exclusively, in the latter half of the long nineteenth century. The advent of the rotary press and the ability to mass produce brochures and bibles increased the need for extra-ecclesiastical organisations that combined efficiency with enthusiasm and energy. The Norwegian *Lutherstiftelsen* (1868), which later became the *Norske Lutherske Indremisjonsselskap* (1891), invested heavily in tract distributors and lay preachers. In England the Salvation Army was evangelising with its most famous publication *The War Cry*, from December 1879. All organisations, whether intra- or extra-ecclesial, profited from the possibility to produce publications in large quantities and sell them cheaply. The long nineteenth century was very much an age of periodicals and brochures, with all the opportunities for reform which such media afforded.

In Roman Catholic quarters, 'worldly' (in the sense of non-ecclesiastical) societies and associations were less common, since confraternities and religious orders fulfilled a similar need. The Napoleonic period was a major setback in this respect: many if not most monastic communities were closed in Germany and Belgium, and also in the Netherlands. In the course of the period, however, religious orders revived, intellectually as well as in practice. Belgium is a case in point: after 1830, the 'unholy alliance' with the Northern Netherlands ended, orders and congregations were re-established, the greater majority active rather than contemplative, and often with the objective of alleviating social needs. Monastic communities even began to be established within the Church of England, although the major developments in religious orders took place within the Catholic Church. In Britain alone twenty seven Roman Catholic monastic foundations for women and thirteen for men were founded between 1850 and 1920. By the end of the period, religious orders were again strongly present in and around the church, in some cases (such as the Netherlands) more so than at the beginning. Moreover, even in the Catholic world associations had grown rapidly in number and importance after about 1880, setting the stage, in Germany, Belgium and the Netherlands, for the 'pillarised' society that flourished after the First World War.[8]

---

[8] The best comparative treatment is still McLeod, *Religion and the People of Western Europe.*

It is illuminating to contrast piecemeal ecclesiastical reformism, perhaps most pronounced in England, Wales and Ireland, as a result of that peculiarly British constellation of church and state, with state interventionism in Protestant Germany. Here whole churches and confessions (that is, Lutherans and Reformed) were pressured to unite after 1817. That issue is treated at greater length in Part I and need not be discussed here; we are more concerned with the internal effects of such processes within the churches. Not surprisingly, there was much resistance in some quarters to a process that could well be seen as deforming rather than reforming age-old practices and customs. Such dissatisfied groups could take recourse to one rather drastic method of ensuring spiritual and administrative reform within the church: schism. When reformist arguments had fallen on barren ground, separation from the established church seemed to be the only option left. Often actual separation was unsought. Reform movements pursued one of two strategies: either they reorganised themselves within the church, as did the Methodists originally and many Pietists in Germany and the Nordic countries; or they reorganised themselves outside the church, claiming that they, in fact, represented the 'true' church. The effects were similar. Wesleyan Methodists in England went their own way after the 1790s; Calvinistic Methodists in Wales ordained their first ministers in 1811 and adopted a formal constitution in 1823. As with Methodism the Swedish Mission Covenant (1878) did not actively seek separation from the Swedish Church but finally found it inevitable.

Separation was epidemic among Presbyterians and Evangelicals. In Britain before 1850, Welsh and English Methodism and Scottish Presbyterianism produced a confusion of minor independent ('dissenting') churches and communities, based on local characteristics (the presence of a charismatic leader, for instance) or doctrinal differences, but showing a high degree of similarity in other respects. After 1850, however, both Methodist and Presbyterian churches began to stress reunion rather than separation (although, as a rule, every reunion left a surviving rump which distrusted its basis). The two largest independent churches in Scotland were the Free Church of Scotland (1843) and the United Presbyterian Church (1847), which came together in 1900 to form the United Free Church of Scotland. The call for reunion eventually resulted in a united Church of Scotland in 1929. In Methodism a similar process occurred, with various churches uniting between 1863 and 1907, ultimately bringing about the Methodist Church in 1932. In each case, small conservative fractions continued independently. Such developments took place also in the Netherlands, in Protestant Germany, and in the Scandinavian countries.

Pietism did not necessarily lead to separation between mainstream churches and revivalist *ecclesiolae*. In Denmark, Sweden and Norway the old Lutheran church accommodated Pietist currents, as did the Protestant churches in the German states - the *Evangelische Brüdergemeinde Korntal* was specifically founded in 1819 with the blessing of the king to control unrest. Danish revivalism was partially channelled through Grundtvigianism and partly through the *indre mission*. Both lay movements were eventually integrated into the institutional church, the Grundtvigian movement somewhat less so than the *indre mission*. On the other hand, the latter formed a cultural enclave within the church and within society, while Grundtvigians were much more open to the 'world'. Grundtvig's commitment to reform was considerable. He shared the traditional revivalist suspicion of the close bonds between church and state. Yet he never radicalised, and contributed to the development of a popular, 'national' church that was able to accommodate a range of religious leanings, from staunchly orthodox to Pietist. In England, too, Evangelicals largely remained within the fold. Equally, the Oxford Movement, which like other reformist groups sought to convert (in this case, to a specific brand of 'catholicity') the mainstream church in which it evolved, was mostly accommodated within that church. Unavoidably, the established churches reformed themselves in the process, in the sense that they became religiously plural. Grundtvigianism may have been peculiarly Danish but the rise of a broad, national church was not. All mainstream confessions in all the countries discussed in this volume entertained the ideal of a national church, which in some cases was interconfessional (as in Germany, where Lutherans and Reformed began to cooperate more and more after the 1840s, partly in response to the reorganisation of Catholicism) but in all instances seeking to accommodate often very diverse currents.

As well as a growing pluralism within the established churches and new groups which had seceded from them, many 'pre-Pietist' and 'dissenting' religious groups that remained independent grew in size and significance. In England and Wales the Baptists and Independents, who had remained outside the established church after the restoration of the monarchy in 1660, experienced significant growth in a second wave of the Evangelical Revival towards the end of the eighteenth century and continued to grow thereafter. To some extent the Remonstrants and Mennonites in the Netherlands followed the same pattern. Throughout the period, new groups emerged. Suffice it to mention the Salvation Army. An off-shoot of one of the many Methodist denominations, it soon set down roots in all the North European countries covered in this volume.

In Protestant countries such as Britain and the Netherlands, with Roman Catholic minorities small or large, Catholics had been used to keeping a low profile; to some extent the same applied to the Scottish Episcopal Church (an Anglican offshoot). Roman Catholics had been subsumed under missionary districts presided over by vicars apostolic. They generally tried to avoid irritating their Protestant countrymen and certainly did not plead openly for organisational reform. Despite the lack of a proper diocesan structure, they gradually made their presence felt before 1850, if often only through numerical increase. The real organisational expansion of Roman Catholic minorities took place after 1850. That may be inferred from the dates signalling the restoration (as Catholics would have it) or imposition (as Protestants claimed) of national episcopates. Catholic bishops were (re)instated in England and Wales in 1850, in the Netherlands in 1853, in Scotland in 1878. Like their counterparts elsewhere, the new Catholic bishops diligently pursued reform, often completely rebuilding the church's administrative and organisational infrastructure. And in accordance with developments within the Catholic Church as a whole, they centralised. In the case of English and Dutch Catholicism, this resulted in the emergence of what Frances Knight calls "a doctrinally orthodox, well-organised, highly disciplined and increasingly well resourced community". Ireland, of course, had a Roman Catholic majority but was a rather different case, since Ireland was a Catholic country within a Protestant state. Furthermore, until the Irish Church Disestablishment Act of 1869 Ireland had a Protestant established church. Reform was pursued nonetheless. The goals were better instruction, increase in the attendance of ceremonies, an expansion of confraternities and religious orders, and a more efficient organisation.

In countries with Roman Catholic majorities, such as the German states and Belgium, the centralisation of the church is a theme that applies to the whole century. The major overhaul, to which 'Germany' was subjected at the beginning of the nineteenth century, and which resulted in a substantial reduction of the number of states and a redrawing of boundaries, required a new organisational structure. Claus Arnold shows how in Germany new ecclesiastical provinces and dioceses were established which reflected these political changes, and examines what their effects were on the longer term. For one thing, organisational reform in this respect had the effect of strengthening the authority and power of bishops. From this point of view, the closing of the monasteries by state decree was not an unmitigated disaster for everyone. The elimination of religious orders at the beginning of the century meant that parish priests had less competition as pastoral care givers. In the course of the long nineteenth century the parish in many ways became more central to the religious life of Catholics than it had been. Whether in the majority or the minority, the Roman Catholic communities across Northern Europe were affected by a wave of ultramontanism in the period under discussion. Conservative everywhere, in Catholic Belgium and Germany the movement provided a response to liberal views and a way to claim the loyalty of lay people as links with the state were curtailed. The rise of ultramontanism after, say, the 1830s thus tied in with debates on religious freedom and the separation of church and state. In Belgium the church (as Jan Art, Jan De Maeyer, Ward De Pril and Leo Kenis point out) had "grasped every chance offered by the new constitution" of 1830 to put into position the framework that allowed ultramontanism to enjoy its heyday in the four decades after 1850. In Britain and the Netherlands ultramontanism helped to create a confident, thriving and exclusive minority community, strongly clerical in leadership and resisting engagement with modernist views.

In all cases, the established churches became more confident in their position and role vis-à-vis the state. This occurred even in countries like England and Sweden where the church did not formally separate from the state. It was this ecclesiastical self-sufficiency, coupled with an increasing reluctance of Parliament to allow time for the discussion of church legislation, which resulted in the setting up of the National Assembly of the Church of England following the Enabling Act of 1919. Thus the Church of England was provided with its own legislature, though one still ultimately subordinated to Parliament. In the case of state churches full independence is by definition out of the question. The financial reforms implemented in Denmark in the two decades before 1920 had the paradoxical effect of giving the clergy financial security while binding the church even more firmly to the state. There was more religious freedom and ecclesiastical autonomy everywhere, but such things, as always, came at a price.

Introduction

Clergy

At the level of the parish, especially in rural areas, time passed slowly, although the rate of change increased as the long nineteenth century progressed. At the beginning of the period, priests and pastors were religious specialists working on government-endorsed mandates. The majority of clergymen were under-paid, often struggling with local elites for adequate stipends and maintenance of the church. To be sure, there were differences between rich and poor livings. In Denmark, Sjaelland was better-off than Jutland; in Sweden, the south better than the north; in Germany, the west better than the east. Here the clergy commonly worked the land to provide an income for their families. Everywhere, town parishes were richer than those in the countryside. Opportunities for reform by melioristic clergymen lacking in ready cash and moral support were few and far between. In a late eighteenth-century tour through Pomerania, the Lutheran reformer Johann Friedrich Zöllner (1753-1804) noted the poor condition of the parishes. In Denmark things were not much better, even during the period of state Enlightenment between 1780 and 1815.[9] The problems became increasingly visible in the early decades of the nineteenth century, in the wake of agricultural reforms. In Denmark these eventually undermined the local authority of the clergy, as their role as state officials was taken up by civil administrations. In England and Wales the financial difficulties of poor livings was tackled by the Ecclesiastical Commission from the 1830s. This began a redistribution of endowments, though inequalities still remained.

In the first decades of the long nineteenth century, reform of the clergy was on the mind of most religious leaders. The reform-minded clergy formed a generation that put great store both by the patriotic spirit prevalent in the literature of the time and by religious ideals, whether Enlightened or revivalist. Mosheim's restructuring of the theological curriculum at Göttingen chiefly emphasised the ability to teach the catechism, exercise pastoral care, and preach.[10] Such reforms for university training were often supported by the Pietist clergy; in Denmark, Pontoppidan put forward similar views of clerical training. On the Catholic side in Germany, Ignaz von Wessenberg tried to realise similar reformist ideals. The idea that clergy should be knowledgeable and well trained was, then, practically universal. In most countries, educational ideals enjoyed the warm support of the state, if for somewhat different reasons. Since the church was still seen in many respects as an extension of the state, and the clergy as civil servants, the state was loath to lose control over the universities.

The political realignment in the German Empire in the decades around 1800 led to the dissolution of quite a few universities.[11] Ten Catholic and eight Protestant universities and seminaries disappeared in this period; three Catholic and twelve Protestant universities remained. A similar process took place in the Nordic countries.

---

[9] Hope, *German and Scandinavian Protestantism*, 263.

[10] Ibid., 270. For a useful discussion of this whole area see Howard, *Protestant Theology*.

[11] Hope, *German and Scandinavian Protestantism*, 217-219.

After 1811, Norwegian clergymen began to be trained at Christiania (Oslo), following the establishment of the Frediciana (by Frederik VI) there. Thereafter, Copenhagen catered primarily for the Danes. In Germany, state control over universities increased, as did state supervision of academic theologians, who practically became civil servants. State universities were established, for example in Berlin (1809, Protestant) and Munich (1826, Catholic). After 1815, Protestant and Catholic faculties were obliged to coexist at the same university. State control was symbolised by the appointment of special ministries, presided over by ministers of 'religious affairs', such as the *Kultusminister* in Prussia. The church, and by extension the theological faculties, had little choice in the matter. In Sweden after 1831, candidates for ordination were also expected, like other state officials, to get their education from secular universities rather than diocesan colleges as formerly. The church's interests were safeguarded by the fact that lectureships at the theology faculties were usually held by leading churchmen. The Catholic University of Louvain in Belgium, re-founded in the 1830s, is probably the best example of a confessional success story. More generally, it is representative of the central position of universities in the education of clergy, which did not prevent the latter from pursuing further studies and, especially, practical training at seminaries.

The churches were largely successful in professionalising the clergy. In most cases, the seeds were planted in the first half of the period and the fruits harvested during the second (although reforming education is a never-ending process and continued right up until, and beyond, the end of our period). Britain offers an interesting case study in this respect. In some parts, where livings were poor and candidates for ordination could not always afford a university education, bishops had to come up with other measures. Thomas Burgess, bishop of St Davids, in 1804 established a Society for Promoting Christian Knowledge and Church Union. Its aim was to distribute religious reading material and foster education, but also to found libraries for clergymen and improve the training of ministers to be. In England and Wales, the training of clergy was increasingly recognised as a serious matter but for which the solution did not rest only in an academic education. Most reform initiatives were aimed at founding theological colleges or seminaries and bringing about a professional attitude among clergy. Although in England the clergy had mostly graduated at Oxford or Cambridge or one of the very few newer universities, there was a call for additional pastoral training, resulting in an increase in the number of theological colleges after 1850. These colleges each had their own particular colouring in terms of doctrine and practice, buttressing different schools and parties in the Anglican Church. They were so successful that the number of clergy with no university degree began to increase until in 1879 about a sixth of the Anglican clergy in England were non-graduate. The educational standards of the nonconformist (i.e. Protestant, non-Anglican) ministry varied according to denomination with Methodists less likely to have any significant education until the opening of their training college at Hoxton in the 1830s. Nonconformists could not graduate from Oxford or Cambridge but many Congregationalist, and to a lesser extent Baptist, clergy had received higher education from one of the numerous dissenting academies. Originally set up to preserve the puritan tradition by clergy expelled at the restoration

Introduction

of the monarchy, these were already turning out well educated ministers in the eighteenth century. Others sought a university education at one of the Scottish universities, where various scholarships were available to make this possible. Like their Anglican counterparts, nonconformist groups set up training colleges in the search for greater professionalization and in response to the demands of an increasingly well educated population.[12]

In Ireland large numbers of priests were trained after 1850, many of whom were sent to minister to congregations overseas, including elsewhere in Britain. Of the growing Catholic congregations in England, Wales and Scotland, a substantial number were composed predominantly of Irish immigrants and often led by Irish priests. In Belgium a number of minor seminaries were founded or re-founded, allowing many rural candidates to be trained for the priesthood, though this did have a detrimental effect on the overall social standing of the clergy. In Germany, as elsewhere, ordinands were kept away from possible corruption by being educated alongside laymen, especially Protestant laymen, and clerical training was kept strictly within the seminaries. Plans from the 1860s to found a Catholic University for training German ordinands finally failed for lack of funding.

Theology

The long nineteenth century produced some very colourful religious thinkers. One was Nicolai Grundtvig. This Pietist writer and leader combined various currents of thought into a home-grown, practical Danish philosophy, dubbed 'Grundtvigianism' by the experts. His impact on Denmark, and to some extent Norway, was considerable. His aphorism "first a human, then a Christian" testified to the influence of the Enlightenment on him. As a Pietist, however, he simultaneously stressed the 'living word', rejecting any reduction of the Word into abstruse doctrine.[13] Søren Kierkegaard was as adamant a critic of the established clergy as Grundtvig, but he, by contrast, spurned the identification of Christianity with humanism, which he found to be prevalent in the Copenhagen of his days. Grundtvig and Kierkegaard show that some of the more interesting theologies and philosophies of the nineteenth century emerged out of the clash between Pietism and Enlightenment. The same applies to Friedrich Schleiermacher and Joseph Görres, German thinkers often associated with that heady mixture of Pietism and Enlightenment called 'Romanticism' by some. Interestingly, it is possible to interpret the Oxford Movement, one of the intellectually most impressive of nineteenth-century reform movements, in the same way. In an in-depth account of the movement's origins, implications, and moral fibre, Peter Nockles discusses the theological and spiritual revival of orthodox Anglicanism. The movement's reform agenda

---

[12] Brown, *A Social History of the Nonconformist Ministry*.

[13] Jespersen, *History of Denmark*, 103-105.

was doctrinal and liturgical but also cultural, in the sense that its aim was to imbue church and society with a revived Christian ethic, providing religious depth to what was seen as an all too secular age.

Reformers like Grundtvig and the Tractarians had to contend with liberal theology, which, if it did not dominate the theological agenda, at the very least posed a serious threat to orthodoxy and revivalism. At the beginning of the period, various theologians in all denominations had sought to integrate 'Enlightenment' into their thought: the German Catholic Johann Michael Sailer, whose books were read outside Germany, is a good example. 'Liberal theology' is hard to define in terms of our North European context. It built on Enlightenment theology in its various guises: latitudinarianism, supranaturalism[14], and neology; it is that form of nineteenth-century theology we could perhaps best describe as 'liberal', 'left-wing' or 'modernist'. It has often been judged, first and foremost by its orthodox (or ultramontane, as the case may be) opponents, as rationalistic, optimistic, humanistic and therefore deficient; liberals went too far for the orthodox (including the various brands of Pietists and Evangelicals) but not far enough for the radicals, let alone the outright secularists. Yet in many ways liberal theologians reformed theology to suit the age of progress and science, by making theology more 'scientific' (although theologians of all kinds of persuasions and leanings laboured to remodel the theological faculties according to the 'sciences'), thinking through the implications of historical criticism (miracles and prophecies were much in dispute in the nineteenth century) and gauging Christian truths and values by the standard of comparative religion. Outside the academies, liberal thought had an impact that could be quite substantial. Different groups of liberal Protestants organised themselves in various ways, ranging from the Friends of Light (*Lichtfreunde*) in Germany to the *vrijzinnigen* (literally, 'those of free sentiments', akin to the German *freireligiös* or 'religiously free') in the Netherlands. Later in the period, the term *Kulturprotestantismus* was used in Germany to denote the kind of Protestantism that engaged directly with the needs of the 'modern' educated classes. 'Liberalism' faded into 'modernism', when, after 1850, fundamental theological issues were raised, including, above all, the consequences of biblical criticism and the theory of evolution. At Cambridge and Oxford, the implications of biblical criticism were discussed and elaborated in relative academic peace by theologians, although several churchmen, both Anglican and nonconformist, were involved in controversies and required to account for their ideas. Some Anglican contributors to *Essays and Reviews* (1860) were prosecuted for heresy. Like historical criticism, Darwinism upset orthodoxies everywhere in the 1860s and 1870s, though attempts to respond theologically in a positive way were produced.

However, liberal theology largely failed to catch on in the Catholic and Nordic-Lutheran countries. At the newly founded University of Christiania a friend of Grundtvig

---

[14] 'Supranaturalism' is a theological term that originated in Germany and refers to a theology emphasising a 'rational' approach to religion while claiming that, in the end, revelation prevails over reason. Miracles and prophecies were not dispensed with but the pursuit of virtue was deemed rather more relevant to the Christian life than maintaining traditional doctrine.

introduced the 'theology of repristination', the traditional theology of Lutheran orthodoxy. Later, Gisle Johnson developed a revivalist theology there, which would prove to have a large impact on Norwegian society, which, like Grundtvig's rather less orthodox thought would have a large impact in Denmark. Roman Catholics everywhere rejected the new theological developments, at least officially, and certainly after the pope had condemned modernism in 1907. Informally, of course, there were Catholics who sympathised with modernism. In Britain the prominent modernists, St George Jackson Mivart and the Irish Jesuit George Tyrrell, were both finally excommunicated, in 1900 and 1907 respectively. But in these quarters, the open pursuit of theological reform would not occur before the 1960s. In Germany ultramontanism ultimately triumphed, but this, again, did not mean that alternative currents did not exist. In South West Germany the *Deutschkatholiken* (that is, 'German Catholics') at an early stage resisted the wave of ultramontanism that washed over Europe, offering a serious alternative to Roman Catholic orthodoxy. Later, in the years around 1900, Herman Schell was one of the leading figures in a reformist movement (*Reformkatholizismus*) that tried, even if it largely failed, to break through the ultramontane mould. Much more could be said on theology, including neo-Thomism at Louvain and neo-Calvinism in Amsterdam, but the general point should be clear. Within the different theological camps the pursuit of intellectual reform, whether through the re-invention or renovation of theology, was taken seriously.

Conclusions

Clearly, the countries treated in this volume were in many ways very different. In the Nordic countries, for example, the Lutheran established churches were virtually indistinguishable from the state and their ministers were effectively civil servants. In England and Wales the Anglican established church was also dependent on the government to legislate for change but received no funding except for being able to apply for some grant aid towards church and school building. Another important difference was that, whereas several of the countries under study retained a substantially agricultural economy despite increased industrialisation, parts of England, Belgium and Germany experienced huge shifts in population from the countryside to urban areas, with manufacturing and trade forming the core of their economies.

Nevertheless, there are so many parallel developments between 1780 and 1920 that it is difficult not to speak of a common 'politico-cultural space'. This has already been shown to be the case for the 'culture wars' of the nineteenth century. The *Kulturkampf* in Germany, the annexation of the Papal States in Italy, the emergence of a conservatively religious as well as an anti-clerical France, and the 'school wars' in Belgium and the Netherlands were all connected with the mobilisation of Catholics around a transnational ultramontane standard.[15] Can we claim something similar

---

[15] Clark and Kaiser, *Culture Wars*, 3.

for church reform in the predominantly Protestant countries of Northern Europe? If we exchange 'Catholic Church' for something like 'traditional churches' it becomes clear that there were parallel developments in all countries treated in this volume. The nation became contested terrain. So did the historical established churches rooted in that nation. All established churches tried to accommodate new groups or mobilise old ones or do both at the same time. Some succeeded better than others. The Lutheran nations - Denmark, Norway, Sweden - were successful in accommodating critics, both on the revivalist and the liberal side. The Anglican Church failed to accommodate Methodism at the beginning of the century but developed a breadth which would ultimately allow both catholic ritualism and revivalist evangelicalism to exist side by side with 'broad church' liberal ideas and worship.

This ability to absorb change, and actively respond to it, is the *sine qua non* of ecclesiastical reform in any period. The nineteenth-century churches did so in specific ways, by giving more voice to the laity, by making use of the greater freedom and autonomy they had gained to put in order their affairs, by training the clergy to cope with the demands and exigencies of the modern world, and by developing theologies that provided answers to new questions. This has not been the story of a church triumphant; a tale of spirited idealism and adroit management is probably more to the point. But perhaps we could say that the rapidity and density of change in the 140 years after 1780, and thus the unprecedented degree to which church reform needed to be, and was in fact, addressed, is what really made the long nineteenth century an age of ecclesiastical reform.

Bibliography

Beales, Derek. *Enlightenment and Reform in Eighteenth-Century Europe*. London, 2005.

Brown, Kenneth D. *A Social History of the Nonconformist Ministry in England and Wales 1800-1930*. Oxford, 1988.

Burns, Arthur and Innes, Joanna, eds. *Rethinking the Age of Reform: Britain 1780-1850*. Cambridge, 2003.

Clark, Christopher and Kaiser, Wolfram. *Culture Wars: Secular-Catholic Conflict in Nineteenth-Century Europe*. Cambridge, 2003.

Hope, Nicholas. *German and Scandinavian Protestantism 1799-1918*. Oxford, 1995.

Howard, Thomas Albert. *Protestant Theology and the Making of the Modern German University*. Oxford, 2006.

Jensen, De Lamar. *Reformation Europe: Age of Reform and Revolution*. Lexington (MA), 1992.

Jespersen, Knud J.V. *A History of Denmark*. Basingstoke, 2004.

Louthan, Howard P. *Conciliation and Confession: The Struggle for Unity in the Age of Reform, 1415-1648*. Notre Dame, 2004.

MacLeod, Hugh. *Religion and the People of Western Europe, 1789-1989*. Oxford, 1997^2.

Ozment, Steven. *The Age of Reform 1250-1550: An Intellectual and Religious History of Late Medieval and Reformation Europe*. New Haven (CT), 1980.

Rich, Norman. *The Age of Nationalism and Reform 1850-1890*. London, 1971.

Saunders, David. *Russia in the Age of Reaction and Reform, 1801-1881*. London, 1992.

Turner, Michael J. *British Politics in an Age of Reform*. Manchester, 1999.

THE UNITED KINGDOM OF GREAT BRITAIN & IRELAND

Until the last quarter of the twentieth century the prevailing view of the established churches in the British Isles was that in the late eighteenth and early nineteenth centuries they were largely antipathetic to reform and had to be forced to reform themselves by parliamentary legislation and government initiatives. This view is no longer tenable. It is now becoming clear that there was a strong movement for reform within the established churches from at least the last quarter of the eighteenth century and that, although the objectives of reform might change, this continued throughout the nineteenth and into the twentieth century. This section is divided into three chapters: the first deals with internal ecclesiastical reform in Britain in the late eighteenth and the first half of the nineteenth century; the second provides a detailed study of the High Church theological reform movement known as the Oxford Movement, which was highly influential, especially in the middle part of the century; the third looks more widely at internal reform in the second half of the nineteenth and early twentieth centuries.

Internal Church Reform, 1780-1850
Establishment under Fire

Nigel Yates †

The work of scholars such as Arthur Burns, Jeremy Gregory, W.M. Jacob, Frances Knight, F.C. Mather, Mark Smith and myself, has largely discredited the traditional view of the nineteenth century, that reform had to be forced on an unwilling church by parliament, and has shown, I hope convincingly, that the Anglican churches of England, Ireland and Wales had been committed to reforming themselves well before the government took a hand.[1] Unfortunately there has been little equivalent research on the Presbyterian established church in Scotland and it has been assumed, perhaps not entirely accurately, that reform was supported by Evangelicals in the face of opposition from the ruling 'moderates' in the General Assembly. In this chapter we will examine the nature of the internal church reform process across Britain and Ireland between 1780 and 1850 and at the various contributions to it made by pressure groups within the established churches. We will also look at equivalent reform movements in the Roman Catholic and Protestant Dissenting Churches, and at various issues arising from the reform process: the role of minority languages, the education and professionalisation of the clergy, lay participation in reform and the campaigns for home and foreign missions.

---

[1] Burns, *The Diocesan Revival in the Church of England*; Gregory, *Restoration, Reformation and Reform*; Jacob, *The Clerical Profession in the Long Eighteenth Century*; Knight, *The Nineteenth-Century Church*; Mather, *High Church Prophet*; Smith, *Religion in Industrial Society*; Yates, *The Religious Condition of Ireland*; Williams et al., *The Welsh Church*; for a slightly more negative view of internal church reform see Virgin, *The Church in an Age of Negligence*.

The Impact of Internal Church Reform

From the last quarter of the eighteenth century there appears to have been a reform movement which spread across England, Ireland and Wales from one diocese to another, starting in Ireland in the 1770s, and spreading to Wales by the 1780s and England by the 1790s. This movement was not, as far as we can tell, centrally directed and is contrary to the perceived expectation that reform tends to begin in London, or at least England, and spread outwards to the periphery. This may suggest that internal reform, in the early period, was at least partly a practical response to local conditions. In Ireland the church was struggling to act as a national church with only a minority of the population as adherents. In Wales bishops were faced with difficulties in communication, poor parishes and a rather greater threat from nonconformity than in England. Reform initiatives seem to have been the work of bishops acting independently of one another, but clearly influenced by initiatives in neighbouring dioceses. There is, however, certainly evidence of correspondence between bishops on diocesan and parochial reform and it is likely that bishops exchanged ideas with one another, for example when they were in London for meetings of the House of Lords.

In Ireland, the initial pioneer of the reform movement was Charles Agar (1736-1809), successively bishop of Cloyne, archbishop of Cashel and archbishop of Dublin.[2] His example was followed by his successor at Cashel, Charles Broderick (1761-1822), and by Thomas Lewis O'Beirne (1749-1823), bishop of Ossory and, later, Meath, Archbishop William Stuart (1755-1822) of Armagh and Richard Mant (1776-1848), bishop of Down and Connor. Agar, who had inherited rural deans at Cloyne, saw them as a vital element of diocesan middle management. He introduced them at Cashel and persuaded many of his fellow bishops to follow his example. By 1820 the office had been revived in 16 out of the 22 dioceses of the Church of Ireland. Agar also persuaded his fellow bishops that training standards for Irish clergy needed to be improved, by requiring candidates for ordination to produce a certificate stating that they had attended at least one complete course of divinity lectures at Trinity College, Dublin, and by agreeing a list of books to be prescribed for the examination of such candidates. Agar tightened the requirements for clerical residence in the diocese of Cashel and in his primary charge to the diocese of Dublin he urged clergy, not just to reside in their parishes, but to visit their parishioners, particularly those who were sick. An insistence on clerical residence was also promulgated by Bishop O'Beirne at both Ossory and Meath; he also implemented programmes for the repair of churches and glebe houses, required the incumbents of urban parishes to hold regular weekday services, and urged the establishment of parochial schools. Bishop Mant's chief priorities were an improvement in standards of worship, an increase in the number of services and more frequent celebrations of Holy Communion.[3]

---

[2] An excellent biography is Malcomson, *Archbishop Charles Agar*.

[3] Yates, *The Religious Condition of Ireland*, 63-99.

Internal Church Reform, 1780-1850

H. Meyer, Samuel Horsley, *engraving after the portrait by J. Green, 1813.*
[Carmarthen, Carmarthenshire County Museum]

S.W. Reynolds, Thomas Burgess, *oil on canvas.*
[Lampeter, University of Wales, Lampeter]

In Wales bishops followed very similar patterns of promoting reform, especially in their strengthening of the powers of the existing rural deans. At Bangor, John Warren (1730-1800) refused to appoint non-graduates to benefices in the diocese and emphasised in his charges the importance of clerical residence, of preaching and catechising and of clergy being an example, through their 'sober and unblemished life', to their parishioners. H.W. Majendie (1754-1830) used his visitation process to initiate an extensive programme of diocesan reform, including the repair of churches, an increase in the number of services and the establishment of schools. At St Davids, Samuel Horsley (1733-1806) personally examined his ordination candidates, maintained a strict discipline over clerical appointments, issued instructions for the proper observance of holy days and encouraged the holding of monthly celebrations of Holy Communion. One of his successors, Thomas Burgess (1756-1837), was an even greater innovator. In 1804 he established a 'Society for Promoting Christian Knowledge and Church Union' in the diocese with five primary objectives: to distribute bibles, prayer books and religious tracts; to establish libraries for the use of the clergy; to improve the education of ordinands; to establish schools for the education of the poor; and to promote Sunday schools. He also encouraged his rural deans to form clerical societies in their deaneries, "to organise Sunday schools, to promote theological study, and support each other in their clerical work". A major problem in the St David's diocese, caused primarily by the poor monetary value of benefices, was a serious lack of graduate clergy. Determined to improve clerical education, Burgess stipulated that he would in future only ordain non-graduate clergy who had studied divinity at one of nine licensed grammar schools in the diocese. This measure was meant to be a temporary one pending the establish-

C.J. Smith, St David's College, Lampeter, in 1827, engraving.
[Lampeter, University of Wales, Lampeter]

ment of a college to educate ordinands, with a syllabus similar to that followed by students at Oxford, Cambridge and Trinity College, Dublin. The foundation stone of St David's College, Lampeter, was laid in 1822 and the first students were admitted in 1827. For most of the nineteenth century it provided the diocese with the majority of its clergy, but its influence was even more widely felt with Lampeter-trained clergy eventually serving in most other dioceses in England and Wales.[4]

Compared with Ireland and Wales, the established church in England rather lagged behind, though it was to make up for it during the early years of the nineteenth century. The first English bishop to revive rural deaneries was James Yorke of Ely (1730-1808). They were not revived until much later in most English dioceses: Salisbury 1811, Chichester 1812, Bristol 1824, Lincoln 1829, Oxford 1831, Canterbury and London 1833, Worcester 1834, Lichfield 1837, Hereford 1838, Chester 1840, York 1843.[5] Samuel Horsley of Rochester, who had been translated there in 1793 from the Welsh diocese of St Davids, issued a printed circular to his clergy instructing them in the proper method of preparing candidates for confirmation, and as Dean of Westminster he increased the frequency of chapter meetings and made important contributions towards improving the services as well as the financial viability of the abbey church.[6] Internal church

---

[4] Williams et al., *The Welsh Church*, 223-265.
[5] Burns, *The Diocesan Revival in the Church of England*, 76-80.
[6] Mather, *High Church Prophet*, 177-191.

reform was, by the early years of the nineteenth century, following a fairly standard pattern across the Anglican dioceses of Britain and Ireland: parochial schools and societies, more frequent services and communion, a greater emphasis on clerical residence and a desire to ensure that where clergy had more than one benefice, both or all of them were served either personally or by a resident curate paid a proper stipend.

From the late 1820s, within what had become in 1801 the United Church of England and Ireland, the programme of internal ecclesiastical reform within the church was hampered, both by government legislation, and by party controversy within the church. There was much resentment, particularly among High Churchmen, at government legislation which appeared to threaten the status of the established church, even when some of the measures had been supported by reforming bishops in the past. Four reforms attracted particular anger: the repeal in 1828 of the Test and Corporation Acts, which had restricted the right to hold public office to members of the established church; Catholic Emancipation in 1829; the Irish Church Temporalities Act of 1833, which reduced the number of Irish archbishoprics and bishoprics from 22 to 12; and the reform of tithes. It was opposition to the Irish Church Temporalities Act that inspired Keble's Assize Sermon and the *Tracts for the Times*, and led to the Oxford Movement (or Tractarianism), the radical reinterpretation of Anglican High Churchmanship in the 1830s and 1840s, which will be dealt with in more detail in the next chapter. Some bishops, such as C.J. Blomfield (1786-1857) of London, John Kaye (1783-1853) of Lincoln and J.H. Monk (1784-1856) of Gloucester, were, however, prepared to work with the government in the newly-established Ecclesiastical Commission, to protect the interests of the established church. Not surprisingly, many clergy felt that the bishops were betraying them, none more so than those in the cathedrals, as a result of the reforms proposed by the Dean and Chapter Act of 1840, which amongst other things gave considerable powers over cathedral appointments to the Crown and the Ecclesiastical Commissioners.[7] The attempt to regularise diocesan boundaries was also extremely controversial. In the end the new diocese of Ripon was created in 1836, financed by the merger of the former dioceses of Bristol and Gloucester. Attempts to unite the dioceses of Bangor and St Asaph, and to suppress the diocese of Sodor and Man, however, were not successful and the diocese of Manchester had to be created in 1847 without a seat being provided, as of right, to its bishop in the House of Lords.[8]

Tensions between church parties, which grew as a result of the strengthening of Evangelicals within the church after 1800 (see below) and the development of Tractarianism in the 1830s (see next chapter) also, inevitably, drew in the bishops and the other higher clergy. Initially the Tractarians had shared the ecclesiastical agenda of other reformers, including more frequent services and celebrations of Holy Communion, but by the late 1830s they were beginning to desire further innovations: the placing of a cross, candles and vases of flowers on the altar, the use of coloured stoles

---

[7] Knight, *The Nineteenth-Century Church*, 153-157.

[8] Burns, *The Diocesan Revival in the Church of England*, 156-161, 192-198.

and frontals, taking the eastward position at Holy Communion, preaching in a surplice instead of a black gown, chanting the services and recommending the use of private confession. These were seen as 'popish' by those who wanted to defend the purity of Protestantism. When some bishops defended some of these innovations and required clergy to preach in their surplices, there was dramatic opposition from both clergy and laity, leading to riots in some places.[9]

Nevertheless, by the middle years of the nineteenth century diocesan administration was becoming much more efficient. In most cases it was based on a four-tier structure with the bishop at the top, archdeacons and rural deans as the new layers of middle-management, and the parochial clergy at the bottom. The cathedrals, despite the 1840 Act, still remained outside the diocesan structure and their personnel largely hostile to reform until well after 1850. Archdeacons were key figures in diocesan administration for it was they, rather than the bishop, who maintained knowledge of the parishes in their archdeaconry through regular visitations and inspections. Rural deans provided a further layer of inspection and, under the Church Discipline Act of 1840, they were responsible for clerical discipline within their rural deaneries. Clergy in remote parishes, who might have been able to hide their incompetence or indiscretions from their bishops in the eighteenth century, were no longer able to do so.[10]

Although a great deal of recent research has now been done on the internal management of the established churches in England, Ireland and Wales, far less has been done on the Church of Scotland. Partly this is because some of the long-standing problems of the other established churches, such as pluralism (the holding of more than one benefice) and clergy not residing in their parishes, were not a problem in Scotland. The only incidences of pluralism were the holding of parochial ministries at the same time as occupying a university professorship, and this was modified by the General Assembly in 1817 when it was stipulated that if a university professor also held a ministerial appointment it had to be within the boundaries of that university town. All parish ministers were obliged by the Assembly to reside in their parishes, conduct at least one service each Sunday, catechise the youth of the parish and visit their parishioners regularly. Ministers who failed to carry out their duties to the satisfaction of their kirk sessions[11] would be reported to their presbytery for disciplinary action to be taken against them.[12] There is clear evidence that kirk sessions generally were keen to ensure that discipline was maintained and that no outside forces should weaken it.

---

[9] Yates, *Anglican Ritualism in Victorian Britain*, 179-183.
[10] Knight, *The Nineteenth-Century Church*, 167-182; Burns, *The Diocesan Revival in the Church of England*, 41-107.
[11] Kirk sessions are the lowest in the hierarchy of church courts in the Church of Scotland, the court of the parish.
[12] Brown, *The National Churches of England, Ireland and Scotland*, 25-26, 78-79.

Evangelicalism and Separation

Evangelicalism in Britain and Ireland was part of the movement for spiritual revival which swept through virtually all the Protestant churches of Europe and North America, at varying dates, between the late seventeenth and early nineteenth centuries.[13] In Britain, Ireland and North America this movement is generally termed Evangelical, whereas in continental Europe it is often termed Pietist. In England and Wales Evangelicalism first began to have an impact in the 1730s; in Scotland there was some early impact, for example in the revival at Cambuslang in 1742, but its full force was not felt until towards the end of the eighteenth century; in Ireland too, Evangelicalism only began to make some headway in both the Church of Ireland and the Presbyterian churches from the late eighteenth century.[14] The essential ingredients of Evangelicalism have been well defined by David Bebbington: "There are the four qualities that have been the special marks of Evangelical religion: *conversionism*, the belief that lives need to be changed; *activism*, the expression of the gospel in effort; *biblicism*, a particular regard for the Bible; and what may be called *crucicentrism*, a stress on the sacrifice of Christ on the cross. Together they form a quadrilateral of priorities that is the basis of Evangelicalism."[15]

Opponents of Evangelicalism, especially Anglican bishops of the late eighteenth and early nineteenth centuries, generally added a fifth, and in their eyes most dangerous, characteristic of Evangelicalism. This was its tendency towards 'enthusiasm', as marked by styles of preaching and worship and the emphasis on the perceptible experience of conversion. Opponents felt that the enthusiasm of Evangelicals might lead all too easily to doctrinal heterodoxy and even political radicalism.

Evangelicals in return regarded the established churches as lacking in spirituality and in urgent need of the gifts of the Holy Spirit to reawaken them. Where they could, they tried to work within the structures of the established churches, but where this was not possible they felt no compunction about preaching their message outside them through itinerant preaching. Evangelicals did not, however, form a united front in their onslaught on what they perceived to be the shortcomings of the established churches. For a start, they were divided doctrinally. The group led by John and Charles Wesley, the Wesleyan Methodists, were Arminian in doctrine; those led by George Whitefield, and in Wales by Howell Harris and Daniel Rowland, were Calvinist. In England and Ireland the Wesleyan Methodists had considerable success, but in Scotland and Wales relatively little impact. Within the Presbyterian churches of Ireland

---

[13] See Ward, *The Protestant Evangelical Awakening* and Campbell, *The Religion of the Heart*.
[14] On Britain generally see Bebbington, *Evangelicalism in Modern Britain* and Ditchfield, *The Evangelical Revival*; on Wales see Morgan, *The Great Awakening in Wales* and Jones, *"A Glorious Work in the World"*; on Scotland see McInnes, *The Evangelical Movement in the Highlands of Scotland*; Ansdell, *The People of the Great Faith* and Brown, *Thomas Chalmers*; and on Ireland see Hempton and Hill, *Evangelical Protestantism in Ulster Society*; Acheson, *"A True and Lively Faith"* and Bowen, *The Protestant Crusade in Ireland*.
[15] Bebbington, *Evangelicalism in Modern Britain*, 2-3.

and Scotland, and the Anglican Church in Wales, Evangelicals were, almost without exception, Calvinists. In terms of their *modus operandi* there was much greater similarity, itinerant preaching leading in due course to the setting up of their own chapels and, eventually, separation from their parent churches.

In England Methodism tended to be concentrated in specific areas of the country. Wesleyan Methodism had some 77,000 adherents in 1796, but about a fifth of these were in Yorkshire, and there were significant groups of Methodists in Cornwall and Lincolnshire. In other parts of England, especially across the southern counties, the impact of Methodism was negligible. Whilst the Wesley brothers remained alive (Charles dying in 1788 and John in 1791) Methodism was no more than a sect within the established Church of England. However, even before their deaths, actions were taken that formed the prelude for schism. In 1784-1785 John Wesley ordained ministers for his adherents in the former American colonies and in Scotland. In 1788-1799 a small number of English local preachers[16] were also ordained. This was in clear breach of Anglican canon law, which insisted on episcopal ordination. In 1793 the Methodist Conference voted that in those societies in which all the members wished to receive Holy Communion from a local preacher they might do so. Even then there was no desire to separate formally from the Church of England and in 1796 the leader of the anti-church party, Alexander Kilham (1762-1798), was expelled from the conference, taking three preachers and about 5,000 members with him to form the Methodist New Connexion.[17]

Thereafter there was a gradual parting of the ways, but there were several parts of the British Isles, notably Ireland and the Isle of Man, where Methodists attended both Anglican parish churches and their own chapels until well into the second half of the nineteenth century. A similar process to that in Wesleyan Methodism took place amongst the Calvinistic Methodists in Wales. Here the organisation itself was somewhat looser and Anglicans themselves were divided about the extent to which they should compete with them. The final catalyst for separation was the decision to ordain some of the local preachers, so that they could baptise and celebrate Holy Communion in Calvinistic Methodist chapels. These first ordinations took place at Association meetings in Bala and Llandeilo in 1811. It was not, however, until 1823 that a formal constitution was adopted for what eventually became known as the Presbyterian Church of Wales. Even after these events there was cooperation between Calvinistic Methodists and Anglicans in some parts of Wales and some Evangelical clergy within the established church continued to minister in, and act as a trustee of, local Calvinistic Methodist chapels.[18]

It is important to emphasise that secessions by both Wesleyan and Calvinistic Methodists did not remove all Evangelicals from the established church in England

---

[16] Methodist local preachers were lay people permitted to lead worship and preach but not to administer the sacraments.

[17] Rack, *Reasonable Enthusiast*, 508-521; Walsh, "Methodism at the End of the Eighteenth Century"; Ward, *Religion and Society in England*, 30, 54-62.
[18] Williams et al., *The Welsh Church*, 209-218.

and Wales. Many chose to remain within the establishment and work for reform from within. Typical of the Evangelical clergy within the established church was John Venn (1759-1813), who became rector of Little Dunham, in Norfolk, in 1783. Here he introduced two Sunday services and a monthly communion service even though the population of the parish was only 172. In 1792 he established a clerical society for sympathetic neighbouring clergy. In 1793 Venn moved to be rector of Clapham, now a suburb of London. His first innovation there was a Friday lecture, quickly replaced with a third Sunday service, in the evening, in addition to those in the morning and afternoon. Monthly communion was also established. The parish became the nucleus of a group of sympathetic Evangelical laity, the so-called Clapham Sect.[19] In 1799 Venn was one of the co-founders of the Church Missionary Society.[20] Another influential Evangelical clergyman was Charles Simeon (1759-1836). Vicar of Holy Trinity, Cambridge, from 1783, he was a strong influence on Cambridge undergraduates and organised classes for intending ordinands. He also set up religious societies for his parishioners and was a co-founder of the Church Missionary Society, the British and Foreign Bible Society, the Colonial and Continental Church Society and the Church Mission to the Jews. He scandalised much of the Anglican establishment by his friendliness to Protestant Dissenters in England and his willingness, when on holiday, to preach and even receive communion in the Presbyterian Church of Scotland. Towards the end of his life he set up a trust to purchase the advowsons of Anglican parishes so that Evangelicals could be presented to them at the next vacancy.[21] William Wilberforce (1759-1833), MP for Hull, and Hannah More (1745-1833), were leading figures in the London Abolition Society, established in 1787 to campaign for the abolition of the slave trade, and which eventually secured parliamentary legislation to this effect in 1807. Evangelicals were also prominent in the Society for Distributing Religious Tracts, founded in 1782, the Proclamation Society, established in 1787 to advocate "the moral regeneration of the ruling elite and the restoration of its sense of responsibility", and the Society for the Suppression of Vice, founded in 1802. They attacked sexual promiscuity, nude bathing at seaside resorts and offensive passages in the plays of Shakespeare and other dramatists, prosecuted the publishers of allegedly obscene material, and strongly supported Sabbath-day observance.[22]

Evangelicalism took on a particular, virulently anti-Roman Catholic stance in Ireland, which caused considerable discomfort to the leaderships of both the Anglican and Presbyterian churches. In 1786 a number of wealthy Evangelicals in Dublin established the Bethesda Chapel, which had become fully Calvinist in its theology by 1794 and to which successive archbishops of Dublin refused to license its clergy until 1825. Evangelical ministries were established at Mary's Abbey Presbyterian church in Dublin in 1778, at Donaghmore Presbyterian church in County Donegal in 1798, and at Rose-

---

[19] The Clapham Sect comprised Henry Thornton, William Wilberforce, Hannah More, James Stephen, Lord Teignmouth and Zachary Macaulay.
[20] Hennell, *John Venn and the Clapham Sect*.
[21] Smyth, *Simeon and Church Order*.
[22] Bristow, *Vice and Vigilance*, 33-41.

J. Heath, William Wilberforce, *line engraving after J. Russell, 1807.*
[London, National Portrait Gallery: D37511]

mary Street Presbyterian church in Belfast. The minister at Donaghmore, Samuel Dill (1772-1845), was a strong opponent of both drinking and gambling. Evangelicals within the Anglican and Presbyterian churches collaborated to establish the General Evangelical Society in Dublin in 1787, the Ulster Evangelical Society in 1798, the Hibernian Bible Society in 1806 and the Hibernian Church Missionary Society in 1814. Two specifically Anglican Evangelical societies were the Association for the Discountenancing of Vice and Practice of Virtue and Religion, a counterpart to the English Proclamation Society, founded in 1792, and the Ossory Clerical Association established by Peter Roe (1778-1842), minister of St Mary's, Kilkenny, in 1800. By the 1820s Evangelicals had gained control of the principal Presbyterian organisation in Ireland, the Synod of Ulster. In the Church of Ireland before 1840 only Archbishops Trench of Tuam and Magee of Dublin (though not himself an Evangelical) supported Evangelical initiatives and their fellow bishops remained distinctly hostile. After 1840 two of the Church of Ireland's leading Evangelicals were elevated to the episcopate: James O'Brien (1792-1874) to Ossory in 1842, and Robert Daly (1783-1872) to Cashel and Waterford in 1843. In the Church of England Evangelicals had been appointed as bishops somewhat earlier: Henry Ryder (1777-1836) at Gloucester in 1815 (later translated to Lichfield), Charles Sumner (1790-1874) at Llandaff in 1827 (later translated to Winchester) and John Bird Sumner (1780-1862) at Chester in 1828; the last of these became archbishop of Canterbury in 1848.

By far the most important consequence of the growth of Evangelicalism in Ireland was the 'Second Reformation' movement launched in the 1820s. This was a deliberate attempt by Evangelicals within the main Protestant churches to proselytise among the Roman Catholic population. Evangelical landowners, such as Lord Farnham in County Cavan, were prominent in the movement and used aggressive conversion methods, such as bribing their tenants to become Protestants with offers of money, food, clothing, bedding, work, housing or land. Initially the movement seemed to have some success. There were 511 conversions on Lord Farnham's estates between October 1826 and February 1827, and later mass conversions at Dingle in County Kerry and on Achill Island in County Mayo. Most of these conversions were short-lived and successfully terminated by equally aggressive counter-missionary work undertaken on behalf of the Irish Roman Catholic bishops. In the long term it soured relations between Catholics and Protestants in Ireland, as the non-Evangelicals within both the Anglican and Presbyterian churches had warned it would, and was a major contributory factor to increasing inter-denominational rivalry in Ireland from the 1840s.[23]

In parts of Scotland too, Evangelical initiatives took a similarly missionary approach, especially in the western highlands and islands, where there were still substantial remnants of both Roman Catholics and Scottish Episcopalians, and where the Church of Scotland had had great difficulty in obtaining ministers. There were 'revivals' in the Argyll parishes of Kilbrandon and Kilchattan in 1786, on Skye in 1806-1812 and Lewis in 1824. The Evangelical revival in these areas encouraged much stricter

---

[23] Yates, *The Religious Condition of Ireland*, 260-279.

conditions being placed on admission to Holy Communion and also laid emphasis on the maintenance of penitential discipline by the kirk sessions. At Uig in Lewis the communion roll was reduced from 800 to 6 and at Bracadale in Skye from 150 to 20. The minister of Lochcarron in Wester Ross secured the fining of the major landowner of the neighbouring parish of Gairloch in 1792 for adultery with his maid, and the deposition of his own schoolmaster, in 1821, for fornication. Evangelicals were contemptuous of the 'moderate' leadership of the Church of Scotland, regarding the moderate clergy as worldly minded and neglectful of their spiritual and pastoral duties. Evangelical ministers, however, as was the case with Methodists in England and Wales, had little regard for parochial boundaries and were not averse to preaching in parishes in which they thought the gospel was not being adequately proclaimed. John Macdonald, minister of Urquhart 1813-1849, undertook preaching tours throughout the highlands and islands, including four visits to the remote island of St Kilda, and he also preached in Ireland.[24]

Before 1800 Evangelicals had made relatively little impression on the Church of Scotland outside the highlands and islands. Thereafter their influence began to permeate the lowland parishes and they found a vocal and highly organised leader in Thomas Chalmers (1780-1847). In 1803 Chalmers became minister of Kilmany in Fife and eight years later experienced a conversion to Evangelicalism, beginning a programme of visiting his parishioners and seeking new methods of poor relief. In 1814 he was called to the ministry of the Tron parish in Glasgow where he continued the programmes of visitation and poor relief he had begun at Kilmany. By then he was also developing a national reputation as a powerful preacher and reformer. Part of his plan for reform included the division of large parishes. In Glasgow he recommended an increase in the number of parishes from 9 to 39, and was successful in persuading the Town Council to create two of these, including the new parish of St John's of which Chalmers was to be the first minister, largely out of the former Tron parish. At St John's, Chalmers introduced a Sunday evening service at which the seat rents were much reduced so as to attract more working-class worshippers. The new church was crippled with financial problems, however, and in 1823 he accepted appointment to the professorship of Moral Philosophy at St Andrews.

By the 1820s Evangelicals within the Church of Scotland were concerned about three major issues, which they felt were preventing the conversion of the people. These were the retention of private patronage, whereby the heritors (landowners) could frustrate the wishes of the parish in calling a minister; the inadequacy of the British government's support for church growth and increased church building in Scotland compared with its much more generous support for the building of new churches and parsonages in England, Ireland and Wales; and the failure to enable new parishes to be created, with seats for the minister and elders in presbytery, for the newly-built churches. This meant either that new church communities could not be established or

---

[24] Ansdell, *The People of the Great Faith*, 47-50, 114-116; Brown, *Religion and Society in Scotland*, 72, 87.

Internal Church Reform, 1780-1850

T. Duncan, Thomas Chalmers, *oil on canvas, c.1840.*
[Edinburgh, National Galleries of Scotland:
PG 1394]

that, where they were set up, they could not play a normal part in church governance. In 1834 Chalmers became chairman of the Church Accommodation Committee of the General Assembly of the Church of Scotland. A year later he could report that 64 new churches had either been completed or were in the course of erection. By 1841, 222 new churches had been built but it was not enough and Chalmers felt that the British government had betrayed the church. The Evangelicals felt that the General Assembly was not putting enough pressure on the government to change its attitude and that the only solution was to establish a 'Free' Church of Scotland. On 18 May 1843 the retiring Moderator, David Welsh (1793-1845), Chalmers and a large number of Evangelicals walked out of the annual meeting of the church's governing body, the General Assembly. Thereafter 470 Church of Scotland ministers signed the 'Act of Separation and Deed of Demission'. In the northern presbyteries a majority of the ministers and their congregations joined the new Free Church, the highest being 75.8% in the Synod of Ross. A majority of ministers seceded in the four major Scottish cities, Aberdeen, Dundee, Edinburgh and Glasgow, but there were far fewer secessions in the southern presbyteries, with only 19% in the Synod of Dumfries, 22.5% in the Synod of Galloway and 25% in the Synod of Merse and Teviotdale.[25]

The Education and Professionalisation of the Clergy

One of the most dramatic changes that took place in the period between 1780 and 1850 was the recognition that clergy had to be trained to carry out their pastoral responsibilities. Before the early nineteenth century the clergy of all the established churches, Anglican or Presbyterian, were generally educated at one of the two universities in England, one in Ireland or four in Scotland. There were exceptions in some parts of the country, notably North-West England, South-West Wales and the Isle of Man, in which the poverty of benefices made it impossible to attract a graduate clergy, and bishops were compelled to ordain those who had had only a grammar school education. In some cases such Anglican ordinands might have received their education at one of the many Protestant dissenting academies, which provided an alternative to the grammar school as well as training older youths and men for the dissenting ministry, though in practice many dissenting ministers had little training and frequently combined ministerial posts with another job to maintain themselves and their families. Roman Catholic priests were generally educated at one of the continental seminaries. All clergy were much more integrated with secular society than became the norm during the nineteenth century. Many were farmers, schoolteachers or private tutors. Anglican clergy tended to serve as magistrates and were frequently the most diligent members of the bench. The government saw the role of the clergy as helping to educate the laity

---

[25] Brown, *Thomas Chalmers*, 49-84, 91-116, 119, 122-123, 131, 140, 235-337.

to be good citizens and much of the preaching of the eighteenth century, across all denominations, had emphasised the importance of good citizenship in the life of the individual Christian.

All this was to change in two respects during the early nineteenth century. In the first place there began to be a recognition that clergy needed training for the job and not just a good education. At Cambridge, the Lady Margaret Professor of Divinity began lecturing in English instead of Latin in 1809. Clerical education societies were set up by Evangelicals at Bristol, Creaton, Elland and London. Charles Simeon provided sermon classes for Evangelical ordinands at Cambridge from 1790 and 'conversation parties' from 1812. Colleges were established to provide courses for ordination candidates, who could not afford to go to one of the existing universities, at St Bees in 1817 and Lampeter in 1827. The new university at Durham, established by Bishop Van Mildart and the cathedral chapter in 1836, had a divinity school to offer a one-year course to graduates of Oxford and Cambridge and a two-year course to non-graduates. Seminaries for Anglicans were first suggested by Bishop Blomfield of London in 1830 and two were founded, both run by Tractarians, at Chichester in 1839 and Wells in 1840. In 1841 new Regius professorships of pastoral theology and ecclesiastical history, annexed to canonries at Christ Church, were established at Oxford. The Roman Catholics too began to establish their own seminaries for clergy training since access to the European ones proved difficult after the French Revolution. Colleges were established at Carlow and Maynooth, the latter with government finance, in Ireland, and at Oscott, Ushaw and Ware in England. The Irish Presbyterians established a school of divinity at the Belfast Academical Institution founded in 1810 and no longer had to send their ministerial candidates to the Scottish universities to be educated. Theological colleges were also established by some groups of Protestant Dissenters. In addition to changes in professional training, there was an acceptance across all denominations that the position of the clergyman in society also had to change. Clergy should no longer be involved in secular pursuits, whether economic or social, and should no longer be seen as acting on behalf of government, in ways such as serving as magistrates. During the course of the early nineteenth century the role of the clergy in all the main churches of Britain and Ireland became much more pastoral, the role of the clergyman being seen as a full-time job which should not, except in certain special circumstances, such as teaching in schools and universities, or managing charitable institutions, be combined with other, essentially non-spiritual, duties.[26]

---

[26] See especially Kitson Clark, *Churchmen and the Condition of England*, 29-43, 141-224; Haig, *The Victorian Clergy*, 1-135; Jacob, *The Clerical Profession in the Long Eighteenth Century*, 41-60, 144-149, 155-157, 165-170, 203-235. On the Roman Catholic clergy in Ireland see Connolly, *Priests and People in Pre-Famine Ireland*, 56-78. On the Irish Presbyterian ministry see Holmes, *The Shaping of Ulster Presbyterian Belief and Practice*, 135-138, and Yates, *The Religious Condition of Ireland*, 138-140. On the training of Scottish Presbyterian ministers see Whytock, *An Educated Clergy*. On the training of English and Welsh dissenting ministers see Brown, *A Social History of the Nonconformist Ministry*, 56-79.

The Role of the Laity

Before 1850 the role of the laity in the Anglican established churches of England, Ireland and Wales was very limited. Effectively they had no real say in the government of the church unless they were members of either House of Parliament, in which case they had a role in ecclesiastical legislation. The management of the dioceses was almost entirely in the hands of the bishops and the senior clergy. At parish level lay people had a greater role to play. Decisions involving expenditure and the raising of a local church rate or cess had to be made by the parish vestry and unpopular clergy might find themselves frustrated by their parishioners, especially if there were large numbers of Protestant Dissenters in the parish, as there was no requirement for those attending vestry meetings to be worshipping Anglicans. The vestry also elected the parish officers: the churchwardens, the overseers of the poor and the surveyors of the highways. A major function of the parish vestry was poor relief but this ceased to be a parish responsibility in England and Wales in 1834, and in Ireland in 1838, when responsibility was transferred to new bodies and the parish became a largely ecclesiastical unit. The extent to which the laity was involved in church government at parochial level was very much a matter for the incumbent and many saw their principal contribution to ecclesiastical affairs as being through their membership of various voluntary organisations set up at national, diocesan or parochial level to support the work of the established churches.

In Scotland both clergy and laity shared in the government of the established church at every level, from the General Assembly, through synods and presbyteries, down to the individual kirk sessions which comprised the minister and the lay elders of each parish. Whilst lay people could not determine the nature of the services and the preaching, for which the minister alone was responsible, they had a major role in the maintenance of spiritual and social discipline.

"The elders were responsible for discovering moral and religious infractions, including extramarital sex, drunkenness, lying, quarrelling, profanity, and unfair business practices. Offenders would be summoned to appear before the kirk-session, examined, and if found guilty, admonished and assigned a penance, which usually involved paying a fine to the poor relief fund or having to stand or sit, sometimes dressed in sackcloth, before the congregation for a specific number of Sundays [...] most kirk-session discipline involved cases of extramarital sex, with elders pressing unmarried pregnant women to reveal the names of the fathers, who could then be forced to contribute to the children's support."[27]

Examination of kirk session records shows very clearly that their disciplinary authority was maintained throughout the first half of the nineteenth century. Another important role in the parish was exercised by the heritors (landowners). They were

---

[27] Brown, *The National Churches of England, Ireland and Scotland*, 27; see also Id., *Religion and Society in Scotland*, 69-73.

responsible for the erection and maintenance of church buildings, for the provision of a manse and glebe for the minister, for the provision of a school and schoolmaster, and for paying the minister's stipend out of the tiends (equivalent to tithes in other parts of the British Isles) of which they themselves paid the major part. Some heritors did their best to keep expenditure as low as possible, particularly when it came to the maintenance of church buildings, a fact revealed only too clearly in the *Statistical Account of Scotland* in the 1790s. However, there is strong evidence from the *New Statistical Account* in the 1840s that the naming and shaming of heritors fifty years previously had had the desired effect of increasing their willingness to live up to their responsibilities.[28]

Protestant Dissenters and Roman Catholics

The years between 1780 and 1850 were ones of expansion both for Protestant Dissenters and for Roman Catholics. A major reason for the increase in Protestant dissent was the number of secessions from the established churches, though the emergence of what is generally termed 'new dissent' also had a major impact on 'old dissent'. These earlier Protestant bodies, especially the Baptists and Independents, began to grow in strength from the 1790s and this was reflected in the increasing vehemence of their attacks on the established churches.[29]

Throughout the British Isles relief measures were passed for the benefit of Roman Catholics between the 1770s and 1790s, which allowed them to worship freely and without fear of prosecution. This culminated in the emancipation legislation of 1829, which gave Roman Catholics full political rights. There was a significant growth in the number of Roman Catholics in certain parts of England and Scotland fuelled largely by the first waves of emigration from Ireland. The total Roman Catholic population of the Lancashire towns of Liverpool, Manchester, Preston and Wigan increased from 4,000 in 1767 to 22,000 by 1810. In Scotland there were equally significant increases in the Roman Catholic populations of Dundee, Edinburgh and Glasgow. These increases in the Roman Catholic population created severe tensions within the existing Roman Catholic community, which had been organised as missionary districts under vicars-apostolic, rather than proper dioceses, and had been dominated by the aristocratic and gentry families who had kept the 'old faith' for themselves and their tenants throughout the penal era. The old Roman Catholic community had deliberately kept their services and pastoral operations low key, for fear of upsetting their Protestant neighbours, and found the desire for British Roman Catholicism to move into the European mainstream distinctly disturbing. Nevertheless, some of the leading clergy, such as John

---

[28] Brown, *Religion and Society in Scotland*, 68-69; Yates, *Preaching, Word and Sacrament*, 51-64.

[29] By far the best survey of Protestant nonconformity in England and Wales is Watts, *The Dissenters*.

Maynooth College, *engraving published in J. Warburton et al.,* History of the City of Dublin *(London, 1818), 1316.*
[Dublin, National Library of Ireland: Ir 94133 w2]

Milner (1752-1826), vicar-apostolic of the Midland District, from 1803, were responsible for imposing changes on clergy and laity which had precisely this effect.[30]

The situation in Ireland was rather different. Here between three-quarters and four-fifths of the population, at any one time, were Roman Catholics, the remaining Protestants being divided roughly three-fifths to the established Church of Ireland and two-fifths to the Presbyterians. The Roman Catholic Church had preserved at least an embryo hierarchy throughout the penal period and by the second half of the eighteenth century all the dioceses had been filled and a programme of reform initiated. This programme was spearheaded by a small group of extremely influential bishops: Francis Moylan (1735-1815), initially at Kerry and then at Cork, John Thomas Troy (1739-1823) and Daniel Murray (1768-1852) at Dublin, William Crolly (1780-1849) at Armagh and James Warren Doyle (1786-1834) at Kildare and Leighlin. The reform movement was also assisted by the establishment of the seminary at Maynooth in 1795. By 1844 no fewer than 19 of the 27 serving Roman Catholic bishops in Ireland had

---

[30] Some of the important work on Roman Catholicism in England, Scotland and Wales is now rather dated and in need of revision; a useful beginning has been made by Mullett, *Catholics in Britain and Ireland.* Older studies include Bossy, *The English Catholic Community*; Johnson, *Developments in the Roman Catholic Church in Scotland*; and Norman, *The English Catholic Church in the Nineteenth Century.*

been educated at Maynooth. From 1788 there were periodic meetings of the four Irish archbishops and from 1823 at least annual meetings of all the bishops. The agenda of the Roman Catholic bishops in Ireland covered very similar concerns to those of their Anglican counterparts: more services, preaching and catechising; improved figures for Mass attendance, confession and reception of Holy Communion; the establishment of parochial confraternities and religious orders; the holding of diocesan conferences for the clergy; improved standards of building maintenance for churches; parochial reorganisation; regular visitation of the parishes; the establishment of schools and libraries. By the 1830s all four archbishoprics, and the vast majority of the bishoprics in Ireland, were in the hands of committed reformers and their programmes of reform were consolidated and implemented throughout Ireland following measures taken to this effect at the Synod of Thurles in 1850.[31]

Between 1780 and 1850 the Scottish Episcopal Church also grew in numbers and influence. The restrictions imposed on it for its Jacobitism after the failed risings of 1715 and 1745 drastically reduced its membership but it survived to benefit from the legal toleration granted, after it formally abjured its Jacobitism, in 1792. Thereafter the church expanded considerably. Those Anglican chapels that had previously not been part of the Episcopal Church, but had been served by clergy ordained by the Churches of England or Ireland had, with one exception, joined the Episcopal Church by 1850. In the same year, all the former dioceses had been resurrected and were served by a total of seven bishops, and a cathedral was established for the diocese of St Andrews, Dunkeld and Dunblane. The landowning classes in Scotland, and those moving to Scotland from elsewhere in the British Isles, were particularly attracted to Scottish Episcopalianism and there were even some converts from the Presbyterian Church of Scotland, attracted by Episcopalianism's more solemn liturgy.[32]

Home and Foreign Missions

Before the nineteenth century the main agencies for missionary work in the Church of England were the Societies for the Promotion of Christian Knowledge (SPCK) and the Propagation of the Gospel in Foreign Parts (SPG), established at the end of the seventeenth century. These two bodies collaborated with the Royal Danish Mission to employ missionaries in India, and print material for their use. Both home and foreign missions received a new impetus from the Evangelical revival during the second half of the eighteenth century. As we have noted, the adoption of itinerant preaching was to cause great conflict between Evangelicals and the church authorities and, once the initial phase of itineracy was over, the chief vehicle for home mission became the

---

[31] Yates, *The Religious Condition of Ireland*, 99-125; see also Connolly, *Priests and People in Pre-Famine Ireland*.

[32] See Strong, *Episcopalianism in Nineteenth-Century Scotland*.

No. 22.   April 1827.

Quarterly Papers,

FOR THE USE OF THE

WEEKLY AND MONTHLY CONTRIBUTORS

TO THE

Baptist Missionary Society.

CHRISTIAN FRIENDS,

In the first of our series of Quarterly Papers we gave you a representation of a *Suttee*; that is, of a Hindoo widow burning herself alive on the funeral pile with the dead body of her husband. More than five years have past away since that paper was published; and it is affecting to think how many wretched females during that time have been sacrificed to this infernal rite! At length, however, the subject is beginning to attract the notice of the benevolent and the humane in this country, so as to produce an effort for its abolition. It is expected, that, very shortly, attention will be called to it, both in the British Parliament, and in the Court of Directors of the East India Company. We are persuaded that many of our readers will rejoice to hear this, and be glad to unite their efforts, by petitioning and other-

Title page of the *Quarterly Papers* of the Baptist Missionary Society, *April 1827*.
[London, British Library: RB.23.a.18345(16)]

publication and distribution of bibles and tracts, either by the churches themselves or by societies set up for the purpose. Evangelicals also made a major contribution to foreign missions, setting up new organisations to take on work that they felt had been neglected by the SPCK and SPG. These new organisations in turn resulted in the reinvigoration of the older bodies and the setting up of missionary organisations by the various groups of Protestant Dissenters. The Baptist Missionary Society was established in 1792 and within a year had set up a mission in Bengal. In 1795 a group of Evangelical Anglicans and Independents formed the London Missionary Society, which sent missionaries to Tahiti in 1796, South Africa in 1798, Ceylon in 1804, Canton in 1807, Demerara in 1808, Malacca in 1815 and Madagascar in 1818. Missionary societies were founded in Scotland at Edinburgh, Glasgow and Paisley in 1796. In 1799 a group of Anglican Evangelicals established the Church Missionary Society, sending out its first missionaries to Sierra Leone in 1802. An Irish branch of the Church Missionary Society was formed in 1814. By the 1820s the society was working in India and the Pacific islands as well as West Africa. The Wesleyan Methodist Missionary Society was founded in 1818 and sent missionaries to West Africa, India, the Caribbean and the Pacific. In 1804 the inter-denominational British and Foreign Bible Society was established to support both home and foreign mission by printing and distributing bibles at minimal cost. Support for missions grew throughout the churches with regular reports of the activities they were supporting being brought back to even the most remote rural congregations. By the middle of the nineteenth century a strong link was being made between missionary work and the expansion of the British Empire.

Members of the missionary public were appalled (and sometimes titillated) when they read missionary accounts of the heathens - including tales of cannibalism, polygamy, nakedness, promiscuity, child sacrifice and idolatry - and they were genuinely horrified by the image of African souls being daily lost to the eternal torments of hell. For the missionary public, there was little doubt that Britain was an elect nation, chosen and raised up by providence for the work of Christianising the globe.[33] It was a religious preoccupation that was to continue right through the nineteenth century.

The one section of British Protestantism that held aloof from this new campaign was the High Church wing of Anglicanism. During the eighteenth century many Anglican High Churchmen had grown increasingly uncomfortable about cooperation with non-episcopally-ordained Protestants, especially if this was to result in the establishment of mission stations outside episcopal control. Until the 1780s all Anglicans outside the British Isles were the responsibility of the bishop of London. Although successive archbishops of Canterbury had tried to persuade the British government to establish bishoprics overseas they had been unsuccessful. Faced with the consecration of Samuel Seabury as bishop of Connecticut by the bishops of the Scottish Epis-

---

[33] Brown, *Providence and Empire*, 196. See generally on this topic Ibid., 31-39, 195-205; Knight, *The Church in the Nineteenth Century*, 101-124 and Strong, *Anglicanism and the British Empire*, 118-282.

copal Church in 1784, the British Government eventually allowed the archbishop of Canterbury to consecrate two further bishops for the former American colonies in 1787. A bishop was also consecrated for Nova Scotia in the same year. However, it was not until 1814 that the first bishop was consecrated for a country with a predominantly non-Christian population; this was Thomas Middleton of Calcutta. Further bishoprics were established in India at Madras in 1835 and Bombay in 1837, in Africa at Cape Town in 1847 and at Hong Kong in 1849.[34] The attempt to establish what turned out to be a short-lived joint Anglican-Lutheran bishopric in Jerusalem in 1841 created severe divisions among Anglican High Churchmen, which effectively sealed the fate of any cooperation between Anglicans and other Protestants in the mission field for the best part of a century. Anglican missionary work took on an increasingly 'party' approach, with Evangelicals channelling their work through CMS and its affiliated organisations and High Churchmen operating through a reinvigorated SPG.

There is no doubt that the period 1780-1850 was a crucial one for internal church reform in British and Irish history, through the theological initiatives of the Evangelical Revival and of the High Church revival whose contribution will be dealt with in the next chapter, and also through administrative reform initiatives within the churches, especially the steps taken to improve the education and professional status of the clergy. The churches themselves had changed dramatically in this period. In the case of the established churches this was just as much the result of internal reform initiatives as of those measures imposed on the churches as part of the programme of political reforms between the 1820s and 1840s.

---

[34] See Jacob, *The Making of the Anglican Church Worldwide*, 62-143.

The Oxford Movement and the Legacy of Anglican Evangelicalism

Peter Nockles

The previous chapter referred to the contribution of the Evangelical Revival to reform in the nineteenth century. The literature on 'evangelical revival', especially in regard to its origins and genesis, is vast. It is matched by a no less substantial literature on the subject of organic and institutional church reform in the long eighteenth century. However, the treatment of church reform has been primarily in institutional or structural rather than theological or spiritual terms. This essay will focus on the Oxford Movement, the High Church religious movement within the Church of England that emerged in the 1830s.

The Oxford Movement (1833-1845), led by a coterie of individuals from within the University of Oxford including John Henry Newman (1801-1890), John Keble (1792-1866), Richard Hurrell Froude (1803-1836) and later Edward Bouverie Pusey (1800-1882), was a religious and intellectual revival in defence of the Church of England as a divine institution, a branch of the wider Catholic Church and a repository of the apostolical succession and of sacramental grace. It aimed to reassert the doctrine of the authority and independence of the church in the face of interference by the state. In its appeal to 'first principles', the movement aimed to restore the faith and practice of the Early Church and the High Church ideals of seventeenth-century Anglicanism. The term 'Tractarian' or 'Tractarianism' soon became shorthand for followers of the Oxford Movement and to describe the principles enshrined in a series of publications called the *Tracts for the Times*.

This chapter will seek to highlight the Oxford Movement's 'reformist' credentials in theological, ecclesiological, liturgical, and devotional terms. Comparisons will also be drawn with the earlier Evangelical Revival, discussed in the previous chapter, and with its nineteenth-century adherents within the Church of England.

Peter Nockles

Evangelical and Tractarian Movements

Religious revival has been mainly studied with a focus on 'evangelical' individual spiritual conversions for which certain criteria were laid down. However, an 'evangelical' revival could also manifest itself in institutional terms. One dimension of an 'evangelical' revival, that of renewal of the church as a whole after a period of neglect or decline, can be applied to the Oxford Movement. A key criterion for "a genuine revival of religion" laid down in 1851 by Daniel Wilson (1805-1886), vicar of Islington, was that of "a return to vigour and energy after a state of torpor and inactivity". Another criterion was the raising up of individuals as agents of revival endowed with special gifts.[1] The early Tractarian leaders were conscious of the need for another criterion, not normally found in the evangelical understanding of revival - a renewal and reform of the church's corporate practical life as well as of her theological resources. The idea of a 'church' or 'catholic' institutional revival was to become a commonplace in the literature on Tractarianism from at least the 1860s onwards. This broader understanding of revival was arguably more akin to the notions of religious reform which characterise the theme of this series.

The language and terminology of reform in the so-called Age of Reform has been explored in recent scholarship, notably by Joanna Innes and Arthur Burns.[2] Drawing on their insights, I will argue that the term 'reform' might be used interchangeably with that of 'revival' in a certain sense. The Swedish Lutheran author, Yngve Brilioth's masterly *Anglican Revival: Studies in the Oxford Movement*, published in 1925, has been one of the few studies to treat the Oxford Movement in terms of a theological and religious revival (in both individualist and corporate terms) that can accommodate the term 'reform'. For the Tractarian reinvigoration of the Church of England as a whole after 1833 to a large extent was nourished on a preceding renewal of the individual interior life of its leading participants, a renewal sometimes fostered as much by the influence of Evangelicalism as by traditional High Churchmanship. However, the 'church revival' not only depended on a preceding individual religious revival in a sense recognisable to writers of 'revival' literature, but Brilioth's approach also enables us to see the Oxford Movement more clearly as one of 'reform' in theological terms.

It is possible, however, to get behind the well-rehearsed polemics which divided Tractarians and Evangelicals and which solidified in succeeding generations, and to view the real spiritual affinities which both movements originally had in common; a fact perhaps the less surprising when it is realised just how many adherents and followers of the Oxford Movement had come from Evangelical households or had had an early Evangelical career. A motivating factor was a desire for 'reform' as well as 'revival' of the religious *status quo*. Moreover, certain individuals such as the Irish High

---

[1] Wilson, *The Revival of Spiritual Religion*, 4-5. Daniel Wilson was the son of Daniel Wilson, bishop of Calcutta, whom he had succeeded as vicar of Islington in 1832.

[2] See Burns and Innes, eds., *Rethinking the Age of Reform*, esp. Burns, "English 'Church Reform' Revisited".

Churchman, Alexander Knox (1757-1831) and his friend and life-long correspondent, John Jebb (1775-1833), bishop of Limerick, acted as bridge figures who managed to span the Evangelical/High Church divide and ensured that what became known as Tractarianism retained components of Evangelicalism and even elements characteristic of Wesleyan Methodism: such common features included an emphasis on a 'religion of the heart' and 'vital religion', on the importance of dogma, and the necessity of the pursuit of holiness. It was one of Knox's contentions that the Church of England since the Reformation had neglected an emphasis on the interior life partly out of an excessive fear of 'popery'. He regarded Evangelicalism and Methodism as supplying that deficiency but his real hope for was for a reinvigoration of a dormant High Church Anglicanism which might harness the best in both competing spiritual traditions. For this reason, Knox and Jebb have been regarded as precursors of the Oxford Movement. It was with them in mind that Brilioth maintained that the Oxford Movement might be better and more broadly described as the 'Anglican Renaissance' or the revival of 'Neo-Anglicanism'. Newman himself characterised the Tractarian movement as "in fact a second Reformation", designed to correct or amend, if not undo, the first.[3]

The Oxford Movement

The Oxford Movement (at least in its classic first phase covering the years 1833-1845) cannot be understood without regard to the context of the University of Oxford. The movement had been preceded at Oxford in the 1820s by a purely intellectual and academic revival, associated with a group of liberal-minded but orthodox Anglican divines centred on Oriel College called the 'Noetics'. The importance of the Noetics has tended to be overshadowed by the ensuing Oxford Movement. In the historiography of the movement they have come to be represented as exponents of a theological liberalism against which the Tractarians reacted. This representation, the product of later theological differences which were latent rather than explicit in the earlier period, is in need of correction. The Noetics anyway were never a coherent or organised party in the way their future opponents, the Tractarians would become. They are best understood in their own right as leading agents in the wider process of Anglican renewal. Mark Pattison (1813-1884), later rector of Lincoln College, even claimed that the Noetics provided an intellectual position on which the Oxford Movement could rest, arguing that the Noetics taught the future Tractarians 'to think' and develop those logical and analytical skills which they were to employ with such effect on behalf of orthodoxy and against theological liberalism.[4]

---

[3] See Stokes, "Alexander Knox and the Oxford Movement"; Brilioth, *The Anglican Revival*, 331-333, chs 3 and 4; Gunstone, "Alexander Knox"; Newman, *Via Media*, I, 2.

[4] Brent, "The Oriel Noetics"; Corsi, *Science and Religion*; Pattison, *Memoirs*, 78-81.

F. Mackenzie, The Hall & Chapel, Oriel College, engraving, 1834.
[Oxford, University of Oxford, Oriel College, Archives]

The Oxford Movement soon attracted able and articulate supporters both within and without the confines of the University. The atmosphere and *ethos* of Oxford itself, with all its historical associations, monastic, Cavalier, Tory, Nonjuror and Jacobite, made it, in Matthew Arnold's immortal words, a city of "lost causes and [...] impossible loyalties". Oxford was a *genius loci* which exerted a potent spell on a rising generation already infused with the influence of Romanticism. As Newman made clear, the popularity of Romantic authors such as Scott was symptomatic of "a growing tendency to that character of mind and feeling of which Catholic doctrines are the just expression".[5]

In his 1839 Crewean Oration (an endowed University of Oxford lecture) as Oxford's professor of Poetry, Keble argued that Wordsworth's poetic depiction of the poor and of rural life and Scott's recapturing in vivid prose of the spirit and values of the age of chivalry and feudal custom, had encouraged a reaction in favour of ancient institutions and stirred emotions that were conducive to a religious revival within the Church of England. Newman and Keble built upon and utilised this 'catholic' spirit, a spirit that went far deeper than merely reactionary nostalgia or an assertion of Romantic sensibility. Keble's celebrated sacred verse, *The Christian Year* (1827), provided a

---

[5] Arnold, *Essays in Criticism*; Newman, "State of Religious Parties", esp. 399-416.

new religious "music, the music of a school long unknown in England", and one which resonated with the rising generation, not least those reared within the Evangelical tradition.[6] Many commentators have regarded this publication as the true moment of the Oxford Movement's spiritual genesis. Nonetheless, the Oxford Movement represented much more than a 'churching of Romanticism', having its intellectual roots in eighteenth-century Counter-Enlightenment and anti-rationalist thought as exemplified by Bishop Butler and William Law.[7]

The Oxford Movement was the heir of a long and rich High Church tradition within Anglicanism, which endured through the eighteenth century when the forces of latitudinarianism and heterodoxy are often assumed to have been dominant. The exact relationship between so-called 'old High Churchmanship' and 'Tractarianism', and how far the Oxford Movement was indebted to a pre-existing tradition continues to be the subject of scholarly focus.[8] One can conclude from the varying evidence that there was to be continuity as well as divergence, but that there needed to be certain ingredients or sparks to produce a religious movement capable of drawing from the well of that older tradition. The 'sparks' were provided by the events of the late-1820s and early-1830s that revolutionised the relationship between church and state.

The question of why the Oxford Movement commenced when it did has been discussed by various historians and is inextricably bound up with political context, both ecclesiastical and secular. In order to gain a sense of its genuinely timeless 'Everyman', transcendent quality, it is important to understand the inner dynamic force of the Oxford Movement, rather than viewing it as a mere reaction or negative recoil from hostile political events of the day. Nonetheless, some explanation here of the immediate background and reasons for the Oxford Movement's date of birth is necessary.

Constitutional Reform

Although the dawn of the Oxford Movement is often dated to John Keble's Oxford Assize Day sermon, entitled *National Apostasy*, delivered in 1833, the timing of its birth can be located within the wider continental political context of responses to recent revolutions in Europe. Within England itself the movement emerged as a reaction to the 'constitutional revolution' in church and state between 1828 and 1833, discussed in detail in volume I. These measures effectively ended an Anglican confessional hegemony. However, these constitutional reforms also had the effect of forcing the church to fall back on its own inner spiritual integrity and inherent powers and providing the spark or trigger that ignited the Oxford Movement. The future Tractarians, though they

---

[6] Newman, *Apologia pro via sua*, 77. Sheridan Gilley has used an apt phrase to describe the process of the Tractarian harnessing of a pre-existing Romantic sensibility: "the Victorian Churching of Romanticism". See Gilley, "John Keble and the Victorian Churching of Romanticism". For the broader relationship between Romanticism and the Oxford Movement, see Prickett, *Romanticism and Religion*.
[7] Pereiro, *"Ethos" and the Oxford Movement*, 79-80.
[8] See Nockles, *The Oxford Movement in Context*.

later accepted them, fiercely resisted these constitutional changes at the time. They were the heirs to the inherited Toryism characteristic of the High Church tradition and in their private correspondence tended to identify the opposing political creed of Whiggery (the Whigs, along with the Tories, forming the historic English political parties) with low churchmanship, latitudinarianism and the forces of secularism.[9]

It would be misleading, however, to view early Tractarianism merely as the ecclesiastical arm of Toryism. While it was certainly the ideological heir to a long tradition of 'High Church' Anglican 'political theology', the Oxford Movement also pushed for the Church of England's complete emancipation in the changed constitutional environment from earlier High Church orthodoxies on the subject of establishment: a trend which paralleled the contemporaneous emergence of 'ultramontanism' on the ruins of *ancien régime* politics on the continent. Moreover, far from being a force for merely conservative reaction, the Oxford Movement's assumption of the primacy of the church over the state was applied in a vigorous social concern over what contemporary commentators called the 'condition of England' question[10] and in a rejection of the prevailing economic philosophy of political economy and Benthamite utilitarianism in favour of the quasi-medieval ideal of what Hurrell Froude labelled the *Pauperes Christi*.

Political events, however, cannot alone account for the rise of a movement which was, at its core, theological, spiritual, and devotional. The movement's religious origins can be traced to a wider religious reaction against the rationalism of the so-called Age of Enlightenment that was pan-European in scope.

A Church in Crisis

Criticism of the late-eighteenth and early-nineteenth-century church was by no means confined to the Tractarians but was made by Anglican Evangelicals, old High Churchmen, and others. In particular, there remains much contemporary evidence for a decline or stagnation in both theological learning at the ancient universities and a perceived need to improve the standard of clerical education. Such educational and spiritual deficiencies can be construed to make out a case for a 'church in crisis', a somewhat different concept to that of the more perennial one of a 'church in danger' where the primary challenge was perceived to be to the church's temporalities. Narrow definitions of 'usefulness' characteristic of potentially destructive state-sponsored church reform were rejected in favour of a recapturing of the original spirit and deeper meaning of apparently decayed institutions. The Oxford Movement's reformist impulse also found expression in the Tractarian advocacy of a counter model of university reform to that of the liberal or secular one.

---

[9] Clark, *English Society*; Nockles, *Oxford Movement in Context*, ch. 1.

[10] See Skinner, *Tractarians and the "Condition of England"*.

Ethos and the Tractarian Reform of the Academy

Liberal and secular critics of the Oxford Movement often portrayed it as a distraction and dislocation of the natural functioning priorities of a university - the pursuit of learning. It was a charge which the Tractarian protagonists who were in the forefront of debates over reform of the universities repudiated with disdain. From its origins, the Oxford Movement possessed a clear and definite vision and ideal of a university and its relation to both church and nation. The University of Oxford was a bulwark of Anglican privilege and monopoly, with even undergraduates being obliged to subscribe to the Thirty-Nine Articles (the doctrinal *formulae* drawn up in 1563 and to which clergy had thereafter to subscribe). However, Tractarian protests in the mid-1830s against liberal reforming plans (emanating from within as well as without the university) were theologically motivated and not mere defensive reactions in favour of an academic *status quo*. The Tractarians opposed liberal or Whig party and parliamentary attempts to reform the university and its collegiate statutes because they rejected the basis and assumptions on which such reforms were formulated. On the other hand, the Tractarians engaged in a reform or counter-reform of their own, attempting to restore and restate statutes that had fallen into abeyance or were not being observed.[11] The Oxford Movement was portrayed as anti-intellectual as well as 'clericalist' by some of its critics but even they conceded that it sought to revive the spirit of learned research in Oxford.

The Oxford Movement was something much more than a rearguard reaction in defence of existing privileges in church and university. In fact, the Tractarians can be regarded as "radicals who deplored the formalism and laxity of current academic practices and stood for their rejuvenation".[12] For example, the Tractarians pressed for the wider study of church history and liturgy within the university. As early as 1834, Benjamin Harrison urged that professors of church polity be created at Oxford and Cambridge. In 1837, conscious of the need to improve clerical training at Oxford, the Tractarians supported a private offer to found a liturgical chair. It was the heads of colleges who rejected the offer. Moreover, by 1840 the Tractarians supported the creation of two new chairs, in ecclesiastical history and biblical criticism, in the University of Oxford, on the grounds that the course of studies at the university were, "of a character too general and vague to have any sufficient bearing on the future usefulness of the Christian minister".[13] The Tractarians only opposed university reform when they perceived that it would have a secularising tendency. In short, there was a dynamic religious motivation at work here which threatened the old *status quo*.

The Tractarian theory of religious knowledge, allied to the concept of *ethos*, underpinned the movement's counter-reform agenda; an agenda which enshrined a positive vision and ideal of a university. At the core of the Oxford Movement, which made it different from the prevailing Anglican high or orthodox churchmanship, lay a

---

[11] See Nockles, "An Academic Counter-Revolution".
[12] Jones, *Intellect and Character in Victorian England*, 29.
[13] See Nockles, "An Academic Counter-Revolution", 193 n. 114.

new emphasis on the concept of *ethos*, a distinctive theory of religious knowledge. The notion of *ethos* has not always been well understood or emphasised in literature on the movement. The problem of definition has been heightened by the paucity of references and explanations of the term by the movement's leading actors. It was defined by Newman's brother-in-law Thomas Mozley (1806-1893), as a "dominant moral habit or proclivity".[14] Asceticism, self-denial, self-resignation, obedience, reverence, awe, submissiveness to authority, and an openness to the divine will, were all characteristics of a Tractarian spiritual *ethos*. An apostolical *ethos* disdained intellectual pride, self-sufficiency and speculation, the claims of private judgment, and a mere mental or logical ability and dialectical skill. It was also rooted in a theory of religious knowledge by which orthodox belief was bound up with moral conduct and behaviour. Moral or ethical flaws could be productive of doctrinal error or heresy. As Pereiro shows, the Tractarians imbibed deeply and reapplied certain key precepts of Aristotle's *Nicomachean Ethics* and Bishop Joseph Butler's *Analogy of Religion, Natural and Revealed* (1736)[15], both prominently taught in Oxford University's curriculum.

Aristotle's *Ethics* and Butler's *Analogy* inculcated the importance of moral habits in the formation of opinions, virtue and orthodox belief going hand in hand. Butler taught that life was a trial or probation for man, with progress towards ascertaining religious truth related not so much to an intellectual reception of the 'evidences' for Christianity on the basis of human reason but to man's own spiritual progress from blindness to light. Both works appealed to the generation of pupils under Newman's care at Oriel College, such as Samuel Francis Wood (1809-1843), gifted younger brother of Charles Wood, first Viscount Halifax, and later a prominent London lawyer. For Wood, such works helped make up for what he regarded as religious deficiencies in the standard religious teaching of the day which he found "wanting in practical reality".

Newman and his followers put into practice at Oriel their high ideal of the pastoral office of a college tutor. The idea that there should be greater intercourse between tutor and pupil had been developed at Oriel before Newman's time and was a by-product of the academic revolution represented by the university reforms of 1800s Oxford. However, it became a cornerstone of Newman's and Tractarian educational philosophy. For Newman, a college was a living entity or *milieu* and not a mere institution or place of abstract teaching. It was the medium of the personal religious and moral as well as intellectual influence of a teacher. Any academic system which lacked this essential element, for Newman was but "an arctic winter [...] ice-bound, petrified, cast iron". Newman's pastoral concept of the tutorial office had reformist implications. Newman effectively overturned the dominance of what he called "a lax traditional party in the College"[16], and did not scruple to regard the improvements in academic organisation

---

[14] Mozley, *Reminiscences, Chiefly of Oriel College and the Oxford Movement*, 211-212.

[15] Pereiro, *Ethos and the Oxford Movement*, 87-95.

[16] The first quotation is cited in Ker, *The Achievement of John Henry Newman*, 188 n. 39. The second is from Dessain and Gornall, eds., *Letters and Diaries of John Henry Newman*, 419.

W. Ross, John Henry Newman, *oil on canvas, 1845*.
[Birmingham, The Birmingham Oratory]

G. Richmond, John Keble, *engraving (detail)*.
[Leuven, K.U.Leuven, Centrale bibliotheek]

and discipline which he initiated as a reform. Newman's practice was not unique, but he helped set Oriel apart from laxer colleges still wedded to older ways.

The Tractarians countered external government-based attempts to reform the university's statutes in the 1830s. However, whereas many of the old 'high and dry' elements ignored calls for statute revision, the Tractarians advocated a restoration of the full observance of original statutes and the spirit of 'our Founders'. In Oriel College, Newman advocated a return to the spirit of its fourteenth-century founder, Adam de Brome. His ideal was for the head of College and fellows living together as a brotherhood, sharing a common table, all devoted to the life of study and using their learning in the service of God.

Newman's conflict with Provost Hawkins and his own subsequent secession to Rome ultimately prevented him from realising the fulfilment of his educational ideal within Oriel itself, but it found an echo in his community at Littlemore (the village in St Mary's parish outside Oxford to which Newman increasingly retired after 1840) and in other Tractarian inspired educational reform proposals of university extension in favour of better provision for poor scholars in Oxford.[17] Above all, these ideals found eloquent expression and a lasting legacy in Newman's *Ideal of a University* (1854), inspired by his attempts to establish a Catholic University in Ireland.

---

[17] Culler, *The Imperial Intellect*, 90; Marriott, *Letter to the Rev. E.C. Woollcombe*.

The Principle of Reserve

Tractarian *ethos* also found expression in the theological principle as well as moral temper of 'reserve'. This was a distinctive Tractarian contribution and amounted to a 'reform' of the prevailing 'religion of the day'. The notion of 'reserve' propounded by Isaac Williams (1802-1865) in two of the *Tracts for the Times* (numbers 80 and 87), in reaction against what the Tractarians regarded as the emotional excesses of popular Evangelical religiosity, manifested itself in an unwillingness to speak of religious experience and sacred matters in familiar discourse; it was a principle which dictated strict reticence when communicating religious knowledge, especially in relation to the doctrine of the Atonement which Evangelicals tended to place at the forefront of their teaching and evangelisation.[18]

The Evangelical manner of preaching the Atonement was deplored by Tractarians who contrasted this method with the reverence with which the Early Church treated the doctrine. Newman's *Arians of the Fourth Century* (1833) claimed that a *Disciplina Arcani* or 'secret teaching' had operated in the pre-Nicean Church (i.e. before the Council of Nicea, A.D. 325) and he also justified its continued use from the precedent that in the Church of Alexandria the catechumens were not taught all the doctrines of the Christian faith. The more vitriolic Evangelical critics of the Oxford Movement claimed that Newman's *Arians* and Tractarian advocacy of Reserve planted the "seed from which many a noxious weed has grown".[19] Even traditional High Churchmen were critical of the Tractarian emphasis on a 'secret tradition' within the church. However, recent scholarship suggests that Newman's fondness for the secret tradition, as expressed in his *Arians,* was an aspect of his 'radicalism', rather than 'Romanism'.

Implications of the Appeal to Antiquity

The sense of crisis among Anglican churchman in the early-1830s was heightened by the apparent threat posed by church reform proposals emanating from latitudinarians and by those from the Protestant Dissenting camp. These proposals included suggestions for reform of the liturgy and Articles, so as to conciliate Protestant Dissenters. The movement of reaction in 1833, of which the Tractarians initially formed but one component, thus had a defensive emphasis. The Tractarians were not initially inclined to go beyond defence of the existing formularies of the church, the Thirty-Nine Articles included.

The Oxford Movement's appeal was primarily to the Ancient or Early Church in its religious practice as well as its formal doctrine and teaching of the Fathers. It is significant that Newman and Froude soon utilised the self-description of 'Apostolicals' for themselves and referred to this or that aspirant potential follower as having

---

[18] See Selby, *The Principle of Reserve in the Writings of John Henry Cardinal Newman.*

[19] Walsh, *The Secret History of the Oxford Movement,* 1.

acquired or being in the process of acquiring an 'Apostolical *ethos*' or a 'Catholic *ethos*'. Tractarian creative patristic scholarship was reflected in Newman's *Arians of the Fourth Century* (1832), in the 'Library of the Fathers' project (begun in 1836) and in Newman's own prolonged research especially in the Christological controversies of the Early Church as reflected in his edition of *The Select Treatises of St Athanasius* (1842). Such scholarship had a conservative aim in vindicating Trinitarian and credal orthodoxy, but by no means employed a merely conservative methodology. In theological terms, the dynamic Tractarian appeal to tradition and the Early Church as a final court of appeal rather than merely a corroborative testimony to the truth of the Church of England's current formularies as was the case with most traditional High Churchmen, had radical implications. For it ultimately had the effect of raising a sense of dissatisfaction with existing Anglican liturgical and doctrinal standards.[20] The Tractarians were bent on a 'second Reformation' aimed at correcting faults and omissions left over from the first. In liturgical terms, this translated into a preference for the first Edwardian Prayer Book of 1549 over the 1662 version, and a desire to restore various primitive practices and usages such as prayers for the dead, while in worship it found expression in a revival of the weekday service and the offertory.

The implications of the Tractarian quest for anchoring the contemporary Church of England more closely to Antiquity were also evident in its evolving attitude to the Thirty-Nine Articles. The Tractarians supported the principle of subscription to the Articles, not only for ordination candidates but for undergraduates and fellows of colleges in the universities of Oxford and Cambridge, as conducive to a requisite submission to church authority, though privately Newman and others by the mid-1830s were already no friends to the theological content of the Articles themselves.

The Tractarians were not primarily concerned with the disputes between Calvinist and Arminian interpretations which had divided Anglican churchmen of a previous generation. Newman's concern in his notorious Tract 90 (1841) was with the Protestantism of the Articles *per se*. Recognising this as a stumbling block for many of his increasingly extreme followers, he aimed in Tract 90 to show that, while the product of an 'un-catholic age', the Thirty-Nine Articles were 'patient' of a 'catholic' interpretation. The principles of interpretations set forth in Tract 90 were condemned by an alliance of old High Churchmen and Anglican Evangelicals. However, the significance of Newman's advocacy of a 'catholic latitude' in interpreting the Articles was not lost upon a rising generation of latitudinarian or broad churchmen such as A.P. Stanley (1815-1881). 'Broad church' was a popular term, coined by the second half of the nineteenth century on the analogy of 'High Church' and 'Low Church', for those in the Church of England who objected to rigid doctrinal definition and sought to interpret the Anglican formularies in a broad and liberal sense. Such broad churchmen used the precedent of Tract 90 for their own later attempts to widen or relax the terms of subscription to Articles and Creeds in ensuing decades.

---

[20] Nockles, *Oxford Movement in Context*, 217-223.

Tract by John Henry Newman *(1841)* and sermon by Edward Bouverie Pusey *(1843)*.
[Leuven, K.U.Leuven, Centrale bibliotheek: 4A5835]

The Rejection of 'Evidence' Theology

The Tractarian theological *ethos* also encompassed a rejection of the evidential and utilitarian method of Christian apologetic associated with such figures as William Warburton (1698-1779) and William Paley (1743-1805) in favour of an emphasis on the sacramental principle and the mystical or typological interpretation of Holy Scripture. This was another manifestation of a theological reforming impulse that challenged a prevailing apologetic that emphasised human reason, natural theology, and utility in the preservation and communication of religious knowledge. In contrast, for the Tractarians, the prerequisites for the reception of the truths of the gospel were the humility and receptivity of a child as well as reserve, and not mere intellectual attainment or rational enquiry. For Newman, the Paleyite emphasis on a study of the physical evidences encouraged an "evil frame of mind" whereby "the learner is supposed external to the system".[21] For the Tractarians, Paley's argument from design was superficial because it failed to engage with those deeper moral truths that lay above and beyond nature, in the unseen world. The Tractarians argued that material phenomena were both the types and instruments of things unseen. As Pusey maintained in his unpublished "Lectures on Types and Prophecies" (1836), God had created "a sort of sacramental union between the type and the archetype, such that the type is meaningful only to the extent that it expresses the archetype, and the archetype can be grasped only by means of embodiment within the type".[22]

In Tract 89, *On the Mysticism attributed to the Early Fathers of the Church* (1841), Keble emphasised the patristic basis of an allegorical understanding of external or material things. The Tractarians were also greatly indebted to Butler's arguments from probability and analogy. The Tractarians absorbed and reapplied Butler's view that man's knowledge was partial and based on probable arguments and that right moral temper was his true guide on the path in search of truth.

Conclusions: the Oxford Movement and Religious Reform

In conclusion, the Oxford Movement represented a struggle for the reassertion of the historic autonomy and institutional freedom of the church against the restrictions and compromises concomitant on religious establishment. The implications of the anti-Erastianism of the movement took some while to work themselves out but by the 1840s many followers of the 'catholic revival' accepted the multi-confessional nature of society, while the foundations of what has been called 'liberal catholicism' were laid.

The crisis in church and state of 1828-1833 served as a catalyst but the movement had a life and spirit of its own which transcended contemporary temporal and political realities. While in origin its vision was to 'catholicise' the Church of England as a whole, its long term accommodation as a 'party' within the church was dependent on eventual acceptance of the idea of religious pluralism and freedom. The active thrust of the movement was also evident in its theological principles but its contribution was most significant in relation to the promotion of theological learning and academic reform. In short, in reacting to contemporary political crisis in church and state, deeper religious forces were unleashed. Tractarianism, like earlier continental Pietism and Anglo-American Evangelical revivalism, was a reaction against a 'dead' orthodoxy and an agency of religious reform.

The Oxford Movement was both an intellectual movement and one of spiritual revival. It was its intellectual dimension which probably attracted many sons from Evangelical households, for whom the religion of the day, even 'Evangelical' religion, was found wanting in practical 'reality'. For those from this tradition, the 'Catholic

---

[21] J.H. Newman to A.P. Perceval, 11 January 1836, Gornall, ed., *Letters & Diaries of John Henry Newman*, V, 197.

[22] Pusey, "Lectures on Types and Prophecies", 1836, Pusey Papers, Pusey House Library, Oxford.

Revival', unlike its Evangelical precursor, awakened a sense of the independent and corporate life of the church in relation to the state. It also represented a much needed revival of theological studies and learning; a much needed liturgical renewal; stricter attention to the rubrics (i.e. ritual or ceremonial directions printed at the beginnings of service books); architectural improvement; improvement of education, a revival of the religious life and also the value of self-denial; a renewed missionary impulse based on a corporate view of the church rather than freelance zeal; and greater recognition of Christian art and culture. According to William Stubbs (1825-1901), the famous medieval historian and later bishop of Oxford, the results were "wonderful" and "to be seen in every village church, to be heard in every sermon, to be felt in the administration of every parish. Never since the Reformation had there been such a change, and the influences that wrought it were more intellectual and more spiritual than those which affected the Reformation."[23]

In his 1842 Bampton Lectures at Oxford which had challenged Tractarian theological principles, James Garbett had this to say of the *Tracts for the Times*: "Whatever judgment may be formed of their ultimate tendency [...] so wide an influence could never have been exerted, or the approbation, however qualified, of wise and good men have been obtained, unless they had successfully struck some deep chord - had hit on some real wants of the period - and brought out distinctly into light certain substantive principles [...] they [...] probed unsparingly the religious and political deficiencies of the times."[24]

It was a moving tribute. If it were intended as an epitaph on a movement of genuine religious reform which corrected wants and deficiencies, it would be one of which the leaders of the Oxford Movement could have been proud.

---

[23] Stubbs, *Visitation Charge*, 54.

[24] Garbett, *Christ as Prophet, Priest, and King*, 1, 462-463.

Internal Church Reform, 1850-1920
An Age of Innovation in Ecclesiastical Reform

Frances Knight

The previous two chapters have examined reform in Britain in the first half of the nineteenth century. In this chapter we shall examine how reform developed in the second half of the century.

The Context of Church Reform

For as long as historians of British Christianity have been studying the nineteenth century, they have been talking about church reform. In part, this is because the participants in nineteenth-century British Christianity, and particularly the Anglican ones, became obsessed with it. As Geoffrey Best put it, "Untold dozens of churchmen buckled down to the self-imposed task of communicating to the world their views, and their views on other writer's views, on this engrossing subject."[1] More recently, Arthur Burns has noted that "'Church reform' is one of the most widely deployed concepts in ecclesiastical historiography. In the modern English context, it moved seamlessly during the late nineteenth and early twentieth centuries from being of central importance in the discussions of ecclesiastical policy-makers to assume a place as a key category in the conceptual apparatus of historical inquiry into the shaping of the Victorian Church of England."

What was true for the Church of England was also true of other ecclesiastical bodies, most of which became caught up in similar processes of reform, readjustment, revival and renewal. Equally, the 'reform' motif was widely applied in a whole range of other nineteenth-century British institutions, as they underwent various processes

---

[1] Best, *Temporal Pillars*, 278.

of modernisation. Indeed, in the volume Burns edited with Joanna Innes, the authors explore reform in the context of opera, the London stage and national art institutions, as well as in relation to Ireland and empire, and to more obvious topics such as parliament, the church, medicine and the law. Their volume provides the most methodologically complete treatment of the aspiration for reform in Britain in the first half of the nineteenth century, and its 'holistic' approach is much to be welcomed. It echoes at least some of the preoccupations of John Wade, whose *Extraordinary Black Book* (1831) is often cited as one of the most significant contributors to the reform clamour of the 1830s. Wade dealt with a range of issues including parliamentary representation, the church, the crown establishment and the civil list, diplomats, the peerage, law, debt, taxation, the East India Company, the Bank of England, and sinecures.[2] In stimulating ways, then, the Burns and Innes volume provides an interesting British counterpoint to our current endeavour to place the dynamics of ecclesiastical reform in a comparative European perspective.

An obvious point about the Burns and Innes volume is that it concludes in 1850. So if 'the age of reform' had indeed concluded by about 1850, what was it followed by? From an ecclesiastical point of view, 'the age of decline' seems to have been the leading contender for several decades in the recent past, a perspective influenced by what has since become the increasingly complex territory of the secularisation debate. Originally, this phenomenon was accepted as having taken hold by the 1850s, after Horace Mann, who had been responsible for writing the preface to the Report on the 1851 Religious Census, described the working classes as "unconscious secularists". Then newer thoughts about secularisation led to 'the age of decline' being shunted forward. So if, following Simon Green, Callum Brown and others, the age of religious decline in Britain is to be pushed firmly into the twentieth century, and older studies, for example P.T. Marsh's *The Victorian Church in Decline* (1969), which argued that the Church of England had "declined unmistakably" by the 1880s, are to be retired from use on the grounds that they are out of date, where does that leave the period 1850-1920? It can be argued that, in ecclesiastical terms at least, the 'age of reform', as conventionally defined, was succeeded by a seventy-year period that was characterised by extraordinary energy and innovation, together with what we may begin to discern as the making of the modern religious mind.

This is a view that would certainly be endorsed by those with an interest in the intellectual development of the period, for as James C. Livingston has noted, "In the study of *religious thought*, it certainly would be incorrect to describe it as simply a time of secularization. The late Victorian period can best be viewed as a time of religious change - change that had profound and enduring influences."[3] On the one hand, during this time religious identities and practices continued to be centrally important

---

[2] Burns, "English 'Church Reform' Revisited", 136 (quotation); Burns and Innes, eds., *Rethinking the Age of Reform*, 2-3.

[3] Livingston, *Religious Thought in the Victorian Age*, 4.

to large numbers of people. Sometimes these were looser and less rigid, but at others more tightly defined. Christians began to define themselves more carefully in relation to what they were not (for example secularists, or other types of religious people of whom they disapproved) and to fight for the most effective use of whatever ground remained available to them, in a world where politics was moving to the centre, and religion to the periphery. On the other hand, a number of recognisably contemporary approaches to religion began to emerge, ranging from a much more pragmatic attitude to religious pluralism, to a recognisably modern approach to theological questions. At the outset, we need to remember that the 'reform and decline' language owes more to what Burns terms "the conceptual apparatus of historical enquiry", rather than to the progressive, decade-on-decade continuity that was the actual experience of most of the British churches in the nineteenth and early twentieth centuries. This chapter will consider the key themes that have been identified as axiomatic for the dynamics of internal ecclesiastical reform, focussing in turn on the experiences of the established churches, the Nonconformist churches, and Roman Catholicism.

Church Organisation: the Established Churches

In the couple of decades before 1850, the Church of England had felt the full force of politically-originated, structurally-focussed ecclesiastical reform. Parliamentary measures had been brought in to bring about the ending of sinecures, non-residence and pluralism; improvements in conditions for curates; the creation of mechanisms such as the Ecclesiastical Commission; the redistribution of episcopal revenues; adjustments in diocesan and parochial boundaries; adjustments in the operation of church patronage and reform of the ecclesiastical courts. By 1840, the external pressure for church reform was waning, and to a remarkable degree, the church had itself internalised the processes of reform which had been originally proposed to it by politicians. After 1850, parliamentary time was still needed to enact major structural changes, such as the creation of new dioceses, but now more often than not ecclesiastical irritation was expressed at the slowness and delay in bringing about reform through the parliamentary process, rather than at the fact of government 'interference' in church affairs.[4] The government's response to this came at the very end of our period, in 1919, when the Enabling Act was passed and the Church Assembly was created. This was intended to give the Church of England far greater control over its own affairs without the need for such regular recourse to parliamentary processes. The era of parliamentary church reform was over, although there would continue to be occasional skirmishes

---

[4] For example, in relation to the reorganisation of the Church of England in East Anglia, which required the creation of a new diocese (Bury St Edmunds and Ipswich) and significant modifications to the boundaries of the existing ones. This proposal was already being enthusiastically spoken of by church people in the 1880s, but insufficient parliamentary time was forthcoming to make it a reality until 1914.

Banner of the Mothers' Union of Alresford (Essex).
[Private collection]

between the Church of England and Parliament, most notably in 1927 and 1928, when Parliament twice rejected revisions to the Prayer Book, and the church decided to use it anyway.

One particular organisational feature of the Church of England in the period from 1850 to 1920 was the very large number of new Anglican societies that were founded. It also became increasingly common for national bodies to have both diocesan and parochial branches - for example the Church of England Men's Society, the Mothers' Union and the Church of England Temperance Society. As we shall see later, the Church of England supported a whole variety of evangelistic and missionary developments. Another innovation of this period was the extraordinary expansion of monastic communities for women, and to a lesser degree, for men. In the period from 1850 to 1913, a total of 91 communities for women and 24 for men were founded.[5] Men's communities tended to be established later, with the 1890s being a particularly prolific decade, and with the founders, for example R.M. Benson (1824-1915), Charles Gore (1853-1932), Herbert Kelly (1860-1950) and Aelred Carlyle (1874-1955), becoming well known names within the church. Although sisterhoods were being established at the rate of several a year for much of the period, and although they often made a considerable impact in their local communities at the time, they have generally left a shallower imprint on the historical record, and some did not last very long. Nevertheless, Susan Mumm has estimated that approximately 10,000 women passed through the Anglican communities in the period from 1845 to 1900, although some stayed for only a short period.[6]

In addition to feeling the effects of Westminster-inspired reform (such as the Irish Church Temporalities Act, 1833) the established churches in Ireland and Wales faced the very major organisational challenges of disestablishment, both in prospect and actuality, in 1869 in Ireland and in 1920 in Wales. In Ireland, the Church of Ireland could claim the allegiance of only 12% of the population in 1860, and its relationship with the Church of England was different from that of the Welsh church, as it had only been united with its sister church as a result of the Act of Union of 1800. In Wales, support for the established church was larger, and indeed growing, in the period under discussion here. The relationship with the Church of England was organic. In institutional terms, there was no difference between the Welsh diocese of Bangor and the neighbouring English diocese of Chester, although in cultural terms, the differences were very considerable. After 1869, therefore, the Church of Ireland assumed the status of an independent voluntary organisation, and Ireland became one of the few places in Europe without an established church.

In 1850, the established Church of Scotland was still reeling from the effects of the Disruption of 1843, in which 38% of its ministers and between 40 and 50% of its lay adherents had left it, in order to form the Free Church of Scotland under the leadership of Thomas Chalmers. Many of those who had left had been among the church's most active members, and so their departure was felt even more acutely than is implied simply from the percentages. In the space of just over one hundred years, the Church of Scotland had, to a greater extent than any of the other established churches, been

---

[5] Data supplied by Dr Melissa Wilkinson.   [6] Mumm, *Stolen Daughters, Virgin Mothers*, 4.

reduced from a position of near monopoly to being simply one Presbyterian denomination among several. By the last quarter of the nineteenth century, the Church of Scotland could claim the allegiance of less than 15% of the total population[7], a situation that was not all that far removed from that of the Church of Ireland. As we shall see later, it was to experience reunion, after the period of separation.

Church Organisation: Nonconformity

In 1854, the publication of the Religious Census revealed that roughly half of those who had attended worship on 30 March 1851 had attended a service in a Nonconformist place of worship, and as the process of recording attendances gave greater weighting to those who worshipped in the morning, it is likely that the Nonconformists, with their emphasis on evening services, were under-represented by the official statistics. The Census also revealed for the first time the regional distribution of the major Nonconformist bodies, although the picture would not be fully uncovered until the arrival of late-twentieth century historians with powerful computer programmes. Methodism, which by 1851 had fragmented into eight different denominations, was dominant in the Midlands, North Norfolk, the North-East, West Yorkshire, Cornwall and Wales. The Independent tradition, known as Congregationalism by this time, was strongest in the South-East of England, the Central Midlands, parts of the South-West and Wales. Baptist strongholds were Southern Wales, and Central and South-East England. Between them, the major Nonconformist denominations had achieved a thick blanket of national coverage, with some of the smaller and older denominations still hanging on to their pockets of regional significance.[8] In Scotland, where the Census was less reliably administered, it appears that 59% of church attendances were taking place within the dissenting communities. The variety of Presbyterian groups could almost rival English Methodism in their number and familial resemblances. Collectively, Nonconformists provided very serious rivalry to the established churches, and in some regions they were strongly in the ascendant. Each denomination differed, in part because differing ecclesiology gave rise to differing approaches to organisation, administration and finance, but in the second half of the nineteenth century, although still buoyant, most were facing the fact that the years of extraordinary growth which had been witnessed in earlier decades were beginning to tail off. Many local congregations were left servicing debts arising from over-optimistic chapel building schemes. The evangelical ethos which marked most, but not all of the Nonconformist bodies, created waves of revivalist expectation; the new chapel, which would often also include a series of function rooms and an adjoining manse, needed to be large, so that when the next revival came, there would be room for everyone to respond to

---

[7] Brown, *Religion and Society in Scotland*, 21-22.
[8] Snell and Ell, *Rival Jerusalems*, 93-172. This is currently the most significant study of the data using computer technology.

the message of salvation. The reality was that congregations, and denominational bodies, found themselves increasingly bogged down with the kinds of organisational and financial issues that they would rather not have faced. In addition to building projects, there was need for money to fund overseas missions (lest the whole world be converted to Roman Catholicism while Nonconformists prevaricated), to establish and enhance training colleges, upgrade ministerial salaries, establish pension provision and pay for growing central bureaucracies. As with all the denominations in Victorian Britain, although there is plenty of evidence of great generosity and sacrifice on the part of lay members and clergy alike, there was never enough money to fund all the extremely ambitious plans which characterised nineteenth-century Christianity, and this provoked a (somewhat self-generated) sense of crisis.

Whilst some denominations were beginning to struggle, there remained in the mid-Victorian ether sufficient evangelical zeal for new ones still to be created. The Salvation Army was the most significant new religious movement of this period, first emerging as yet another off-shoot of a Methodist denomination in 1865, and poised to become a world-wide movement by the end of our period. Organisationally, it borrowed unashamedly from the language and structures of the military world. General Booth presided with absolute authority over the ranks of his officers and soldiers, who waged war on the enemy (godlessness, but also poverty and despair) from their barracks and citadels, strategically positioned in areas of the greatest deprivation. The Salvation Army, in its early days, was strikingly different from much of Victorian Nonconformity and at the other end of the spectrum from the genteel world of thoughtful, suburban Congregationalism.

Church Organisation: Roman Catholicism

In terms of organisation and expansion within British Christianity, the greatest success story of the nineteenth and twentieth centuries was that of the re-rooting of the Roman Catholic Church within British society, to the extent that by the mid-twentieth century, it had become the major denominational alternative to the Church of England. At the time of the 1851 Religious Census, the Catholic population in Britain was experiencing sudden expansion as a result of a wave of migrants arriving from Ireland following the Famine, but it still only amounted to four percent of the population. These people, rather than arriving for seasonal work and then returning home, as had been the pattern in the past, suddenly required year-round and life-long pastoral care. Catholicism still remained very regionally concentrated, north of a line from the Wash to the Bristol Channel, and south of Cumberland and the Pennines, as well as in London. Lancashire was a particular stronghold, with the indigenous population now reinforced by Irish migrants. Catholicism remained very weak in Wales. In Scotland, the initially small Catholic population was boosted by a dramatic expansion in arrivals from Ireland, who settled around the south western seaboard, and particularly in Glasgow. In organisational terms, the major event at the beginning of the period was the restoration of a local hierarchy of bishops, which in England and Wales occurred in

1850, and in Scotland in 1878. Prior to this time, Catholicism in Britain had been organised as a mission territory, administered by vicars apostolic of episcopal status under the direct control of Rome. The re-establishment of the Catholic hierarchy prompted a short flurry of anti-popery rhetoric, together with some limited outbursts of violence. This was in part because the implementation was poorly handled by the first archbishop of Westminster, Nicholas Wiseman (1802-1865), who seemed quite insensible to the visceral Protestant climate that pervaded mid-nineteenth-century Britain. Nevertheless, the tension was short lived, and within a few decades the new structures had become embedded and accepted. Indeed, churches announcing themselves to be 'in the archdiocese of Westminster' soon provoked as little comment as neighbouring churches proclaiming their location within 'the diocese of St Albans'.

Once the long standing issue of the organisation structure of British Catholicism had been resolved, the Catholic community could get on with the business of developing its infrastructure, with church building projects ranging from the modest to the lavish. There was also the challenge of attempting to create a homogenous group of orthodox, practising believers out of the diverse constituencies of Catholics now resident in Britain, which included the Irish, the existing English community, and some Anglican converts. Strong leadership was provided by the first three cardinal archbishops of Westminster, who each came from a different one of these constituencies. Wiseman, with his Irish-Spanish-Roman roots, represented 'foreignness'; Henry Edward Manning (1808-1892) was an Anglican convert; Bernard Vaughan (1847-1922) came from an old established English Catholic family. Under the leadership of these three men, English Catholicism emerged as a doctrinally orthodox, well-organised, highly disciplined and increasingly well resourced community. In Scotland, strong leadership came from Charles Eyre (1817-1902), who became the first archbishop of Glasgow. In Ireland, Cardinal Paul Cullen (1803-1878), whose period in office as archbishop of Armagh, and then Dublin, almost exactly coincided with the pontificate of Pius IX, has traditionally been seen as the dominating figure. In reality, however, his two immediate predecessors, John Thomas Troy (1739-1823) and Daniel Murray (1768-1852), were equally important in achieving Ireland's organisational revolution, as were some of the other bishops, particularly Francis Moylan (1735-1815), William Crolly (1780-1849), James Warren Doyle (1786-1834) and John MacHale (1791-1881). During the second half of the nineteenth century, record numbers of priests were recruited, trained and then sent forth to lead the Irish diaspora, which by this point was expanding all over the world.

Ireland produced large numbers of religious sisters, and following the restoration of the hierarchy in England and Wales, there was also a rapid development of monastic communities in England. These tended to be located in London and the Home Counties, and in Catholicism's strongholds in the North West. The period from 1850 to 1920 saw the foundation of a total of 27 monastic foundations for women and 13 monastic foundations for men.[9] The 1860s and the 1880s were the key decades for this expansion.

---

[9] Data supplied by Dr Melissa Wilkinson.

Internal Church Reform, 1850-1920

J. Dinnewet, Nicholas Wiseman, *oil on canvas, 1861.*
[Mechelen, Great Seminary / © IRPA-KIK, Brussels: X010905]

The Clergy: the Established Churches

The transformation of clerical performance has been seen as one of the central dynamics needed for the achievement of church reform, both by churchmen at the time, and by historians at the present. This intensified once the external clamour for reform began to ebb, and the process became internalised within the minds of churchmen.[10] There is a significant literature devoted to chronicling the transformation of the Anglican clergyman from gentleman dilettante to hardworking professional.[11] By the 1850s, there was a clear expectation (not universally fulfilled until the 1870s) that a beneficed clergyman would be working according to the terms set out in the Pluralities Act of 1838, which meant that he would be resident in one parish and serving that parish only, unless he were serving two neighbouring parishes that were less than ten miles apart, with a combined value of less than £1000, and a population of less than 3,000 souls. Curates were expected to be resident less than three miles from their church, and additional curates had to be appointed when parishes were being held in plurality, unless the combined value of the livings was very low.[12] Essentially, then, the model of (at least) one man at work in each parish had been established as the pastoral ideal which planted itself deep into the psyche of the late Victorian and Edwardian church. It would strive very hard to maintain it, in the face of the increasing expense of this way of working, and the declining numbers within the ordained ministry. In heavily urbanised areas, staff parishes employing teams of curates under the direction of an incumbent became seen as the ideal. In early-twentieth-century Leeds, there were 91 curates employed in 18 parishes, but this density of clergy was exceptional.[13]

By the 1880s, there was an expectation that a largely graduate clergy would have had some further period of training in one of the newly-established theological colleges, but this did not become an actual requirement until after the First World War. Theological colleges were founded in response to a number of changing circumstances, the chief of which was the realisation that a period of residence at Oxford or Cambridge did not equip a man for the realities of parish ministry, whether that was conceived as avoiding such elementary theological blunders as the equation of childhood naughtiness with the absence of baptismal regeneration, or with holding the baby safely at the moment of baptism. Nor was the tone of the increasingly secularised ancient universities seen as helpful in forming clerical character. But the intention was to supplement, rather than replace, what the universities offered. Traditional university education was still seen as important in the development of gentlemanliness, and as providing a general form of educationally-focussed life experience. The period after 1850 witnessed the major growth of theological colleges aimed at graduate or non-graduate ordinands, with the foundation of eleven such institutions in the period up until 1881.

---

[10] Burns, "English 'Church Reform' Revisited", 158-162.
[11] Heeney, *A Different Kind of Gentleman*; Russell, *The Clerical Profession*; Haig, *The Victorian Clergy*.
[12] Knight, *The Nineteenth Century Church and English Society*, 119-122.
[13] Haig, *The Victorian Clergy*, 234.

All but two of these, Wycliffe Hall in Oxford, and Ridley Hall in Cambridge, were firmly High Church institutions, and the majority were founded in cathedral cities. Some of these colleges were very small, with little more than a principal, a vice-principal, and a dozen or so students. But a remarkably large number survived until well into the twentieth century, and made their mark on the Church of England by producing men who conformed to (or who were at least expected to conform to) Anglican churchmanship of the particular texture and shading associated with the institution. Theological colleges became a key element in the institutionalisation of church party, but (and this was equally true for Roman Catholic and Nonconformist institutions) they also engendered powerful feelings of loyalty, community, fellowship and esprit de corps.

One of the paradoxes of the rage for theological education, including for nongraduates, was that at a time when other professions were moving towards a graduate-only entry, the church began to open itself up to increasing numbers of non-graduates. In England by 1879, about one in six had no degree, whereas fifty years earlier, graduate status would have been almost universal. A further paradox was that as other professions developed and lengthened their training arrangements because there was an increasing body of knowledge which new recruits were required to master, there remained uncertainty about what the clergy should be required to know. Theological colleges were seen as imparting a certain ecclesiastical tone to their students; much less certain was the notion of a shared curriculum. There was also some criticism of them for failing to teach anything about science, economics, or social conditions.

In Wales, the expectation of ordination straight from an English university, or after completing studies at St David's College Lampeter remained stronger for much longer. St Michael's, the largely post-graduate theological college for the Welsh church, was not founded until 1892. Originally located in Aberdare, it moved to Llandaff in 1903.[14]

The Clergy: Nonconformity

For the Nonconformist ministry, the shift to professional status in the second half of the nineteenth century was more marked than that among the established churches, because the journey to be travelled was far longer. Early-nineteenth-century Nonconformist ministers had been at risk from arrest, verbal abuse and sometimes even physical assault. Although violence was directed at the Salvation Army, the last recorded attack on a Primitive Methodist was in 1843, by which time the connexion was already distancing itself from its revivalist, working-class roots, and was well on the way to acquiring all the institutional trappings of a full-blown denomination.[15] Nevertheless, life could remain extremely challenging, particularly in those denominations that

---

[14] Williams et al., *The Welsh Church*, 349-353.

[15] Brown, *A Social History of the Nonconformist Ministry in England and Wales*, 8.

required ministers to engage in a constant round of itineration and pastoral visitation, with the expectation that much of the travelling would still be accomplished on foot. Most of the Methodists Connexions moved their ministers every three years, although occasional exceptions were made to allow a man to stay for five. This could place huge strain on domestic arrangements and was undoubtedly one reason why men left the ministry. Indeed, the utter dependence of ministers on the whims of stationing committees or congregational calls was a factor which mitigated against the trend towards professionalisation, which included the notion of the independence of the professional gentleman.

Kenneth Brown's research has revealed the extraordinary extent to which men dropped out of the Nonconformist ministry during the nineteenth century. Between 1831 and 1851, almost one third of the Wesleyans who entered ministry were lost to it within four years, while half of the Baptists who began between 1861 and 1881 did not last for more than fourteen years. These heavy losses did not seem to cause undue worry to the Nonconformist denominations until the last years of Victoria's reign, presumably because the overall numbers in the ministry were continuing to go up, with numbers rising steadily in major Methodist denominations, and among the Baptists and Congregationalists, until the First World War.[16] This presented a rather different demographic from that within the Church of England, where ordinations peaked in 1886, and a 'crisis' in clergy numbers had been detected and was being regularly commented upon by the following decade, and in every decade thereafter. In reality, however, because Anglican priests were much less likely to abandon the ministry than their Nonconformist brethren, there continued to be large numbers of clergy available until the intake from the 1880s reached death and retirement, towards the end of the 1920s.

Within Nonconformity, year on year ministerial growth was regarded as a given for the whole of this period, and the fact that many of these men were in effect 'fresh supplies', replacing those who had dropped away, seems to have caused little anxiety. The absence of belief in the indelibility of orders prevented this pattern causing the kind of outcry that it would have aroused in Anglican or Catholic circles. It is also worth stating that rather than simply dropping out, large numbers of Nonconformist ministers left for work abroad, either as missionaries, or to serve congregations in the New World, and many switched from pastoral to educational work. Furthermore, having an exit route out of the home-based pastoral ministry was highly desirable, given the fluctuations in funding to pay for ministers. Whereas some Anglican clergy ended up in circumstances of severe destitution, Nonconformist ministers facing similar problems simply seem to have opted for new career choices.

The historic exclusion of Nonconformists from England's ancient universities meant that there was a well-established network of Nonconformist colleges, although

---

[16] Brown, *A Social History of the Nonconformist Ministry in England and Wales*, 103, 124-169.

there was a much greater emphasis on learning among some denominations, for example the Congregationalists, than among others, for example the Primitive Methodists. But for all groups, the period after 1870 represented something of an educational turning point. The combined impact of the opening up of Oxford and Cambridge, the 1870 Education Act and the growth of school boards, technical education, public libraries and public examinations, meant that it was now seen as essential for a Nonconformist minister to be a learned man, if he was to have any hope of retaining his increasingly well-educated congregation within the Nonconformist fold. Educated, suburban congregations demanded high quality preaching, and certainly not the 'ranting' of former days, and they expected their ministers to be knowledgeable about the intellectual revolutions that were occurring in the scientific world and in the field of biblical criticism. Those traditions which continued to make heavy use of lay preachers tended to retain more of the old, Bible-thumping, ethos, but what could happen was that a wider gulf than previously opened up between the local preachers who effectively kept the cause going, and the college-educated minister who visited from time to time. It would also be misleading to suggest that all Nonconformist ministerial training colleges were at the vanguard of conveying new ways of thinking to their students, any more than the Anglican theological colleges did. The Congregationalists were better at this, but there was frequent criticism about the old-fashioned and uninspiring tone and content of the teaching offered in some denominational colleges.[17]

The Clergy: Roman Catholic

We have already noted that in Ireland, the period after 1850 saw record numbers of priests being trained, with large numbers being sent to minister all over the world. Eight seminaries were in existence by the end of the period, some of which, for example Holy Cross, Clonliffe, Dublin, were for particular dioceses only, and others (most particularly Maynooth) were for all of Ireland. Such were the numbers seeking ordination in Ireland that a new institution, All Hallows, Dublin was founded specifically in order to train men for other parts of the world. Significant numbers of Irish clergy ended up in mainland Britain. For the Anglican converts, it may have come as a surprise to discover that "the Church of the Fathers would have a Kerry accent"[18] but that was the reality.

The expansion in the priesthood that came in the wake of the restoration of the hierarchy of bishops was striking: in 1850 there were 587 Catholic churches in England and Wales and 788 clergy; in 1900 there were 1,529 churches and 2,812 clergy.[19] The Irishmen in mainland Britain were joining a number of mainly Italian mission priests, whose arrival in Britain had been encouraged, although not always helpfully supported, by Cardinal Wiseman. Prominent among these orders were the Passionists,

---

[17] For an account of Nonconformist training in the years 1860-1914, see Ibid., 80-123.

[18] Norman, *Roman Catholicism in England*, 73.
[19] Ibid., 71.

Belgian and English Friars Minor in West-Gorton,
near Manchester, *photograph, c.1870.*
[Leuven, KADOC]

whose founder, Paul Francis Daneo (1694-1775) had felt a particular call to try to bring about the conversion of England. Wiseman's gullibility in believing that English society in the 1840s was on the brink of conversion, an absurd view that was fuelled by the Anglican converts Ambrose Phillipps de Lisle (1809-1878) and George Spencer (1799-1864), resulted in his summoning the Passionists under Fr Dominic Barberi (1792-1849) to England in 1842. Together with the Rosminian Luigi Gentili (1801-1848), Barberi became the most celebrated retreat-giver and missioner in nineteenth-century Britain. The Italian missioners, although small in number were large in impact, as they moved from parish to parish conducting their high profile missions. Although very different in theology and ecclesiology from their Protestant revivalist counterparts, there were distinct similarities in tone. As the century progressed, large-scale evangelism began to give way to attempts to rekindle the faith of existing, but backsliding Catholics. Meanwhile, missions aimed specifically at children (a specialisation of the Redemptorists) ground to a halt in the 1870s, after it began to be seen as unacceptable to threaten children with lurid and horrifying descriptions of their eternal fate in hell, if they failed to be good.[20] Clerical converts to the Catholic priesthood were relatively few in number, there were 572 from the Church of England and only 23 from all the Scottish denomi-

---

[20] Sharp, "Juvenile Holiness".

nations.[21] Nevertheless, they had influence, particularly intellectual influence, and indeed on-going fame, out of all proportion to their size. The most famous were the two cardinals, Henry Edward Manning and John Henry Newman. Also worthy of mention is Frederick William Faber (1814-1863), who converted a few weeks after Newman in November 1845. Faber became leader of the London branch of the Oratorians, Newman having founded the Birmingham house. Unlike Newman, Faber became fully identified with Italianate, ultramontane religious devotion of the most extreme variety, and he was widely known as a hymn writer and author of devotional books. His style found its architectural expression in the Brompton Oratory, which he founded.

Very large numbers of male and female religious orders were involved in education for children of all classes. Significant late-eighteenth or early-nineteenth-century foundations at Stonyhurst, Ushaw, Oscott, St Edmund's Old Hall, Sedgeley Park, Ampleforth and Downside provided education for boys, and three of these schools - Ushaw, Oscott and St Edmund's Old Hall - also had seminaries, to which boys could progress for vocational training for the priesthood. The education of lay students together with intending future clerics - something which occurred also within the Church of England until the widespread foundation of non-graduate theological colleges in the second half of the nineteenth century - was seen in the Catholic context as fraught with dangers and pitfalls, although even in Ireland, four of the eight seminaries also had a lay wing.

The perceived problem was that the influence of lay students threatened the seminarians with a secular tone. Lay students enjoyed drinking and smoking, and required a curriculum that included music, fencing, dancing and gymnastics. Those in St Edmund's, in Hertfordshire, tended to want to make the most of their proximity to London entertainments. But the cost of endowing diocesan seminaries on the Tridentine model was prohibitive, and was successful only in Liverpool and Southwark.[22] Some diocesan seminaries seemed notably unsuccessful, producing far higher levels of ministerial drop out than would normally have been expected within Catholicism at this date. At Nottingham, the 'Diocesan College of our Lady and St Hugh' which lasted for only twenty years produced a total of 47 priests over the lifetime of its operation, of whom twelve left the priesthood and another nine attracted public notoriety at some point during their careers. The problems of the Nottingham clergy reached a peak around 1900, when a quarter were reckoned to be mentally unstable.[23] There was a considerable price to be paid when the need for additional priests was met by over-hasty ordinations.

---

[21] Aspinwall, "Another Part of the Island", 200.
[22] Norman, *The English Catholic Church*, 178-181; Holmes, *More Roman than Rome*, 171-175.
[23] Ibid., 173-174.

Separatism and Reunion

There are several narratives that could be explored under the heading of separatism and reunion, the most significant of which concern Scottish Presbyterianism and Methodism. In both cases, separation belonged more to the period before 1850, as a series of new revivalist Methodist denominations broke away from the Wesleyan parent, and as the Scottish Disruption rent asunder the established Church of Scotland, in 1843. In the period after 1850, the emphasis switched gradually from fissures and separations, to the reunion of those churches which had split from a common parent. The culmination of this process was the reunion of the Church of Scotland in 1929, and the creation of the Methodist Church in 1932. Elsewhere in the British Isles, the established churches were also involved in separation during this period, in the form of severance of their special relationship with the state, which, as already noted, took place in Ireland in 1869, and in Wales in 1920. The separation entailed by disestablishment was not followed by reunion, but rather by a re-evaluation of the Anglican Church's sense of itself in each part of the British Isles.

We have already seen how the Free Church of Scotland was formed as a result of Thomas Chalmers, David Welsh and a large number of other evangelical Church of Scotland clergy walking out of the General Assembly of the Church of Scotland on 18 May 1843. The new Free Church won immediate support, particularly in northern Scotland and the major cities. Within four years it had 730 churches throughout Scotland, over 500 schools, two teacher training colleges and a ministerial training college. It also had the full structure of Presbyterian church government, from kirk session to General Assembly.[24] Although it had been remarkably successful in creating a new national structure, the Free Church began to develop an increasingly sectarian ethos, picturing itself as a gathered community of true believers. As such it identified more with the third major constituency within Scottish Presbyterianism, the United Presbyterian Church, which had been formed in 1847 as a result of union between the Secession Church and the Relief Church, two denominations which themselves had separated from the Church of Scotland in the eighteenth century. By the 1860s, the Free Church and the United Presbyterians were beginning to explore the possibility of reunion, with negotiations, which in the event were unsuccessful, lasting from 1863 to 1873. The sticking point was voluntaryism; from the perspective of conservative Free Church Highlanders, embracing the voluntary principle seemed totally unacceptable.

This was not the end of the matter, however. It would have been surprising if the disestablishment question, which had just been settled in Ireland, and was beginning to rage in Wales, and (in a more short-lived form) in England, had failed to leave its mark on Scotland. The prospect of disestablishment for the Church of Scotland flared again in 1874, with the passing of the Patronage Act as a catalyst. By passing the Patronage

---

[24] Parsons, "Church and State in Victorian Scotland", 116.

Act, Disraeli's Conservative government agreed to the Church of Scotland's request to end patronage as it had traditionally been understood (something which Gladstone's Liberals had refused to do) thus eliminating the historic issue which had provoked the Disruption. From the point of view of the Church of Scotland, disposing of this historic bone of contention was intended to be a step on the road to reunion. It was hoped that other Presbyterians would feel able to reunite, in a less contentious climate, with the 'Auld Kirk', which was now thoroughly recovered from the trauma of the Disruption, and was a growing denomination. But they had expressed their sentiment too early: the United Presbyterians, the majority of the Free Church and other Scottish Dissenters saw the abolition of patronage as a dangerous attempt to shore up the establishment by reforming it, when the proper response was to abolish it. The stage was set for a disestablishment campaign, which rumbled on for the next twenty years.

Although it might have seemed as if the Church of Scotland was less bothered by the establishment principle than were its counterparts elsewhere in the British Isles, its commitment to it was deeply rooted. As A.C. Cheyne put it, "It is, quite simply, the old Reformed conviction - eloquently enunciated by John Calvin, adhered to by John Knox, battled for by the Covenanters and in no way denied by the settlement of 1690 - that an established Church stands, as no 'sect' can, for the sovereignty of God and the headship of Christ over the nations."[25] In the light of these convictions, and of subsequent events, it was fortunate that the Scottish disestablishment campaign faded away in the 1890s, and unlike its Welsh counterpart, which also encountered a lull at the same period, it did not come back to life in the early years of the twentieth century.

Instead, as the new century dawned, the Scottish Presbyterians took a path unique to themselves, as they began to move towards reunion based on a reformed establishment. The Free Church and the United Presbyterians were united in 1900, with a small group of mainly Highland conservatives, staying out of the reunion and styling themselves as the Free Church Continuing, or more popularly as the 'Wee Frees'. In 1905, parliamentary legislation was passed to permit the Church of Scotland to change its terms of subscription to the Westminster Confession, independently of the state, thus making it immediately more acceptable to the non-established Presbyterian constituency. By 1909, the negotiating committees of the Church of Scotland and the United Free Church were ready to begin discussions for reunion. The outcome they had in mind was not so much an established church, as traditionally conceived within the British Isles, but a national church, which they hoped would articulate Christian faith meaningfully to the people of Scotland. The context for this was the knowledge that all the Scottish Protestant denominations were facing a crisis of decline. Crucially, the state would not interfere in its affairs, and therefore the criticisms of state control, which the established Church of Scotland had faced in the previous two centuries would fall away. The negotiations prospered. In the 1920s, various Acts of Parliament were passed to ease the merger. In 1929 the churches united with only a small group

---

[25] Cheyne, *Studies in Scottish Church History*, 158.

seceding, as the United Free Church Continuing. Thus the mainstream of Scottish Presbyterianism moved relatively smoothly from separation to reunion in the space of 86 years.[26]

For the Methodists, the movement from separation to reunion bore some similarities with the Scottish experience. The timescale was not hugely dissimilar, with the 'separation' phase in Methodism lasting from 1797, when the Kilhamites (also known as the Methodist New Connexion) broke away, until 1857 when the United Methodist Free Churches formed themselves out of an amalgamation of the Wesleyan Methodist Association and the Wesleyan Reformers. This was one of the most damaging secessions, with an estimated loss of membership to the Wesleyans of upwards of 100,000 people. During the sixty year 'separation' period, seven major new Methodist denominations were born, together with several smaller off-shoots, such as the Teetotal Wesleyan Methodists (1841). Separations most frequently occurred as a result of zealous church members falling foul of the Wesleyan authorities over their freelance preaching activities. Disputes centred on the nature and conduct of revivals, and on matters relating to discipline and polity. Doctrine was rarely an issue, something which again links the Methodist experience with that of the Scottish Presbyterians.

The United Methodist Free Church amalgamation of 1857 marked the end of the emergence and consolidation of anti-Wesleyan forces in Methodism. Hostilities remained, but no further splits took place, apart from those of a purely local character.[27] David Easton has shown that from as early as 1860, the thoughts of Methodists turned in the direction of reunion, and the divisions between them, rather than being a source of pride, gradually began to be seen as a source of shame. Four denominations, the Bible Christians, the Primitive Methodists, the Methodist New Connexion and the United Methodist Free Churches, engaged in negotiations with a view to reunion at various points in the years between 1863 and 1900. In all the debates that took place, emphasis was placed on the 'growth of fraternal feeling' and the desirability of lessening the 'reproach of denominational division', as well as on more pragmatic factors, such as the reduction in costs and duplication.[28] When the Wesleyan Methodists enacted the principle of lay representation, thus conceding their previously cherished principle that authority should be exercised within an all-ministerial conference, many people thought that the major obstacle to reunion had been removed. Finally, the view of the non-Wesleyans had triumphed, that ultimately, authority should rest in the hands of the lay majority. But in fact it took a further fifty years for Methodist union to be achieved.

Talks began again in 1901, and by 1907 they had come finally to fruition, with the merger of the Methodist New Connexion, the Bible Christians and the United Methodist Free Churches, to form the United Methodist Church. The Union of 1907 was met with enthusiasm throughout Nonconformity, and seen as possibly heralding the complete

---

[26] Parsons, "Church and State in Victorian Scotland", 117-120.

[27] Easton, *'Gathered into One'*, 36.
[28] Ibid., 320.

Internal Church Reform, 1850-1920

W.H.Y. Titcomb, Primitive Methodists at Prayer, *oil on canvas, 1889. The painting shows the Fore Street Chapel in St Ives, Cornwall.*
[Dudley, Dudley Museum & Art Gallery]

union of Methodism, or perhaps of Nonconformity more generally. Secondly, it demonstrated that significant union could take place without the Wesleyans; the children of the mother church could resolve their differences and live peaceably together, without the leading of their Wesleyan parent. Thirdly, although United Methodism, with a membership in 1907 of 165,500 was still far smaller than the Wesleyans, and even than the Primitives, the newly-founded denomination had a greater confidence, and knew that it would have a greater parity in any future negotiations.[29] Perhaps this showed that even in an increasingly ecumenical climate in the early-twentieth century, reunion could only really be successful among those who regarded themselves as in some sense equal. Negotiations began again almost straight away, to continue for a further twenty years, demanding the attention of most influential figures within the three Methodist denominations. The final denouement was the union of the Wesleyan Methodist, United Methodist and Primitive Methodist Churches, to create the Methodist Church in Great Britain, in 1932. But beyond the formal unions of 1907 and 1932, research into the post-1907 and post-1932 churches has shown that achieving practical amalgamation locally was an on-going, and often painful process. There was a far greater readiness to vote for union, than to implement it in the districts, and especially, the circuits.[30] For Methodists themselves, the question of whether the Union had been beneficial was one which sometimes seemed to hang in the air. There was, however, less of a dissentient tradition than was the case within Scottish Presbyterianism. Only the United Methodists and the Wesleyan Reform Union remained separate bodies.

Theology and Doctrine: the Church of England

Peter Nockles has argued that above all, the Oxford Movement's contribution was most significant in relation to the promotion of theological learning and academic reform, in the universities, and through the foundation of theological colleges. As we shall see, men who may be described as the third generation offspring of the Oxford Movement, the liberal Anglo-Catholics of the late-nineteenth century, continued to be at the forefront of theological change. But by 1860, the discussion of theological issues had broadened out from its hitherto limited constituency of the clergy of the Church of England. It was now involving well-informed Nonconformists, Roman Catholics and Freethinkers. Their deliberations were assisted by the growth of a very considerable periodical press, with titles such as the *Fortnightly Review*, the *Contemporary Review* and the *Nineteenth Century* providing a steady diet of informative articles. These journals devoted many column inches to the discussion of what were essentially theological questions, opening up the debate to the educated middle classes, without reference to their religious affiliation.[31] But although the climate in which theological discus-

---

[29] Easton, '*Gathered into One*', 84-87.
[30] Ibid., 311.
[31] Livingston, *Religious Thought in the Victorian Age*, 1.

sion was taking place was changing faster than it had for many decades, the British state was still seen to be regularly wading in, when the secular judicial committee of the Privy Council overturned the judgements of the ecclesiastical courts in doctrinal matters, as it continued to do on a number of occasions.

Our survey begins in March 1850, with the judicial committee of the Privy Council declaring that Bishop Henry Phillpotts (1778-1869) of Exeter had been wrong to refuse to institute an Evangelical clergyman called George Gorham (1787-1857) to the living of Bampford Speke, on the grounds that Gorham was unsound on the Anglican understanding of the doctrine of baptismal regeneration. The decision of the judicial committee, which was a recently-founded body, caused shock waves among many High Churchmen, who believed both in baptismal regeneration, and in the right of a bishop to veto the nomination of clergymen judged to be of unsound orthodoxy. It prompted the conversion to Roman Catholicism of a further small wave of Anglicans, including Robert Wilberforce, and most significantly, Henry Edward Manning. The dispute at Bampford Speke crystallised perfectly the increasingly large chasm which had opened up between those members of the Church of England who were firm believers in sacramental grace, and those who were staunch advocates of the need for the individual to make his or her own response of faith to God. Catholic and Protestant Anglicans eyed each other nervously, while the courts did their work. It was a strange state of affairs from the perspective of history, and it was seen as a strange state of affairs at the time. Clashes over doctrine and theology between some sections of the Church of England, and the judicial committee, continued for much of the nineteenth century, although as time went on the focus tended to move from doctrinal matters to church discipline and ritualism. Perhaps even more incongruously, whilst this was going on in London, detailed work on new translations of Scripture, the exploration of the history and construction of the canon, and the birth of the modern Bible commentary, were all taking place in the universities. With this came the arrival of a recognisably modern theological agenda, which raised questions which still concern some theologians today.

The acceptance of biblical criticism was the largest tidal wave to hit the coastline of British theology at this period, spraying the British with its bracing saltiness several decades later than it had the Germans. The debates which began in the 1850s and 1860s took place at two different levels. At the more popular level, they were punctuated with the publication of a series of writings which, in the contemporary climate, were seen as being notorious and shocking. At the more academic level, these decades marked the beginning of what was to be (to use a phrase now much over-used) groundbreaking scholarship, in particular associated with B.F. Westcott (1825-1901), F.J.A. Hort (1828-1892) and J.B. Lightfoot (1828-1889), the trio of Cambridge scholars who did a very great deal to establish an English theology with a distinctive style and content in the second half of the nineteenth century. Not surprisingly, it was to be the Cambridge trio, rather than the writers whose work resulted in shock and legal proceedings, that were

Publications by John William Colenso *(1862)* and W. Robertson Smith *(1882)*.
[Leuven, K.U.Leuven, Maurits Sabbebibliotheek]

to have the most sustained influence on British theology. Indeed, David Thompson has argued recently that the Cambridge theology Tripos (the undergraduate theology degree) remained fundamentally shaped by Westcott's priorities until as late as 1999.[32]

The three Cambridge theologians were closely linked by deep associations of intellectual sympathy and friendship. They corresponded over many years, and together with E.W. Benson, the future archbishop of Canterbury, Lightfoot and Westcott regularly holidayed together. Westcott, Benson and Hort even dreamed of setting up a Coenobium, a religious community for their families and a few others, possibly in Peterborough.[33] Such a development would have been a radical departure for a group of prominent clergy families in mid-Victorian Britain. As it was, only the unmarried Lightfoot remained at Cambridge and focussed on his scholarly endeavours until his elevation as bishop of Durham in 1879. The others combined marriage with country parishes and posts in public schools, until Westcott and Hort were recalled as professors, in 1870

---

[32] Thompson, *Cambridge Theology in the Nineteenth Century*, 95. Chapter 5 of this work provides the best recent overview of the work of Westcott, Hort and Lightfoot.
[33] Ibid., 137.

and 1878 respectively. Benson became bishop of Lincoln, and never returned formally to Cambridge. According to Thompson, their correspondence "reveals a shared vision of an Anglican response to contemporary theological scepticism, which required an institutional expression, but which was clearly distinct from that of Evangelicals and Tractarians".[34]

Part of that response was a thorough-going attempt to understand the first-century Palestinian context of Christianity, in a manner that would not embarrass a modern scholar. Another was to provide an informed reply to the scepticism of the Tübingen School, a distinctive British response founded on both open questioning and theological orthodoxy. Both were endeavours with which Lightfoot was particularly associated. Above all, however, Lightfoot's Pauline commentaries - *Galatians* (1865), *Philippians* (1868) and *Colossians with Philemon* (1875) - set a new standard for biblical scholarship, and together with Westcott, he is credited with inventing the biblical commentary in its modern form. Westcott and Hort also started writing commentaries, with Westcott's on St John's Gospel, the Johannine Epistles and Hebrews appearing during the 1880s. Hort's commentaries never appeared, although some of his work on James and 1 Peter was published after his death.[35] Westcott and Hort also produced a new critical Greek text of the New Testament, launching "a process of continual revision in the light of new manuscript discoveries".[36] They were also heavily involved in the translation process which produced the Revised Version in 1881. In addition, Westcott wrote a number of other widely-regarded works on biblical inspiration and miracles.[37]

In contrast with the exceptionally creative and productive endeavours of the Cambridge trio, there appeared a number of other early sallies into the field of biblical criticism. A notorious early salvo was *Essays and Reviews* (1860), which was a collection of essays by Anglicans. The point about *Essays and Reviews* was not its content, but the attention it attracted, first from the bishops and then from the ecclesiastical courts, which was followed by the acquittal of two of its authors by the judicial committee of the Privy Council. *Essays and Reviews* was more of a plea that biblical criticism should be done, than an attempt to do it, and it was to be left to Bishop John William Colenso (1814-1883) of Natal to be the first high profile Anglican to nail his colours to the mast, with the publication of *The Pentateuch and Book of Joshua Critically Examined* (1862).[38] This was, in many ways, an embarrassing false start, a book which attracted notoriety because its author was a bishop, and censure because of its very inadequate

---

[34] Ibid., 98.
[35] Ibid., 109-111.
[36] Ibid., 113.
[37] The first work was published as *The Elements of Gospel Harmony* (1851) and later revised as *An Introduction to the Study of the Gospels* (1860, with further editions published later). Westcott's *A General Survey of the History of the Canon the New Testament* appeared in 1855, again with regular new editions published at intervals in the years which followed. His *Characteristics of Gospel Miracles* appeared in 1859 and a *History of the English Bible* in 1868.
[38] Larsen, "Biblical Criticism and the Desire for Reform".

methodology. Colenso's hermeneutic (if it may be so described) was relentlessly mathematical. He set himself the task of proving that the early books of the Old Testament were unreliable because the figures contained within them were nonsensical. Starting off with a statement derived from passages in the Book of Numbers that Israel had around 600,000 warriors, Colenso concluded that the population of Israel must have been in the region of two million. But if this were so, they would have been a large unwieldy group to encamp, would have required huge numbers of lambs to celebrate Passover, which in turn would have needed unfeasible amounts of grazing pasture. It could not be so, and therefore the numbers given in the Bible could not be relied upon, and the historical veracity of the Mosaic narrative in the Bible was called in question. Strangely, Colenso had read the German biblical critics, but he chose to adopt simplistic mathematical formulae instead. His status as a bishop gave the book far greater publicity than it would otherwise have attracted.[39] Colenso was to remain an awkward embarrassment to the developing community of biblical scholars. Lightfoot remarked that "a more frank and liberal treatment of the difficulties of the Old Testament, if it had been general, would have drawn the sting of Colenso's criticism" but the effect of the book was to "discredit reasonable enquiry" and "to divide men into two extreme parties, who will wage fierce war against each other and trample the truth underfoot between them".[40] Nervousness about *Essays and Reviews* and *The Pentateuch and the Book of Joshua* was heightened because the publications were interspersed by those from scientific or free thinking authors who were either hostile to or detached from orthodox Christianity, such as Henry Mansel, Charles Darwin, Max Muller and Thomas Huxley. The Cambridge theologians were also ill-equipped to respond to work on the Old Testament; trained as classical scholars, the Semitic languages were foreign to them. Thomas Jarrett (1805-1882), Regius Professor of Hebrew 1854-1882, might have been expected to answer Colenso, but he spent much of his time transliterating oriental languages into roman characters according to a system of his own devising.[41] The lack of facility with Hebrew was one reason why British theologians found it so hard to answer Colenso.

The second wave of Anglican biblical criticism broke more gently on the shoreline. On the one hand, Westcott, Lightfoot and Hort became increasingly revered as the heroes of late-nineteenth-century scholarship. On the other emerged the group of liberal Anglo-Catholic scholars, the third generation off-spring of the Oxford Movement alluded to earlier, who authored *Lux Mundi: A Series of Studies in the Religion of the Incarnation* (1889) under the editorship of Charles Gore. The *Lux Mundi* men, although still youthful, either were or had been theologians at Oxford University, and had met together for periods of discussion, study, prayer and relaxation during long vacations for over a decade. They had developed a strong sense of commitment to a shared theo-

---

[39] Larsen, "Biblical Criticism and the Desire for Reform", 61-62.
[40] Letter to Bishop Tait, 19 November 1862, Davidson, *Life of Tait*, I, 338, cited by Larsen, "Biblical Criticism and the Desire for Reform", 76.
[41] Knight, "Life at the Cathedral 1836-1980", 286.

logical project, and a sense of freedom arising from their belief that Christianity was a religion focussed on a person, rather than on a book. The implications of their incarnational theology led them to an interest in democracy and social justice, and several contributors were at the forefront of church-sponsored work among London's poor. They took for granted that there was value to be found in evolutionary theory, science, socialism and even in other faiths; Catholicism was seen as large enough to embrace all things new. As Gore wrote in the Preface: "The real development of theology is [...] the process in which the church, standing firm in her old truths, enters into the apprehension of the new social and intellectual movements of each age [...] shewing again and again her power of witnessing under changed conditions to the catholic capacity of her faith and life."[42]

The influence of both the Cambridge and the Oxford scholars produced a climate in which a whole group of Anglicans were able to embrace a critical, and usually an orthodox and critical, approach to a variety of theological questions. Taken as a whole, *Lux Mundi* was more about doctrine than biblical criticism, although the sections of Gore's essay on "The Holy Spirit and Inspiration" that dealt with the allegorical nature of parts of the Old Testament, and that asserted that Jesus's knowledge was limited by the fact of his incarnation, received a disproportionate amount of unfavourable attention from the older generation of Anglo-Catholics. Some, particularly Archdeacon George Anthony Denison (1805-1896) and H.P. Liddon (1829-1890), were horrified at what they saw as Gore's capitulation to liberalism and rationalism, particularly because, as the Principal of Pusey House, he was seen as standing in the shoes of the great E.B. Pusey, who had sternly resisted such ideas. It became apparent, however, that the older, more conservative Anglo-Catholics had had their day, and *Lux Mundi* became a sort of manifesto for a new form of liberal Catholic tradition within Anglicanism, and one which was so influential that one hundred years after the book was first published, many of the leading figures in late-twentieth-century Anglican theology became associated with publications to mark the centenary.[43] Meanwhile, the rising generation of Old Testament scholars, including J.B. Mozley (1813-1878), S.R. Driver (1846-1914), T.K. Cheyne (1841-1915) and A.F. Kirkpatrick (1849-1940), and New Testament scholars, including William Sanday (1843-1920) and F.C. Burkitt (1864-1935), were able to pursue their scholarly interests without fear of persecution or condemnation.[44] And through all this, Anglican theology and doctrine remained closely wedded to the interests of the church. Benson, Westcott, Lightfoot and Gore all became bishops, as did Frederick Temple (1821-1902), a contributor to *Essays and Reviews*, and Francis Paget (1851-1911), Arthur Lyttleton (1852-1903) and E.S. Talbot (1844-1934), all of whom wrote in *Lux Mundi*.

---

[42] Gore, ed., *Lux Mundi*, ix.
[43] Anglican scholars who felt a sufficient sense of continuity with the *Lux Mundi* tradition to write for the centenary volumes included Paul Avis, John Barton, David Brown, Tim Gorringe, Daniel Hardy, Brian Hebblethwaite, Peter Hinchliff, Andrew Louth, Alister McGrath, Robert Morgan, John Mudiman, David Nicholls, Geoffrey Rowell, Stephen Sykes, Keith Ward, Maurice Wiles, Rowan Williams and Trevor Williams. The volumes in question were Morgan, ed., *The Religion of the Incarnation* and Wainwright, ed., *Keeping the Faith*.
[44] Parsons, "Biblical Criticism in Victorian Britain", 247.

Theology and Doctrine: Nonconformity

Protestant Nonconformity faced its own struggles to come to terms with biblical criticism, with well-publicised cases involving Samuel Davidson (c.1806-1898) and William Robertson Smith (1846-1894) to some extent paralleling Anglican uproar over Colenso and *Essays and Reviews*. Samuel Davidson was born in the north of Ireland, but was Scottish by descent, and initially at least, Presbyterian by religion. He began his academic career in Belfast, in a chair of biblical criticism at the Belfast Academical Institution, and with a knowledge of German biblical scholarship that was regarded as unrivalled.[45] It was, however, as a Congregationalist that Davidson took up a chair at the newly-founded Lancashire Independent College in Manchester, in 1842. He published solidly, on both Old and New Testaments, for a decade and a half, until the College authorities began to receive complaints about his orthodoxy, particularly in relation to his work *The Text of the Old Testament Considered: With a Treatise on Sacred Interpretation, and a Brief Introduction to the Old Testament Books and the Apocrypha* (1856). A committee was appointed to investigate whether the views expressed in this volume were 'unsound', and after finding Davidson's explanations unsatisfactory, he resigned from his post in 1857. As well as being accused of unsound doctrine and of denying Mosaic authorship of the Pentateuch, he was also accused of plagiarising the works of German authors. Davidson continued with his writing, but retired initially to Cheshire, and later moved to London after being elected a Scripture examiner in the University of London, a post which gave him a form of academic rehabilitation. Nevertheless, although his adopted Congregationalism was to be at the forefront of new intellectual developments within Nonconformity, Davidson remained distanced from it, choosing in his later years to worship in Anglican or Unitarian churches.

William Robertson Smith was also caught up in an intra-denominational controversy. He was a Scot, who, like Davidson, was a youthful devotee of German theological scholarship - in the 1860s, he had been able to spend two summers attending lectures in Germany, where he was particularly impressed by Albrecht Ritschl.[46] Smith was ordained in the Free Church of Scotland at the time of his election to the chair of Hebrew and Old Testament exegesis at the Aberdeen Free Church College, in 1870. It can be argued, therefore, that the Free Church knew the man that they were getting, and should not have been disconcerted by his openly expressed views on the importance of an historical and critical approach to the Bible, and on the status of biblical texts as edited versions. This seems to have been the case whilst Smith remained focussed on academic projects; the crisis came when he contributed some articles on biblical subjects to the ninth edition of the *Encyclopaedia Britannica*, a publication which was intended for a general and domestic readership. The Free Church ruled that Smith's views were, if not heretical, at least incompatible with his position as a teacher of ministerial students. Smith retorted that they were nothing beyond what he had

---

[45] Hawke, "Samuel Davidson".

[46] Sefton, "William Robertson Smith".

been taught as a student at New College, Edinburgh. Smith demanded a formal trial for libel, and used the full range of his intellectual and rhetorical powers to tie up the church courts in protracted legal proceedings. Although the libel failed, Smith was removed from his chair in 1881.

In contrast to Davidson, Smith's career was enhanced rather than damaged by his biblical controversy. During his trial, people flocked to his public lectures in Edinburgh and Glasgow, and after his dismissal, he became editor-in-chief of the *Encyclopaedia Britannica*. From 1883, he was a professor of Arabic at Cambridge, and then became chief librarian of Cambridge University. He ended his days as a highly respected Semitics scholar. The Free Church of Scotland, meanwhile, had managed to maintain some semblance of unity on the issue of biblical criticism, thus avoiding the risk of a potentially hugely damaging split. By the turn of the century, however, critical approaches to the Bible were being discreetly accepted, and although Free Church scholars were sometimes warned to be careful, censure was a thing of the past.[47]

Theology and Doctrine: Roman Catholicism

The obvious difference between Roman Catholic approaches to theology and doctrine and those of Anglicans and Nonconformists was that, whatever view points they might be seeking to advance, Roman Catholics in Britain and Ireland found themselves in a reactive role, responding to directives which stemmed from Rome, rather than to ideas independently generated from within their own community. Catholic thinkers at this period could not avoid taking a position at some point on the spectrum of approval or non-approval for infallibility, and for liberal Catholicism, or modernism, as it became known by the 1890s. As occurred elsewhere in the Christian world, journals became associated with particular theological causes, with *The Rambler* (founded 1848) at the vanguard of disseminating liberal positions, particularly those emanating from France and Germany. It also courted controversy among the hierarchy with its open criticism of Catholic academic and educational standards, and with its belief that literary, intellectual and political positions should be adopted without direct reference to ecclesiastical authority.[48] At the opposite end of the spectrum, *The Dublin Review* became transformed into a vehicle for extreme ultramontane opinions under the editorship of W.G. Ward (1812-1882) in the 1860s.

Because Roman Catholicism had little regard for the opinions of German Protestant scholars, or the responses that these opinions provoked among English-speaking Protestants, it was, officially at least, less troubled by developments in biblical criticism than was the rest of late-nineteenth-century European Christianity. Unofficially, the reality was rather different, and pressure built up among Catholic modernist think-

---

[47] Parsons, "Victorian Britain's Other Establishment", 130-132.

[48] Norman, *English Catholic Church*, 304-305.

ers all over Europe who wished to see a critical and scholarly engagement with the theological issues of the day, and who were reacting against the revival of scholastic theology which was then in favour in Rome. Prominent among the modernist movement in Britain was St George Jackson Mivart (1827-1900), a zoologist who was the only English natural scientist of any reputation among the Roman Catholic community, who had once been a close associate of Huxley, but became increasingly sceptical of the Darwinian position. His growing distance from the Darwinians did not, however, prevent him from censure within the church, particularly as he was by this time writing in favour of biblical criticism, and expressing the view that there was hope even for those in hell. Mivart was finally excommunicated, six weeks before his death, in 1900.[49] The other leading figures were the theologian Baron Friedrich von Hügel (1852-1925), a man of Austrian and Scottish parentage, and strongly international outlook, although also firmly wedded to English culture (he became a naturalised British subject in 1914) and the Irish Jesuit George Tyrrell (1861-1909). Whereas Tyrrell was excommunicated the year after the papal condemnation of modernism in 1907, von Hügel managed to escape a similar fate, no doubt because of his respected status and aristocratic connections. The papal condemnation of modernism as the 'synthesis of all heresies' stopped Roman Catholics' dynamic engagement with theology and doctrine for decades. It was not until the Second Vatican Council that the greatest British theologian of the period, John Henry Newman, became properly celebrated and recognised for his contribution to Catholic thought. At the same period, the Roman Catholic Church embarked on that conscious pursuit of renewal with the aim of adaptation, the renewal which lies at the heart of religious reform.

---

[49] Gruber, "St George Jackson Mivart".

Bibliography

Acheson, Alan R. *"A True and Lively Faith": Evangelical Revival in the Church of Ireland*. Belfast, 1992.

Ansdell, Douglas. *The People of the Great Faith: The Highland Church 1690-1900*. Stornoway, 1998.

Arnold, Matthew. *Essays in Criticism*. First Series, preface. London, 1865.

Aspinwall, Bernard. "Another Part of the Island: Robert Montieth and the Roman Catholic Revival in Nineteenth Century Scotland" in: Dominic Aidan Bellenger, ed. *Opening the Scrolls: Essays in Catholic History in Honour of Godfrey Anstruther*. Bath, 1987, 199-215.

Bebbington, David. *Evangelicalism in Modern Britain from the 1730s to the 1980s*. London, 1989.

Best, Geoffrey F.A. *Temporal Pillars: Queen Anne's Bounty, the Ecclesiastical Commissioners, and the Church of England*. Cambridge, 1964.

Bossy, John. *The English Catholic Community 1570-1850*. London, 1975.

Bowen, Desmond. *The Protestant Crusade in Ireland 1800-1870*. Montreal, 1978.

Brent, Richard. "The Oriel Noetics" in: Michael G. Brock and M.C. Curthoys, eds. *The History of the University of Oxford*. 6: *Nineteenth-Century Oxford*. Vol. 1. Oxford, 1997, 72-76.

Brilioth, Yngve. *The Anglican Revival: Studies in the Oxford Movement*. London, 1925.

Bristow, Edward J. *Vice and Vigilance: Purity Movements in Britain since 1700*. Dublin, 1977.

Brown, Callum G. *Religion and Society in Scotland since 1707*. Edinburgh, 1997.

Brown, Kenneth D. *A Social History of the Nonconformist Ministry in England and Wales 1800-1930*. Oxford, 1988.

Brown, Stewart J. *Thomas Chalmers and the Godly Commonweal in Scotland*. Oxford, 1982.

Brown, Stewart J. *The National Churches of England, Ireland and Scotland 1801-46*. Oxford, 2001.

Brown, Stewart J. *Providence and Empire: Religion Politics and Society in the United Kingdom*. Harlow, 2008.

Burns, Arthur. *The Diocesan Revival in the Church of England, c.1800-1870*. Oxford, 1999.

Burns, Arthur. "English 'Church Reform' Revisited, 1780-1840" in: Arthur Burns and Joanna Innes, eds. *Rethinking the Age of Reform: Britain 1780-1850*. Cambridge, 2003, 136-162.

Burns, Arthur and Innes, Joanna, eds. *Rethinking the Age of Reform: Britain 1780-1850*. Cambridge, 2003.

Campbell, Ted A. *The Religion of the Heart: A Study in European Religious Life in the Seventeenth and Eighteenth Centuries*. Columbia, 1991.

Cheyne, Alec C. *Studies in Scottish Church History*. Edinburgh, 1999.

Clark, Jonathan C.D. *English Society 1688-1832: Ideology, Social Structure and Political Practice During the Ancien Régime*. Cambridge, 1985.

Connolly, Sean J. *Priests and People in Pre-Famine Ireland*. New ed. with new intro. Dublin, 2001.

Corsi, Pietro. *Science and Religion: Baden Powell and the Anglican Debate, 1800-1860*. Cambridge, 1988.

Culler, Arthur Dwight. *The Imperial Intellect: A Study of Newman's Educational Ideal*. New Haven-London, 1955.

Dessain, Charles Stephen and Gornall, Thomas, eds. *Letters and Diaries of John Henry Newman*. Vol. 30. Oxford, 1976.

Ditchfield, G.M. *The Evangelical Revival*. London, 1998.

Easton, David. *'Gathered into One': The Reunion of British Methodism 1860-1960, with Particular Reference to Cornwall*. Thesis PhD University of Wales. Lampeter, 2007.

Garbett, James. *Christ as Prophet, Priest, and King. Being a Vindication of the Church of England from Theological Novelties.* The Bampton Lectures for 1842. Vol. 1. Oxford, 1842.

Gilley, Sheridan. "John Keble and the Victorian Churching of Romanticism" in: John Richard Watson, ed. *An Infinite Complexity: Essays in Romanticism.* Edinburgh, 1983, 226-239.

Gore, Charles, ed. *Lux Mundi: A Series of Studies in the Religion of the Incarnation.* London, 1890.

Gornall, Thomas, ed. *Letters & Diaries of John Henry Newman.* Vol. 5. Oxford, 1981.

Gregory, Jeremy. *Restoration, Reformation and Reform, 1680-1828: Archbishops of Canterbury and their Diocese.* Oxford, 2000.

Gruber, Jacob W. "St George Jackson Mivart" in: *Oxford Dictionary of National Biography.* Oxford, 2004.

Gunstone, J.T. "Alexander Knox, 1757-1831". *Church Quarterly Review,* 157 (1956), 466-472.

Haig, Alan. *The Victorian Clergy.* London, 1984.

Hawke, Joanna. "Samuel Davidson" in: *Oxford Dictionary of National Biography.* Oxford, 2004.

Heeney, Brian. *A Different Kind of Gentleman: Parish Clergy as Professional Men in Early and Mid-Victorian England.* Hamden (Conn.), 1976.

Hempton, David and Hill, Myrtle. *Evangelical Protestantism in Ulster Society 1740-1890.* London, 1992.

Hennell, Michael. *John Venn and the Clapham Sect.* London, 1958.

Holmes, Andrew R. *The Shaping of Ulster Presbyterian Belief and Practice 1770-1840.* Oxford, 2006.

Holmes, J. Derek. *More Roman than Rome: English Catholicism in the Nineteenth Century.* London, 1978.

Jacob, William M. *The Making of the Anglican Church Worldwide.* London, 1997.

Jacob, William M. *The Clerical Profession in the Long Eighteenth Century.* Oxford, 2007.

Johnson, Christine. *Developments in the Roman Catholic Church in Scotland 1789-1829.* Edinburgh, 1983.

Jones, David Ceri. *"A Glorious Work in the World": Welsh Methodism and the International Evangelical Revival.* Cardiff, 2004.

Jones, Stuart. *Intellect and Character in Victorian England: Mark Pattison and the Invention of the Don.* Cambridge, 2007.

Ker, Ian. *The Achievement of John Henry Newman.* London, 1991.

Kitson Clark, G. *Churchmen and the Condition of England 1832-1885.* London, 1973.

Knight, Frances. *The Nineteenth-Century Church and English Society.* Cambridge, 1995.

Knight, Frances. "Life at the Cathedral 1836-1980" in: Peter Meadows and Nigel Ramsay, eds. *A History of Ely Cathedral.* Woodbridge, 2003, 281-304.

Knight, Frances. *The Church in the Nineteenth Century.* London, 2008.

Larsen, Timothy. "Biblical Criticism and the Desire for Reform: Bishop Colenso on the Pentateuch" in: Larsen Timothy. *Contested Christianity: The Political and Social Contexts of Victorian Theology.* Waco, 2004, 59-77.

Livingston, James C. *Religious Thought in the Victorian Age: Challenges and Reconceptions.* London-New York, 2006.

Malcomson, A.P.W. *Archbishop Charles Agar: Churchmanship and Politics in Ireland, 1760-1810.* Dublin, 2002.

Marriott, Charles. *Letter to the Rev. E.C. Woollcombe, Fellow and Tutor of Balliol College, on University Extension, and the Poor Scholar.* Oxford, 1848.

Mather, Frederick Clare. *High Church Prophet: Bishop Samuel Horsley (1733-1806) and the Caroline Tradition in the Later Georgian Church.* Oxford, 1992.

McInnes, John. *The Evangelical Movement in the Highlands of Scotland 1688 to 1800.* Aberdeen, 1951.

Morgan, Derec L. *The Great Awakening in Wales.* London, 1988.

Morgan, Robert, ed. *The Religion of the Incarnation: Anglican Essays in Commemoration of Lux Mundi.* Bristol, 1989.

Bibliography

Mozley, Thomas. *Reminiscences, Chiefly of Oriel College and the Oxford Movement*. London, 1882, 2 vols.

Mullett, Michael. *Catholics in Britain and Ireland, 1558-1829*. Basingstoke, 1998.

Mumm, Susan. *Stolen Daughters, Virgin Mothers: Anglican Sisterhoods in Victorian Britain*. London, 1999.

Newman, John Henry. *Via Media* no. I. Tracts for the Times I/38. London, 1833-1834.

Newman, John Henry. "State of Religious Parties". *British Critic*, 25 (April 1839), 399-416.

Newman, John Henry. *Apologia pro vita sua*. London, 1864.

Nockles, Peter B. "An Academic Counter-Revolution: Newman and Tractarian Oxford's Idea of a University". *History of Universities*, 10 (1991), 137-197.

Nockles, Peter B. *The Oxford Movement in Context. Anglican High Churchmanship in Britain 1760-1857*. Cambridge, 1994.

Norman, Edward. *The English Catholic Church in the Nineteenth Century*. Oxford, 1984.

Norman, Edward. *Roman Catholicism in England from the Elizabethan Settlement to the Second Vatican Council*. Oxford, 1985.

Parsons, Gerald. "Biblical Criticism in Victorian Britain: From Controversy to Acceptance?" in: Gerald Parsons, ed. *Religion in Victorian Britain*. 2: *Controversies*. Manchester, 1988, 238-257.

Parsons, Gerald. "Church and State in Victorian Scotland: Disruption and Reunion" in: Gerald Parsons, ed. *Religion in Victorian Britain*. 2: *Controversies*. Manchester, 1988, 107-123.

Parsons, Gerald. "Victorian Britain's Other Establishment: The Transformations of Scottish Presbyterianism" in: Gerald Parsons, ed. *Religion in Victorian Britain*. 1: *Traditions*. Manchester, 1988, 117-145.

Pattison, Mark. *Memoirs*. London, 1885.

Pereiro, James. *"Ethos" and the Oxford Movement. At the Heart of Tractarianism*. Oxford, 2008.

Prickett, Stephen. *Romanticism and Religion. The Tradition of Coleridge and Wordsworth in the Victorian Church*. Cambridge, 1976.

Rack, Henry D. *Reasonable Enthusiast: John Wesley and the Rise of Methodism*. London, 1989.

Russell, Anthony. *The Clerical Profession*. London, 1980.

Sefton, Henry. "William Robertson Smith" in: *Oxford Dictionary of National Biography*. Oxford, 2004.

Selby, Robin C. *The Principle of Reserve in the Writings of John Henry Cardinal Newman*. Oxford, 1975.

Sharp, John. "Juvenile Holiness: Catholic Revivalism among Children in Victorian Britain". *Journal of Ecclesiastical History*, 35 (1984) 2, 220-238.

Skinner, Simon. *Tractarians and the "Condition of England": the Social and Political Thought of the Oxford Movement*. Oxford, 2004.

Smith, Mark. *Religion in Industrial Society: Oldham and Saddleworth 1740-1865*. Oxford, 1994.

Smyth, Charles. *Simeon and Church Order: A Study of the Origins of the Evangelical Revival in Cambridge in the Eighteenth Century*. Cambridge, 1940.

Snell, K.D.M. and Ell, Paul S. *Rival Jerusalems: The Geography of Victorian Religion*. Cambridge, 2000.

Stokes, G.T. "Alexander Knox and the Oxford Movement". *Contemporary Review*, 3 (1887), 184-205.

Strong, Rowan. *Episcopalianism in Nineteenth-Century Scotland: Religious Responses to a Modernising Society*. Oxford, 2002.

Strong, Rowan. *Anglicanism and the British Empire c.1700-1850*. Oxford, 2007.

Stubbs, William. *Visitation Charge Delivered to the Clergy and Churchwardens of the Diocese of Oxford, May-June 1899*. Oxford, 1899.

Thompson, David M. *Cambridge Theology in the Nineteenth Century: Enquiry, Controversy and Truth*. Aldershot, 2008.

Virgin, Peter. *The Church in an Age of Negligence: Ecclesiastical Structure and the Problems of Church Reform 1700-1840.* Cambridge, 1989.

Wainwright, Geoffrey, ed. *Keeping the Faith: Essays to Mark the Centenary of Lux Mundi.* London, 1989.

Walsh, John. "Methodism at the End of the Eighteenth Century" in: Rupert Davies and Gordon Rupp, eds. *History of the Methodist Church in Great Britain.* Vol. 1. London, 1965, 284-289.

Walsh, Walter. *The Secret History of the Oxford Movement.* London, 1898.

Ward, W. Reginald. *Religion and Society in England 1790-1850.* London, 1972.

Ward, W. Reginald. *The Protestant Evangelical Awakening.* Cambridge, 1992.

Watts, Michael. *The Dissenters: The Expansion of Evangelical Nonconformity.* Oxford, 1995.

Whytock, Jack C. *An Educated Clergy: Scottish Theological Education and Training in Kirk and Secession 1560-1850.* Milton Keynes, 2007.

Williams, Sir Glanmor et al. *The Welsh Church from Reformation to Disestablishment 1630-1920.* Cardiff, 2007.

Wilson, Daniel. *The Revival of Spiritual Religion the Only Effectual Remedy for the Dangers which now Threaten the Church of England.* London, 1852.

Yates, Nigel. *Anglican Ritualism in Victorian Britain 1830-1910.* Oxford, 1999.

Yates, Nigel. *The Religious Condition of Ireland 1770-1850.* Oxford, 2006.

Yates, Nigel. *Preaching, Word and Sacrament: Scottish Church Interiors 1560-1860.* Edinburgh, 2009.

THE LOW COUNTRIES

Belgium and the Netherlands have gone down in history as the 'Low Countries'. In terms of geography (a considerable part is deltaic) and politics (the Burgundian states in the later Middle Ages, the Benelux now), they to some extent still form a unit. As was pointed out in Volume I, however, the Southern and Northern Netherlands went their different ways once the dust of the Reformation had settled. The former developed as a southward-looking territory within the Habsburg Empire, the latter emerged in the late sixteenth century as a federation of autonomous provinces. Apart from a brief but notoriously unsuccessful attempt to reunite the south and the north between 1815 and 1830, the two countries continued along two culturally separate paths, the one almost uniformly Roman Catholic, the other predominantly Calvinist. Such dissimilarities had obvious consequences for the way internal church reforms were implemented in either country. The differences have also influenced the approaches taken in each of the two sections that make up this chapter. The first section discusses church reforms within a fairly homogeneous religious context: that of Roman Catholic Belgium. The second deals with church reforms within a context that was much more diverse, since the dissolution of the Dutch ancien régime was accompanied by the emancipation of some churches and a proliferation of others.

Church Reform and Modernity in Belgium

Jan Art, Jan De Maeyer, Ward De Pril & Leo Kenis

Belgium lies on the southernmost border of Northern Europe, but it could also be described as being the most northerly part of Southern Europe. The country has therefore somewhat Latin characteristics which are hardly, if at all, to be found elsewhere in the North. In the sixteenth to seventeenth century the Southern Netherlands was considered to be a bridgehead of the Counter-Reformation, from which the British, Dutch and Germans, who had 'fallen away' from the Catholic faith, would be brought back on the right path. That 'baroque' stamp would last for a long time, especially in Flanders, the northern part of Belgium. For centuries the region was far removed from the capital of the empire (Madrid or Vienna), and was therefore able to maintain a relative autonomy from the monarchy and the central authority. That autonomy was manifested in the region's close attachment to ancient 'liberties' and class privileges, an attachment encountered by the enlightened Emperor Joseph II, the French Republic (which governed the *Départements réunis* longer than any other region), as well as Willem I, King of the United Kingdom of the Netherlands. Once the period of 'occupation' (c.1780-1830) was over, the Catholic Church made good use of the new Belgian liberties - and the shortcomings of the minimal or so-called night watchman state - to restore its influence in society. *In politicis*, this was the period of Unionism, and *in religiosis*, the period of the Revival (1830-1850). Once the young Belgian state was consolidated, the old internal differences re-emerged: the liberals formed a political party and would for decades, almost continuously, utilise the state system to implement their views. Catholics responded to this campaign by extending their own network of ultramontane-oriented periodicals, associations and all sorts of charitable work: it was the heyday of ultramontanism (1850-1884), which was dominated by the clerical-anticlerical opposition. After 1884 the country remained in the hands of Catholic governments for thirty years, and during the interwar period also the Catholic party remained in the majority, leading opponents to speak of a *régime clérical*. From a

Catholic viewpoint the period was characterised by the development of a huge number of voluntary charities and the implementation of social legislation, which resulted from the introduction of universal male plural suffrage (1893), the rise of the socialist party as well as the encyclical *Rerum novarum*.[1]

1780-1830
Forms of State Religion and Accompanying Reactions

The Austrian rulers attempted to make religious worship part of the state system, following the model of their Protestant colleagues. The church reforms launched by Joseph II led to a period of unrest in the Southern Netherlands. In particular, the dissolution of 'useless' (that is, contemplative) monasteries (1783) and the imposition of a civil marriage law (1784) led to a lot of disturbance. In 1786 the storm broke with the foundation of a general seminary in Louvain and a daughter seminary in Luxembourg. These were intended to replace all existing forms of priestly education in the diocesan seminaries, the university colleges and the formation centres of the regular clergy. In the spring of 1787 ultramontane opposition to the general seminary became one of the elements in the wider ecclesiastical and political opposition to the reforms of Joseph II, the so-called 'Minor Brabant Revolution'. Under increasing political pressure, Joseph II repealed the obligatory character of the general seminary and the bishops could henceforth open their own seminaries again.[2] Ultramontanism spread further among Catholics during the Brabant Revolution (Spring 1789). During the short-lived Republic of the United States of the Netherlands (1789-1790), the democratic forces in the Catholic camp were eliminated and driven into the group that would become the basis of the later liberal party. The Brabant Revolution was conceived as a counterrevolution: it restored the established order that had been disrupted. The ultramontanes were extremely hostile to the founding ideas of the French Revolution, and their convictions were validated by the events that took place during the period of French domination - both the anti-religious regime of the Republic (1795-1799) and the increasingly cesaropapist regime of Napoleon (1799-1814).

The period of the French Republic saw the gradual introduction of religious laws intended to de-christianise public life. In the autumn of 1796 all monasteries and abbeys were closed, their possessions seized and most of them sold at public auction (the so-called 'black goods'). One year later the University of Louvain was closed as were all church institutions still in existence (chapters, seminaries and other religious communities). At the same time the clergy were bitterly divided between those who

---

[1] Art, "Pourquoi la christianisation de la Flandre a-t-elle si bien réussi?". For a general introduction to the context, see Blom and Lamberts, *History of the Low Countries*, 269-384.

[2] See Roegiers and Van Sas, "Revolution in the North and South"; Hasquin, *Joseph II*, 181-292; Roegiers, "Routine, réorganisation et révolution".

had taken an oath of fealty to the constitution (a minority of *prêtres assermentés*) and those who had refused (a majority of *prêtres insermentés*). It was a period when the church seemed to be coming to an end (*Beloken Tijd* or 'low time'), and many saw its situation as hopeless.

Nevertheless, this period of oppression and persecution of the church did not have negative consequences solely. In many places the connection between the parish clergy and the faithful was reinforced, and many of the faithful were inspired to become involved in protecting persecuted priests, and in purchasing church goods and valuables with a view to later restitution. It was, in short, a period of quiet opposition. The majority of the rural population opted for the side of the church, and people chose to fight *pro aris et focis*, for 'altar and hearth', just as they had during the Brabant Revolution. The interests of the church coincided with those of the individual, and were seen as two sides of the same coin. Clerical opposition quickly linked up with that of population groups who felt short-changed by other governmental regulations, and priests frequently became the instigators of rebellious movements. Nobility and clergy, the two classes that had lost their privileges with the revolutionary legislation, formed a conservative block, an alliance that would hold out for the whole nineteenth century.

After Napoleon's coup (9 November 1799), the church's position quickly improved. Recognising the social usefulness of the church, Napoleon negotiated a concordat with Pope Pius VII in 1801 that would determine the organisation of the church and church-state relations for a long time to come. Of course, the Napoleonic reform was primarily aimed at incorporating, if not subordinating, religion within the imperial system, but it was also intended to rationalise and adapt the church's administration thoroughly. Of course, this meant that legally speaking the church would lose its quasi-monopoly over education and poor relief, something it would continue to fight tooth and nail, and with success. On the other hand, a clean sweep was made of many traditional and habitual customs, whose inefficiency was already evident by the end of the eighteenth century and had at least partly justified the intervention of the enlightened monarchs. Diocesan and parochial borders were brought into line with administrative borders. The maintenance of church buildings (church fabric or *fabrica ecclesiae*) no longer depended on the goodwill of the tithe-levying patron, but was put in the hands of the local population, in this case the local elites and dignitaries. The stipends of priests would henceforth be the responsibility of the state and, in principle, would be standardised, thus putting an end to the great divergences and nepotism of past times. The tensions between the *prêtres assermentés* and the others gradually disappeared. Above all, the bishop, the 'purple prefect', could from then on have absolute control over his personnel at will; priests could henceforth be dismissed, and there was no mention anymore of universities, abbeys or even secular patrons being involved in appointing parish clergy. The bishop was given an official residence, a seminary building was put at his disposal and he became lord and master of the secular clergy - though not, however, of the religious orders, that is if they still existed and had not been amalgamated with the parish clergy, a point that would later become the cause of dissension. The religious communities, which had been under fire since the time of the Austrian regime, were all dissolved at a certain point during the French regime. Under Napoleon, only communities involved in education and health care could be recognised. In this period also the first 'new' congregations came into existence, often founded by priests who brought together a few devout girls to open a school or to care for the sick in a village. The most famous were those congregations founded by Canon Petrus Jozef Triest from Ghent (Sisters of Charity, 1803; Brothers of Charity, 1807), all of which were attuned to the needs of the time.[3]

During the period of the United Kingdom of the Netherlands (1815-1830), the struggle to safeguard the social position of the church, which the ultramontanes had carried on for almost forty years, was continued under the leadership of the bishop of Ghent, Maurice de Broglie (1766-1821). With their *Jugement doctrinal* (September 1815), the then bishops in what would be the future territory of Belgium (Ghent, Malines, Liège, Namur and Tournai), condemned the indifferentism of the new constitution and forbade Catholics to swear allegiance to the constitution. In the succeeding years opposition focused on the educational policy of the government, in particular the decisions of 14 June 1825 which put the minor seminaries under state control and established a *collegium philosophicum* in Louvain. Before beginning their theological studies, all candidates for the priesthood had to spend two years in the new college, which was to be supervised by the government of the Netherlands.

Whereas in 1814 the clergy had requested the mere reintroduction of the old regime, by the end of the Dutch period they were almost completely won over to "liberté en tout et pour tous" (freedom in everything and for everyone). The final recognition of the religious freedom written into the constitution of the Netherlands actually meant that the clergy had reconciled themselves to the free market principle *in religiosis*. That Catholics had closed ranks in their opposition to the government's policy did not imply that they in fact formed a solid monolithic block. On the eve of the September revolt of 1830, there were various tendencies within Catholicism that in the succeeding years would more clearly emerge as separatist and ultimately hostile. From that time on there were liberal Catholics who, inspired by the ideas of the French priest, apologist and journalist Félicité de Lamennais (1782-1854), believed that Catholicism had the inner strength to continue on its own, even given the conditions of modern liberal society. Their ranks included not only lay people but also young priests who trusted the persuasive power of the faith more than the protection that the secular power could offer. Without identifying completely with the liberals, they shared an enthusiasm for the great possibilities of freedom. Some even went so far as to call on their personal freedom of action with regard to episcopal instructions or on their personal freedom of interpretation with regard to theological tradition. Over against the liberal Catholics were the conservatives, who absolutely refused to recognise the naturalness of an alliance between Catholicism and liberalism, and as loyal royalists hoped for a quick

---

[3] On what follows, see also Tihon, "La restauration".

return of the age-old unity between throne and altar. The nobility and the higher clergy constituted this Catholic right wing. In between was a group sometimes referred to as the 'Malines School'.⁴ Though small in number, this group was extremely influential. Its main driving forces were Archbishop François-Antoine de Mean (1756-1831), his vicar-general Engelbert Sterckx (1792-1867) and the new bishop of Liège, Cornelis Van Bommel (1790-1852). Supporters of this third way were generally not well-disposed towards Lamennais' theories, but realistically concluded that a return to the *ancien régime* was no longer possible or even desirable, since the close tie between church and state made incursions into ecclesiastical life unavoidable. The Malines School attempted to link the advantages of the liberal system with those of the *ancien régime* by allowing the church to enjoy a certain protection from the state, in particular on the level of financial support.⁵

1830-1850
The Revival: a 'Modern' Restoration

The Catholics were easily able to push through their demands at the national congress that drew up the constitution of the independent Belgian state. That constitution, the most liberal of the time on the continent, opened the door for free, and, thus also Catholic, initiatives. The Belgian church would virtually be the first in Europe to be confronted with this aspect of modernity, and instead of struggling with it, succeeded in using it for its own advancement. In the aftermath of the Belgian Revolution, the church blossomed, and became a model for Catholics in other countries. In the time of the United Kingdom of the Netherlands, the Catholic Revival was limited to the upper classes centred on aristocrats like Henri de Mérode (1782-1835) and Ernest de Beauffort (1782-1858), but around 1839 it developed into a mass movement, supported by both ultramontane and liberal Catholics. The sudden outburst of religious energy reached its high point in the early 1840s. This movement of religious renewal aspired to no less than 'to restore all things in Christ'.⁶

However, first things first: care had to be taken that the country's governance remained in good hands. The clergy would, directly or indirectly, attempt to influence electoral results until the end of the twentieth century. Priests regularly hold seats in the House of Representatives and in the Senate, but the actual body that attempts to move governments towards a church-friendly legislation is the Conference of Bishops, where the *ordinarii*, under the chairmanship of the archbishop and in the presence

---

⁴ See Simon, "L'École de Malines".
⁵ Aubert, "Die erste Phase des katholischen Liberalismus".

⁶ Tihon, "La Belgique (de l'Indépendance à la fin de l'unionisme)"; Viaene, *Belgium and the Holy See*; Id., "Katholisches Reveil und ultramontane Pietät in Belgiën", 111-113; Id., "L'épanouissement d'une Église 'libre'".

A. Tessaro, Pope Gregory XVI and the Belgian episcopate, *lithograph*, 1833.
[Leuven, KADOC: KPC34]

of the nuncio, come together at least once a year to determine their position towards outstanding problems. The Belgian bishops were amongst the first in Europe to found this institution. In the unionist period, due consideration was given to their advice. Later when liberal cabinets came to power, opposition was organised from within the Conference, and after 1884 almost every important initiative of the Catholic government was first submitted to the *nihil obstat* of the bishops. At the same time the Conference constituted the Board of Governors of the Catholic University, which was re-established first in Malines in 1834 and after 1835 in Louvain.

Conscious of the importance of public opinion, the bishops not only issued an annual communal pastoral letter to be read in all the churches condemning the reading of 'bad newspapers and books', they also started their own periodicals and attempted to silence dissonant Catholic periodicals. In that way the small number of those taxpayers who were eligible to vote would be brought to the correct views. The rest of the population was kept on the right track through education, preaching and Catholic societies.

The Provisional Government, comprising the founders of the newly-independent Belgium, had proclaimed complete freedom of education, which led to a proliferation of primary schools especially. This was brought under control by the law of 1842, but until 1879 the clergy exercised a great deal of control over the education and appointment of personnel, the inspection of schools and the content of the curriculum. The quasi-monopoly of the church in the primary education of both boys and girls, whether in primary, vocational or Sunday schools, was all but restored. The authority of the clergy at the level of secondary and normal schools was also overwhelming.

From the 1830s on Belgium saw the advent of popular missions, which had been forbidden during the Dutch regime though they had taken place on a large scale in France at the same time. They can be seen as one of the principal expressions of the Catholic Revival in Belgium. During these missions, one or more preachers descended on a parish for seven to ten days and the faithful were expected to come and listen for a few hours every day. The missions had a great impact, particularly in the more rural Flanders, until the 1870s. The mission in a parish ended with confession and general communion, and often with the erection of a large mission cross. Initially, irregularities from the previous period (such as buying national goods or marrying relatives) were set to right. Later, when each parish priest was required to organise such a mission at least once every ten years, it acquired more the character of a renewal and was intended to show the mobilising power of Catholicism. The confessors-preachers, who were mostly regular priests, came across as being less rigorous than the often very strict older parish priest, and they spread the more lenient Liguorian moral theology.

The popular mission was often the occasion for the founding or re-founding of a new confraternity or pious lay congregation. The religious associations, which had been abolished by Joseph II and replaced by one single association, led a slumbering, hidden and often unworldly existence until the time of the Concordat. The Concordat bishops would attempt to inject new life into them, for example by furthering devotion to the Holy Sacrament. The Belgian bishops would do their utmost to bring these associations back into the hands of the clergy and to root out all profane phenomena (e.g. feasts following the 'reading of the accounts' or following the funeral of a member of the society). In the period following the 'regularisation' of the old confraternities, voluntary charities, which were centrally directed either by the diocese or the papacy, were promoted or even made compulsory.[7]

Where did the bishops get the manpower necessary to staff all those parishes and educational institutions, to arrange all those days of preaching and hearing confessions, not to mention all the many foundations caring for old people, the sick and orphans? Because of the hold they had on secondary education and the (re-)foundation of the minor seminaries, the secular clergy were in a favourable position to recruit suitable candidates for the priesthood. The minor seminaries particularly often gave pupils from a modest background an academic secondary education paid for by

---

[7] Art, "Social Control in Belgium".

the parish priest or a benefactor, thereby enabling the clergy to take advantage of what until then was largely unexploited intellectual capital hidden in the countryside. There were years when there were more ordinations than conferrals of university degrees. The reverse of this was that the secular clergy increasingly came from a rural and often modest background, not the kind of background that would enhance their standing in the eyes of the prejudiced and more intellectual urban bourgeoisie. However, the succession to the often very old parish clergy was guaranteed, and most parish priests felt at home in rural areas.[8]

Moreover, the bishops made efforts to raise the level of priestly education. They reopened the major seminaries, which had been closed since 1825. Between 1842 and 1848 they organised meetings between the professors from the various diocesan seminaries and tried to implement a coherent structure for the education of the clergy, with special attention to the continuity between the minor and major seminaries and to a consistent methodology in theological formation.[9] The main emphasis, however, lay not on intellectual but on moral and spiritual formation. Aided by annual spiritual exercises and monthly retreats, the Belgian clergy were noted for their strict moral piety, which evinced little mysticism but was methodically regulated. The parish clergy had to edify the faithful more by their piety and exemplary lives than by their learning.

The re-founding of the Catholic University of Louvain and the foundation of the Belgian College in Rome in 1844 brought about a striking improvement in theological studies.[10] The theology faculty of Louvain grew steadily in the 1840s. One of the most notable figures there was Jean Baptiste Malou (1809-1864), who was professor of dogmatic theology from 1837 to 1849. As a former student of the *Collegium Romanum*, he set himself up in Louvain as the defender of scholasticism and classical theology against his colleagues, the philosopher Gerard Casimir Ubaghs (1800-1875) and the theologian Arnold Tits (1807-1851). These Louvain professors aimed at developing a new apologetic, which would be able to show the truth of the Christian faith in confrontation with contemporary rationalistic thought.[11] Their ideas have been characterised as a mitigated form of traditionalism, later as ontologism. The ideas of Ubaghs and Tits were well received in the seminaries and in *Revue Catholique*, which was started in 1843 as the in-house periodical of the Louvain professors. However, they had to reckon with the increasing opposition of the Jesuits, of Lamennais' opponents and finally also of Rome. In 1843 some of Ubaghs' works were submitted to an investigation by the Holy See. This was the beginning of a process of growing opposition against Ubaghs and his Louvain colleagues, which would end in a condemnation of Ubaghs in 1866.

---

[8] On what follows see Viaene, "L'épanouissement d'une Église 'libre'"; De Maeyer, Leplae and Schmiedl, eds., *Religious Institutes in Western Europe*; Tihon, "Le prêtre et le religieux"; Van Dijck, De Maeyer and Henneau, eds., *Historiographie et perspectives de recherche des ordres et congrégations*.

[9] Kenis, "Movements toward Renewal".
[10] The Belgian College in Rome was founded to enable Catholic University of Louvain graduates with a license or doctorate in theology and the top students from the major seminaries to pursue religious studies for a number of years.
[11] Kenis, *De Theologische Faculteit te Leuven*.

J.B. De Noter, The Great Seminary of Mechelen, aquarelle, 1848.
[Mechelen, Great Seminary / © IRPA-KIK, Brussels: X010948]

The constitutional right of association made possible the (re-)foundation of orders and congregations, an opportunity that Belgian Catholics enthusiastically embraced. Between 1830 and 1850 in the diocese of Ghent alone, 36 new diocesan-approved congregations and old exempt orders were (re-)established. Still, this did not constitute a complete restoration of the regular clergy; in contrast to the situation before the French Revolution, truly contemplative orders now became the exception. No Carthusian monastery was re-established in Belgium; only the strictly enclosed Carmelites and Poor Clares and the Trappist Abbey of Westmalle remained as a reminder of the *ancien régime*.[12] Almost all the new foundations, like their rare predecessors in the French and Dutch periods, came into existence in order to alleviate an acute social need: in many places and for various reasons, governments seemed not to be prepared or able to guarantee elementary social services.[13] In order to meet that need, congre-

---

[12] Viaene, "L'épanouissement d'une Église 'libre'", 55-56 and 64-67; Van Dijck and Dusausoit, "Hommes visibles et invisibles"; see also Suenens and Marcelis, "Vrouwelijke religieuze instituten".

[13] All representatives at the levels of legislative and executive power were chosen by wealthy taxpayers. The question was if those elected would be re-elected if they were to use 'their' tax money for purposes other than those of their voters, who themselves could pay for the education of their own children and for their old age.

gations of sisters and brothers were founded here and there, sometimes initiated by lay people but increasingly in consultation with the clergy, in order to provide for the educational and other needs of the local population. Paradoxically, the vow of poverty included in the rule of every order, the support of benefactors and the subsidies offered by the authorities who accepted these inexpensive workers as a gift from heaven, ensured that many congregations would grow into large international organisations in the second half of the century. However, in this heroic period of new beginnings, many of them had a precarious existence, in the service of the poor ... and of the bishop who was their lord and master.

This however was not the case with the exempt orders which fell under papal protection.[14] The Jesuits had been back in the country since before 1830, albeit under another name. After 1830 they launched into education, by opening up colleges and by taking over the popular missions, a task they shared with the Redemptorists. Initially they wanted to resume their old traditions and provide only free education at the request and expense of the urban councils, but they quickly had to adapt to new circumstances and impose school fees. These enabled them to register some non-paying students, a strategy that would be followed by many other congregations. The Jesuits clashed with the archbishop on a number of occasions, including the foundation of the Namur faculty of philosophy which was intended as a counterweight to that at the Catholic University of Louvain. In order to prevent such conflicts, the opening of each school, including those run by exempt orders, would in the future require the bishop's approval.

Other exempt orders that had been re-established also presented the bishops with problems. After Rome rejected the request that they be subject to episcopal supervision, the bishops still agreed that an apostolic visitor would be appointed to ensure proper governance among the Norbertines, Dominicans, Franciscans, and others, whose early years were frequently unsettled because of their thorny financial situation. Indeed, because these communities were not incorporated, they had to resort to constructions based on trust, and were more than once betrayed in that trust. The malaise in the relations between the bishops and the exempt orders would drag on until the end of the 1860s.

In short, in the years from 1830 to 1850, the church grasped every chance offered by the new constitution: it succeeded in insisting on a favourable *modus vivendi* with the secular authority, including the monarchy; it was prominent in all the public sectors that it traditionally held dear, namely education and social welfare; it exercised a strong influence on public opinion through preaching and the press; the parish clergy were getting younger and new religious congregations, adapted to the needs of the time, were coming into existence. Catholicism had become if not *de iure* then *de facto* the state religion of Belgium.[15]

---

[14] See Simon, *Le Cardinal Sterckx*, 48-93.

[15] Lamberts, "Belgium since 1830", 324-328.

1850-1884
The Heyday of Ultramontanism

Liberal opinion, the other partner in the unholy alliance of 1830 began to make itself felt in the 1840s. The liberals saw Catholic domination in the new Belgium as excessive, endangering the neutrality and prerogatives of the state. A liberal congress was held, liberal voters' associations were founded, and a victory was garnered at the ballot box. In 1847 the first distinctly liberal cabinet came to power and many large cities were no longer in Catholic hands. With only a few short breaks, the liberals held on to power until 1884, and made every effort to expand the presence of the state in public life. This led inevitably to an ever sharper confrontation with the church authorities, who felt the position they had acquired after 1830 to be under threat. The signals from Rome, where the new, young and media-savvy Pope Pius IX (1846-1878) was 'beleaguered' by Italian nationalists, were not reassuring. Given this climate, it is not surprising that ultramontane ideas, which had also been resurrected in previous periods, would now get a new lease of life.[16]

Striking here is the increasing lay contribution to and influence on church life. The more the state scaled down its support for and cooperation with the Catholic project, the more the ecclesiastical authorities relied on the support of benefactors and the contributions of the faithful, 'the real country'. This financial dependence would bolster the connection between the conservative nobility and bourgeoisie and the clergy.

The cradle of the many initiatives undertaken to christianise the working class lay in the Societies of St Vincent. These initially paternalistic charitable 'conferences' of wealthy Catholic dignitaries were founded in a number of large cities at the beginning of the 1840s, following the French example. In 1852 there were 52 conferences in Belgium, and by 1881 there were 625 (in 1912: 1,273). By then the conferences had become the meeting place and heart of a network of committed ultramontanes, who undertook numerous initiatives alongside charitable ones. They were responsible for a number of important press initiatives, such as the leading Ghent paper, *Le Bien Public* (1853-1940) or the Brussels daily, *Le Courrier de Bruxelles* (1861/1871-1914), and for numerous educational initiatives, such as the St Luke Schools where, under the direction of the Brothers of the Christian Schools, artists and craftsmen were trained who would go on to create neo-Gothic art works in the second half of the century. The art and programme of the neo-Gothic movement summarised what the ultramontanes stood for: a restoration of the 'old' order, and a return to what was seen as having existed during the Middle Ages, while still making use of the achievements of modern times.[17]

The members of the Society of St Vincent were also involved in successive Catholic congresses (the 'Malines Congresses'), which were organised in Belgium by

---

[16] Tihon, "La Belgique (de la fin de l'unionisme à la Première Guerre mondiale)"; Witte, "The Battle for Monasteries, Cemeteries and Schools".

[17] See De Maeyer and Wynants, eds., *De Vincentianen in België*, passim; De Maeyer, "The Neo-Gothic in Belgium".

J. Géruzet, The officers of the Catholic Congress in Malines, *photograph, 1863*.
[Leuven, KADOC: KFB2369]

Edouard Ducpétiaux (1804-1868) in 1863, 1864 and 1867, along the lines of the German *Katholikentage*. The goal was to coordinate the activities of the different kinds of Catholic voluntary work and to unleash a powerful public opinion. The Belgian primate Engelbert Sterckx gave his full support, realising that the prestige of the episcopacy no longer sufficed with the 'liberal' government to ensure religious liberties. He therefore called on the help of an organised laity: in accordance with democratic logic and apostolic need, Christian people had to set out to use the constitutional freedoms to defend their faith against other hostile-minded citizens.[18] The decisions passed in those gatherings included surveys of everything that was alive in Catholicism and plans for what had to happen in the future. The Malines Congresses were a great success. They gave a strong impetus to the activity of ideologically convinced Catholics who would henceforth join forces, and the very contemporary character of the congresses' concerns gave a modern look to the Belgian church. They also drew up outlines for the educational programme of the later Catholic party, the foundations of which lie in the Malines Congresses.[19]

Finally, as their name indicates, the ultramontanes were the mediators of papal interests in these parts. They did this in various ways: through the press, not only their own favourite paper *Le Bien Public*, but also by actively cooperating with the 'Black International' which wanted to defend papal interests in the international press; by organising pilgrimages to the prisoner of the Vatican and by supporting papal initiatives, ranging from St Peter's Pence to attending the many processions and jubilees that were being celebrated; and by continuing to demand that their views of

---

[18] Aubert, *150 ans de vie des Églises*, 21.

[19] Simon, *Le Cardinal Sterckx*, 132-133; Viaene, "L'épanouissement d'une Église 'libre'", 89-99.

the encyclical *Quanta Cura* and the *Syllabus errorum* (1864) be put into effect. Those views ensured them the support of the Curia in Rome, but also formed the basis of their endless disagreement with liberal Catholics and of divisions within the Catholic party. It even led on occasion to a clash with the older, more pragmatically inclined bishops. Some ultramontanes raised the question whether a convinced Catholic was permitted to discharge a public function since that presupposed an oath of loyalty to liberal laws, or if a convinced Catholic could even take part in elections since that implied approval of a bad liberal constitution.[20]

The former domination of the episcopacy was curtailed from various angles. The liberal cabinets cut back on everything they saw as intruding on the separation of church and state and preventing the modernisation of society. This included the administration of burial places, the granting of scholarships, work on church maintenance and, not least, the dominating influence of the clergy in the organisation of the educational system. As far as primary education was concerned, the law of 1879 had to be the crown of the liberals' work: every district was to have a neutral school, under the direction of teachers with a degree from a state normal school, with an up-to-date curriculum and with religious instruction being offered only outside of school hours. The bishops reacted furiously: Catholics could not send their children to 'Godless schools'; teachers had to resign and move to Catholic primary schools that were set up very quickly almost everywhere. The school struggle, which in 1884 was settled in favour of the Catholics, was the highpoint of the ultramontane-marked Catholic mobilisation that had been carried out in the preceding decades as a reaction to the liberal offensive. It restored unity in the Catholic ranks, but at the same time it illustrates the clergy's great dependence on the laity, not least in matters financial.[21]

Rome also aimed at keeping a closer eye on what happened in the Belgian church province. Pius IX nominated bishops who were strongly pro-Rome, who in their turn would appoint Rome-trained priests to influential positions. The nuncio was present at every episcopal conference and did not hesitate to put forward the views of the Holy See. In 1869, in the run-up to the first Vatican Council, he listed all the weak points in the Belgian church that, in his view, showed the need for papal guidance but that also highlighted the way in which the Belgian bishops had adapted to their 'modern' situation.[22] Many of those deviations from Tridentine regulations had to do with the bishops' concern to maintain their own authority, and the nuncio often had to conclude that "given local circumstances, it is best to allow matters to stand as they are". So, in 1870 no diocesan or provincial synods had yet been held (except for one in Namur), even though they should have been held once every year or every three years respectively. Instead the bishops came together at least once a year (the Bish-

---

[20] De Maeyer, "La Belgique: un élève modèle de l'école ultramontaine".
[21] Lory, *Libéralisme et instruction primaire*; Lamberts and Lory, *1884: un tournant politique en Belgique*; Viaene, "L'épanouissement d'une Église 'libre'", 89-99; De Maeyer, "L'Église se tourne vers le peuple", 126-141.
[22] Art, "Documents concernant la situation de l'Église catholique en Belgique".

ops' Conference) and 'important' priests were brought together once a year in every diocese (the decanal meeting). The papal envoy saw this as a good solution and even proposed that a provincial synod could be held only with papal approval. Since proper courts of canon law did not exist, the bishop was the superior and sole judge, a situation that could lead to difficulty when incumbents were removed or transferred at his pleasure. Here too it was best to maintain the existing situation and not extend the right to tenure that had been the privilege of the main churches since the French period, given that the parish priests were already inclined to rule over their parishes in an autocratic way. For the same reasons the *concursus* (a special examination for particular vacancies), which was still being organised in Liège for the main churches, would not be reintroduced. It was better to require young priests to take an annual examination, and then when a vacancy arose the bishop could nominate the most suitable candidate as parish priest from a reserve pool. In the system of the *concursus*, however, poor parishes were left sometimes for years without a priest, for want of candidates. In dealing with the chapters, the bishops tried to take over completely, and nominated all the canons, even though the Holy See had the right to appoint the first titular canon. A final Belgian peculiarity, which the nuncio highlighted, concerned the seminaries and minor seminaries. The latter were not housed in the major seminaries and admitted students who were not preparing for the priesthood. They therefore did not wear a soutane (!) and their curriculum focused too much on the official requirements for admission to higher education, to the neglect of Latin. The Italian official here overlooked the fact that the 'mixing' of the student body had one great advantage, to be later highlighted by Canon Jacques Leclerq (1891-1971): in those schools future priests often made lifelong friendships with the rising intelligentsia of the land, which enhanced their influence once they were ordained.

Despite their attempt to keep a tight rein on matters, the bishops could not keep an eye on everything. This was due not only to the opposition of the government, the anticlerical press cabal or the stubbornness of lay benefactors, but was also the result of more structural factors. According to the nuncio, their dioceses were too large and/or too densely populated with the result that the bishops were not in a position to exercise the necessary personal supervision. The episcopal visitation of parishes and religious communities had become a formality and this could be set right only by creating new dioceses or by appointing auxiliary bishops responsible for parish and monastery visitations. As a result of this inadequate oversight, the typical Belgian secular priest saw himself as lord and master of the parish; was too involved in worldly affairs, much to the glee of the 'bad' press; opposed the splitting off of new parishes even when this was required by the increase in population; reluctantly tolerated the work of regular clergy in 'his' territory; and preached badly. All of this meant that he enjoyed little standing among the upper classes, who moreover very rarely sent their sons to the seminaries and gave the impression of being profoundly ignorant about the church's teaching and organisation.

Nor did the bishops have everything in hand in dealing with the regular clergy. Since the apostolic visitation had been abolished, the exempt orders and congregations were themselves responsible for the supervision of their members. However, this duty was properly observed only among the Jesuits, Dominicans, the Discalced Carmelites and the Redemptorists, but not, for example, in the four Trappist monasteries in Belgium at the time. And what about the 153 different women's congregations and the approximately 15 congregations of brothers, almost all of which were subject to episcopal jurisdiction and therefore to the supervision of the *ordinarii*? In fact, there were far too many of them, and given that almost all had been founded with the same objective, would it not be better to amalgamate them into larger and more viable entities? The bishops opposed this proposal, fearing they would no longer have the same power over the members of religious orders and would have to reckon with powerful general superiors. They put up with the negative consequences of that strategy and tried to remedy it by nominating priests as directors alongside the congregation's mother (or brother) superior. Nevertheless, the small-scale congregations were rarely able to vouch for a thorough novitiate formation and so brothers and sisters were often sent out unprepared, more sister houses were founded than the congregation could either staff or financially support, large loans were taken on and there were no clear rules concerning dowries and inheritances. In short, after the death of the often charismatic founder, many congregations had difficulty in finding a suitable and competent superior, especially the congregations of brothers which almost exclusively recruited poorly educated people of modest background.

On the other hand - something the nuncio could not know in 1869 - these congregations would in 1880 provide the necessary personnel for the extension of a Catholic primary school network. Small communities of, for example, three or four religious, would be set up even in the smallest villages. The foundation was laid in this period for the extension of what would later develop into the Catholic pillar. The school struggle of 1879-1884 was the catalyst for this process: all squabbling was pushed to the background, a larger Catholic front was formed on the political level, an election was won, to be followed by a thirty-year period of successive Catholic governments. The school struggle could only have been won by a synergy of various players: a wealthy ultramontane elite, an army of available nuns and brothers, a secular clergy, which despite everything was tightly under the control of the bishops, and a militant faithful subservient to the clergy but nonetheless concerned or even outraged. The bishops did not succeed in bringing a friendly government to power at this time, but in the parish societies they had a powerful means to mobilise the country. Following the honeymoon of unionism, the Belgian bishops had learned that in the wrong hands the state system could also be directed against them and they were forced to proceed in creating their own structures that could also function without state aid.[23]

---

[23] De Maeyer, "La Belgique: un élève modèle de l'école ultramontaine".

Jan Art, Jan De Maeyer, Ward De Pril & Leo Kenis

1884-1920
Rerum novarum: the Rise of Christian Democracy

The first concern of the Catholic cabinet in 1884 was to revise the education laws. The Ministry of Education, which had been formed during the previous legislature, did not continue as an independent department and the local authorities could henceforth again 'adopt' the existing free schools. In practice this meant that almost all the Catholic primary schools founded after 1879 would from then on receive subsidies from the local authorities; the 'official' school was abolished or converted to a boys' school with 'reliable' teachers. The extension of official secondary education was slowed down; the Missionaries of Workers and the Salesians devoted themselves to the burgeoning technical and vocational schools; religious institutes and especially those of women invested heavily in agricultural and home economics schools, while the bishops tried - admittedly in vain - to acquire corporate status for the Catholic University of Louvain. All these measures guaranteed Catholic domination of education, certainly in Flanders, for many decades. However, this did not mean that the school question disappeared from the political agenda and it would continue to be an electoral issue until the 1950s. In the years after 1884 the free schools would be supported by the state, in so far as was politically feasible without their autonomy being endangered.[24]

In 1886, however, castles in Wallonia were being plundered by rebellious workers and the socialist party, which was strongly anticlerical, was coming increasingly to the fore. Its main demand was universal suffrage, which the conservative government, with the support of the more conservative liberals, would be forced to accede to gradually. In 1893 universal plural voting for men was introduced (thereby increasing the number of electors fourteen times); then after the First World War, one-man one-vote male suffrage was introduced, and only after the Second World War were women given the vote.

From the point of view of the church authorities, it was of primary importance that the government did not come into anticlerical hands; developments in neighbouring France illustrated the disastrous results such a development could have for the church. This led to a double concern: maintaining unity within Catholic ranks and damming the threatening tide of socialism. The church's success with the latter enhanced its authority over the former and enabled it to keep control of affairs. However, it was not easy to keep the internally divided Catholic party in line: the opinions of conservatives and Christian democrats differed fundamentally with regard to state intervention in labour relations, military investments, the taking over of the Congo Free State, the development of the embryonic social security system, not to mention the granting of Flemish linguistic demands. Even the bishops themselves differed on

---

[24] Tihon, "La Belgique (de la fin de l'unionisme à la Première Guerre mondiale)", 538-554; De Maeyer, "L'Église se tourne vers le peuple", 126-141; Gerin, "Catholicisme social et démocratie chrétienne".

many of these issues, and within the regular clergy also there was a world of difference between pro-Flemish priests, teachers and parish priests on the one hand and, on the other, the Jesuits and many congregations of sisters who were unwilling to allow their schools to become Dutch-speaking. That the Catholic majority could hold out till 1914 was to a large degree thanks to the influence of the bishops and above all of the archbishop, and to the success of the charitable social work that was started by the clergy, especially in the countryside.[25]

Long before *Rerum novarum* (1891) the ultramontanes, concerned about the salvation of the 'poor' and preserving public order, had become involved with the working classes by organising working men's associations, guilds and Sunday school activities for the young (*patronages*). Those associations had a distinctly charitable character but brought about little change in the precarious living conditions of a great deal of the population. The successful advance of the socialist party in cities and industrial centres could largely be attributed to the fact that it concerned itself with the material improvement of people's present lot by organising workers' unions, cooperatives and health insurance associations ('mutualities'), and with their future betterment by holding out the prospect of workers' participation in the governance of the country. The shock of 1886, the encyclical *Rerum novarum* and above all the introduction of universal plural voting brought Catholic dignitaries (often the ultramontanes from before 1879) and the bishops to the realisation that the socialist threat could no longer be averted by paternalistic charitable work.[26] Following consultation among each other, the bishops in 1893 ordered their parish clergy to set up working men's guilds in all the industrial centres, Xaverian societies in all rural villages, accompanied in both cases by "societies of mutual assistance, health funds, savings associations and farmers' unions", *ut minaces socialistarum conatus repellantur*, "so that the threatening ventures of the socialists may be repelled". The provincial of the Belgian Jesuits summarised the situation pithily: "The bishops and principal Catholics wish to create syndicates and cooperatives to take over the working classes [...] This is both an economic and a political undertaking because of the role they are called to play in elections."[27] The strategy was a rewarding one as the Catholic cabinet remained in power even after 1893. Through its legislation and policy, including its policies on health insurance and pensions, it would support free and therefore above all Catholic initiative. On the eve of the First World War, between the Association of Christian Mutualities of Belgium, the National

---

[25] The Belgian bishops did not hesitate to make the party's unity into a question of conscience or to issue disciplinary sanctions against clergy who threatened it, as in the case of the priests Adolf Daens (1839-1907) and Antoine Pottier (1849-1923). See Simon, *Le parti catholique belge*, 51; see also De Maeyer, "L'Église se tourne vers le peuple", 117-126.
[26] Indeed, census suffrage meant that Catholic action addressed itself mainly to those who were entitled to vote, and the remaining groups (workers, lower middle class and small farmers) became, above all, objects of Christian charity.
[27] Translation of: "Les évêques et principaux catholiques veulent créer des syndicats et des coopératives pour s'emparer de la classe ouvrière [...] ce seront des œuvres économiques et même politiques à cause du rôle qu'elles sont appelées à jouer dans les élections".

Secretariat of Christian Unions (1904) and the Farmers' Union (*Boerenbond*), there was a strong framework of charitable work in place, with local branches in all the villages. It was the envy of Catholic countries elsewhere. That all this could be realised in one decade was due to the favourable attitude of the government, but above all to the effort of Catholic lay people, secular priests and regular clergy.

The parish priests, whom the nuncio in 1869 had described as living at their ease, were now expected to retrain as social workers. For example, the pension offices which, following the legislation of 1900, the bishop of Ghent ordered to be established in all parishes of his diocese, were managed by the parish priest "for the benefit of working men, who through this priestly action would come to see that their real friends were to be found not among the socialists but in the church and religion". The parish clergy, some of whom saw themselves above all as 'celebrants of religious services', now had to come out into the public arena, recruit members, and care also for those sheep that had strayed. This made their daily work considerably more onerous, with the charitable work coming on top of their religious duties.

Similar efforts were made by the male regular clergy (who in this period were more numerous than the secular clergy), including the Jesuits, who were the largest group. They deliberately did not become too involved in charitable work as this might alienate them from the target audience of their colleges and Marian congregations, but they did embark on retreats for working men. Long before Joseph Cardijn (1882-1967), they were convinced that the 'working man' could more successfully be brought to the right views by a fellow worker than by a priest. 'Good' workers therefore got the chance to spend a number of days together in 'spiritual seclusion' at the expense of the Catholic employer, and to listen to the preacher, so that they could afterwards be sent out into the field and influence their fellow workers in a positive way. The Jesuits also took charge of the Societies of the Sacred Heart, which especially during the interwar years would propagate monthly group confessions and communion among the traditionally church-shy menfolk.

The Dominicans devoted themselves to apologetics, while the Franciscans expanded their network of third orders. In 1909, the Benedictine Abbey of Mont César in Louvain took over the leadership of the liturgical movement, which aimed at increasing the involvement of the faithful in the celebration of the Eucharist. The Flemish Norbertine abbeys became centres of 'the good press', distributing countless periodicals and brochures; they also coordinated the 'Eucharistic Crusade' that had been founded by the beatified priest Edouard Poppe (1890-1924) and was directed to young children who needed special attention ever since the lowering of the communion age.[28]

For Leo XIII a Christian reform of society was not conceivable without a reform of the study of religion, both of which had to be based on Thomism. In the encyclical *Aeterni patris* (1879) and elsewhere, Thomism was recommended as the authority in

---

[28] De Maeyer, "L'Église se tourne vers le peuple", 141-156; Id., "Les hommes d'oeuvres"; Gerard, "L'épanouissement du mouvement ouvrier chrétien".

Désiré Mercier, *photograph*, c.1910.
[Mechelen, Archbishopric of Mechelen-Brussels, Archives]

the area of philosophy, in particular for the education of young priests. However, the Thomist offensive did not immediately raise the intellectual level of seminary formation in any noticeable way. In 1890 the Belgian nuncio complained that priestly formation usually lasted only three years instead of four, and that during those three years students were not urged to study or read on their own, but were required mainly to listen and be docile. The report drawn up in 1891 by the later cardinal, Désiré Mercier (1851-1926) about the situation in the different Belgian seminaries exposed the many weak points in the clerical formation of the time: seminarians were allotted a merely passive role, without any room for individual spontaneity; the numerous religious exercises made intensive study impossible; above all, the seminarians were overly enclosed in their own small world without any contact with what was happening outside. Their formation did not include any discussion of the burning problems of the day - rationalism, biblical criticism, socialism, evolution, materialism, etc. As a result, young priests were not prepared for the real world and were not in a position to give any leadership to the faithful living in a sophisticated society.[29] In 1892 Mercier

---

[29] Boudens, "The Parish Priest", 112-113; see Sauvage, *Jacques Leclercq*, 24-27.

got permission to establish a seminary himself, the Leo XIII Seminary where promising young priests would get a neo-Thomist formation that they would later pass on as professors at the universities and major seminaries.

On the academic level, Thomism succeeded in making a quicker breakthrough and developed more productively. From the 1880s on, the Catholic University of Louvain became an important centre for the revival of Thomism. In 1882, at the request of Leo XIII, the Belgian bishops established a chair of Thomistic philosophy in the Theology Faculty and entrusted it to Mercier. In 1889, with the approval of the pope, Mercier extended this into a Higher Institute of Philosophy. The Institute was to educate an intellectual elite (both clerical and lay!) who would raise the prestige of the church in the world and rescue Catholics from their intellectual isolation. In the succeeding years Mercier attempted to realise his ideal of neo-Thomism, one characterised by a respect for scholarly freedom, openness to contemporary philosophical and scientific problems and close contact with the experimental sciences.[30] With the launch of the *Revue néo-scolastique* in 1894, the Catholic University of Louvain with its vision of an 'open' Thomism was given a voice that further enhanced its international influence. At the same time, opponents of neo-Thomism on the ideological and social level expressed their views in the influential monthly periodical *Revue sociale catholique* (1897-1927).[31]

The study of theology was also revised in these years. Since the condemnation of traditionalism, research in systematic theology at Louvain had become very conventional, conforming to the model of Roman theology. The renewal in methodology was first introduced in the historical disciplines of theology.[32] In 1890 Albin Van Hoonacker (1857-1933) was appointed to a new chair in the 'Critical History of the Old Testament', and began to apply the historical-critical method to the study of the Hebrew Bible. He was later joined by Paulin Ladeuze (1870-1940), who used the same critical approach in his research on the New Testament. The study of church history also integrated the new historical criticism, and through young professors such as Alfred Cauchie (1860-1922) earned Louvain a reputation for its sound critical historiography. Actually, this renewal of historical study was also carried out by other Catholic scholars, such as the Jesuits Charles De Smedt (1831-1911) and Hippolyte Delahaye (1859-1941), the successive editors of the *Acta Sanctorum*. During the modernist crisis, these professors remained untouched by the Holy See's condemnations thanks to the protection of Mercier, who in 1906 had become Belgium's archbishop.

Since the seminary professors were generally educated in Louvain, the new scholarly trends eventually came to have an influence on priestly formation in the seminaries. This is evident in the scholarly journals that were started in various dioceses at this time, with the goal of bringing the intellectual level of priests up to standard and making them into a cohesive group, both intellectually and spiritually. These

---

[30] Aubert, *Aspects divers du néo-thomisme*.
[31] De Maeyer, "L'Église se tourne vers le peuple", 118-119; Id., "Katholische Soziallehre und Christliche Arbeiterorganisationen".
[32] Aubert, *Le grand tournant de la Faculté de théologie de Louvain*, 73-109.

journals included *Collationes Brugenses* (1896), *Collationes Gandavenses* (1909), *La Vie diocésaine. Bulletin du diocèse de Malines* (1907) and *Revue ecclésiastique de Liège* (1905). At the same time Cardinal Mercier aimed at a spiritual formation of the clergy, aware that in time of war the apostolate had to be adapted so that the living example of priests would be at the forefront. To that end, from 1917 on he encouraged the formation of small movements or communities that brought priests together with a view to furthering a fuller spiritual life. In 1919 Mercier, together with Canon Allaer founded the *Fraternité sacerdotale des Amis de Jésus* (Priestly Fraternity of the Friends of Jesus), which was recognised as a sodality of priests by Rome in 1926. The members took an oath of personal poverty and absolute obedience to the bishop, devoted themselves to an intensive life of prayer and put great emphasis on helping one's neighbour. The objective was not so much to further the personal sanctity of the members as to bring about an improvement in the apostolate.[33]

Conclusion

The period of foreign domination (1780-1830) coincided with a severe crisis for the strongly ultramontane church in the Southern Netherlands. With these traumatic experiences stamped on its memory, from 1830 to 1920 and even later the church's aim was 'to restore all things in Christ'. It adapted its strategy for achieving this aim to the changing political and socio-economic parameters.

In combining freedom and protection for the national religion, the new Belgian regime created an original context that seemed to be extraordinarily favourable for the social development of Catholicism.[34] The Belgian bishops accepted the modern freedoms - in particular freedom of worship and of association - as an effective means of realising their religious objectives. As a consequence, the young Belgian state offered a favourable terrain for the re-establishment of old congregations and orders, and for the founding of new, often female religious institutes, which played a crucial role in the Catholic Revival in the decades after 1830. Between 1830 and 1870, the numerous new congregations responded to the challenges of their time and to the needs of a society that had gone through the industrial revolution. Their many initiatives show that the church in fact did contribute to the shaping of modern society. At the same time the religious institutes played an essential role in the modernisation of church life. Thanks to the exponential growth of the religious communities, the churche succeeded in taking over the social welfare arena (education, health care, care of the poor), while with its popular missions it succeeded in its goal of a spiritual conquest of the people. At the same time the extension and consolidation of the Catholic Revival depended on

[33] Simon, *Le Cardinal Mercier*, 90-91, 102; De Maeyer, "L'Église se tourne vers le peuple", 149-151.

[34] Viaene, "L'épanouissement d'une Église 'libre'", 42-44 and 94-99.

a body of secular clergy that was kept tightly under episcopal authority and that had been given a strong moral and spiritual formation.

The conflict with the liberals, which intensified after 1860 and reached its zenith with the school struggle (1879-1884), finally broke the model of the Revival (that of unity between religion and nation) and signalled the beginning of organisational Catholicism and pillarisation.[35] From then on the life of the church was devoted to protecting and maintaining the working class and its links with the church, and this within a multifunctional organisation adapted to the times. The network of Catholic organisations, guilds and societies made it possible to protect a large section of the people against socialism and thereby keep the Catholic party in power. The church addressed all sectors of the population: the working class, the middle class, the poor, women, young people and children. Organisational Catholicism ensured not only the social emancipation of workers but also their integration in the life of the church. Lay people were increasingly called on to defend and support the church, primarily by voting for the Catholic party. In involving the laity the role of the clergy was of great importance: the secular clergy served the farmers and petit bourgeoisie, while the regular clergy and their lay colleagues focused on the world of the workers.

On the eve of the First World War, the initiatives were already in place that would come to fruition during the interwar years: in 1914 Joseph Cardijn started in Laeken what would later become the JOC-KAJ (*Jeunesse Ouvrière Chrétienne-Katholieke Arbeidersjeugd*, i.e. Christian Working Youth). With a view to winning over the youth intellectually, Canon Abel Brohée (1880-1947) started the *Oeuvres Apologétiques* in 1909. In 1919 he founded the ACJB (*Association Catholique de la Jeunesse Belge*, i.e. Catholic Association of Belgian Youth) and so laid the foundations of modern Catholic youth clubs. Thanks to their key position in almost all the Catholic organisations, the clergy, headed by the bishops, were clearly in charge and their influence was everywhere to be felt. This influence would be further enhanced by Cardinal Mercier's opposition to the German occupation during the First World War, and by the role of chaplains and stretcher-bearers in the trenches.[36]

---

[35] Viaene, "L'épanouissement d'une Église 'libre'", 98-99.

[36] De Maeyer, "L'Église se tourne vers le peuple", 166.

Contested Unity
Church, Nation and Reform in the Netherlands

Joris van Eijnatten

On 6 August 1863, Alexander Ver Huell (1822-1897) spent a rainy day in the Wolfhezer Woods near Arnhem in the east of the Netherlands. "I've just come from a General Evangelical National Mission Feast", he wrote that evening in the diary he kept: "a renewal of the Old Hedgerow Sermons". He felt that he had been witness to a revival of the open-air meetings that long ago had sparked off the iconoclastic storms of the Dutch Reformation. Ver Huell was much impressed by the event. The day had begun quietly. Rustic pulpits and benches had been placed here and there and the stalls sold buns and coffee at 5 cents apiece. The scene, wrote Ver Huell, was quite poetic. That idyllic prospect rapidly changed as it became busier and "old-fashioned *Dominees*[1] with fat bellies and cocked hats" went to work. Nevertheless, it was a pleasant, homely event, where one could find "a farmer's wife from Gelderen sitting next to a woman from North Holland, her hair done with golden clasps".[2]

A wealthy Amsterdammer, Ver Huell travelled around the country as a writer and artist. His pseudonym, aptly, was O. Veralby, since he wanted to be in on everything - in Dutch, *overal bij* literally means 'present everywhere'. This time he had journeyed to the site of the first mass evangelisation meeting in the Netherlands. His description of that gathering in the Wolfhezer Woods is eminently recognisable. It marked both the new-found unity of the nation and, paradoxically and ironically, its division into mutually exclusive religious groups. As passive objects of, and active contributors to, political and social change, the Dutch churches were deeply involved in this double-edged process. They had to deal with the gradual extension and growing cohesion, through

---

[1] A *dominee* is a Reformed minister. The word is derived from the vocative (*domine*) of the Latin *dominus*.

[2] Ver Huell, *Het dagboek van Alexander Ver Huell*, 96.

various social and economic processes, of a public sphere centred on the nation. The emergence of that public sphere, in the Netherlands as elsewhere, was connected with such things as the rise of mass media and the consumer society; the development of nationalism and the invention of a national culture; the renewed emphasis on the individual religious consciousness and attempts to mould and guide it through education and 'enlightenment'; the growing participation of people in governing the society to which they belonged; the expansion of the middle class, followed by that of the working class; and a growing consciousness among people of a shared citizenship based on notions of equality and liberty, and supported by political and legal institutions and regulations.

Many of these elements are present in Ver Huell's account of the 1863 mission feast. Mass meetings, held annually until the Second World War (with the exception of 1866, due to the cholera epidemic of that year) had been made possible by the liberal constitution of 1848.[3] Crucial to the success of evangelisation meetings was the railway expansion between 1860 and 1880. People came by train, often travelling on early schedules in order to pay the lower rates negotiated beforehand by the organisers. They disembarked on temporary wooden platforms and when they left they checked the colour of their ticket against that of the flags temporarily hung out on the platforms; blue might be the train to Den Helder, yellow the one to Rotterdam. Communication networks, linking towns and cities, enabled women from Gelderen and North Holland to sit side by side in traditional costume, praying and singing and listening to the sermons of preachers of certain renown. This religious togetherness of people from all over the country contributed towards a sense of national identity. But the 1863 meeting was at the same time a gathering of self-consciously orthodox Protestants. It was symbolic of the dynamic revival of organised religion and of the deliberate pursuit of religious reform in the second half of the century.

For the nineteenth-century elite, the mass meetings took some getting used to but they were there to stay. The fact that 6 August passed in an orderly fashion did not prevent Ver Heull from wondering anxiously in his diary whether "this would be the case again next time". Mass meetings of the orthodox symbolised the contestation for public power; they were part of a process of religious empowerment which came to the fore when technological, cultural and intellectual innovation in combination with political and legal change opened up the public sphere to ever larger groups. Religious leaders were keen to gain access to the national stage and began to reach out to, and mobilise, the population. The arena in which they did so was not so much the institutional church itself as the associations and societies established by church members. With the exception of Catholic bishops, those who did the instigating and mobilising were not so much the administrative elites responsible for the ecclesiastical organisation as individual members of the clergy, the religious orders, and the laity, most of whom belonged to the upper and middle class.

---

[3] For the following, see Houkes, *Christelijke vaderlanders*.

A. Allebé, Revival Meeting in Wolfheze, *1863*,
aquarelle.
[Boston, Museum of Fine Arts: 1993.134]

The national scramble for social and political influence largely took place in the second half of the long nineteenth century. During the first half of that period the pursuit of ecclesiastical reform had been somewhat less obviously self-conscious; it was aimed not so much at the construction and preservation of competing organisations and group identities as at the establishment of the spiritual and organisational principles that unified the nation (but which were repudiated by some groups, as we shall see). This neat division of the long nineteenth century into two halves does not, of course, do justice to the complicated political and ecclesiastical history of any country, let alone the Netherlands. A simple rule of thumb could be that ecclesiastical reform during the first half of the century concentrated on buttressing national unity; whereas during the second half a renewed focus on church organisation which had the effect, unintended or not, of carving the nation into segments with specific religious identities was much more pronounced.[4]

Anyone reading up on the ecclesiastical history of the Northern Netherlands would be wise regularly to pose the question, "which church?"[5] In 1780 the situation was still relatively straightforward. There was one large Reformed Church, its doctrines definitively established at the Synod of Dort in 1618-1619 and comprising about 55% of the population according to the census of 1809. It was usually called the 'public church' at the time although it was not fully a state church. There was a dissenting church, the Remonstrant Brotherhood, representing the party that had lost out at that synod. There were Walloon churches, widely regarded as an extension of the public church, to which many Huguenots reckoned themselves. There were Mennonite assemblies (called *vermaningen*, which literally means 'admonitions') and there was a Lutheran Church, which had long functioned as an immigrant church but whose members had more or less been assimilated into Dutch society. Together these smaller churches represented no more than 5% of the population. Finally, there were in practice two Catholic churches. The Roman Catholic Church represented a very substantial minority (about 38% of the population). While Catholic religious life had become less clandestine by 1780, it was nonetheless still only 'tolerated', informally and not by official decree. The 'old-episcopal cleresy' was a very minor group which still regarded itself as part of the (Roman) Catholic communion. Known as the Old Catholics in the nineteenth century, the cleresy had originated in a complicated quarrel between Dutch bishops and the Roman curia in the early eighteenth century.[6]

This, then, was the situation in 1780. By 1920 what was once the public or 'established' church, while still largely intact, had witnessed at least five major schisms and

---

[4] Older accounts describe nineteenth-century change, not in terms of 'loss of unity', but more triumphantly as 'Resurrection and Development' (Knappert, *Geschiedenis der Nederlandsche Hervormde Kerk*) and 'The Emancipation of the Church' (Reitsma and Lindeboom, *Geschiedenis van de Hervorming en de Hervormde Kerk der Nederlanden*).

[5] Overviews include Wintle, *Pillars of Piety*; Van Rooden, *Religieuze regimes*; Van Eijnatten and Van Lieburg, *Nederlandse religiegeschiedenis*; Selderhuis, ed., *Handboek Nederlandse kerkgeschiedenis*.

[6] See Schoon, *Van bisschoppelijke cleresie tot Oud-Katholieke Kerk*.

sub-schisms and produced as many churches, with the promise of more to come (they did). To distinguish between the many later offshoots of the former public church, all of which were in some sense 'Calvinist', I will use their Dutch names; the term 'Reformed Church' will be reserved for the semi-established public church as it existed before 1796. This chapter on ecclesiastical reform in the Netherlands is divided into two parts, the one covering the period between about 1780 and 1852, the other dealing with the remaining seven decades until 1920.

State Patronage

In the Dutch Republic, each of the Provincial States had taken care of the Reformed churches in its domain, paying ministers' salaries as well as retirement pay and widows' pensions, and ensuring the church's ability to provide religious services on the local level. This changed in 1795 with the separation of church and state and the ratification of the *Staatsregeling* or constitution of 1798. The Reformed Church was given three years to find financial support for its own organisation, the theological faculties, the maintenance of its buildings, and the payment of its 1,500 ministers in addition to the parish clerks (*kosters*), readers, organists, catechisers and other church officials.[7] Shocked into action, the Reformed Church turned to its one million members for assistance. It submitted petitions to the government to prevent the 'nationalisation' of church property. This led to a stipulation in the *Staatsregeling* of 1801 permitting churches to retain their properties. These favourable terms laid the foundation for subsequent decrees and laws put into effect in 1808, 1814 and 1815, and guaranteeing state support for the salaries of church ministers. The 1798 decision to 'privatise' the church led to an enormous amount of deliberation and consultation by church officials, who often travelled large distances for meetings with colleagues and wrote endless notes and reports. One positive effect was that the church gained experience in fundraising. It employed newspapers, the pulpit, pamphlets and circulars to raise awareness among church members and collect money. It obtained financial resources to pay for the upkeep of church buildings when these were transferred to the church after 1810. No less importantly, the flurry of ecclesiastical activity during the period of French domination fostered a feeling for nationhood and a sense of belonging to a unified, national church - which henceforth was called the *Nederlandse Hervormde Kerk*.[8]

The consternation over the separation of church and state eventually subsided with the government-imposed *Algemeen Reglement* (General Directive) of 1816. The *Algemeen Reglement* was the culmination of the newly centralised state's policy after 1801 to patronise the church. For the *Hervormde Kerk*, the directives boiled down to the abolition of the Presbyterian system established at the 1618-1619 Synod of Dort. Ecclesi-

---

[7] Den Ouden, *Kerk onder patriottenbewind*, 38-49.   [8] Ibid., 223-228.

astical reforms in this period therefore meant the establishment of centralised administrations on a national level. Similar measures were taken with regard to the smaller Protestant churches. The Evangelical-Lutheran Church was given a directive in 1818; arrangements had already been made for Jews in 1816. The centrally organised *Algemeene Doopsgezinde Sociëteit* (General Mennonite Society) of 1811, which consisted of about 26,000 members, likewise obtained government approval. For the *Hervormde Kerk*, the general synod became the most important governing body, its members appointed by the Crown. The synod developed into a meeting place for representatives of the three main parties who figured prominently in the new kingdom's religious configuration: the state, or more precisely the Ministry of Church Affairs (*Ministerie van Eeredienst*, literally 'Ministry for Public Worship'); the theological faculties and their professors; and the professional elite, consisting mainly of influential ministers from the larger towns. If the result of these measures implied a loss of influence for local congregations, a large majority of the clergy were perfectly happy to accept them because they guaranteed financial security and national uniformity in a church which only two decades before had been almost as fragmented in organisational terms as the Dutch Republic itself. The government, moreover, was presided over by no less a person than a prince from the house of Orange, the member of a dynasty of leaders for whom the Protestant (and Jewish) clergy traditionally had the greatest respect.[9]

The most common term used by Dutch state officials to designate the church in this period was *kerkgenootschap*, which literally means 'church association'. This was a legal rather than theological concept, and in any case far removed from the ecclesiology of the Calvinist Reformation and the Reformed scholastics.[10] The notion of a 'church association' or 'religious society' conveyed a sense of legal separateness from the state, the idea that as a private institution the church too was committed to public utility, and the realisation that the church was now a single organisation standing aloof from regional political interests. For the first time since the Reformation there was the possibility of a single, unified church in the Netherlands. Hence the clergy warmly applauded the *Algemeen Reglement*. Synod members were expected solely to fulfil administrative duties, although the General Directive was clear as to the spirit in which they should acquit themselves of this task. All administrators, stipulated article 9, were to take care of the interests of Christianity in general and the Reformed Church in particular, uphold its doctrine, spread religious knowledge, foster Christian morality, and maintain order. Meanwhile the "nourishment of love for King and Country" would be their chief aim.[11] The *predikanten* or *dominees* in the field (this applies to Remonstrants, Mennonites and Lutherans as much as it does to *hervormden*) were not so much representatives of the state as the state's spiritual assistants.[12] Their salaries were paid by the central government and they were much less dependent on local patrons. Entry into the ministry was direct, in the sense that those who aspired to a clerical profession

---

[9] Bos, *In dienst van het Koninkrijk*, 93-128.
[10] Van Eijnatten, *Liberty and Concord in the United Provinces*, 102-117.
[11] Van Loon, *Het Algemeen Reglement van 1816*.
[12] For the following, see Bos, *In dienst van het Koninkrijk*.

no longer needed to begin as assistant (i.e. a 'curate'; the Dutch term is *proponent*). This fostered a sense of professional autonomy. A career in the church often ran in the family; in 1858 no less than 40% of all *hervormde* theology students had been fathered by a church minister, a number that varied between 25 and 40% throughout the nineteenth century. There was, in consequence, a measure of social homogeneity among ministers, who frequently married their older colleagues' daughters.

Clergymen had been recognisable socially in the eighteenth century, dressing according to their station, with cocked hat, knee-breeches, tail coat, and shoes with silver buckles. In 1796, under the 'revolutionary' Batavian regime, they were forbidden to use professional dress in public. When the French occupation ended and the ban was lifted many continued to do without the uniform - or put it on again intentionally, usually as a sign of orthodoxy (cf. Ver Huell's description of pot-bellied *dominees*). Traditionally, the main task of the *predikant* (the word is derived from *preken*, 'to preach') was to deliver sermons and visit parishioners, inviting them to participate in the Lord's Supper, which was celebrated four times a year. After the introduction of public education in 1806 he also was expected to catechise, so that confirmation classes grew in importance. The transfer of religious duties from school to church did not mean that the clergy lost their influence on education; on the contrary, they were often appointed as school supervisors by the government.

Fractures

The first major secession took place against this background of state patronage and national churchhood.[13] It is a poignant detail that educated *hervormde* clergymen thwarted the attempt of the political and religious elites to forge national unity through orchestrated ecclesiastical reform. Hendrik de Cock (1801-1842), an erstwhile liberal theologian stationed at Ulrum, a minor village in the province of Groningen, had initially pursued his traditionalist agenda through the church's administrative bodies, arguing for abolition of the church order of 1816. Ultimately, separatist sentiments came to a head in 1834, a result in part of dissatisfaction with the way liberal churchmen neglected, if not rejected, the tenets of Dort. Those who cherished the Pietist traditions that had developed within the eighteenth-century public church felt marginalised. Beginning in the 1820s, reissues of the *oude schrijvers* or Old Pietist Writers of the seventeenth and eighteenth centuries had begun to appear as part of a canonisation process that would continue well into the twentieth century. Orthodox believers joined conventicles and itinerant preachers travelled the country. The result was what De Cock and his supporters regarded as a temporary separation, one that would last as long as it took the *Hervormde Kerk* to genuinely reform and return to the true service

---

[13] Literature on the secession in English is sparse and not particularly up to date; but see e.g. Bouma, *Secession, Doleantie, and Union*; De Jong and Kloosterman, eds., *The Reformation of 1834*.

of the Lord. But to all intents and purposes this was a secession, whose self-conscious leadership shocked the establishment. These years witnessed the rise of the highly charged soubriquet *gereformeerd* (literally 'reformed'), which would soon be claimed by a variety of orthodox groups both in the *hervormde kerk* and the free churches. The term *gereformeerd* had connotations ranging from pietistically inclined (or *bevindelijk*, i.e. experiential) to confessionally precise as well as triumphantly nationalist, and sometimes all of these.

De Cock was suspended and then dismissed. But he was not the only clergyman to join the secession. Ten mostly very young colleagues followed suit. Demands from within the *Hervormde Kerk* that the government undo the secession fell on deaf ears. The government did require secessionists to register as a separate church, since the law forbade more than twenty people to congregate unless they were formally recognised as a church (which then allowed them to appeal to the right to freedom of religion). The secessionists refused point blank, since this would compel them to give up their claim to the name and status of the *Hervormde Kerk* and their identity as the rightful heirs to the reformed tradition. As *gereformeerden* they considered themselves as truly reformed, and their church was, therefore, the only reformed church. State officials harassed them by fining them, billeting troops with them, and even using violence against them, but to no avail. By 1836 there were 130 secessionist (*afgescheiden*) congregations comprising a few thousand people, mainly, but not exclusively, from the lower middle class. Their churches were financed wholly by the congregations themselves. They formed a tight-knit group, partly because their ministers tended to intermarry. The persecution ended when in 1839 most of the *afgescheiden* churches complied with government demands. They then registered themselves as the *Christelijke Afgescheiden Gemeenten* (Christian Secessionist Congregations). Those that persevered in rejecting the government aspired to martyrdom and aptly called themselves the *Gereformeerde Kerken onder het Kruis* (Reformed Churches under the Cross). The vision of national unity that had defined the *Hervormde Kerk* as the church to which all churches in the kingdom would ultimately turn or return, had been shattered.

Even Catholics had been expected, in the end, to form an attachment to the *Hervormde Kerk*; the Protestant elite saw this largely as a matter of properly educating what they looked upon as a backward minority. For the Roman Catholics themselves the *Staatsregeling* of 1801 had meant that they could not lay claim to the church buildings they had lost during the Reformation. In social rather than legal terms, Catholics were subject to neglect, if not discrimination, even under French occupation[14]; and they, too, were the object of regulation. Catholics posed a particular problem because there were so many of them in the Kingdom of the United Netherlands (1815-1830): practically the whole population of the formerly Austrian Netherlands was Catholic, and more than a third of the former Dutch Republic. As far as the northern-based government was

---

[14] Clemens, "De terugdringing van de rooms-katholieken uit de verlicht-protestantse natie".

concerned, the Roman Catholic Church in the Southern Netherlands for the time being was acceptably organised according to the Napoleonic concordat of 1801. Catholics in the Northern Netherlands, however, were difficult to regulate through state directives; they still mostly lived in what Rome regarded as missionary territory. They were oriented towards their local communities and tried to avoid state interference as much as possible. The *missio Hollandica*, comprising the larger part of the Northern Netherlands, consisted of seven archpriesthoods (Holland and Zeeland, Utrecht, Gelderland, Twente, Drenthe-Salland, Groningen and Friesland). The southern part of the Northern Netherlands was divided into four apostolic vicariates (the larger ones were Breda and 's-Hertogenbosch, the smaller ones Megen and Grave). So-called 'stations' (from *statie*, the territory presided over by a priest) from the time of the Republic still existed; they were usually run by a priest and sometimes by one or more *kapelaans* (curates in the sense of assistant priests). The state tried to ensure its grip on this loose Catholic organisation through a concordat concluded in 1827. The concordat signified, in theory if not in practice, the end of the *missio Hollandica*. Aiming to bring about two new bishoprics, in 's-Hertogenbosch and Amsterdam, it was never implemented because the Dutch-Belgian War of 1830 put things in a totally new perspective. For almost a quarter of a century, the only bishops in the Northern Netherlands would still be itinerant bishops *in partibus infidelium*, so that the Catholic organisation remained fragmentary and decentralised.

After the French closed the university at Louvain in 1797, Dutch Catholics in 1799 began to establish their own seminaries, at Warmond for Holland and Zeeland, and at 's-Heerenberg for the six remaining archpriesthoods. Seminaries that had been shut down in the Southern Netherlands were continued in the Brabant vicariates of 's-Hertogenbosch, Breda and Roermond (the Old Catholics had long had a seminary in Amersfoort). But higher theological education soon experienced setbacks. The so-called *kleinseminaries*, Latin schools and colleges from which future priests were usually drawn, were abolished by law in 1825. A second law enacted in that year stipulated that all priests were to follow courses in philosophy, church history and canon law, given by government-appointed professors, at the new *collegium philosophicum* in Louvain. After protests by Dutch Catholics and in the context of negotiations over the concordat of 1827, King Willem I dropped the requirement that theology students attend the *collegium philosophicum*. Future priests could now receive their training at the seminary at 's-Heerenberg. Dissolved in 1842, this seminary had been a little broader in outlook than its more conservative sister seminaries, which banned all references or reminiscences of *katholische Aufklärung* from the curricula. In terms of scholarship and learning all Catholic seminaries fell far behind the Protestant theological faculties, which themselves did not exactly belong to the European avant-garde. Catholic leaders did not, however, regard the use of traditionally scholastic textbooks as a serious deficit requiring institutional reform. They expected the seminaries to produce priests, not pedants. Meanwhile, the religious orders (such as the Jesuits, Dominicans and Franciscans) relied on their own international networks, which supported high-level teaching.

Joris van Eijnatten

Liberal Theology

For the Protestants, the situation regarding higher education was much better, although those who aspired to a university education had limited choice (the options being law, medicine and theology). About half of all applicants chose divinity, which could be studied at the universities of Leiden, Utrecht and Groningen; in the 1880s, two theology faculties would be established in Amsterdam, at the *Gemeente Universiteit* (a new 'Municipal University', now the University of Amsterdam) and the *Vrije Universiteit* ('Free University', now VU University). After 1815, following a reorganisation of university education, future theology students were required first to obtain a preliminary ('propedeutic') degree. Their intensive academic training allowed them to mingle easily with the cultural and political elites. For example, *dominees* ruled the literary scene of the 1840s and 1850s, giving rise to the phenomenon of the *dominee-dichter* (clergyman-poet). Protestant clergymen were, in a sense, products of the state, since the government exerted control over theological education, among other things by appointing professors. The other churches educated their clergy at seminaries that had been re-established early in the century, for Mennonites in 1811, for Remonstrants in 1816 and for Lutherans in 1816.

'Liberal' Protestant theology was dominant at the universities and it formed a body of teaching that was crucial to the success of the state's national policy *vis-à-vis* the churches. Liberal theology grew out of the later 'Enlightenment', which had been moderate in nature. It was inclined to defuse apparent conflicts between reason and revelation by assuming that mankind, being for the moment insufficiently enlightened, in the future would resolve most contradictions between biblical claims and rational truths. Christian apologetic had been the main thrust of Protestant theological practice in the 1780s and 1790s; its central message was that Christianity was true because it was reasonable, trustworthy, and convincing. Through the first three or four decades of the nineteenth century, Protestant theology remained 'supranaturalist' in content, apologetic in strategy, and unabashedly nationalist in tone. It was a theology thoroughly dedicated to moulding morally responsible citizens loyal to the kingdom, to generating believers who were both civilised (*beschaafd*) and enlightened (*verlicht*). An influential figure in this respect was the philosopher Philip Willem van Heusde (1778-1839), who as the so-called *Praeceptor Hollandiae* produced the philosophical foundation for the educational reform programme fostered by the state. Van Heusde's concept of encyclopaedia, his interlinking of systematic and applied sciences, and his view of 'Christian humanism' as the historical soul of the Dutch nation served as a theoretical basis for the newly united kingdom.[15]

One important nineteenth-century off-shoot of liberal theology was the so-called *Groninger richting* (literally the 'Groningen orientation'; in shorthand its

---

[15] De Valk, *Philip Willem van Heusde*. In a sense, Van Heusde could be compared to Grundtvig in Denmark, although the latter is, of course, reckoned to the Pietist tradition.

W. van Senus, Philip Willem van Heusde, engraving, 2nd quarter 19th century.
[Utrecht, Museum Catharijneconvent]

J. Ensing, Petrus Hofstede de Groot, lithograph, 1840.
[Groningen, University of Groningen, Museum of the University]

adherents are often called the 'Groningers'). The initiator of this theological school within the *Hervormde Kerk* was Petrus Hofstede de Groot (1801-1886), a professor at the University of Groningen between 1829 and 1872. Under his leadership the Groningers stressed the emotional experience of faith, rejected subscription, and advocated popular education; indeed, their theology took much of its rationale from education.[16] The history of humanity in their view was a learning process supervised by Providence, with Jesus acting as the supreme Pedagogue and ministers as educators of the people. They, too, attempted to integrate notions of national identity into theology. Calvinism they considered to be a foreign element in the nation's religious history, which in their view was characterised by leniency, tolerance and humanitarianism. Such national traits had first come fully to the fore (they suggested) among leaders of the *devotio moderna* and northern humanism, among men like Geert Grote, Wessel Gansfort and Erasmus. The Groninger theology became so influential that orthodox leaders initiated an appeal (it went down in history as the 'petition of seven gentlemen from the Hague'), which in 1842 was submitted to, and subsequently rejected by, the *hervormde* synod. The synod regarded itself more as a professional association or even a learned society than a council invested with disciplinary authority, and refused to decide on theological issues.

By the end of the century, the Groninger orientation petered out, crushed in the battle between orthodox and moderns. As a theology it had epitomised the unity of the

---

[16] Vree, "Petrus Hofstede de Groot".

kingdom, thoroughly identifying with the centrally led, state-oriented *Hervormde Kerk*. Its intention, characteristic of early liberal theology as a whole, had been to achieve unity not through church discipline, but through organisational control and doctrinal leniency. This ideal was reflected in practice: youthful *predikanten* who embarked on a career in the church were no longer required to interpret the confessions in the way their sixteenth and seventeenth-century authors had intended. Instead, they were asked to teach 'according to' (*overeenkomstig*) the Word of God. But did *overeenkomstig* mean that something was true 'because' (*quia*) it was said in the Bible, or 'to the extent in which' (*quatenus*) the Bible made mention of it? Liberals and orthodox disagreed. The result was the so-called *quia-quatenus* debate. All parties referred to the Bible as the touchstone of truth but differed on the status of confessions.

Self Organisation

The religious associations that appeared on the eve of the nineteenth century had a distinct distaste for confessional allegiance. Liberal Protestants were dominant among the founders, and their objective was unity, national and religious. They considered subscription a thing of the past, unsuited to churches that were true to Christianity's original message - a message they believed to be both enlightened and liberal. The new associations and societies that sprang up after the 1760s emphasised interdenominational membership. Characteristic of the 'ecumenical' mood was a relatively small but successful initiative called *Christo Sacrum* (1797-1838), a society of laymen in Delft in Holland that welcomed all Christians. The mostly upper middle class members (94 in 1810) belonged to the Walloon and *Hervormde* churches. *Christo Sacrum* is illustrative of how cross-confessional elite lay initiatives gradually emerged into the open once the public church had been 'disestablished' and strictures were removed. Most if not all religious associations originated outside the church, but not all of them were necessarily lay-led. A large and long-lived organisation (it still exists) was the *Maatschappij tot Nut van 't Algemeen* (Society for Public Benefit). Founded in 1784 by a Mennonite minister, its aim was to spiritually and intellectually elevate the nation by spreading cheap books, organising readings and reforming schools. By 1816 it had more than 6,000 members, by 1830 more than 13,000. The *Nederlandsch Zendeling Genootschap* (Dutch Missionary Society) was established in 1797 by a physician, after the English model; its members included numerous ministers. The *Nederlandsch Bijbel Genootschap* (Dutch Bible Society), founded in 1814 and connected with the British and Foreign Bible Societies, also had many clergy among its members. Transcending the provincial boundaries that had kept the Dutch Republic fragmented for so long, these organisations contributed to the new sense of nationhood, at least among the literate. Also, they assumed functions previously monopolised by the public church, performing tasks for which the institutional church was not equipped or which it failed to see as its duty. From the point of view of the state, private associations like the Society for Public Benefit had the same function as churches. Both associations and churches were legal entities expected to contribute to the moulding of citizens loyal to the national trinity of state, people and Christendom.

Catholics organised themselves somewhat differently. King Willem I followed a moderately Josephinist (or Napoleonic) policy with regard to monasteries, convents and congregations, permitting the establishment only of those institutions that contributed directly to the public weal, for example by providing health care or education. In 1840 Willem II gave permission by decree to twelve monasteries to attract novices. As in the time of the Republic, the religious orders organised their own stations under supervision of an archpriest.[17] In this way they could remain active despite the strict state policy concerning religious congregations. There was a slight growth in the number of congregations (1800: 1 male, 7 female congregations; 1850: 3 male, 13 female congregations). Some were able to establish themselves despite the prohibitions, for example by making use of other legal bodies, such as associations, as a front. Periodicals were another important instrument of 'outreach', if we take this to mean the attempt to develop religious opinion nationwide, or even to mould a traditionally Catholic population into a single, more self-confident whole. Catholic weeklies advocating Christian Enlightenment appeared with the blessing of the government; tellingly, some were heavily state-subsidised. This applies, for example, to *Katholikon* (1827-1830), the content for which was largely supplied by a civil servant of the department for Roman Catholic worship. Less subservient to Willem I's project to create a unified enlightened state were Catholic periodicals like *De Godsdienstvriend* (The Friend of Religion, 1818-1869) and the *Catholyke Nederlandsche Stemmen* (Dutch Catholic Voices, 1835-1874). Both were initially run by the convert Joachim George Le Sage ten Broek (1775-1847), who struggled to raise Catholic self-consciousness. In 1820 he even established a society, the *R.K. Maatschappij* (Catholic Association), the objective of which was to promote "religious knowledge and good morals in the Kingdom of the Netherlands". The government, however, regarded the society as a potential threat to religious-political unity and abolished it in 1831. There were other attempts to give voice to Catholics: *De Katholiek* (The Catholic, 1842-1924), a long-lived periodical founded by a bishop and run by the seminary in Warmond under the slogan *vindicamus hereditatem patrum nostrorum*. It represented a liberal current in Dutch Catholicism and played an important role in the formation of Catholic intellectuals.

On the Protestant side, the gradual Catholic awakening was mirrored in the so-called *Réveil*, the Dutch off-shoot of a broader north-west European revivalist movement that surfaced in Scotland, France, Switzerland and Germany. Although unequivocally Calvinist in its theology, the Réveil did not emphasise doctrine; it usually just stressed sin and conversion. Remaining firmly loyal to the *Hervormde Kerk* (and in some cases the Walloon church) and finding support mainly in upper-class circles, the *Réveil* opposed the liberal Protestant establishment that controlled that

---

[17] Van Vugt, "'Should it happen that God should permit....'"; Roes and De Valk, "A world apart?".

J.G. Schwartze & J. Sluyter, Isaäc da Costa, *engraving, published in I. da Costa,* De mensch en de dichter Willem Bilderdijk *(Haarlem, 1859), frontispiece.* [Leuven, K.U.Leuven, Centrale bibliotheek: 4A22114]

P. Telyn, Willem de Clercq, *engraving, c.1835.* [Amsterdam, VU University]

church's administrative bodies. It organised its activities beyond the strictly ecclesiastical domain. The convert Isaäc da Costa (1798-1860), a scion from a wealthy Jewish family, in 1826 began to hold religious meetings at his home in Amsterdam, where he explained the Bible to an interested audience, who participated by singing. The *Réveil* was made possible through the influence and financial means of an urban elite, which included such figures as Willem de Clercq (1795-1844), a former Mennonite and director of the government-owned *Nederlandsche Handel-Maatschappij* (Dutch Trading Company); and the fabulously rich aristocrat, state historian and later Member of Parliament Guillaume Groen van Prinsterer (1801-1876). These men were intellectuals and the public they sought to convince initially was a literate one. Da Costa and De Clercq ran the periodical *Nederlandsche Stemmen over Godsdienst, Staat-, Geschied- en Letterkunde* (Dutch Voices on Religion, Politics, History and Literature) from 1834 to 1839, Groen the *Nederlandsche Gedachten* (Dutch Thoughts) from 1829-1831. The aim of these reformist leaders was nothing less than to revitalise the nation, including the church; it was reform they intended, not secession. The Christian Friends issued a periodical, *De Vereeniging: Christelijke Stemmen* (The Association: Christian Voices), which lasted from 1846 to 1878 but in the end did not succeed in bringing about a truly ecclesiastical reform movement. Incidentally, the Catholics and the *Réveil* were hardly the only ones to actively propagate their religious 'orientation' by running periodicals. The Groningers published *Waarheid in Liefde* (Truth in Love, 1837-1872: cf. Eph. 4:1), "a theological periodical for civilised Christians", as the subtitle put it. It became clearer than ever that the battle for the soul of the nation, begun in the 1830s, would eventually be won by those who succeeded in mobilising the masses and taking over church leadership.

Clergy

Halfway through the century, pursuing national and ecclesiastical unity in combination no longer seemed to be a realistic option. Communication networks ranging from telegraphs to railways had increased the speed of information exchange and fostered a sense of shared experience among religious groups living at large distances from each other. The first train ran in 1839, between Amsterdam and Haarlem. The introduction of new printing technology had the same effect. It led to an expansion of the periodical press, including newspapers, and the formation of mass, but also group opinion. The tax on newspapers was abolished in 1869. The 'middle groups', who profited from the constitution of 1848, grew in importance. The liberal constitution of 1848 and the laws that followed in its wake enabled middle class leaders to act more freely and mobilise supporters. Ironically perhaps, the very success of the nation state subverted the idea that Christendom and nationhood were, or could be, two sides of one and the same coin.

The friction caused by the *quia-quatenus* debate was only one sign that the status of the *hervormde* synod - that supreme administrative symbol of the unity of state, academia and *vaderlandse kerk* or 'national church' - was being contested. The orthodox *gereformeerden* and the Roman Catholics had begun openly to question the liberal *hervormde* claim to moral leadership. Parishioners became increasingly critical and schoolteachers more outspoken. Conversely, the ministers' spiritual, pastoral and social authority went into decline. Gradually, the pastoral elite who had dominated church life in the first half of the century became alienated from the nation (which did not feel happy with moderate liberal Protestantism) as well as the state (which had begun to retreat from the church, as the constitution of 1848 made clear). The clergy, who until now had functioned as a government-supported body of spiritual caregivers, needed a new basis for legitimacy. They sought this, not in the state, but in the university; they invested in 'cultural capital', as it were, rather than political support.[18] In brief, clergymen turned into academics. The number of ministers who had obtained the equivalent of a Ph D had already increased before 1850 (during the Dutch Republic a minister with a doctorate had been quite rare) but in the second half of the century the number of theological doctors grew substantially. Even the ministers' new professional clothing, the toga, introduced in 1854, was modelled after the robes of academic professors.

This self-reforming investment in cultural capital on the part of the clergy had at least four consequences. Firstly, it opened perspectives for those clergymen who wished to leave the church. Some began a career in journalism or education. Secondly, academic professors began to employ the historical-critical method to develop a more 'scientific' theology that could compete intellectually with other academic disciplines. The new theology, disseminated through students, led to the rise of 'modern-

---

[18] Bos, *In dienst van het Koninkrijk*, 307-356.

ism', which held an appeal to educated laypeople. The clerical elite thus gained status through self-obtained intellectual authority rather than state-supported ecclesiastical rank. Thirdly, the clergy became ever more dependent on their own parishioners. Their salaries, though still paid for by the state, were no longer corrected for inflation, while competition from other 'caregivers', notably socialists, forced them to pay closer attention to their flocks than they had previously done. A personal bond with the parishioners, modelled after the confidential relation between doctor and patient, became the new clerical ideal. Clergymen visited their parishioners to conduct private conversations and establish closer, more informal and personal contacts. This gradually became an important means of 'outreach' within the *hervormde* parish itself, but also led to an expansion of the ministers' job responsibilities.[19] Fourthly, a gulf developed between the urban elite (who had to cater more and more to a demanding laity) and the theological faculties (which concentrated on 'scientific' theology), so that the semi-formal ecclesiastical structure that in the first half of the century had brought together the university, the professional urban elite and the state began to crumble. In brief, the liberal message did not appeal to the masses, the clergy coped with loss of authority, and the laity became more discriminating. If the liberal *hervormde* clergy had acquired a select but loyal following, they were, however, in danger of losing the nation.

The Rise of Orthodoxy

The synod of the *Hervormde Kerk* tried to make the best of the constitutional reforms of 1848. Its task, at least in the eyes of the synod members, was daunting: how to make the best of the new freedoms that had recently universalised the right to associate and congregate? A new church order was passed in 1852. It made possible the election, directly by the parishioners themselves, of pastors, elders and deacons. In 1867, male members of the *Hervormde Kerk* obtained the right to elect ministers, all 1,500 of them, either by direct vote or indirectly via electoral associations. The liberals had counted on the popularity of ministers who adhered to what was, in their eyes, a progressive message. They were deeply disappointed, for it was the orthodox who triumphed, and with a resounding victory. The orthodox march to power had begun, albeit mainly at the level of local congregations, and especially in the larger cities. The higher echelons, where vacancies were filled through indirect elections, remained beyond the reach of the orthodox. On the local level, however, liberal pastors henceforth had to deal with orthodox consistories, while orthodox pastors mobilised grassroots support instead of closing ranks with liberal colleagues. Yet, while the seventy years between 1850 and 1920 reflected the rise of Protestant orthodoxy within the church, even that orthodoxy was unable to find strength in numbers. In the end, neither they nor the liberals were able to dominate the church; and by 1920 all Protestants were reorganised into separate

---

[19] Bos, *In dienst van het Koninkrijk*, 79-86.

groups within the churches, or in separate churches altogether. By then a Dutch Bible Belt had become geographically visible, a band of predominantly orthodox congregations stretching diagonally over the Netherlands from Zeeland through South Holland and Utrecht to Overijssel.

Adjusting themselves to the consequences of (and the possibilities afforded by) the constitution of 1848, religious leaders realised that they possessed the means to mobilise self-conscious groups, and they did not shirk using them. The greatest mobiliser of them all was the formidable theologian and politician Abraham Kuyper (1837-1920) - hence the epithet still often used, 'Abraham the Mighty'.[20] As a young minister, Kuyper (who, incidentally, was a pupil of the modernist theologian Scholten, on whom more below) converted to Calvinist orthodoxy. He developed a blueprint for a church organisation that was rooted in the Reformed tradition, sheltering orthodox believers from the modern world as well as introducing them to it, and last but not least, galvanising them into action. Most orthodox colleagues in the *Hervormde Kerk* disagreed with his vision, which they considered too activist, too worldly and too radical. It was Kuyper who dealt the final blow to the image of the *Hervormde Kerk* as the national church of the Netherlands. In the 1880s the *hervormde* synod had revised the formula for ministers entering office, no longer requiring them formally to subscribe to the three 'formularies of unity'. Kuyper led orthodox protests from his *hervormde* church in Amsterdam. In 1886 matters came to a head when Kuyper and his followers refused to accept as church members people who had not explicitly subscribed to the formularies. The *dolerenden* (complainants or 'protestants'), as they were called, even took hold of church property, to make clear that in their view the real power in the church lay with the local consistory. Eighty complainants were dismissed from church service, and thus the *doleantie* began. Five percent of the *hervormde* ministers, about sixty in all, joined Kuyper; by 1887 no less than 151 consistories and their congregations had seceded. The *Gereformeerde Kerken* were better organised than any other Protestant church, a fact that would distinguish them from the *hervormden* during most of the twentieth century. Despite the drive and activism, the *Gereformeerde Kerken* did not attract many more members from outside the fold once the initial *doleantie* had subsided and the church was secured institutionally.

The institutional history of separatists, free church groups, secessionists or schismatics (the choice of word rather depends on one's point of view), is not an easy one to portray. At the local level there was a continuous series of splits and separations brought about by squabbles and quarrels among local congregations led by authoritative leaders, some of them self-made ministers who capitalised on their status as gifted preachers or guardians of tradition, all of them intent on reforming the *oud-vaderlandsche kerk*, 'the church of the fathers' that had deviated from the path of the Reforma-

---

[20] The only biography is in Dutch: Koch, *Abraham Kuyper*. But see also Van der Kooi and De Bruijn, eds., *Kuyper Reconsidered*. Kuyper has become increasingly popular in recent years among American Reformed, and some of his work is available in translation.

A. Hahn, Abraham Kuyper, *cartoon*, 1904.
[Amsterdam, International Institute of Social History: BGC1/328]

tion. The heirs to the first secession of 1834 shared in the general orthodox sense of revival and rejuvenation. They were somewhat more modest in their aspirations than Kuyper's *gereformeerden*, but nevertheless participated fully in society. One milestone in the process of orthodox ecclesiastical reform was the unification, in 1869, between *afgescheiden* churches and those under the cross. The unified church called itself the *Christelijke Gereformeerde Kerk* (Christian Reformed Church), again with a deliberate appeal to the time-honoured epithet *gereformeerd*. It consisted of some 100,000 members. In 1854 their various preachers' colleges had already been combined in a Theological School in Kampen. Theologically their outlook was moulded, in particular, by Herman Bavinck (1854-1921), who held a position at the Kampen school and shared Kuyper's conviction that seventeenth and eighteenth-century Reformed theology could and should be remodelled to fit the modern world. Bavinck and Kuyper together worked to unify the *afgescheidenen* and *dolerenden*, a project that eventually was completed successfully. In 1892 they united both groups in the *Gereformeerde Kerken in Nederland* (Reformed Churches in the Netherlands - note the conscious use of the Presbyterian plural). They brought together a little under 400,000 church members (190,000 *afgescheidenen* and 180,000 *dolerenden*, to be precise), representing about 8% of the population. It took until 1905 to iron out doctrinal differences between the two groups, mostly concerning the relations between baptism, covenant, regeneration and election. Insiders were well aware of the differences, which did not and would not disappear - there were 'A' congregations, who were *afgescheiden*, and 'B' congregations, who were *dolerend*. The distinction remained intact partly because of the existence of two training centres, one in Kampen, another in Amsterdam (the *Vrije Universiteit*, see below).

Needless to say, not all members of the *Christelijke Gereformeerde Kerken* joined Bavinck's and Kuyper's unified church, and of those who did not all wanted to remain in it. The *afgescheidenen* in the *Christelijke Gereformeerde Kerken* demurred to Kuyper's theology, in particular his doctrine of 'presumed regeneration', according to which baptised children were presumed to be regenerated until their conduct in life showed that this, unfortunately, was not the case. Kuyper's doctrine was considered much too optimistic, so that the more experientially inclined *Christelijke Gereformeerde Kerken* continued as a separate group, expanding from several congregations in 1893 to 60 in 1900 and more than 100 in 1920. By 1894 the *christelijk gereformeerden* had their own theological training centre, located first in The Hague and after 1917 in Apeldoorn. But not all orthodox churches appreciated ecumenism, even with their closest spiritual relatives. Three ultra-Calvinist congregations remained outside the *christelijk gereformeerde* fold. The Reformed Congregations under the Cross or *kruisgemeenten* in 1907 united with former *christelijk gereformeerden* and *dolerenden* to form the *Gereformeerde Gemeenten* (Reformed Congregations), under the leadership of G.H. Kersten (1882-1948). The churches brought together the most pietistically inclined among the orthodox *gereformeerden*.

One consequence of the various secessions was that the *hervormden* became a minority, albeit a substantial one. In 1889 the *hervormden* comprised about 49% of the population, a figure that decreased to 44% within two decades. Leading *hervormde* theologians continued to stress the unity of the church as a people's church (*volkskerk*) comprising the orthodox and the liberals and everyone in between. The *hervormde* Philip Jacob Hoedemaker (1839-1910), for example, even developed a *volkskerk* theology. Hoedemaker, an advocate for church reform, had initially collaborated with Kuyper but later opposed the *doleantie* and the idea that the state could be neutral vis-à-vis the church. "The whole church and the whole people", was his theological motto, suggesting that the Christian state ought to support the *Hervormde Kerk* as *the* national church and that Catholics should be referred to a position of second-rate citizenship. After Kuyper's *Doleantie*, the still quite substantial number of orthodox within the *Hervormde Kerk* (who, unsurprisingly if somewhat confusingly, also claimed for themselves the honorary title *gereformeerden*) began to form a right-wing coalition in the church. The immediate cause was the promotion of Buddhist sentiments from the pulpit by a liberal minister; but the impulse to organise and reorganise was already strong. The *hervormde gereformeerden* did what all the other orthodox groups did: in 1886 they established a periodical (in the case the *Gereformeerd Weekblad* or Reformed Weekly), in 1901 an organisation for outreach (the *Gereformeerde Zendingsbond* or Reformed Missionary Alliance), and in 1906 (or rather 1909, since the first attempt failed) an association of like-minded church members, the *Gereformeerde Bond* (Reformed Alliance). The driving force behind the *Gereformeerde Bond* was Hugo Visscher (1864-1944), and its aim to (literally) 'reform' the *Hervormde Kerk* in such a way that it would regain its place 'in the midst' of the Dutch people. This objective conformed to Hoedemaker's ideal, but the Alliance put more emphasis than he did on the seventeenth-century church order of Dort. Soon the *Gereformeerde Bond* became the largest and best organised group within the *Hervormde Kerk*.

The Decline of Liberalism

The orthodox return to power was all the more pronounced because it led to a minor but noteworthy exodus of liberal Protestants. The latter believed that the reforms they wanted were now impossible to realise within the conservative confines of the *Hervormde Kerk*. Thus, around 1877 a number of liberal 'moderns' defected to the old dissenting churches, especially the Remonstrant Brotherhood, which saw a threefold increase in its numbers, from 0.15% to 0.47% of the total population. New Remonstrant congregations were established; around 1850 there had been about 3,000 Remonstrants, by 1900 there were 12,000, and by 1920 no fewer than 30,000. There had been a relatively substantial group of moderately orthodox Remonstrants earlier in the century, but after 1870 modernism prevailed. Remonstrantism became all but synonymous with *vrijzinnigheid* or religious free-thinking, a change in outlook and ambition symbolised by relocating the Remonstrant seminary from Amsterdam to the hotbed of modernism, Leiden. Reorganised as an association of liberals rather than a brotherhood of believers (let alone a 'church'), the Remonstrant elite came to regard themselves as the core of the Dutch 'thinking public'.[21] There was some truth in this elitism, in so far as several Remonstrant intellectuals achieved international renown, such as Cornelis Petrus Tiele (1830-1902), the first professor of the (comparative) history of religions at the University of Leiden. The modernists likewise overran the Mennonite churches, although not quite to the same degree as they had swamped the Remonstrants. The Mennonites did quite well, growing from 44,000 members in 1869 to 68,000 in 1920. The influence of modernism was evident from the fact that these left-wing churches allowed women to enter church office (Mennonites in 1911, Remonstrants in 1919, Lutherans in 1922).

Other modernists gave vent to their reforming impulse by founding their own religious communities. In 1877 the brothers Peter Herman Hugenholtz (1834-1911) and Philip Reinhard Hugenholtz (1821-1889) established a *Vrije Gemeente* (Free Congregation) in Amsterdam. They rejected binding confessions as well as the sacraments and did not celebrate Ascension and Pentecost. Yet another group of modernist ministers abandoned their profession, either because the reforms they sought were too radical (the abolition of sacraments, for example), or because their congregations pressured them to leave. The literary critic Conrad Busken Huet (1826-1886) claimed to have been one of a hundred ministers to leave their stations. He himself was the first to go, in 1862, after his church council had expressed its anxiety that fewer and fewer people were attending his services (which, apart from the unrest, meant less money in the alms bag). No less sensational was the departure of the Walloon minister Allard Pierson (1831-1896) in 1865. In a public farewell letter to his congregation he explained that due to its clerical, exclusive character, the church was not the proper institution to foster true 'humanity' (*humaniteit*). Meanwhile, those who remained within the church were criticised by both the orthodox and the freethinkers, but also by Huet and Pierson, for not actually believing what they preached. What remained of modernism in the *Hervormde Kerk* organised itself in *vrijzinnige* associations. Henceforth, modernism would stay on the defensive.

Catholic Emancipation

The later nineteenth century witnessed not so much the birth of Protestant orthodoxy as its emergence in the public sphere and the concomitant mobilisation of *gereformeerden*. Much the same could be said for Catholicism. It, too, came out into the open, developed ideas and structures, and mobilised supporters. Dutch Catholicism gave expression to its ambitions as a public force through ultramontanism, which by definition was both ecclesiastical and orthodox. As among the orthodox Protestants, there was little room for new-fangled theologies, let alone modernism. Unity prevailed, while the doctrinal decisions of Rome were accepted and followed: first the Immacu-

---

[21] Barnard, *Van 'verstoten kind' tot belijdende kerk*.

late Conception in 1854, then *Quanta cura* in 1864, and finally papal infallibility in 1870. The concordat of 1827 had envisaged a restoration of the Catholic 'hierarchy' (meaning a full episcopalian organisation), but it was the constitutional reform of 1848 that opened the way for a return to the Northern Netherlands of proper bishops. Rome had not been especially eager to reintroduce the hierarchy, but Dutch Catholic leaders, including archpriests and dignitaries, kept harping on the issue until the pope succumbed. In 1853 the Dutch Catholics finally got their bishops, after having had to do without them for 300 years. They even installed, by unilateral Roman declaration and to the chagrin of both the Dutch government and the *Hervormde Kerk*, an archbishop in, of all places, Utrecht, the academic navel of the Dutch Protestant world.

Once the dust had settled, Archbishop Zwijsen, an administrator and pastor rather than an intellectual and thus well-equipped for the task, set about organising the five new bishoprics founded at Utrecht, 's-Hertogenbosch, Haarlem, Breda and Roermond (Zwijsen himself occupied the first two sees). Slowly but surely, Dutch Catholicism was clericalised: bishops and parish priests waged a successful campaign to gain control of administrative bodies, finances and buildings, which had long been owned or managed by laity. Further unease resulted from the redrawing of territorial boundaries within the bishoprics. The *staties* or stations of secular priests were turned into parishes, as were those run by regulars. Neither the seculars nor the regulars were happy, since they often lost part of their territory and in all cases their autonomy. A fine illustration of the degree to which the episcopates had become regional bastions of clerical power is the organisation of *katholiekendagen* (Catholic Congresses, literally 'Days for Catholics').[22] In Germany such days had been organised by clergy and laity since the middle of the nineteenth century, but their establishment met with considerable delay in the Netherlands. All bishops were wary of too much lay influence and those of Haarlem and Utrecht in particular disagreed on the course of action. The *katholiekendagen* were thus organised on a diocesan level, between 1900 and 1903 in Limburg, 's-Hertogenbosch, Haarlem and Breda, while Utrecht had its first mass meeting to boost the Catholic corporate spirit in 1916. The first really national Catholic day took place only in 1919, on the initiative of the archbishop of Utrecht, and at the end of our period.

The bishops did not hasten reforms, and nationally they kept a low profile. They avoided the international orders and took recourse to Rome only when they needed to. They established their own congregations, more than ten before 1870. After that year the developments in France (anticlerical laws) and Germany (the *Kulturkampf*) led to the influx of foreign congregations, many of them active in education and health care. Dutch Catholics were not unaware of their underdevelopment. The bishops in 1905 founded the *Radboudstichting* (Saint Radbod Foundation); it developed plans for a Catholic university, which was finally established in 1923. The event was perhaps

---

[22] van Xanten, *'Katholieken, wat zijt gij toch een wonderlijk volk!'*.

J. Dunselman & R. van de Pavert, The restoration of the episcopate, *introduction page of* Neerlandia Catholica, *a nineteenth-century miniature work dedicated to Pope Leo XIII, 1888. The restoration is compared with the raising of the daughter of Jairus (Mark 5: 35-43); at the left are the coats of arms of the five bishoprics.*
[Leuven, K.U.Leuven, Maurits Sabbebibliotheek: 282.492/Fo NEER]

representative of the full integration of Catholics into the nation - albeit as a separate, recognisable and cohesive group. By 1920, Dutch Catholics had been successfully moulded into an obedient, clergy-led and Rome-oriented flock. As far as clerical training and theology among the Catholics is concerned, there is little to tell in the way of reform. Late-nineteenth-century neo-Thomism seemed to offer a way to take seriously modern science, and perhaps even to allow for a modicum of modernism in the church. Pius X condemned such developments, so that before 1920 all Catholic attempts at far-reaching theological reform were buried under doctrines and encyclicals.

Modernism

The nineteenth century was very much an age of conscious theological reform and the Netherlands are no exception. In the Dutch Protestant churches the modernist movement attracted a relatively prominent following. Modernists took for granted the progress made in particular by the natural sciences. They were concerned to present modern society with a credible, and consequently viable, form of Christianity. It was in their view a matter of life and death for the churches to reform, to adapt their principles and traditions to the modern world and accommodate themselves to the age of progress. Modernism was influenced to a significant extent by ideas from outside the somewhat provincial world of Dutch Protestantism, by writers like Strauss, Baur, Renan and, of course, Darwin. Hegel and Schleiermacher were of seminal influence on Joannes Henricus Scholten (1811-1885), the man central to Dutch modernism as an intellectual movement. A professor at Leiden, Scholten offered a novel if short-lived basis for theology in his chief study, *The Principles of the Doctrine of the Hervormde Kerk, Presented and Judged from the Sources* (1848-1850), which swept away two and a half centuries of meticulous Calvinist scholasticism and replaced it with the self-evident propositions of human reason. Scholten portrayed Reformed theology in grand Hegelian terms as a system that uniquely combined determinism with evolutionism, as the ineluctable end result of the historical development of Christian thought over a little less than two thousand years. He inspired a large number of students who began as orthodox freshmen but later disseminated modernist theology in the field. Modernism stood for the universal validity of natural law, and thus rejected wonders and miracles, including, above all, the Resurrection; and it supported evolutionary theory and historical criticism. Another leading modernist at Leiden was Abraham Kuenen (1828-1891), who achieved international renown for his historical-critical dissection of the Old Testament. Utrecht, too, produced a modernist theologian of repute: Cornelis Willem Opzoomer (1821-1892). Much of their academic work was popularised by Conrad Busken Huet, for example in his *Letters on the Bible* (1857-1858).[23]

---

[23] Busken Huet, *Brieven over den Bijbel*.

Orthodox theologians were adamantly opposed to modernism. Often called *confessionelen* ('confessionals', i.e. 'confessionally inclined'), they emphasised subscription and the exercise of ecclesiastical discipline. This group (Groen van Prinsterer was one prominent member) saw confessions rather than the insights of modern science as standards of truth. But there were other intellectuals who were not particularly enamoured of the modernist gospel of human autonomy and natural law. One important group of theologians were the so-called 'ethical' theologians, who adhered to the *ethische richting* or 'ethical orientation'. Leaders such as Daniël Chantepie de la Saussaye (1818-1874) and Johannes Hermanus Gunning Jr. (1829-1905) resembled the *Réveil* in that they favoured an affective, orthodox faith; ethical meant as much as 'inward-looking'. Influenced by Friedrich Schleiermacher and Alexandre Vinet, ethical theology stressed spiritual development rather than objective truth; it valued conscience and the heart over hard facts and analytical reason; and it tried to be 'modern' without dispensing with the Reformed tradition. Ethical theology was founded, not directly on the Bible as revelation, but on the testimony of the Holy Spirit in the heart of the believer. Hence the *ethischen* or 'ethicals' focused on the individual conscience and the relevance of faith for the here and now, showing relatively little interest in the history of theology. But to the moderns and the orthodox, the *ethischen* were really neither fish nor fowl. In fact, orthodox students preferred to study under modern professors, since at least it was clear where they stood, even if they stood in the wrong place. "Among the moderns the devil walks on clogs", it was said, "but among the ethicals he walks on stockings".

The failure of modernism to catch on led to the development of 'ethical modernism'. Taking his cue from the ethicals, the Mennonite S. Hoekstra (1822-1898) suggested that scientific rationality had to be complemented by religious feeling, and that the one area of human experience should not encroach upon the other. Man, believed Hoekstra, had an ingrained ('ethical') need to believe. In this way Hoekstra and other ethical moderns distanced themselves from Scholten's deterministic and monistic modernism, in which rational science, causality and the divinity itself were seen as aspects of the same reality. In their enthusiasm to stress personal religious experience and moral conduct, the ethical moderns began to draw apart the realms of science and religion; in effect, they subverted the original thrust of modernism.

Neo-Calvinism

Theologians were now bound to develop ideas that took issue with the nation's disintegration into a potpourri of spiritual orientations and alignments in and outside the churches. Hoedemaker had elaborated precisely such a theology in his views on the *volkskerk*. However, no thinker succeeded better in theologically rationalising and justifying religious and ecclesiastical disunity than Abraham Kuyper. He had successively sympathised with the liberal modernists and the *confessionelen* in the *Hervormde Kerk* before becoming a secessionist leader, and consequently was in an excellent position to develop an all-encompassing 'neo-Calvinist' theology that did justice to the modern world. In the process he more or less singlehandedly provided the ideological basis on which his brand of *gereformeerden* could develop as a church and a socio-cultural group.

Kuyper developed an impressive theology of culture (as others did at the time: one thinks of Paul Tillich's *Kulturtheologie*), a theory of 'common grace' which justified Christian involvement in culture. Common grace made clear that God, who voluntarily bestowed particular grace on the elect, held the whole world in his hands. This implied that Christians, as a minority, could still joyfully cultivate the world in spite of its having fallen into sin. Christians belonged to the church, but the church was not the only or even the primary means by which they could christianise culture. The church proper, said Kuyper, was the 'church as institute'. But the church also manifested itself as 'organism', by virtue of the fact that Christians were members of all kinds of extra-ecclesiastical organisations and associations. It was through the church as organism that the nation in due course would be reconquered. To achieve that victory, Christianity (i.e. Calvinism) would have to confront modernity. Hence Kuyper suggested that there is an 'antithesis' between Christianity and other 'ideologies', in particular 'liberalism' and 'paganism'. His programme was basically one of stepping back to jump better, by having a close-knit band of free Christians work under a religiously neutral government. Kuyper's vision was a broad one. He campaigned successfully for the removal from the sixteenth-century Belgic Confession of a passage that called upon the government to eradicate heresy (i.e. papism). The *Gereformeerde Kerken* adapted the article concerned (no. 36) in 1905.

Kuyper in 1880 even established his own university, the *Vrije Universiteit* or 'Free University', as an academic institution free from both church and state; its theological faculty was, however, bound to the Reformed confessions. The *Vrije Universiteit* was one of the more striking expressions of Kuyper's theory of *soevereiniteit in eigen kring*, or 'sphere sovereignty'. Each 'sphere' of life, such as the family, the church and the school, was a relatively independent whole, he argued, ordered by its own rules and regulations. This theory resembled in its effects the principle of subsidiarity developed among Catholics after Pope Leo XIII had issued *Rerum novarum* in 1891. As for the theological faculties at the state universities, these were regulated by the Law on Higher Education, passed in 1876. The minister had wanted to relegate theological studies to private institutions: if Mennonites and Remonstrants had their seminaries, why not the *hervormden*? Among the *hervormden*, the moderns were in favour of refashioning theology into 'scientific' religious studies on an academic level, while the orthodox preferred to keep the traditional preserve of theology intact. The compromise of 1876 was the so-called *duplex ordo*. The state (or more precisely, the university) appointed professors in non-ecclesiastical subjects while the church (or more precisely, the synod) designated professors for ecclesiastical topics. The law could be seen as a triumph for orthodoxy as well as modernism, since the academic status of theology was preserved; but also as a fiasco for both, since neither group got what it wanted.

Means of Mass Mobilisation

The mobilisation of various brands of Protestants and Catholics would have been unthinkable without the new means of communication. The invention of the rotary press heralded an era of mass produced and affordable reading material - so much so that one commentator in 1863 noted that the *Hervormde Kerk* was ruled by pamphlets. Again, this was a development that largely occurred outside the church, and sometimes even against the good advice of anxious pastors. The bishops were not particularly enthusiastic about the many books and periodicals being read by the flock, but in the end they could hardly disapprove of such landmarks in the history of the Dutch Catholic press as *De Tijd* (The Times, 1845-1959), which became the Catholic daily par excellence. Other institutionalised publications were *De Maasbode* (The Meuse Messenger, 1868-1959) and *De Katholieke Illustratie* (The Catholic Illustration, 1869-1969). In the competition to affirm or reaffirm the Christian identities of individuals, ministers acted as natural opinion leaders. Modernist clergymen offer a fine example of the way 'outreach' in and outside the church took place, which by 1920 resulted in the ideological segmentation or pillarisation of the nation. Liberal Protestants organised themselves in the *Vergadering van Moderne Theologen* (Meeting of Modern Theologians, 1866), which convened once a year. The Meeting put theological and ecclesiastical issues on the agenda, but debated also on society and science. The liberal *Nederlandsche Protestantenbond* (Dutch Protestant Union), founded in 1870, originated in clerical conventions held in the northern provinces of Friesland, Groningen and Drenthe. The idea was to establish an anti-confessional, modernist alliance similar to the German *Protestantenverein*, to stimulate a 'free development of the religious life'. By the First World War, the *Protestantenbond* had some 20,000 members. It typically published song collections and others writings, founded Sunday schools, and organised lectures and debates.

Modernism was considered appropriate not only for the educated (since it took progress seriously), but also the less educated (since it had no particular liking for doctrine). A substantial part of the modernist audience consisted almost by definition of the educated elite. They had both the opportunity and the inclination to read up on theology. But the moderns were aware of the gap between the intellectual elite at the academies, where theology had progressed far beyond its traditional confines, and the relatively traditional congregations taught by local preachers. Hence liberal ministers were bent on spreading their new insights among the public at large, using every means available to them to reach and teach the 'common man'. They published sermon upon sermon, separately or in collections, on such subjects as historical criticism, the social status of women, technological progress or cholera epidemics. They produced whole series of affordable volumes, such as the *Stuivers-preeken van woordvoerders der nieuwe richting* (Penny Sermons by Spokesmen of the New Orientation), which ran from 1869 to 1874. The aim was to reach the congregations, to convince the sceptics and soothe the anxious, since the modernist message diverged substantially from the kind of teaching people were most familiar with. However, the modernists also understood

Cover of De Katholieke Illustratie, *1873-1874*.
[Leuven, KADOC: KYC195]

Busken Huet's Brieven over den Bijbel, *1858*.
[Leuven, K.U.Leuven, Maurits Sabbebibliotheek: 22.010.1]

that sermons were perhaps not always the best medium to defend their ideas, and that popular lectures gave them rather more freedom. Public lectures for all classes had long been organised by the Society for Public Benefit, which in 1858 began a series of *volksvoorlezingen* (popular lectures) for the labouring class. These Public Benefit lectures were usually very well attended and treated all kinds of subjects, ranging from potatoes and mosquitoes to electricity and the telegraph; sometimes religion was specifically excluded to avoid dissension. Modernist ministers did not always make use of the facilities provided by the Society for Public Benefit for their lecturing, since there were other organisations and associations that afforded them similar opportunities. But their aim was to reach the orthodox churchgoers and unchurched labourers who for different reasons did not attend their sermons.

Popular books on modernist theology disseminated academic scholarship to non-specialists, treating subjects such as miracles, the resurrection, sin or eternal life. Novels, too, were used to spread the modernist gospel. In an attempt to pass on in an entertaining way their message to the audience, the authors situated modernism in recognisable settings such as the church community or a family. The protagonist in Busken Huet's *Letters on the Bible*, with three editions probably the most influential novel written by a modernist clergyman, was a knowledgeable stockbroker who convinces his sister of the truth of historical criticism. In this way Busken Huet portrayed modernist theology as the terrain of lay people, including women. Modernist clergymen naturally spread their creed though periodicals such as *De teekenen des tijds* (The Signs of the Times, 1858-1859). It included articles on, for example, Willem of Orange as a paragon of liberality, but also discussed the church and the theatre, and contained reviews, notes on novelties, and letters to the editor. One long-lived conduit for modernist thought was the weekly *De Hervorming* (Reformation), which ran from 1873 to 1934. Cheap, readable material for the semi-literate was distributed after 1869 by the *Vereeniging tot Verspreiding van Stichtelijke Blaadjes* (Association for the Dissemination of Edifying Leaflets). Children's bibles and catechism books principally served the young. P.H. Hugenholtz's *Sketches and Scenes* (1872) was berated for attempting to initiate the unspoiled youth in Darwin and Spinoza - some critics apparently called it the 'ape book'.

The liberal, modernist attempt to monopolise the nation's theology and spirituality ended in dismal failure. Modernism was too intellectualist to really have the impact it intended; there was only so much optimistic rationality and reasonableness people could take. Not everyone was consoled by the observation that the cholera epidemic of 1866, whatever grief it may have caused, at least had the advantage of forcing mankind to take measures to prevent future outbreaks. But if modernism failed to catch on among most churchgoing people, and did not capture the interest of those on the fringes of the church, it was symptomatic of the way churches 'reformed' their missionary capabilities by reaching out to the nation through a variety of institutions, including the church itself.

A similar story could be told for the *Réveil* and the Groningers who stayed closest to the hearts and minds of 'ordinary' congregations. The landslide victory at the church elections of 1867 in particular stimulated the orthodox to reach out and conquer the world. A campaign of *kerkherstel* or 'church restoration' (rather than 'church reform') was started up by orthodox organisations such as the *Vereeniging Vrienden der Waarheid* (Association of Friends of the Truth, founded in 1863) and the *Confessioneele Vereeniging* (Confessional Association, founded in 1864 as a society for both clergy and laity). Evangelists, some of them itinerant, were hired to persuade and arouse supporters at the grassroots level. Between 1855 and 1875 the number of evangelists' stations grew from 8 to 59. Some chose to evangelise outside the *Hervormde Kerk*, such as Jan de Liefde (1814-1869), who in 1755 established the association *Tot Heil des Volks* (For the Salvation of the People) that combined charity and social work with outreach and training for evangelists. The revival of orthodoxy had repercussions on the missionary field, in the sense that it, too, fragmented. The Dutch Missionary Society (NZG), active in South Africa, India and the Dutch East Indies (Indonesia), had dominated the scene of Protestant missions since 1797. The Groningers had subsequently called the shots, so that the NZG duly developed a reputation in confessional quarters for being less than orthodox. Consequently, in the 1850s the missionary landscape was rapidly transformed. The *Nederlandsche Zendingsvereniging* (Dutch Missionary Association, 1858), the *Utrechtse Zendingsvereniging* (1859) and the *Nederlandsche Gereformeerde Zendingsvereniging* (1859) were three societies that reflected as many orthodox identities. Initially, the *Christelijke Gereformeerde Kerk* was the only church to take matters into its own hands by organising missions on an ecclesiastical basis. In 1896 Kuyper's *Gereformeerde Kerken* similarly took charge directly of missionary activities, employing theologically schooled evangelists. Catholics became increasingly active in the missionary field in the last quarter of the nineteenth century, partly because of the move to the Netherlands of French and German orders.

Conclusion

Little work has been done on the institutional history of the Dutch churches, let alone church reform, in the long nineteenth century. This chapter offers a first impression of the reformist dynamics of the churches. New narratives on the period, taking new approaches and offering new perspectives, would be more than welcome. Perhaps the best approach to a 'dynamics of reform' would be to look at the church as an institution interconnected with other institutions (ranging from government ministries to the commercial press) and organisations (such as semi-private associations, schools, or companies) through middlemen ('mediators' would be a better, more gender-neutral term) who occupied positions at crucial nodes in social networks.

The 'dynamics of ecclesiastical reform' in the Northern Netherlands is not just a story of churches consciously pursuing reform, but also of people within churches creatively responding to the rise of the nation state. In result, churchgoing Dutchmen were moulded into relatively coherent groups and mobilised on the basis of shared religious identities. This process was bound up with the pursuit of reform, reawakening, renewal, or, if you will, reformation; it resulted in the disintegration of the unity of church, state and nation, and the reconstitution of churches within the public domain. All this certainly amounted to a 'dynamics of religious reform', although the term 'reform' (*hervorming*) itself was used in an explicitly institutional context only in the second part of the long nineteenth century - while the related term *gereformeerden*, for those who considered themselves 'Reformed' in a broad sense, abounded throughout the period. Much more could be said: this account should be seen as no more than a first attempt to look at Dutch church history from the perspective of 'reform'.

Bibliography*

Belgium

Art, Jan. "Documents concernant la situation de l'Église catholique en Belgique en vue du concile de Vatican I (1869-1870)". *Bulletin de l'Institut historique belge à Rome*, 1978-1979, 353-563.

Art, Jan. "Pourquoi la christianisation de la Flandre a-t-elle si bien réussi?" in: Jean-Pierre Massaut and Marie-Elisabeth Henneau, eds. *La christianisation des campagnes*. Actes du colloque du CIHEC (25-27 août 1994). Vol. 2. Brussels-Rome, 1996, 511-520.

Art, Jan. "Social Control in Belgium: the Catholic Factor" in: Clive Emsley et al, eds. *Social Control in Europe. 2: 1800-2000*. Columbus (Ohio), 2004, 112-124.

Aubert, Roger. *Aspects divers du néo-thomisme sous le pontificat de Léon XIII*. Rome, 1961.

Aubert, Roger. "Le grand tournant de la Faculté de théologie de Louvain à la veille de 1900" in: *Mélanges offerts à M.-D. Chenu, maître en théologie*. Paris, 1967, 73-109.

Aubert, Roger. "Die erste Phase des katholischen Liberalismus" in: Hubert Jedin, ed. *Handbuch der Kirchengeschichte*. VI/1: *Die Kirche in der Gegenwart*. Freiburg-Basel-Vienna, 1971, 333-334.

Aubert, Roger. *150 ans de vie des Églises*. Brussels, 1980.

Blom, J.C.H. and Lamberts, Emiel. *History of the Low Countries*. New York-Oxford, 1999.

Boudens, Robrecht. "The Parish Priest in Historical Perspective" in: Jan Kerkhofs, ed. *Europe without Priests?* London, 1995, 89-120.

De Maeyer, Jan. "The Neo-Gothic in Belgium: Architecture of a Catholic Society" in: Jan De Maeyer and Luc Verpoest, eds. *Gothic Revival. Religion, Architecture and Style in Western Europe 1815-1914*. KADOC-Artes 5. Leuven, 2000, 19-34.

De Maeyer, Jan. "Les hommes d'oeuvres en Belgique (1875-1919/1921): utopistes néo-médiévaux ou hommes politiques" in: Laurence Van Ypersele and Anne-Dolorès Marcelis, eds. *Rêves de Chrétienté-Réalités du monde. Imaginaires Catholiques. Actes du colloque, Louvain-la-Neuve 4-6 novembre 1999*. Louvain-la-Neuve, 2001, 185-204.

De Maeyer, Jan. "La Belgique: un élève modèle de l'école ultramontaine" in: Emiel Lamberts, ed. *The Black International: the Holy See and Militant Catholicism in Europe / L'Internationale noire: le Saint-Siège et le Catholicisme militant en Europe. 1870-1878*. KADOC-Studies 29. Leuven, 2002, 361-386.

De Maeyer, Jan. "Katholische Sozialehre und Christliche Arbeiterorganisationen in Belgien von der Freiburger Union (1884-1888) zur Union von Mechelen (1921-1960)" in: Claudia Hiepel and Mark Ruff, eds. *Christliche Arbeiterbewegung in Europa 1850-1950. Konfession und Gesellschaft*. Beiträge zur Zeitgeschichte 30. Stuttgart, 2003, 99-119.

De Maeyer, Jan. "L'Église se tourne vers le peuple, 1884-1926" in: *L'Archidiocèse de Malines-Bruxelles. 450 ans d'histoire*. Vol. 2. Antwerp, 2009, 101-171.

De Maeyer, Jan; Leplae, Sofie and Schmiedl, Joachim, eds. *Religious Institutes in Western Europe in the 19th and 20th Century. Historiography, Research and Legal Position*. KADOC Studies on Religion, Culture and Society 2. Leuven, 2004.

De Maeyer, Jan and Wynants, Paul, eds. *De Vincentianen in België. 1842-1992. Les Vincentiens en Belgique*. KADOC-Studies 14. Leuven, 1992.

Gadille, Jacques et al, eds. *Histoire du christianisme des origines à nos jours*. 11: *Libéralisme, industrialisation, expansion européenne 1830-1914*. Paris, 1995.

---

* Note that Belgian authors are listed alphabetically according to the prefix 'De' or 'Van', Dutch authors according to the main part of the surname.

Gerard, Emmanuel. "L'épanouissement du mouvement ouvrier chrétien (1904-1921)" in: Emmanuel Gerard and Paul Wynants, eds. *Histoire du Mouvement ouvrier chrétien en Belgique*. KADOC-Studies 16. Vol. 1. Leuven, 1994, 115-173.

Gerard, Emmanuel and Wynants, Paul, eds. *Histoire du Mouvement ouvrier chrétien en Belgique*. KADOC-Studies 16. Vol. 1. Leuven, 1994.

Gérin, Paul. "Catholicisme social et démocratie chrétienne (1884-1904)" in: Emmanuel Gerard and Paul Wynants, eds. *Histoire du Mouvement ouvrier chrétien en Belgique*. KADOC-Studies 16. Vol. 1. Leuven, 59-113.

Hasquin, Hervé. *Joseph II. Catholique anticlérical et réformateur impatient. 1741-1790*. Brussels, 2007.

Kenis, Leo. *De Theologische Faculteit te Leuven in de negentiende eeuw 1834-1889. With a Summary in English*. Verhandelingen van de Koninklijke Academie voor Wetenschappen, Letteren en Schone Kunsten van België 143. Brussels, 1992.

Kenis, Leo. "Movements toward Renewal: The Belgian Church and the Improvement of Clerical Education 1830-1850". *Dutch Review of Church History*, 83 (2003), 371-389.

Lamberts, Emiel. "Belgium since 1830" in: J.C.H. Blom and Emiel Lamberts. *History of the Low Countries*. New York-Oxford, 1999, 313-384.

Lamberts, Emiel and Lory, Jacques. *1884: un tournant politique en Belgique*. Brussels, 1986.

Lory, Jacques. *Libéralisme et instruction primaire 1842-1879. Introduction à l'étude de la lutte scolaire en Belgique 1842-1879*. Louvain, 1979, 2 vols.

Roegiers, Jan. "Routine, réorganisation et révolution (1759-1802)" in: *L'Archidiocèse de Malines-Bruxelles. 450 ans d'histoire*. Vol. 1. Antwerp, 2009, 231-296.

Roegiers, Jan and van Sas, N.C.F. "Revolution in the North and South, 1780-1830" in: J.C.H. Blom and Emiel Lamberts. *History of the Low Countries*. New York-Oxford, 1999, 282-310.

Sauvage, Pierre. *Jacques Leclercq. 1891-1971. Un arbre en plein vent*. Paris-Louvain-la-Neuve, 1992.

Simon, Aloïs. *Le Cardinal Sterckx et son temps (1792-1867). L'Église dans l'État*. Vol. 2. Wetteren, 1950.

Simon, Aloïs. "L'École de Malines (1826-1830)". *Collectanea Mechliniensia*, 37 (1952), 349-364.

Simon, Aloïs. *Le parti catholique belge 1830-1945*. Brussels, 1958.

Simon, Aloïs. *Le Cardinal Mercier*. Brussels, 1960.

Suenens, Kristien and Marcélis, Anne-Dolorès. "Vrouwelijke religieuze instituten in België in de negentiende en twintigste eeuw. Een historiografisch overzicht". *Revue belge de philologie et d'histoire*, 86 (2008) 3-4, 809-839 and 841-864.

Tihon, André. "La Belgique (de l'Indépendance à la fin de l'unionisme, 1830-1857)" in: Jacques Gadille et al, eds. *Histoire du christianisme des origines à nos jours*. 11: *Libéralisme, industrialisation, expansion européenne 1830-1914*. Paris, 1995, 203-212.

Tihon, André. "La Belgique (de la fin de l'unionisme à la Première Guerre mondiale, 1857-1914)" in: Jacques Gadille et al, eds. *Histoire du christianisme des origines à nos jours*. 11: *Libéralisme, industrialisation, expansion européenne 1830-1914*. Paris, 1995, 545-561.

Tihon, André. "Le prêtre et le religieux: bilan et perspectives historiographiques". *Revue d'histoire ecclésiastique*, 95 (2000) 3, 211-224.

Tihon, André. "La restauration (1802-1830)" in: *L'Archidiocèse de Malines-Bruxelles. 450 ans d'histoire*. Vol. 2. Antwerp, 2009, 7-33.

Van Dijck, Maarten; De Maeyer, Jan and Henneau, Marie-Elisabeth, eds. *Historiographie et perspectives de recherche des ordres et congrégations sur le territoire des Pays-Bas méridionaux/Belgique*. Special issue *Revue belge de philologie et d'histoire*, 86 (2008) 3-4.

Van Dijck, Maarten and Dusausoit, Xavier. "Hommes visibles et invisibles. Thèmes de l'historiographie relatifs aux instituts religieux masculins en Belgique (XIXe-XXe siècle)" in: Maarten Van Dijck, Jan De Maeyer and Marie-Elisabeth Henneau, eds. *Historiographie et perspectives de recherche des ordres et congrégations sur le territoire des Pays-Bas méridionaux/Belgique.* Special issue *Revue belge de philologie et d'histoire*, 86 (2008) 3-4, 809-839.

Viaene, Vincent. *Belgium and the Holy See from Gregory XVI to Pius IX (1831-1859). Catholic Revival, Society and Politics in 19th Century Europe.* KADOC-Studies 26. Leuven, 2001.

Viaene, Vincent. "Katholisches Reveil und ultramontane Pietät in Belgien (1815-1860)" in: Gisela Fleckenstein and Joachim Schmiedl, eds. *Ultramontanismus. Tendenzen der Forschung.* Paderborn, 2005, 111-134.

Viaene, Vincent. "L'épanouissement d'une Église 'libre' (1830-1883)" in: *L'Archidiocèse de Malines-Bruxelles. 450 ans d'histoire.* Vol. 2. Antwerp, 2009, 35-99.

Witte, Els. "The Battle for Monasteries, Cemeteries and Schools: Belgium" in: Christopher Clark and Wolfram Kaiser, eds. *Culture Wars. Secular-Catholic Conflict in Nineteenth-Century Europe.* Cambridge, 2003, 102-128.

The Netherlands

Barnard, Tjaard Roeland. *Van 'verstoten kind' tot belijdende kerk. De Remonstrantse Broederschap tussen 1850 en 1940.* Amsterdam, 2006.

Bos, David. *In dienst van het Koninkrijk. Beroepsontwikkeling van hervormde predikanten in negentiende-eeuws Nederland.* Amsterdam, 1999.

Bouma, Hendrik. *Secession, Doleantie, and Union: 1834-1892.* Transl. Theodore Plantinga. Neerlandia-Alberta etc., 1995.

Buitenwerf-van der Molen, Mirjam. *God van vooruitgang. De popularisering van het modern-theologisch gedachtegoed in Nederland (1857-1880).* Hilversum, 2007.

Busken Huet, C. *Brieven over den Bijbel.* Haarlem, 1859.

Clemens, Theo. "De terugdringing van de rooms-katholieken uit de verlicht-protestantse natie". *Bijdragen en mededelingen betreffende de geschiedenis der Nederlanden*, 110 (1995), 27-39.

De Jong, Peter Y. and Kloosterman, Nelson D., eds. *The Reformation of 1834. Essays in Commemoration of the Act of Secession and Return.* Orange City (IA), 1984.

De Maeyer, Jan; Leplae, Sofie and Schmiedl, Joachim, eds. *Religious Institutes in Western Europe in the 19th and 20th Century. Historiography, Research and Legal Position.* KADOC Studies on Religion, Culture and Society 2. Leuven, 2004.

Eijnatten, Joris van. *Liberty and Concord in the United Provinces. Religious Toleration and the Public in the Eighteenth-Century Netherlands.* Brill's Studies in Intellectual History 111. Leiden etc, 2003.

Eijnatten, Joris van and Lieburg, Fred van. *Nederlandse religiegeschiedenis.* Hilversum, 2006².

Houkes, Annemarie. *Christelijke vaderlanders. Godsdienst, burgerschap en de Nederlandse natie 1850-1900.* Amsterdam, 2009.

Knappert, Laurentius. *Geschiedenis der Nederlandsche Hervormde Kerk gedurende de 18e en 19e eeuw.* Amsterdam, 1912.

Koch, Jeroen. *Abraham Kuyper. Een biografie.* Amsterdam, 2006.

Kooi, Cornelis van der and Bruijn, Jan de, eds. *Kuyper Reconsidered. Aspects of his Life and Work.* Amsterdam, 1999.

Loon, J.C.A. van. *Het Algemeen Reglement van 1816.* Wageningen, 1942.

Ouden, Willem Hendrik den. *Kerk onder patriottenbewind. Kerkelijke financiën en de Bataafse Republiek, 1795-1801.* Zoetermeer, 1994.

Reitsma, Johannes and Lindeboom, Johannes. *Geschiedenis van de Hervorming en de Hervormde Kerk der Nederlanden.* The Hague, 1949⁵.

Roes, Jan and Valk, Hans de. "A World Apart? Religious Orders and Congregations in the Netherlands" in: Jan De Maeyer, Sofie Leplae and Joachim Schmiedl, eds. *Religious Institutes in Western Europe in the 19th and 20th Century. Historiography, Research and Legal Position.* KADOC Studies on Religion, Culture and Society 2. Leuven, 2004, 135-162.

Rooden, Peter van. *Religieuze regimes. Over godsdienst en maatschappij in Nederland 1570-1990.* Amsterdam, 1996.

Schoon, Dick J. *Van bisschoppelijke cleresie tot Oud-Katholieke Kerk. Bijdrage tot de geschiedenis van het katholicisme in Nederland in de 19de eeuw.* Nijmegen, 2004.

Selderhuis, Herman J., ed. *Handboek Nederlandse kerkgeschiedenis.* Kampen, 2006.

Valk, J.M.M. de. *Philip Willem van Heusde. Wijsbegeerte van het gezond verstand.* Baarn, 1989.

Ver Huell, Alexander. *Het dagboek van Alexander Ver Huell 1860-1865.* Ed. Jan Bervoets and Rody Chamuleau. Zutphen, 1985.

Vree, Jasper. "Petrus Hofstede de Groot and the Christian Education of the Dutch Nation (1833-1861)". *Nederlands archief voor kerkgeschiedenis*, 78 (1998), 70-93.

Vugt, Joos van. "'Should it Happen that God Should Permit...'. The Political and Legal Position of Orders and Congregations in the Netherlands" in: Jan De Maeyer, Sofie Leplae and Joachim Schmiedl, eds. *Religious Institutes in Western Europe in the 19th and 20th Century. Historiography, Research and Legal Position.* KADOC Studies on Religion, Culture and Society 2. Leuven, 2004, 277-308.

Wintle, Michael. *Pillars of Piety. Religion in the Netherlands in the Nineteenth Century 1813-1901.* Hull, 1987.

Xanten, Hendrikus Johannes van. *'Katholieken, wat zijt gij toch een wonderlijk volk!'*

GERMANY

This chapter is divided into two sections, one dealing with Catholic, the other with Protestant Germany. Given the political and religious complexity of the German 'bloc', a division along confessional lines seems the most sensible way to discuss 140 years of ecclesiastical reform. As became apparent in Volume I, the intricacy of German political history is daunting: one need think only of the more than 300 states of the Holy Roman Empire (till 1806), the 39 states of the German Confederation (till 1866), the inclusion and subsequent exclusion of Habsburg Austria in 'Germany', the establishment of the German Empire in 1871, and finally the birth of the Weimar Republic in 1919. By contrast, the confessional divide seems more or less clear-cut, with Catholics on the one hand and Protestants on the other. But appearances deceive. The problems begin when one takes a closer look at the individual German states, which after the abolition of the Holy Roman Empire proved to have been much less mono-confessional than they had been, or than their political leaders may have wanted them to be. The complications arising from this historical jumble of political and religious alliances is discussed in detail in each of the two sections that make up this chapter. The first section focuses on Roman Catholic ecclesiastical reform; the second deals with church reforms within the Protestant churches. Each offers a chronological outline highlighting important aspects and major transitions.

Internal Church Reform in Catholic Germany

Claus Arnold

Reform at the Time of the Secularisation, 1780-1803/15

During the last decades of the Holy Roman Empire the Catholic Church with its 23 prince bishops and its 44 imperial abbeys constituted not only a political force of cohesion and a career market where the younger sons of the nobility could live in style, but showed remarkable efforts in the field of internal ecclesiastical reform. The absolutism of the prince bishops was combined with a renewed sense of their episcopal dignity and relative independence from Rome.[1] These episcopal ideas, which were in part similar to French Gallicanism, went in Germany under the label of 'Febronianism', named after the pseudonymous author Febronius - Johann Nikolaus von Hontheim (1701-1790), auxiliary bishop in Trier - whose *De statu ecclesiae et legitima potestate Romani pontificis liber singularis* had appeared in Frankfurt in 1763. Furthermore, the Catholic version of late Enlightenment influenced many of the last prince bishops. The archduke Maximilian Franz of Austria (1756-1801) for instance, who became Archbishop of Cologne in 1784, not only went as far as receiving the higher orders of priesthood and episcopate very quickly and actually fulfilling liturgical functions himself - things unheard of in the older generation of prince bishops who relied for these things mainly on their bourgeois auxiliary bishops - he also tried to enforce an Enlightenment programme of church reform that was similar to the so-called Josephinism of his elder brother, Emperor Joseph II (1741-1790). Although holidays, processions, confraternities, festive liturgies and the activities of mendicant and contemplative orders were reduced and 'popular' pieties like the rosary viewed with suspicion, the enlightened

---

[1.] Cf. the 'Punctation of Ems' of 1786; English translation in Maclear, ed., *Church and State*, 28-31.

reforms were only partly at odds with the former post-Tridentine confessionalisation and the resulting baroque piety. Their core element was the strengthening of pastoral care and education on the parish level, e.g. by regulating the size of parishes. Thus, although the reformist reduction of some elements of Baroque Catholicism caused many conflicts, the overall post-Tridentine trend of social control and religious intensification persisted in the years after 1780 and well into the nineteenth century.[2]

The papal suppression of the Jesuits and their colleges in 1773 paved the way for a reorganisation of the training of priests. On the orders of Empress Maria Theresa (1717-1780), the Benedictine Abbott Franz Stephan Rautenstrauch (1734-1785) developed a new plan of studies with a typical 'Jansenist' character: an anti-scholastic emphasis on biblical studies and ecclesiastical history was combined with a decidedly practical orientation, institutionalised in the new subject of Pastoral Theology. In contrast to the strictly centralised but short-lived 'General Seminaries', introduced by Joseph II, Rautenstrauch's plan had lasting effects and parallels in other German states. Here, a consecutive model was favoured, which was fundamental for the formation of a modern diocesan clergy in Germany: university studies in theology were followed by the immediate preparation for ordination in the episcopal seminary. In the diocese of Münster, for instance, the Vicar-General and Minister Franz von Fürstenberg (1729-1810) prepared the foundation of a new university and a seminary in 1773.

German Catholic theology in these years was partly 'rationalist' and tried to integrate historical criticism. Johann Lorenz Isenbiehl (1744-1818), professor at Mainz University, had studied Oriental languages at the Protestant university in Göttingen (with the approval of his enlightened Archbishop-Elector Emmerich Joseph von Breidbach zu Bürresheim (1707-1774)). In his *Neuer Versuch über die Weissagung von Emmanuel* (1778) he contested the messianic interpretation of Isaiah 7,14 and reaped the most solemn form of ecclesiastical censure, a special papal *Breve* against his book in 1779. Franz Berg (1753-1821), professor of ecclesiastical history at Würzburg University, tried to explain the entire development of Christianity from the standpoint of an immanent human psychology. At Ingolstadt, the ex-Jesuit Benedikt Stattler (1728-1797) demonstrated the rational character of Revelation by using the philosophy of Christian Wolff. But on the whole a moderate religious Enlightenment prevailed. For example, in the case of Johann Michael Sailer (1751-1832), who taught at Ingolstadt, Dillingen and Landshut, a biblical and patristic, anti-scholastic re-orientation was combined with a strict Christocentrism and a pietist interiorisation of religion. Sailer's pastoral theology was implemented as a concrete programme of reform in the Constance Diocese by his pupil, the influential Vicar-General Ignaz Heinrich von Wessenberg (1774-1860). Wessenberg's reform of the Meersburg seminary with stress on biblical, historical and liturgical studies, his introduction of pastoral conferences and theological libraries

---

[2] Klueting, *Katholische Aufklärung*; Schneider, "Katholische Aufklärung"; Holzem, *Religion und Lebensformen*.

Internal Church Reform in Catholic Germany

M. Ellenrieder, Ignaz Heinrich von Wessenberg, *engraving, 1819.*
[Konstanz, Städtische Wessenberg-Galerie]

for the rural chapters, his creation of a 'civic' clergy, his liturgical reforms (compulsory homily during mass, German Vespers, use of German in the administration of the sacraments) remained a model for South Germany and beyond well into the 1830s.

The secularisation of 1803 brought the end of most abbeys and religious orders and had a negative effect on the cultural standard in rural Catholic areas, where the abbeys had been centres of art and education and had offered some degree of vertical mobility to gifted youths. On the diocesan level many prince bishops, who did not want to be mere pastors, resigned; the vacuum was filled by capitular or apostolic vicars, who had to cooperate with the new territorial states and their Protestant monarchs (with the exception of Bavaria and its Catholic Wittelsbach dynasty). The secularisation brought no real disestablishment, but started a re-establishment of Catholicism on a new political basis. In this process the new governments were often influenced by enlightened Catholic clergymen and their ideas of reform. Wessenberg, for instance, was backed by the government of Baden against the Roman Curia and could carry on with his work until 1827.

From Restoration to Revolution 1815-1848

The Vienna Congress did not bring a *Bundeskirche* or 'federal Church' under a German Primate, because the Roman Curia and the new states of the German Federation opposed such relative independence. Thus, after bilateral talks with the states, the pope erected new ecclesiastical provinces and dioceses, which reflected exactly the political situation after 1815 - a reorganisation which remains fundamental until the present day (Bavarian Concordat of 1817; papal bulls for the Protestant states: Prussia 1821, Hanover 1821, Upper Rhenish Church Province for Württemberg, Baden, Hessen-Darmstadt, Frankfurt, Hessen-Kassel and Nassau 1821-1827).[3] As Napoleon had done after the Concordat of 1801, the states introduced, after the canonical erection of the dioceses by the pope, a system of control over the new Catholic *Landeskirchen* which echoed Napoleon's 'Organic Articles' of 1802 (these were a unilateral addition to the French Concordat of 1801 and in themselves an echo of Gallicanism/Josephinism). Before the first new bishops were installed (most of them only around 1830, and rarely recruited from the nobility), the states became active in founding new seminaries, *lycea*, clerical colleges and university faculties for the professional training of their new Catholic 'religious servants'. The Prussian *Kultusminister* (Minister of Religious Affairs) Karl Freiherr von Altenstein (1770-1840) formulated the new situation thus: "The Prussian State is an evangelical State and has one third of Catholic subjects. It is correct behaviour, if the Government provides for the Evangelical Church lovingly and for the Catholic Church dutifully. The Evangelical Church must be favoured. The Catho-

---

[3] Burkard, *Staatskirche - Papstkirche - Bischofskirche*.

lic Church must not be disadvantaged - for its good all provisions must be made."⁴ On the whole, the consecutive model of the late eighteenth century was preserved. After studying at a state university faculty (Tübingen for Württemberg, Freiburg for Baden, Giessen for Hessen-Kassel, Bonn and Breslau for Prussia, Würzburg and Munich for Bavaria) or at a lyceum (e.g. Münster and Braunsberg in Prussia or Regensburg and Passau in Bavaria) the candidates would go to the seminary for ordination.

The states gave subsidies for the new dioceses and cathedral chapters, thus securing a relative financial independence and a modicum of (well-controlled) self-government. The chapters had not only liturgical functions, but assisted the bishop in his care of the diocese. In the dioceses of the Upper Rhenish Church Province they formed the *Ordinariat* - a collegial body of diocesan government, theologically inspired by an enlightened 'presbyterialism' and modelled on the contemporary collegial ministries of state. In the Prussian dioceses Trier and Cologne the cathedral chapters were also integrated in the diocesan government (the *Generalvikariat*), but a strict episcopal control prevailed. The situation in Bavaria was similar. On the whole, the bishops became clearly the ecclesiastical key figures, and a long process of episcopalisation and centralisation began which has continued until the present and has remained unaffected by all changes in theological preferences or church politics. Centralised bureaucratic structures were more and more imposed. The *Ordinariat* or *Generalvikariat* themselves were regulated by a strict order of business with regular conferences and a formalised way of downward and upward communication. This is also mirrored in the increase of personnel in the *Generalvikariat* (diocesan curia): in Trier numbers rose from 5 officials (additional to the canons) in 1824 to 12 in 1832, in Cologne from 13 in 1825 to 54 in 1838. In time more and more laymen were included, some of them in important positions (mainly legal experts). In this process the deans became the intermediaries of episcopal control. The deaneries in Cologne and Trier for instance were reorganised in a 'manageable' size and in correspondence with the administration units of the state. The deans had the obligation of constant control and regular visitation of the parishes; regular reports to the *Generalvikariat* were expected; elaborate questionnaires were developed for the visitations. Episcopal confirmation of the dean's election was necessary; Bishop Hommer of Trier went as far as to simply nominate new deans himself. Also the immediate presence of the bishops in their dioceses increased. Auxiliary bishops were rare now, and episcopal acts like confirmation (often hundreds of young people at a time) or the consecration of churches and altars were executed by the ordinaries themselves. (Not without reason two out of four bishops of Rottenburg in the nineteenth century died when touring their diocese).⁵

The parishes, whose finances had been untouched by the secularisation, were partly reorganised. In Württemberg for instance, parish regulation on the model

---

⁴ Cited after Bachem, *Vorgeschichte, Geschichte und Politik der deutschen Zentrumspartei*, I, 158.
⁵ Wolf, "Generalvikar oder Domdekan?"; Burkard, " Zum Wandel der Domkapitel"; Ebertz, "Ein Haus voll Glorie"; Lill, " Der Bischof zwischen Säkularisation und Kulturkampf"; Schneider, "Entwicklungstendenzen rheinischer Frömmigkeits- und Kirchengeschichte".

of Austrian Josephinism was continued until 1848 in a close collaboration of state and ordinariat: 'unnecessary' parishes were suppressed and 90 new parishes were founded in order to achieve better pastoral care in diaspora areas. In Eastern Prussia, however, the state suppressed parishes in Silesian diaspora areas for merely financial reasons, which led to episcopal protests. An accord was reached by Bishop Melchior von Diepenbrock (1798-1853) of Breslau in 1848. On the other hand, in the Prussian Rhineland many old parishes were reinstated which had fallen prey to the French regulation and its imposition of main (cantonal) and subordinate (succursal) parishes. In a high percentage of parishes, the monarchs had the patronage (the right to nominate the parish priest), thus reducing episcopal influence.[6]

With the end of the 'parallel' religious world of the monasteries and religious orders the parish became the almost exclusive place of pastoral care and the high ideal of the parish priest as the one and only real pastor of his flock could now be enforced effectively. Popular attachment to the old forms of baroque piety persisted nevertheless, at least in some areas (e.g. in Westphalia and Upper Swabia). Theologically, the ideas of the confessionally irenic and moderate Catholic Enlightenment continued to influence clerical education, at least in South and South-West Germany. The hugely popular professor of dogmatics at Bonn University, Georg Hermes (1775-1831), stood for a slightly different orientation. His Restoration theology was simultaneously anti-Enlightenment, anti-Romantic and anti-mystical and tried to establish a new rational basis for the belief in revelation. With the consent of Archbishop Ferdinand August von Spiegel (1764-1835) of Cologne, Hermes and his pupils created a civic, politically conservative and pastorally active clergy in Western Prussia. All dioceses aimed at greater homogeneity in their clergy, whose make-up was still characterised by the difficult situation in the period before 1821-1827.

From the 1830s onwards the ultramontane movement gained ground in Germany. The new call for *libertas ecclesiae* included the reduction of state control, the strengthening of episcopal influence on seminaries and colleges, and the nomination of parish priests. It did not include the wish for a complete separation of church and state, but the older generation of 'cooperative' bishops and theologians came more and more under fire: Hermes for instance was stigmatised as a rationalistic heretic shortly after his death in the papal brief *Dum acerbissimas* of 1833, which took up the denunciations of German ultramontanes. This way of intermingling theology and church politics and of acting (or trying to act) *via Rome* remained popular throughout the century, as shown by the cases of the relatively 'progressive' or merely non-neo-scholastic theologians Anton Günther (1783-1863), Jakob Frohschammer (1821-1893) or Johannes Evangelist von Kuhn (1806-1887) (the posthumous denunciation of Sailer failed).[7] The turn towards ultramontanism was prepared in elitist circles, like the *familia sacra*

---

[6] Gatz, ed., *Die Bistümer und ihre Pfarreien*.
[7] Schwedt, *Das römische Urteil über Georg Hermes*; Id., "Die Verurteilung der Werke Anton Günthers";
Pahud de Mortanges, *Philosophie und kirchliche Autorität*; Wolf, *Ketzer oder Kirchenlehrer?*; Id., ed., *Johann Michael Sailer*.

around the Countess Amalie von Gallitzin (1748-1806) in Münster or the ones around Joseph Görres (1776-1848) at Munich and the Redemptorist Clemens Maria Hofbauer (1751-1820)[8] at Vienna, where historians, philosophers and theologians came together. Roughly speaking[9], 'Romantic-organic' and 'historical' thinking gained ground over against 'Enlightenment' tendencies in Catholicism. A theological representative of 'organic' thinking was the Tübingen theologian Johann Adam Möhler (1796-1838). Although his *Symbolik* (1832) was still irenic in tone, it presented a new apologetic of the Catholic Church with a distinctly anti-Protestant note: the organic unfolding and development of Catholic truth in history stood against the criticism of Protestantism, which remained essentially a negation without substance of its own.

The beginnings of neo-scholasticism in Germany were a result of the French (or rather Alsatian) period in the Mainz seminary under Bishop Joseph Ludwig Colmar (1760-1818). The seminary's new regent Bruno Franz Leopold Liebermann (1749-1844), who taught from 1803 until 1824, and other professors had come from Strasbourg and stood under the influence of contemporary French anti-revolutionary thinking and ultramontanism. In 1821 the Mainz circle founded the influential journal *Der Katholik. Eine religiöse Zeitschrift zur Belehrung und Warnung* (The Catholic. A Religious Journal for Instruction and Admonition) which continued until 1918.

Nevertheless, the ultramontanes were not without opposition. The 1820s and 1830s saw an anti-celibacy and pro-synod movement in South-West Germany, which tried to establish lay participation in church government. Before and around the 1848 Revolution the ultramontane and 'rationalist' mobilisation of lay people competed on an impressive scale. More than 500,000 pilgrims to the Holy Coat of Trier in 1844 - a typical ultramontane re-enactment of baroque piety - were counterbalanced by thousands of *Deutschkatholiken* (literally 'German Catholics'), who formed independent parishes and created 'rationalist' liturgies in German. Recent research has shown that the religious reform impetus of the *Deutschkatholiken* has to be taken seriously; it was not a primarily or merely political movement for freedom under the guise of anti-ultramontane protest.[10]

The ultramontane political movement around the 1848-1849 Frankfurt Parliament used the new civil liberties for their ecclesiastical agenda: 400 *Pius-Vereine für religiöse Freiheit* (Pius (IX) Associations for Religious Freedom) and similar associations were founded. The first national congress of these associations was held at Mainz in October 1848, where - on the model of the Irish Catholic Association - a *Katholischer Verein Deutschland* was founded. Except for war times, similar national gatherings of the associations were from then on held annually and under changing names (the name

---

[8] Weiß, *Begegnungen mit Klemens Maria Hofbauer*; Id., *Kulturen - Mentalitäten - Mythen*.
[9] Theological 'Romanticism' would have been impossible without an antedecent 'Enlightenment' as precondition. The relative continuity between the two is clearly visible in the biographies of Sailer, Möhler or the Countess Gallitzin. Cf. Holzem, *Weltversuchung und Heilsgewißheit*; for a short synthesis see Kustermann, "Romantik".
[10] Smolinsky, "Synoden"; Holzem, *Kirchenreform und Sektenstiftung*.

Keepsake print of the pilgrimage to the Holy Coat
of Trier, *1844*.
[Private collection]

Katholikentag was adopted only in 1948). In order to influence the debates on fundamental rights in parliament, the associations organised 1,100 petitions. Ultramontane bishops like Peter Joseph Blum (1808-1884) of Limburg favoured this kind of mobilisation. Within the Frankfurt Parliament 'bad' and 'good' Catholic members were almost equal in numbers - with lay- and clergymen on both sides. The 'bad' Catholics included for example the *Deutschkatholik* Robert Blum (1807-1848) and the Wessenbergian Dean of Constance, Vincenz Kuenzer (1793-1853); the 'good' Catholics were loosely organised in the 'Catholic Club' initiated by an episcopal Member of Parliament, namely Melchior Diepenbrock of Breslau. Prominent names were here Ignaz von Döllinger (1799-1890) (then a convinced ultramontane) or the future bishop of Mainz Wilhelm Emmanuel von Ketteler (1811-1877). The Catholic Club failed to secure ecclesiastical control of the primary schools, but religious instruction was safeguarded as a regular school subject in the projected constitution. Liberal attempts to prohibit obligatory clerical celibacy and the introduction of the Jesuit and Redemptorist orders in Germany were successfully frustrated. The churches were to be given the right to order their internal affairs themselves, although "within the framework of common law". The ultramontane offensive met with the criticism of the prominent 'enlightened' theologian Johann Baptist Hirscher (1788-1865) at Freiburg, who called for synods made up of laity and clergy alike, in order to introduce some lay participation *within* the institutional church and to compensate for the loss of (lay) government control. Hirscher's pamphlets were quickly put on the Index of forbidden books.[11]

The use of print media for communication within German Catholicism increased continually before 1848.[12] According to a contemporary categorisation there were four types of journals: those with a strictly theological-scholarly orientation, like the *Theologische Quartalschrift* from Tübingen or the Hermesian *Zeitschrift für Philosophie und katholische Theologie* (Bonn), both connected with a university faculty and addressing theologians and the educated clergy in general. The *Jahresschrift für Theologie und Kirchenrecht der Katholiken* or the *Freimüthige Blätter über Theologie und Kirchenthum* had a distinctly enlightened touch, whereas the *Katholische Zeitschrift für Wissenschaft und Kunst* was clearly ultramontane. A second type of journal stood for the propagation of 'Catholic Science' and *Weltanschauung* in the ultramontane sense among an educated lay public: here the two-weekly *Historisch-politische Blätter* of the Munich Görres-circle was most prominent. In the third category many periodicals cared for concrete pastoral needs with sketches for homilies and catechesis. In the fourth category 'the Catholic people' were addressed directly in mostly weekly periodicals (*Kirchenblätter für das katholische Volk*), which combined edification, entertainment and information. Here the already mentioned ultramontane *Katholik* from Mainz was most prominent,

---

[11] Horstmann, *Katholizismus und moderne Welt*; Schwedt, "Die katholischen Abgeordneten der Paulskirche und Frankfurt"; Id., "Vom ultramontanen zum liberalen Döllinger"; Köster, *Der Fall Hirscher*.

[12] Cf. the synthesis in Schneider, *Katholiken auf die Barrikaden?*, 33-94, and Burkard; "Presse und Publizistik".

though not without enlightened and supraconfessional alternatives like the *Badisches Kirchenblatt*. In the end most dioceses had *Katholische Sonntagsblätter*[13] which began as private initiatives (mostly of priests) and - after gaining episcopal approval - ended as official diocesan organs (especially after the Second World War).

Mobilisation and Polarisation, 1848-1870

It has been said that the Catholic Church, or more precisely the bishops, profited most from the 1848 Revolution.[14] Indeed, state control became, sooner or later, less rigid in many states of the German Federation, most notably in Prussia. Bishops were free to meet for national or provincial conferences - even the latter had been regarded with suspicion by the governments. The first German episcopal conference was held at Würzburg in October-November 1848 under the presidency of Cardinal Johannes von Geissel (1796-1864), the archbishop of Cologne. Döllinger was present as theological adviser. The bishops' memorandum of 14 November called for a reduction of state interference, but opted against a separation of state and church. Confessional schools and religious instruction were main concerns as well as complete episcopal control over the training of priests. On the reform side, the celebration of diocesan and provincial synods according to the ordinances of the Council of Trent was to be revived and a national council (*National-Concil*) projected. A joint *Agentur*, a representative office in Rome, was planned. Pope Pius IX was asked for his consent concerning the national council, which he denied after six months' hesitation. The intransigent Munich nuncio Carlo Sacconi (1808-1889) and the extremely ultramontane Munich archbishop Karl August von Reisach (1800-1869) had sown seeds of distrust in Rome by evoking the spectre of an anti-Roman national church. Reisach was the first German bishop who had been trained in the 'new' Roman *Collegium Germanicum* (revived in 1818-1819). Outside Bavaria, so-called *Germanikerbischöfe*[15] were excluded by the governments and became more frequent only after 1918. The national council never met, and diocesan synods remained virtually unknown until 1918. A prominent exception was the Provincial Council of Cologne under Cardinal Geissel in 1860, which not only prescribed disciplinary measures in the ultramontane sense (e.g. by reducing the use of German hymns and favouring Gregorian chant), but also touched on dogmatic matters by defining - against 'Darwinism' - the direct divine creation of Adam and Eve and by invoking the infallible *magisterium* of the Roman Pontiff. Inside the dioceses the trend towards centralisation, episcopalisation and an overall ultramontanisation was strengthened. All bishops now nominated a vicar-general as their *alter ego* and head of the diocesan administration. Apart from this, the bureaucratic structures developed in the first half

---

[13] For instance in Rottenburg: Wolf and Seiler, eds., *Das Katholische Sonntagsblatt*.
[14] Geschichtsverein, ed., *Die Revolution von 1848*.
[15] Peter Walter, in Gatz, ed., *Der Diözesanklerus*, 253-263; Leitgöb, *Vom Seelenhirten zum Wegführer*.

Johannes von Geissel, *photograph, c.1860*.
[Leuven, K.U.Leuven, Maurits Sabbebibliotheek:
05:27*GOER 81/2]

F. Hanfstaengl, Ignaz von Döllinger, *photograph*,
c.1860
[Private collection]

of the century were still functioning. They underwent no essential changes until the huge administrative expansion which came after 1950-1960.[16]

After the failure of the Frankfurt Parliament, the political mobilisation of the laity in 1848 was channelled mainly into the social field, where associations like the male *Vinzenz-Vereine* (on the model of the French *Conférences de Charité*, founded in 1833 by Antoine Frédéric Ozanam in the spirit of Saint Vincent de Paul) and the female *Elisabeth-Vereine* (named after Saint Elisabeth of Hungary) were active. The problems of early industrialisation and pauperism were perceived as *Soziale Frage* (the 'social question'). The priest Adolf Kolping (1813-1865) founded in 1849 the Cologne *Gesellenverein* (Journeymen's Association) which turned into a highly successful movement and effectively improved the living conditions and the religious and educational standards of journeymen. *Arbeitervereine* (workers' associations) were similarly active, and with the public pronouncements of Bishop Ketteler of Mainz the social question was identified as a problem which needed state intervention and could not simply be remedied

---

[16] Cf. the example of Münster: Damberg, *Moderne und Milieu*.

by private or ecclesiastical charity. In the social context, the re-foundation of female congregations (mostly under diocesan law) had begun early in the nineteenth century, but gained considerable momentum now. Their fields were education, child care and care for the sick. The evolution of a modern hospital system in Germany would have been impossible without the dedication of these women. In this *catholicisme au feminine* (Claude Langlois) it was not only energetic founder personalities like Katharina Kasper (1820-1898) of the *Arme Dienstmägde Jesu Christi* (the *Dernbacher Schwestern*) who could be active in an ecclesiastical field, but young women in general found an attractive religious and professional alternative to the vicissitudes of married life.[17] A multitude of Franciscan, Dominican, Vincentian and other congregations were active; and their membership rose quickly to about 67,000 sisters in Germany in 1910.

Under the Prussian Constitution of 1850 even male religious orders were allowed (though not in Württemberg or Baden, where ultramontanes craved for "freedom as in Prussia"). In Bavaria the Romantic sympathy of King Ludwig I for the Benedictines had allowed the re-foundation of a dozen monasteries from 1830 onwards. They were expected to run *lycea*, which became important centres of Catholic education (e.g. the abbeys of St Stephan at Augsburg and Metten near Deggendorf). Even where they were not allowed to settle permanently, the Jesuits and Redemptorists were able to take up their missions again after 1850, thus infringing the exclusiveness of pastoral care by secular parish priests. The mission movement was favoured by ultramontane bishops and parish priests as well as patrons from the Catholic nobility who were often at odds with the central government of their respective state.[18]

The ultramontane movement had had considerable success in reducing state 'interference' in ecclesiastical matters. When the 'common enemy' had thus become less important, the internal diversity of the movement became more palpable. The Romantic interest in history had led to the evolution of historicism - a trend shared at least partly by church historians like Döllinger, who began to deconstruct traditional narratives of church history (e.g. his *Papstfabeln des Mittelalters*, 1863). In addition, the confrontation with Enlightenment and German Idealism had not remained without effect on German university theologians like Kuhn at Tübingen (see above). These aberrations from a strict scholastic approach were regarded with scepticism in Mainz and Eichstätt. The Würzburg university faculty had become another centre of neo-scholasticism: here the bishop sent many seminarians to the *Germanicum* for the study of 'Roman' theology. Thus, alumni of the *Germanicum* like Joseph Hergenröther (1824-1890) and Heinrich Denzinger (1819-1883) (first editor of the famous *Enchiridion symbolorum ac definitionum* (1854), which assembled the source texts for the construction of the 'Roman *magisterium*') were able to dominate the faculty from the 1850s onwards. The tension between 'Roman' and 'German' theologians became public on

---

[17] Gatz, ed., *Klöster und Ordensgemeinschaften*; Meiwes, *"Arbeiterinnen des Herrn"*; Zimmermann and Priesching, eds., *Württembergisches Klosterbuch*.

[18] Geschichtsverein, ed., *Kulturkampf*; Lill, *Der Kulturkampf*; Weiß, *Die Redemptoristen in Bayern*; Burkard, "Volksmissionen und Jugendbünde"; Heitz, *Volksmission und badischer Katholizismus*.

the occasion of the *Münchener Gelehrtenversammlung* (Munich Congress) of 1863. In his programmatic speech, Döllinger compared scholasticism to an old building beyond repair. In opposition to the backward Roman school, he praised the modern 'scientific' German school, which unlike scholasticism was open to historical research and needed real freedom in order to fulfil its role within the church. After Munich, the split between neo-scholastic and 'German' theologians was obvious.[19] Pius IX widened the gap by his letter *Tuas libenter*, sent to Archbishop Gregor von Scherr (1804-1877) of Munich after the congress. The letter had been inspired by Scherr's predecessor Reisach, who had been promoted (perhaps 'a-moted' would be more to the point) to a cardinalship at the Curia, and demanded the subjection of theology under the Magisterium.

The conflict was also fought out on the field of clerical and lay education, with the alternatives: seminary or state faculty, Catholic university or state university. In the first instance, bishops like Reisach and Ketteler praised the exclusive theological training in a seminary, 'away from the world' and under close episcopal surveillance, as the only truly 'Tridentine' solution. Reisach's seminary at Eichstätt had become a model of ultramontane clerical education before 1848, and Ketteler withdrew his seminarians from the Giessen Faculty of Catholic Theology back to Mainz in 1850. However, the Giessen state Faculty was the only one to be eventually dissolved; the other bishops did not follow Ketteler's example. In the second instance, the project of a Catholic university in Germany was formulated at the 14th *Generalversammlung der katholischen Vereine Deutschland* (General Assembly of the Catholic Associations of Germany) at Aachen in 1862. The motivation for the project came from the perceived discrimination against Catholic laymen at state universities, dominated by Protestants and liberals, and the moral dangers inherent in public, non-religious universities. A Catholic university was seen as the only possible means to do away with academic imparity with the Protestants and with the general Catholic educational inferiority. The University of Louvain, re-established in 1834-1835 as the Catholic University of Belgium, served as a model. Opposition against this project of the Catholic laity came primarily from university theologians like Johannes Ev. Kuhn and Carl Joseph Hefele (1809-1893) at Tübingen. Kuhn argued for the autonomy of the arts and sciences; 'Catholic' chemistry, physics, mechanics etc. were nonsense. For Kuhn the university was not a place of an authoritarian education under clerical surveillance, but a space for 'self-thinking and research'. Catholics should try to succeed at the state universities, and not simply leave them in the hands of the Protestants. The project of the Catholic university failed in the end, mainly for financial reasons, and was realised on a small scale at Eichstätt only in 1980.[20]

---

[19] Bischof, *Theologie und Geschichte*.
[20] Garhammer, *Seminaridee und Klerusbildung*; Scharfenecker, *Die Katholisch-Theologische Fakultät Gießen*; Brandt, *Eine katholische Universität in Deutschland?*; Wolf, *Ketzer oder Kirchenlehrer?*, 156-167.

In the New German Empire, 1871-1914

The First Vatican Council created the Old Catholic schism in Germany, which robbed the church of a large portion of its not too numerous lay intelligentsia, and served, together with the 1864 *Syllabus errorum*, as a pretext for Bismarck's *Kulturkampf*.[21] This attempt to re-introduce the pre-1848 state control of the church in Prussia, and the effects of church resistance against it created severe difficulties in diocesan administration and pastoral care. In 1881, of 4,627 Prussian parishes 24% were vacant (without regular parish priest), while 601 parishes were without any priest at all. In Gnesen-Posen with its strong Polish population, 13.2% of the Catholics had no pastoral care.[22] In 1878 only three Prussian bishops were in office, the rest deposed, exiled or in prison. Theological faculties continued to work, but numbers of students fell sharply: at Bonn from 169 in 1870 to 88 in 1880, at Breslau from 132 to 65, at Münster from 199 to 75. Besides, all seminaries, theological colleges and minor seminaries in Prussia were closed. Theology students emigrated west and south: from 1873 to 1887, 78 priests for the Cologne archdiocese were ordained in the seminary at Roermond in the Netherlands. Würzburg, Tübingen and Eichstätt were other popular places of refuge. At the same time, Jesuits and Redemptorists were banned from the German Empire (1872-1917) and had to move their houses e.g. to Austria, the Netherlands or England. In Prussia, all orders and congregations, except those for the care of the sick, were suppressed in 1875; many of them went to the USA with its strong population of German Catholic immigrants (numbering about two million persons around 1900). The ordinary training of priests in Prussia could be slowly resumed only after the *Erste Friedensgesetz* (First Law of Peace) in 1886, when the discriminating *Kulturexamen* (literally 'cultural examination') of candidates for ordination was abolished; for the Polish dioceses of Kulm and Gnesen-Posen the seminaries at Posen (Poznan) could be reopened only in 1889. Similar situations could be encountered in Baden (archdiocese Freiburg) and to a lesser degree in Hessen-Darmstadt (diocese Mainz). Württemberg and Bavaria were relatively untouched, though not without confessional polarisation.

The *Kulturkampf* had some lasting secularising effects like the diminution of church influence on schools and the introduction of registry offices and compulsory antecedent civil marriage (until 2009). On the other hand, it brought a political mobilisation of Catholics on a scale unknown before. The Centre Party, founded in 1870, gained 24.8% in the election for the Reichstag (Imperial Parliament) of 1875, amounting to more than 80% of the Catholic vote. The number of Catholic papers doubled between 1870 and 1885: from 126 to 248. Two national centre papers emerged and remained influential until their suppression by the National Socialists: the *Kölnische Volkszeitung* (1868-1941), owned by the Cologne publisher family Bachem, and the more conservative *Germania* (1870-1938) from Berlin, with its priestly editor-in-chief Paul Majunke (1842-1899), a skilled confessional polemicist and typical 'press chap-

---

[21] Geschichtsverein, ed., *Kulturkampf*.   [22] Gatz, ed., *Der Diözesanklerus*, 105-124.

lain'. The years before 1900 saw the perfection of a veritable Catholic media system in Germany: in addition to the papers and various periodicals there were the printed pastorals of the bishops and the bilingual editions of papal pronouncements. There were also the big Catholic publishing houses: Herder in the first place, but also Pustet, Schöningh, Kirchheim, Aschendorff and many others. Their products comprised popular religious books for use in modest households like the *Kalender für Zeit und Ewigkeit* (first published in 1843) by Alban Stolz, or Goffiné's classic *Hauspostille* (first published 1690 with a multitude of later editions) or the annual *Haus- und Volkskalender* (since 1849) in Rottenburg; but also products for more advanced needs like the Catholic *Geschichte der deutschen Literatur* (1865; 12th edition 1911) by Gustav Brugier or the critical biography *Göthe* (1879-1882) by Alexander Baumgartner SJ (1841-1910). There were the Catholic *belles-lettres* that could be read without danger for religion and morals like the Catholic epic *Dreizehnlinden* (1887) by Friedrich Wilhelm Weber (1813-1894) which saw 200 editions at Schöningh. This wealth of production was presented in special Catholic review journals like the *Literarische Handweiser* (1862-1931) or the *Literarische Rundschau* (1881-1914).

Parallel to the political mobilisation in the Centre Party and the outreach in a Catholic media system, the organisation of Catholics in social, charitable and religious associations saw an unparalleled intensification between 1880 and 1914. Mainstream German social Catholicism, which opted for concrete reforms within the framework of a liberal society and a moderate capitalism, had its mass organisation in the *Volksverein für das katholische Deutschland* (seat: Mönchen-Gladbach). The idea of the *Volksverein* (People's Association) came from Ludwig Windthorst (1812-1891), the leader of the Centre Party, who wanted to create a Catholic counterpart to the social democratic movement. The *Volksverein* reached Catholics of all classes, counting 180,000 members in 1900 and peaking with 800,000 in 1914. It organised social instruction on a broad scale which helped recruit leaders for the Catholic unions and the Centre Party. Besides, the *Volksverein* also did apologetic work by distributing tracts and booklets on religious questions, so as to enable workers to defend their faith in discussions.

Social mobilisation and organisation coincided with an intensification in the religious praxis of Catholics (church attendance on Sundays and reception of sacraments). The entire process shows analogies with the 'pillarisation' of society in the Netherlands, and has been described in recent research as the formation of a Catholic 'milieu'.[23] The overall trend of a Catholic intensification of religious life and socio-political mobilisation, however, varied from region to region: in rural Bavaria (diocese of Regensburg) for instance, the traditional Catholic way of life (*Lebenswelt*) simply persisted whereas in rural Westphalia around Münster a mobilisation was effected. An explanation for this is offered by the 'cleavage-theory': in rural Bavaria the cleavage factors of state-church conflict (*Kulturkampf*) and conflict between centre and periph-

---

[23] Arbeitskreis, "Konfession und Cleavages"; Holzem, "Das katholische Milieu".

ery (western provinces of Prussia versus Berlin) were lacking. Similarly, the formation of a 'milieu' depended on a certain 'critical mass' of Catholics in the cities: in Bochum, the gap between labour and capital and that between state and church were effective, whereas in Prussian industrial cities with very few Catholics they were not. With the lack of a serious state-church conflict in Bavaria the Catholic workers in Munich favoured the social democrats instead of the Centre Party.

The attitudes of Catholics towards the new German nation state were ambivalent. Before the Prussian victory over Austria and its allies in 1866 their mental orientation had clearly been directed towards Vienna and not towards Berlin. The Prussian occupation of Hanover, Nassau, Hessen-Kassel and Frankfurt was regarded with dismay by many Catholics. Bishop Ketteler of Mainz and Bishop Blum of Limburg, however, were quite happy to accept the new situation as they hailed the relative freedom of the church in Prussia. The unifying effects of the war against France in 1870-1871 were also felt among Catholics, although their religious interpretation differed from Protestant Germans: for the latter France was punished as godless and Catholic at the same time, whereas the German Catholics thought that the French Catholics received the just reward only for their religious decadence.[24] The Catholic historical construction of the German identity remained different, too: Luther as national hero of a "Holy Evangelical Empire of the German Nation" (as famously formulated by the Protestant theologian and anti-Semitic social politician Adolf Stoecker (1835-1909)) was unacceptable. Catholics favoured Saint Boniface instead, as the 'apostle of Germany' and father of a Christian nation.[25] The hugely successful charity for diaspora Catholics was aptly named *Bonifatius-Verein* (founded in 1849), whereas the Protestants had struck a more militant note with their *Gustav-Adolf-Werk* (already founded by 1832 and named after the Swedish king and 'saviour' of German Protestantism). After the disillusionment during the *Kulturkampf* the mental need for Catholic integration in the Reich was felt more and more keenly; Catholics wanted to have their fair share in an economically, politically and scientifically successful nation. The Fulda bishops' conference for instance demanded Catholic missions in the German *Schutzgebiete* (de facto colonies) and simultaneously the *Afrikaverein deutscher Katholiken* was founded in 1888 under the protectorate of the archbishop of Cologne. Even the Centre Party paid a posthumous tribute at the grave of Bismarck. The nationalisation of episcopate, clergy and laity made progress under Wilhelm II, who had some pro-Catholic tendencies. Male Catholic orders, e.g. the Steyl Missionaries and the Missionary Benedictines were allowed to take over missions in the new German colonies. On the other hand, Polish Catholics found help in the episcopate against state efforts towards their complete Germanization.[26]

Apart from the national loyalty, Catholics were often strongly attached to their 'local' monarchs: this is evident for Bavaria (with the Catholic Wittelsbach dynasty) and Württemberg, where the *Kulturkampf* had not been grave and where bishops

---

[24] Rak, *Krieg, Nation und Konfession*.
[25] Weichlein, "Religion und Nation". Cf. Smith, *German Nationalism and Religious Conflict*; Stambolis, "Nationalisierung trotz Ultramontanisierung".
[26] Gatz, ed., *Kirche und Muttersprache*.

St Boniface, *devotional image issued by* the Verein zur Verbreitung religiöser Bilder, *Düsseldorf, c.1860.*
[Leuven, KADOC]

and prominent Catholic professors usually received personal nobilitation (i.e. ennoblement, therefore: *von* Döllinger, *von* Hefele, *von* Kuhn etc.). Even in Baden with its strong polarisation and the special situation of a Catholic majority in the population and a Protestant dynasty, the *Großherzog* (archduke) was a popular figure.

Theologically, the religious crisis around 1900 was echoed in the *Reformkatholizismus* ('Reform Catholicism'-movement), which strove to integrate Catholicism into Wilhelmine society. The movement marked also a tendency towards internal pluralisation in German Catholicism and a modification of the ultramontane agenda. The effects of Vatican I and the Old-Catholic schism had severely damaged German Catholic university theology. Entire faculties like Bonn had been paralysed; others like Tübingen sought refuge in a self-imposed sterility and kept clear of controversial questions. The excommunication of Döllinger was a warning signal, and only in the 1890s did the field begin to come to life again. A leading figure was Herman Schell (1850-1906) who taught dogmatics and apologetics at Würzburg. Schell had a strong Thomist orientation, but worked for a modernisation of scholasticism, in order to make it more effective against monist tendencies in the Zeitgeist. He tried to integrate modern concepts of freedom and personality in theology and developed a dynamic notion of God as 'purest act', 'self-ground' and 'self-cause' (*Selbstgrund* and *Selbstursache*). Historical criticism (as found with Alfred Loisy in France) remained foreign to Schell, but he tried to present the traditional Christological notions in an actualised form according to contemporary cultural optimism and its stress on 'fresh vitality': Christ as 'vigorous personality' and 'fountainhead of the Divine which lives in modern culture'. Here, Schell was very close to contemporary Catholic 'Americanism' and its slogan "Church and Age Unite!". With regard to eschatology, Schell opted for milder solutions, which would allow for post-mortem penitence for 'deadly sins' - a rather progressive view in times when the material existence of hell fire was upheld by scholastic theologians like Joseph Bautz (1843-1917) at Münster.[27]

Schell tried to answer the fears and sensibilities of educated Catholics (*Bildungsbürger*), where he made a great impact.[28] Schell's breakaway from ultramontane cultural dualism became even more visible in his programmatic booklet *Der Katholizismus als Princip des Fortschritts* (Catholicism as Principle of Progress, 1897). In the context of a lively debate on 'Catholic inferiority' Schell and other reformers like the church historians Franz Xaver Kraus (1840-1901) and Albert Ehrhard (1862-1940) wanted to demonstrate the potential for modernity in Catholicism: this comprised the demand for free academic research, for theological studies at the universities rather than in 'Tridentine seminaries', and for a disentanglement of the all too close connection between Catholicism and Centre Party politics. Church historians like Ehrhard and

---

[27] Graf and Renz, eds., *Umstrittene Moderne*; Blaschke and Kuhlemann, eds., *Religion im Kaiserreich*; Weiss, *Der Modernismus in Deutschland*; Arnold, *Kleine Geschichte des Modernismus*; Hausberger, *Herman Schell*.

[28] Dowe, *Auch Bildungsbürger*. Similar attempts were made in England by George Tyrrell and St. George Jackson Mivart ('Happiness in hell').

Sebastian Merkle (1862-1945) opted for a revision of the ultramontane view of history: the Middle Ages should serve no longer as an ideal for all things Catholic. Renaissance Humanism and Catholic Enlightenment were rehabilitated and confessional polemics against the Reformation and Luther reduced in order to facilitate Catholic integration in the Reich. In the end, the reform Catholics did believe in Catholic superiority over Protestantism, but aimed at demonstrating this in a fair competition. Their option for inculturation brought sometimes with it a certain affinity with *völkisch* nationalism and liberal Protestant anti-Judaism; on the other hand, they were less prone to ultramontane aversions against freemasons and 'Jewish capitalism'.[29]

Reform Catholicism was not highly organised but internally diverse; loose personal networks which reached out to similar movements of 'liberal Catholicism' in Italy, France, England and the USA were dominant. The *Kraus-Gesellschaft* (Kraus-Association, named after the liberal Catholic Franz Xaver Kraus, who died in 1901) with its journal *Das 20. Jahrhundert* failed to unite the entire movement. More important was the cultural journal *Hochland* (1903-1941; 1946-1971), founded by the layman Carl Muth, a protagonist of the *katholische Literaturstreit* which was waged for and against the confessional character of literature. Muth opted for more literary freedom, though his outlook was not decidedly modern: Schiller and Goethe remained the classic models for him (still a comparatively progressive opinion in German Catholicism). *Hochland* tried to present all fields of culture and science and remained a formative influence on educated Catholics. It was nearly put on the Index in 1911.[30]

Although the bishops of Bamberg and Passau signed the appeal for a memorial of their friend Schell, deceased in 1906 after continued attacks on his orthodoxy, Reform Catholicism met - on the whole - with episcopal scepticism. Bishop Leopold Haffner (1829-1899) of Mainz had denounced Schell at the Roman Curia, where his main works were put on the Index in 1899. Other prominent adversaries were the bishops of Rottenburg and Trier, Paul Wilhelm von Keppler (1852-1926) and Michael Felix Korum (1840-1921). Keppler's public polemic against *Margarinekatholizismus* ('margarine Catholicism') in 1902 became famous; it was inspired by the conservative cultural pessimism of the *völkisch* author Julius Langbehn. The crisis escalated with the Roman measures against modernism after 1907. Critical church historians and historians of dogma like Joseph Schnitzer (1859-1939) were especially vulnerable. Careers within the church were ended or - as in the famous case of Franz Joseph Dölger (1879-1940) - led into other directions, away from theology proper and on more secure and positivistic fields like Dölger's project 'Antiquity and Christianity' with its trend towards cultural

---

[29] Baumeister, *Parität und katholische Inferiorität*; Landersdorfer, "'Hie Staatsschule, dort Kirchenschule'"; Hürten, "Karl Muths 'Hochland' in der Vorkriegszeit"; Blaschke, *Katholizismus und Antisemitismus*.

[30] Haustein, *Liberal-katholische Publizistik*; Arnold, *Katholizismus als Kulturmacht*; Schmidt, *"Handlanger der Vergänglichkeit"*; Osinski, *Katholizismus und deutsche Literatur*; Merlio, "Carl Muth et la revue 'Hochland'"; Weitlauff, "'Modernismus litterarius'"; Busemann, "'Haec pugna verum ipsam religionem tangit'".

history. The Bonn New Testament scholar Fritz Tillmann (1874-1953) changed to moral theology after his reception of literary criticism had been complained about by the Roman Congregation of the Consistory. With the introduction of the anti-modernist oath in 1910, the existence of theological state faculties was endangered. The liberal university establishment and the governments initially refused to accept theologians who had sworn the oath. The episcopate, however, was anxious to preserve the status quo and to avoid another catastrophe like that after Vatican I; Pope Pius X eventually exempted the German professors from the oath. The intellectual problems of 'modernism' remained unsolved, but cropped up again - on a theologically lower level and in a transformed manner - in the various 'movements' (youth, liturgy, ecumenism), after the First World War.

In spite of these difficulties Catholic theology participated in the boom of 'German science' around 1900. Institutionally, 'seminars' were created, both in the sense of specialist libraries with studying facilities within the faculties (as in the splendid new university buildings of Freiburg and Würzburg) and as a new form of teaching, by which the students could be trained in a critical approach towards source documents and their interpretation. A prominent example for the fruitfulness of this innovation were the *Veröffentlichungen aus dem kirchenhistorischen Seminar München* (publications of the seminar for ecclesiastical history at Munich University), edited by Alois Knöpfler (1847-1921), where hopeful young theologians published editions and critical studies. In his speech in celebration of the emperor's birthday in 1907, Adolf Harnack (1851-1930), the prominent liberal Protestant church historian, praised the general scientific progress in Catholic theology as a hopeful sign for an interconfessional détente within the German nation. Harnack singled out Franz Wieland's (1872-1957) critical work on the historical development of the sacrificial character of Mass - which helped to bring Wieland into grave ecclesiastical troubles. Although many of the young talents were thwarted by anti-modernism, the overall innovation persisted. New 'scientific' journals like the *Theologische Revue* (founded in 1902 and modelled on the Protestant *Theologische Literaturzeitung*) or the *Biblische Zeitschrift* (founded in 1903) helped to intensify communication and mutual critique. New theological disciplines emancipated themselves and were institutionalised: *Missionswissenschaft* (missiology) was established as an ordinary chair at Münster in 1914. Its first incumbent, the Alsatian Joseph Schmidlin (1876-1944), was indeed the founder of this new branch in Catholic theology and his seminar at Münster served as a model for similar institutions around the world. Before the background of German colonialism, the project had been favoured by lay Catholics, the episcopate and the Prussian government alike. Christian archaeology as a science had been promoted in Germany by the liberal Catholic Franz Xaver Kraus, with his close contacts to Italy. After Kraus' death in 1901, his library and legacy were used for the creation of a *Seminar für Christliche Archäologie* at Freiburg Theological Faculty. His pupil Joseph Sauer (1872-1949), an important protagonist of Christian iconography, became the first incumbent of the ordinary chair founded in 1916. The impact of 'scientific' theology can also be measured by the increase in doctorates. The university faculties conferred doctorates, which were canonical and state degrees at the same time. Thus, Bonn, Freiburg, Munich, Münster, Tübingen and Würzburg were attractive centres of qualification. In Freiburg, for instance, 209 theological doctorates were conferred between 1870 and 1914 (compared with 60 between 1846 and 1870).[31]

In addition, Catholic chairs for history and philosophy (later called *Weltanschauungsprofessuren*) were established in the philosophical faculties of some universities, and many future priests acquired a doctorate there - often with prominent professors like the historian Heinrich Finke (1855-1938) at Freiburg or the philosopher Georg von Hertling (1843-1919) at Munich. Even the monastic and mendicant orders began to join in this movement in order to qualify their future lecturers. Thus, apart from the university professors a huge reservoir of ordained doctors of theology and/or philosophy was available. These men combined the pursuit of scientific interest with their pastoral work. A monument to their zeal is the *Kirchliches Handlexikon. Ein Nachschlagewerk über das Gesamtgebiet der Theologie und ihrer Hilfswissenschaften*, edited in two large volumes with almost 5,000 columns by Michael Buchberger in 1907-1912. The successor of this *Handlexikon* was the *Lexikon für Theologie und Kirche* (10 vols., 1930-1938) which established itself as the leading Catholic theological encyclopaedia (second edition 1957-1968 by Karl Rahner, third edition 1993-2001 by Walter Kasper). Already in 1902, Franz Xaver Funk (1840-1907), a leading critical church historian of his time, could sum up the success of Catholic theology in Germany rather assertively and with a certain cultural nationalism: "On the entire field of theology a higher scientific activity was developed [in Germany after 1815]. It is sustained by the theological faculties at the universities, to which other institutes of learning [e.g. the Bavarian *lycea*] have since been added. The opposition to Protestantism proved to be a strong incentive; and although this contact has sometimes been not without disadvantages, on the whole far more good for faith and science came out of it. The Romance peoples, who had held the first place in this field before, were now left behind by Germany. [...] They lack the theological faculties, which have shown themselves as so beneficial in Germany. In these countries the clergy is educated almost entirely in seminaries, and these institutes [...] proved to be no places of scientific research and work."[32]

Apart from these overall theological developments it is difficult to generalise about reform in '*the* German Catholic Church' before 1914. The episcopal conferences, which became more regular and important in these years, are a possible focus. After the unique event of the national conference in 1848, the Bavarian bishops met regularly from 1850 at the *Freisinger Bischofskonferenz*. Those from Prussia and the smaller German states did so from 1867 at the *Fuldaer Bischofskonferenz*. A second national

---

[31] Weiß, *Der Modernismus in Deutschland*; Schepers, "Widerspruch und Wissenschaft"; Wolf and Arnold, eds., *Die katholisch-theologischen Disziplinen*; Müller, *Joseph Schmidlin*; Arnold, *Katholizismus als Kulturmacht*; Müller, *Fünfhundert Jahre theologische Promotion an der Universität Freiburg i. Br.*

[32] Kany, "A Century of Catholic Theology"; Franz Xaver Funk, *Lehrbuch der Kirchengeschichte* (1902), 587, cit. after Wolf, "Der Historiker ist kein Prophet", 86. Cf. Arnold, "Konfessionalismus und katholische kirchenhistorische Forschung".

conference was held in 1905, but was established permanently only in 1933, when National Socialism made the need for joint decisions more urgent. A look at the protocols of the *Fuldaer Bischofskonferenz* shows a variety of topics that touch on the question of internal ecclesiastical reform.[33]

For example, the establishment of new parishes was apparently a main concern of the bishops, especially in the industrial Rhine/Ruhr areas.[34] The background is easily explained. The population in the area of the Deutsche Reich increased from 31.7 million in 1850 to 58 million in 1910 (the percentage of Catholics rose only slightly from 36.21% in 1871 to 38.99% in 1910). Mobilisation and urbanisation were concomitant effects of industrialisation. In 1907, 48% of the population no longer lived in their place of birth. This created pressing problems in the growing urban parishes. After the *Kulturkampf* a regular programme for the building of new churches began. As the income of the financially autonomous parishes from their local church tax did not suffice, diocesan offertories were held. In addition, under the presidency of Cardinal Georg von Kopp (1837-1914) the *Fuldaer Bischofskonferenz* made obligatory the formation of parish federations (*Gesamtverbände*) which received the right to raise church taxes, thus putting an end to parish autonomy and creating a system of subsidy for financially weaker parishes. At the same time a diocesan rate for church tax was fixed and an inter-diocesan assistance fund created. It was not only the financial side of pastoral expansion which posed problems; the double juridical difficulty (canon law and state law) of the founding of new parishes had to be overcome. Therefore, apart from the official foundation of a new parish or parish-vicariate (*Pfarrvikarie*) by canonical separation from its 'mother', a variety of models for the creation of semi-dependent *Filialkirchen* (daughter churches) was developed.

The new situation was not only dealt with in financial and legal ways; in 1911 the *Fuldaer Bischofskonferenz* discussed pastoral care in the big cities in a comprehensive sense as a new challenge. Archbishop Nörber of Freiburg presented a new concept of city pastoral organisation: apart from new parishes and vicariates he proposed detailed card files on the faithful in order to facilitate systematic pastoral visits to all Catholic households. A lay apostolate in the strict sense was not envisaged, but in the extension of the associations (*Vereine*) he saw an important help for pastoral care. It was therefore only logical that the bishops tried to establish more control over and more coordination of the Catholic associations. This applied for example to the various mission associations, founded by laymen (*Franz-Xaver-Verein*, *Kindheit-Jesu Verein*, *Bonifatius-Verein*). The *Charitasverband für das katholische Deutschland* founded by prelate Lorenz Werthmann (1858-1921) in 1897 was acknowledged by the conference in 1916 as the official umbrella organisation for all diocesan *Caritas* (charitable) committees.

The importance of the social question for pastoral care was another main concern of the bishops. Already in 1890 Franz Hitze (1851-1921), co-founder of the *Volks-*

---

[33] Gatz, ed., *Akten der Fuldaer Bischofskonferenz*.   [34] Id., ed., *Die Bistümer und ihre Pfarreien*.

The Catholic associations greet the dignitaries at the *Katholikentag* at Mainz in 1911, *photograph*. *[Leuven, KADOC]*

verein, had presented a memorandum to the *Fuldaer Bischofskonferenz* which asked for a special training of priests in this field. A deep division inside the conference was created by the problem of inter-confessional Christian unions which were favoured by the *Volksverein* (the *Mönchengladbacher* or *Kölner Richtung*) and the left wing of the Centre Party, whereas Cardinal Kopp and Bishop Korum (representing the *Berliner* or *Trierer Richtung*) championed the cause of the strictly confessional *Fachabteilungen* in the Catholic workers associations (*Arbeitervereine*). The latter were mostly led by priests and dependent on the hierarchy, whereas the *Kölner Richtung* aimed at a relative independence from the bishops in questions of social politics. Thus, the problem of 'integralism' was raised, which was central in the latter stages of the modernist crisis under Pope Pius X. The pope favoured the *Berliner Richtung*, but under strong political pressure from Germany his encyclical *Singulari quadam* (1912) made possible a toleration of the Christian unions, while the confessional *Arbeitervereine* were still clearly favoured by the pope. On the whole, the majority of German bishops were successful in moderating Roman influence in these years, thus saving social Catholicism and Christian democracy from the grave difficulties they had to undergo in Italy and France.[35]

---

[35] Brack, *Deutscher Episkopat und Gewerkschaftsstreit*.

Apart from the predominant interest in educational matters (confessional primary schools and religious instruction) the conference had to deal with a variety of questions that corresponded with the differentiation and modernisation of society in general. For instance, higher mobility increased the 'problem' of mixed marriages and their validity. Here the conference was successful in obtaining papal assent (1906) for an extension of the *declaratio benedictina* (1741) which had suspended the strict Tridentine rules for Germany. This very generous solution was replaced by a stricter policy only with the new *Codex Iuris Canonici* of 1917. From then on and well into the 1960s the old ultramontane 'battle against mixed marriages' (*Kampf gegen die Mischehe*) was fought more fiercely again. Mixed marriages were regarded as creating religious 'indifferentism' and as endangering the existence of small diaspora parishes.

War and Reform, 1914-1918

The First World War was interpreted by the German bishops as an occasion for the religious purification and self-reform of society. National integration was paramount, and support for the 'just cause' unanimous.[36] With self-confidence the Jesuit Peter Lippert (1879-1936) proclaimed that the edifying national solidarity and religious awakening at the beginning of war in August 1914 had also been prepared for by the pastoral and educational work of German Catholicism, whose priests had, in spite of all difficulties (*Kulturkampf!*), preserved the people mentally sane and physically fit and whose patriotic political and social activity in the associations had contributed to national education.[37] National unity was thus interpreted as a success of ecclesiastical reform and mobilisation. In this sense, the war was a grand opportunity for mission and outreach. The *Militärseelsorge* (pastoral care for soldiers) was well organised: Prussia had a *Feldpropst* (a military vicar-general with the rank of a titular bishop). In Bavaria this function had to be fulfilled by the archbishop of Munich-Freising. The numbers for Bavaria are interesting. Between 1914 and 1918, 401 priests served as army chaplains, while 1,354 theology students and candidates for the priesthood served in the army, many of them as medical orderlies. A disproportionately large number of them were killed: 504 (37.4% as compared to 15% in the army in general).[38] The students often rose quickly to become officers - with effects on their mentality that persisted during their later priesthood or episcopate (a prominent example is the later bishop of Münster, Michael

---

[36] Geschichtsverein, ed., *Christentum und Krieg in der Moderne*; Scheidgen, *Die Deutsche Bischöfe im Ersten Weltkrieg*.
[37] Peter Lippert, "Weltkrieg und religiöses Bekenntnis", *Stimmen der Zeit*, 88 (1915), 4-10, here 7, cited after Schreiner, "Helm ab zum Ave Maria".
[38] The percentage of fallen theology students was even higher in other places: Tübingen 55%; Paderborn 31.8%. Gatz, ed., *Der Diözesanklerus*, 145.

Keller (1896-1961)).[39] The theological faculties and seminaries tried to stay in contact with their students, not only by letter, but also with tracts and booklets.[40]

Theologically, the war created new opportunities for national ecumenism. During the Reformation Jubilee of 1917 a joint committee of Protestant and Catholic (church) historians (amongst others Harnack, Karl Holl (1866-1926), Sebastian Merkle and Martin Spahn (1875-1945)) was formed in order to overcome the confessional stereotypes concerning the interpretation of Reformation and Counter-Reformation (or Catholic Reformation). Catholic war theology itself became less triumphant from 1915 onwards and centred on the meaning of suffering. On the whole, the pronouncements of the German episcopate were more restrained than those of their Austrian colleagues.[41] The 'spectacle' of an open clash with the French episcopate, which had backed the propaganda work *La Guerre Allemande et le Catholicisme* (1915) and its interpretation of the war as an anti-Catholic Prussian aggression, was narrowly avoided and the task of anti-propaganda delegated to a working group of Catholic theologians, philosophers, historians and Centre Party politicians.[42] Christian universalism did not become entirely extinct, though reservations regarding the war were rare among the Catholic elites.[43]

'A New Time'

In contrast to Protestantism, the downfall of the German monarchies in 1918 left the Catholic Church institutionally untouched; unwavering feelings of allegiance to the monarchy were more or less confined to Bavaria. But implicitly, many dioceses had to 're-invent' themselves in terms of their identity, as their *raison d'être* had referred directly to the nineteenth-century monarchies. The solution was often inner mobilisation and further episcopalisation.[44] The Weimar Constitution brought the necessary 'liberty' for these developments, while preserving the privileged legal status of the churches. The inner mobilisation of the dioceses could profit from the anti-individualistic 'Zeitgeist' after 1918 and its predilection for the 'objective' which favoured the Catholic Church as a 'given' institution. The *Liturgische Bewegung* (liturgical movement), which strove to facilitate the 'active participation' (*actuosa participatio*: Pope Pius X) of the faithful in the Latin Mass (for instance by the German-Latin missal of Anselm Schott OSB) and the *Jugendbewegung* (youth movement) with its anti-bourgeois attitude and its option for 'freshness' and 'vitality' were amalgamated in German Catholicism by the

---

[39] On him Damberg, *Moderne und Milieu*.
[40] For instance Heinrich Finke, ed., *Kraft aus der Höhe. Ein Pfingstgruß ehemaliger und jetziger Universitätsprofessoren an ihre Kommilitonen im Felde*. Kempten-Munich, 1915; cf. Arnold, *Katholizismus als Kulturmacht*, 311.
[41] Holzapfel, "Krieg als 'heilsame Kreuzes- und Leidensschule'"; cf. Krumeich, "Gott mit uns"; Achleitner, *Gott im Krieg*.
[42] The so-called '*Arbeitsausschuss zur Verteidigung deutscher und katholischer Interessen im Weltkrieg*'; Scheidgen, *Die Deutsche Bischöfe im Ersten Weltkrieg*, 258-269; Arnold, *Katholizismus als Kulturmacht*, 310-317.
[43] Fuchs, *Vom Segen des Krieges*.
[44] Arnold, "Bistumsjubiläen und Identitätsstiftung".

theologian Romano Guardini, who gained influence in the *Bund Quickborn* (Quickborn Youth). The renewed perception of the church as *Gemeinschaft* ('community') became essential for the post-war generation of clergy and the educated laity. This coincided with a theological reorientation. The Barthian turn away from liberal Protestantism had its analogy in Catholic theology, where the old ultramontane anti-liberalism was now amalgamated with the anti-individualism of disillusioned 'modernists'. A typical product of this process was Karl Adam's (1876-1966) *Das Wesen des Katholizismus* (The Spirit of Catholicism, 1924) with its vitalistic and communitarian orientation.[45]

The liturgical movement gained additional momentum by the refoundation of monasteries after 1918, when the last obstacles against male orders and contemplative orders were removed. In Württemberg, for instance, the old Benedictine abbeys of Neresheim (1919) and Weingarten (1922) could be resettled. Bishop Keppler of Rottenburg and his colleagues favoured this 'holy Catholic spring' (*ver sacrum catholicum*) of the early Weimar Republic. On the diocesan level, purely clerical synods under episcopal control were held according to the new Codex of 1917 (e.g. Cologne 1919, Rottenburg 1919) which dealt with pastoral (e.g. catechism) and administrative (e.g. payment of parish priests) problems. In the diocese of Cologne in 1919-1920 several regional *Katholikentage* demonstrated the strength of organised Catholicism[46], even in times of crisis, when a national *Katholikentag* was not yet possible (the first after the war was held at Frankfurt in 1921). Eugenio Pacelli (from 1917 nuncio for Bavaria, after 1920 for the entire Deutsche Reich) was much impressed by the high degree of organisation in German Catholicism.[47] His aim, however, was to conform the German situation to the Roman ideals of theological neo-scholasticism, the centralistic *Codex Iuris Canonici* of 1917, and of the hierarchically controlled *Actio Catholica* (from 1922).

---

[45] Krieg, *Romano Guardini*; Ruster, *Die verlorene Nützlichkeit der Religion*; Raffelt, "Die Erneuerung der katholischen Theologie"; Wolf, "Der Historiker ist kein Prophet"; Arnold, "Konfessionalismus und katholische kirchenhistorische Forschung"; Krieg, *Karl Adam*; cf. Bucher, *Hitlers Theologie*.
[46] Klöcker, *Katholikentage im Erzbistum Köln*.
[47] Wolf and Unterburger, eds., *Eugenio Pacelli*.

The Protestant Churches in Germany and Ecclesiastical Reform

Klaus Fitschen

Enlightenment, Pietism and Political Crisis

Within Protestantism, Enlightenment and Pietism shared certain essential points. Both movements aimed at intensification of individual piety as well as at new forms of social contextualization of religion. The middle-class appetite for reading was used by both Pietists and Enlightenment thinkers to spread their particular concerns. Enlightened societies, such as the *Lesegesellschaften* (reading clubs) promoted literature and culture as a sophisticated surrogate for religion. Reading in Pietist conventicles, havens for people seeking a more intense form of Christianity, was concentrated on the Bible and pious tracts. In addition, both movements shared a critical stance towards the tradition of state churches - church and state were to be more strongly differentiated. On the other hand, the same tendencies led to impulses for reform from inside the church as well. Church practice was reformed and adapted to new needs. Sermons were versatile. They could address practical issues in agriculture just as easily as the promotion of piety. Funerals were held in the morning or in the evening to save time for the daily work and to avoid unnecessary expenses. Pastoral education was influenced by theologians inclined to either Pietism or Enlightenment.

There were also external influences. The Protestant churches in Germany completely reorganised themselves at the beginning of the nineteenth century. The reasons for this were the substantial changes in the political topography of Germany following the promulgation by the Holy Roman Empire of its final law, the *Reichsdeputationshauptschluß* of 1803, which secularised property and power. While the majority of German states had previously been coloured by a particular confession, now they were all confessionally mixed. Prussia had gained large Catholic populations in Rhineland-Westphalia, and Bavaria large Protestant areas in Franken (Franconia) and Swabia. The Catholic king of Bavaria was now the *summus episcopus* of the Protestants in his territory. The prince-bishoprics, which had been a fundamental part of the empire since the Middle Ages, had disappeared, along with several small secular territories. Germany was still not a nation state, but the large number of small states had now given way to a more manageable number. This new constitution for the states also required a new constitution for the churches within their borders. Lutherans and Reformed now had the same rights everywhere and the collective term for both, Protestants, became customary. At the same time, the question arose as to whether the increased self-organisation of the churches should occur within the framework of state churches, or bring with it a modification of that framework. Developments typical of the nineteenth century are exemplified by Prussia, the largest state in Germany and the vanguard of Protestantism. In Prussia, home to very diverse traditions of church administration, church reforms were discussed along with the political reforms which arose out of the defeat of the Prussian army by the French.[1] The central idea in this discussion was the self-administration of the church by means of synods in which not only ordained ministers, but also the laity would be represented. Within the individual congregations the synods were to be paralleled by *Presbyterien* (councils of elders) or parish councils which led and administered the congregation along with the pastor.

Friedrich Schleiermacher (1768-1834) played a leading role in these debates and was soon to become prominent as a university reformer and theologian. In 1808 Schleiermacher recommended a fundamental revision of the church constitution which would also serve to invigorate church life.[2] Members of the congregation and pastors, rather than state authorities, were to take responsibility for the church. The church would again be 'a self-regenerating living whole'. One significant goal of Schleiermacher's project of reform was to make the church more independent of state subsidies by allowing churches to own property and accumulate wealth. In addition, pastors were not to be appointed by the state or local patrons - landowners who were also responsible for the upkeep of the church building - but rather by the councils of elders and synods. In the synods, as Schleiermacher envisaged them, there would be no lay representatives, and the synods themselves would not actually be organs of self-governance. Rather, the synods were to perform the function of a pastors' conference, in which pastors could deepen their education. Schleiermacher's plans were generally very extensive. He even considered the possibility of a full Prussian synod to be called on a case-by-case basis and suggested that the church could have a spiritual head, an individual bishop, as its leader. In any case, each Prussian province was to have such a head cleric. A full disassociation from the state was, however, not what he wanted. Instead, the state was to appoint a representative who would have the ultimate control over the church and attend synods. Similar suggestions to those of Schleiermacher were made by 22 superintendents from the province of Kurmark in June 1814. In their plans for reform, synods also played a role, and were conceived as educational forums

---

[1] Goeters, "Die Reorganisation der staatlichen und kirchlichen Verwaltung".

[2] Nowak, *Schleiermacher*, part 3, ch. 13; Huber and Huber, eds., *Staat und Kirche*, I, no. 257.

F. Elias, Friedrich Schleiermacher, *lithograph, 1820.*
[Stuttgart, Württembergische Landesbibliothek]

for priests. The elders had fewer responsibilities in this plan than in Schleiermacher's. According to the superintendents, church elders were to have an advisory function and to be nominated by the pastor. As a result, this reform plan was accused of trying to establish clerical dominance.

Attempts at Ecclesiastical Self-organisation

The realisation of such plans encountered state and ecclesiastical resistance. Pastors did not find the prospect of sharing church leadership with a council of elders attractive, not least because rural pastors who occupied farms as tenants were already dependent on wealthy farmers. The state approved councils of church elders in 1816, but the patron was to have a seat and a vote. Synods were to be established at the level of the Prussian provinces and counties. A general synod would only be called five years later. The plans thus formulated by the state were only put into practice to a limited degree. In 1817, district synods met at the bidding of the state to confer on the drafting of a synodal constitution. It then became clear that there were both advocates and vehement opponents of the synods among the pastors. Provincial synods were held in the years 1818 and 1819, but they expressed very different positions on the question of separating the church administration from the state. The synod in the recently annexed western provinces went farthest in this regard. The synod in the capital city Berlin advocated an independent church administration, but also a continuation of the state's right of supervision. A spiritual head of the church was not proposed. It would be decades before synods and *Kirchenvorstände* (parish councils) were accepted by the state as self-governing organs. In the period of restoration after 1815, there was concern on the part of the state that synods would serve as breeding grounds for democratic-republican ideas. The state wanted synods only where these were conceived as pastoral conferences for the development of spirituality. Thus the provincial synods were not called a second time and the planned general synod only met in 1846.[3]

The Protestant church in Prussia continued to be led and administered by state ministries which worked even more efficiently than they previously had, since church administration was made uniform. The church remained financially dependent on the state. A particular concern of the in-church reform was the improvement of clerical training. At the behest of the Prussian king a *Predigerseminar* was founded in Wittenberg in 1817 on the occasion of the 300th anniversary of the Reformation. The seminary was open only for exceptionally qualified *Kandidaten* (candidates for the ministry) in order to give them an additional space of time for further studies and practical training. Wittenberg became a pattern for other institutions of the same kind. Clerical training all in all was controlled by the state. Protestant pastors and Catholic priests were regarded as state officials. They had to study theology at the faculty of a state university (independent faculties did not exist from the *Reichsdeputationshauptschluß*) for at least three years. Free churches or other religious groups were not allowed to run schools for the training of their preachers until the end of the nineteenth century.

However, state officials did have to take the particularities of the provinces into consideration. This can be seen especially in the province of Rhineland-Westphalia,

---

[3] Geck, "Die Synoden und ihre Sistierung in der Reaktionszeit".

which became part of Prussia in 1815.⁴ Here, especially in the Rhineland, there were old synodal traditions and long-standing precedents in the matter of church elders. King Friedrich Wilhelm III had recognised these traditions in 1816, and especially in Westphalia this encouraged a hopeful attitude. On the other hand, the synods and councils of elders were soon caught up in the process of restoration, which hindered their development. The Prussian system of state administration of the church by consistory officials limited the amount of influence available to synods and elders significantly. Protests by pastors and congregations at first had no effect. Particularly in the Rhineland, where republican ideas coming in from France were still a lively force, the self-organisation of the church led to suspicions on the part of the state that political power was being accumulated. Accordingly, even in Rhineland-Westphalia, efforts towards ecclesiastical self-governance were also suppressed after 1819. The synods in these provinces were to have only an advisory function.

The Prussian state very soon found it necessary to take a more moderate approach. The occasion for this change was the massive resistance encountered by the introduction of a new service book in 1822 which was supposed to cement the unification of the Reformed and Lutheran churches. Pastors and congregations in Rhineland-Westphalia made their acceptance of the new service book dependent on the recognition of synods and elders by the Prussian state, because the synods had been responsible for liturgical matters up to that point. In 1835 the *Rheinisch-Westfälische Kirchenordnung* (Rhenish-Westphalian Church Constitution) was approved by the Prussian king.⁵ The ultimate supervision of the church remained with the state, but the church had greater rights of self-governance than in other provinces. Councils of elders as well as county and provincial synods had significant responsibilities, and non-theologians also took part in them. The relationship with the state administration remained problematic, since it persisted in making life difficult for the heads (*Praeses*) of the provincial Rhenish and Westphalian synods. The state insisted on the right to approve decisions taken by the synods and protests against this position had no effect at first. When King Friedrich Wilhelm IV took power in 1840, there was an occasion for fresh hope. Although he was a conservative monarch, he was basically open to the idea of ecclesiastical self-organisation. State supervision of the church in Rhineland-Westphalia would thus be rescinded and the church supervisory office, the *Konsistorium*, more closely integrated into organs of church self-administration. Decisive steps were only taken after 1848 when the Prussian constitution granted the churches substantial rights of self-governance. In 1849 the provincial synods of Rhineland-Westphalia met but did not achieve consensus on the matter of how much authority they should leave with the state. The provincial synod of the Rhineland came very close to advocating separation of church and state, while the Westphalians held fast to the supervision of

---

⁴ Goeters, "Die kirchliche Reformdiskussion".

⁵ Neuser, "Die Entstehung der Rheinisch-Westfälischen Kirchenordnung".

the church by the state.[6] In March 1850 delegates of both synods met to promulgate a common plan for reform. The matter of state supervision was left to one side for that purpose, but the decision was still reached that the synods should elect the *Konsistorium*, the state office for supervision of the church. Since the Revolution had also come to an end, the plan for reform was never realised.

The position taken by Friedrich Wilhelm IV led to a discussion of reform involving greater independence for the church beyond the provinces of Rhineland-Westphalia from 1843 to 1846. Thus the Prussian state explicitly encouraged the holding of county and provincial synods in 1843 and 1844. The questions of the unification of Lutherans and Reformed and a common creed continued to be essential topics. It is striking that the king advocated ecclesiastical self-governance through synods in 1845. In 1846 a Prussian general synod finally met.[7] Thirty-seven members were clergy, and thirty-eight were laymen. The majority had been elected by provincial synods and sent as delegates. The general synod, however, did not really contribute to the self-organisation of the church, but instead concerned itself with the question of whether the Lutheran and Reformed theologians could produce a common creed which would be binding for the pastors. The resolutions of the synod were not accepted by the king and thus never took effect. The discussions on the reform of the church constitution likewise failed to deliver results. The attempts of representatives of the synods from Rhineland-Westphalia to encourage the use of the church constitution valid since 1835 as a guideline were fruitless. If they had borne fruit, the strong position of the elders and synods would have been put into effect in the eastern provinces of Prussia as well, which would have limited the influence of patrons in local congregations. The draft of the constitution which was accessible to the synod also maintained the *Konsistorium* as the highest office. Resistance on the part of representatives of the system of state churches was substantial. It was, however, still possible to strengthen the presbyterial-synodal element. The king would remain the head of the church and *Konsistorien* would have ultimate supervision of the churches in the provinces with an *Oberkonsistorium* at the top. Councils of elders and synods were to have authority only at the level of the congregations and counties. The decisions of the General Synod, particularly those regarding the presbyterial-synodical element, were never put into practice because of the revolution which soon followed. Only the plan for an *Oberkonsistorium* was realised in January 1848, producing the *Evangelischer Oberkirchenrat* in 1850.

---

[6] Neuser, "Die Revision der Rheinisch-Westfälischen Kirchenordnung".

[7] Id., "Landeskirchliche Reform-, Bekenntnis- und Verfassungsfragen"; Huber and Huber, eds., *Staat und Kirche*, I, no. 274.

The Erweckungsbewegung

Revival is not a clearly defined term. What is meant is a Protestant pattern of piety which linked into Pietism in the first half of the nineteenth century and was organised in societies or associations. This took place throughout Europe. The revival intended to fill religious life with new liveliness, new organisation, and new content. Part of the new content was the expectation of the Kingdom of God and the desire to promote its arrival through human activities. Another essential element was personal faith based in the experience of sin, conversion and forgiveness. Thus, as in Pietism and the Enlightenment, both the individualisation of faith and its contextualisation in the community played an important role. Both could take place independently of the state and the organised churches. The fact that members of the revival movement denounced the Enlightenment does not contradict their observable similarities.

The *Erweckungsbewegung* or revival movement showed great regional variation in its distribution.[8] It was ahead of its time in so far as it attached little value to the confessional boundaries among Protestant groups, between Lutherans, Reformed, the United Church in Prussia, Herrnhut Brethren, and others. Above all, in this movement, the impetus came from individuals, often working together. One of these was Johann Hinrich Wichern (1808-1881), whose main agenda was solving the social issue through a religious and moral revival amongst working-class people as well as amongst the middle-class. The *Innere Mission* (or Inner Mission: see below) was an influential expression of this revivalist concern. The revival movement fitted in well with the flourishing culture of civic associations in the nineteenth century and made full use of it. An early example of this can be found in the *Verein der Freunde in der Not* (literally, Association for Friends in Need) which was founded in Weimar in 1813 by Johannes Falk (1768-1826). In the revival, societies or associations were organised for distributing the Bible and pious writings, for doing missionary work among Jews and 'heathen' and also for caring for displaced children, for young people and others in precarious situations. A main engine of the revival movement was the *Christentumsgesellschaft* (literally, Society for Christianity) located in Basel.[9]

The goal of revival was not directly related to church organisation. What representatives of the revival movement wanted to influence was individual faith. Indirectly, however, this was bound to touch on the organisational forms of the churches. Since there were close relationships between the revivalists and the Herrnhut Brethren, the question arises as to whether the Brethren were not a sort of role model for many in the revival movement. In other countries, the revival led to non-established churches. This was not the case to the same degree in Germany, but the boundaries between the non-established churches or free churches (see below) and the revival were open.

---

[8] Benrath, "Die Erweckung innerhalb der deutschen Landeskirchen"; Gäbler, "Erweckung"; Ruhbach, "Die Erweckungsbewegung und ihre kirchliche Formation".

[9] Greschat, *Vom Konfessionalismus zur Moderne*, no. 46.

Johann Hinrich Wichern, *photograph, c.1860.*
[Stuttgart, Württembergische Landesbibliothek]

Gustav Werner, *photograph, c.1880.*
[Reutlingen, Bruderhaus Diakonie]

An example of this can be found in the Old Lutherans (see below) and their leader, the theology professor from Breslau, Johann Gottfried Scheibel (1783-1843). Another split came with the *Evangelischer Brüderverein* (Protestant Association of Brethren) which was founded in 1850 in Elberfeld near Wuppertal. Accordingly, the state had a critical view of revival groups. Religious self-organisation outside the established churches was hardly possible.

On the other hand, there were many followers of the revival who were integrated in established church structures and who tried to saturate both church and state with the priorities of the revival. Friedrich Julius Stahl (1802-1861), an important advisor to King Friedrich Wilhelm IV of Prussia, developed the concept of a Christian state. Johann Hinrich Wichern, the leader of the *Innere Mission*, was pleased to accept support from the Prussian king for his aims. Aristocrats who joined the revival movement and were patrons of church congregations introduced new forms of piety like prayer meetings and household devotions to the people on their landholdings and their congregations. These congregations did not, however, separate themselves from the established church. In Württemberg, the revival linked directly into Pietism. Here again separatist tendencies are noticeable, and these gained momentum through their millenarian expectations. To prevent emigration and to channel unrest, the *Evangelische Brüdergemeinde Korntal* was founded in 1819 with royal permission to organise itself. It was supervised not by the *Konsistorium* but by the ministry in Stuttgart directly. These forms of faith could not be completely integrated, however, so that in 1868 a group of Pietists from Württemberg emigrated to Palestine where they awaited the arrival of the millennium. In Reutlingen, Gustav Werner (1809-1887) also played a particular role with a form of faith which integrated both older forms of Pietism and teachings of the eighteenth-century mystic Emanuel Swedenborg. Werner, who tried his hand as an entrepreneur and social reformer, was supported by his own congregation. In the wake of growing conflict between Lutherans and members of the United Church in Prussia, confessional distinctions became important even among the revivalists. Among the *Altlutheraner* (Old Lutherans), the revival entered into a close relationship with Lutheran confessionalism.

Self-organisation of Dissenters: The Old Lutherans and Non-Established Churches

Friedrich Wilhelm III of Prussia had encouraged the unification of Lutherans and Reformed since 1817. In general, this programme had been successful, but in the following years and decades conflicts persistently arose, generally from the side of the confessionally-conscious Lutherans. The attempt of the king to introduce a binding service book was particularly exasperating. Their criticism could only be allayed by allowing for modifications to the service book according to confessional tradition.

Bitter resistance was maintained by confessionally loyal Lutherans in Silesia when it came to the question of union.[10] The Silesian Lutherans had held their own against the Austrian Catholic authorities until their integration into Prussia in 1740, and were not about to give up their confessional position for a union. While most accepted the offer of permission to modify the unionist service book given in a special addition to the document valid for that particular province, the hard core refused and was prepared to split. In a state church system based on confessional conformity, these determined Old Lutherans found themselves in the same position as any other minority confession, and they lost their right to the public practice of their religion. In 1834 even home services were limited to individual families, and failure to comply could mean a fine or imprisonment. Friedrich Wilhelm IV changed course when he took the throne in 1840. In 1845, the Old Lutherans gained the right to organise themselves into congregations. Many had since emigrated to North America or Australia. The Prussian Old Lutherans were not the only ones to choose to form a Lutheran non-established church. In other established churches there were similar splits, for example in 1878 in the state church of Hanover.

On the Protestant side, the *Verein der Protestantischen Freunde* (Protestant Friends), also called *Lichtfreunde* (Friends of Light), were basically the Protestant version of the *Deutschkatholiken* (an oppositional movement of German Catholics) and organised themselves as *Freie Gemeinden* (free parishes).[11] Many school teachers

---

[10] Nixdorf, "Die lutherische Separation"; Roensch and Klän, eds., *Quellen*, document 1, 17.

[11] Brederlow, *"Lichtfreunde" und "Freie Gemeinden"*, ch. 4; Obst, "Lichtfreunde, Deutschkatholiken und Katholisch-apostolische Gemeinden".

who had resented supervision of their school by the local pastor were members. Their leader was the Pastor Leberecht Uhlich (1799-1872) who was active in Pömmelte near Schönebeck and then in Magdeburg, and had been relieved of office in the Prussian state church in 1847. The programme of the movement was coloured by rationalistic ideas opposed to both revival and compulsory church confessionalism. Their main concern can be seen in the case of the Magdeburg pastor Wilhelm Franz Sintenis (1794-1859) who was reprimanded by his church leadership in 1841 because he rejected the worship of Christ, whom he considered a morally admirable human being. The Pastor Gustav Adolf Wislicenus (1803-1875) in Halle was more radical and more political. His aim was not the reform of church life or a rational interpretation of the Bible, but rather a decisive individualisation of faith. The improvement of society was an important goal, and so Uhlich and Wislicenus were both involved in the Revolution in 1848. Political and ecclesiastical protests were equally of high priority with both the Friends of Light and the German Catholics. Accordingly, both were legislated against. Private individual practice of religion was allowed to them, but not organised assembly as religious associations. A ban on the Friends of Light in 1845 did not go through without resistance and provoked a wave of protest in liberal circles. In 1846 the Friends of Light began to organise themselves into non-established churches, thus making a split with the state churches official. Like the German Catholics, the non-established churches also provided a forum for women. Thus the women's rights activist, democrat, and author Malwida von Meysenbug (1816-1903) joined the non-established church in Hamburg, which also ran a women's college.

Since the movement of religious dissent could not be broken by legislation, Friedrich Wilhelm IV found it necessary to allow freedom of worship, association, and conscience in a *Religionspatent* (edict on religion) of 1847. This religious freedom was then expanded from the individual to the corporate levels. With this edict of toleration, the Prussian state could establish continuity with the *Allgemeines Preussisches Landrecht* (General Prussian State Law) of 1794[12], which was still valid, and leave the recognition of new ecclesiastical or religious associations of the future open. After the Revolution of 1848-1849, the German Catholics and Protestant Friends soon found themselves marginalised and persecuted as democrats and rabble-rousers. The remnants of both movements joined together in 1859 in Gotha, forming a *Bund freireligiöser Gemeinden* (Union of Free Religious Congregations). They did not agree to a common confession, but made freedom of conscience their standard. Their meetings often did without conventional forms for church services. The congregations concerned themselves with criticism of religion. Although they deliberately continued to refer to themselves as *freireligiös* and originally preferred to have nothing to do with the non-religious freethinkers, both groups joined together in the 1880s.

---

[12] Goeters, "Bekenntnis und Staatskirchenrecht".

The 1848-1849 Revolution and its Consequences

The European revolutionary movement manifested itself in Germany in March 1848. There were demonstrations in Berlin which were violently suppressed. In order to placate forces of political unrest, King Friedrich Wilhelm IV ordered a memorial service for those killed in the conflict. The majority of Protestant theologians rejected the revolution as rebellion against the monarchy, since in their view monarchs derived their authority from God, while the fourth commandment demanded obedience to them.[13] The question was whether the revolution would provide the church with more freedom from the state. In Prussia, a commission was supposed to determine how self-governance through councils of elders and synods could be expanded. A full synod for all of Prussia was to be called to consider these questions. The plans for this originated with King Friedrich Wilhelm IV, but he encountered resistance in church circles, where the possible renewal of controversy about the union of Lutherans and Reformed was looked upon with apprehension. In the end there was only a conference which was held in 1856 at Schloss Monbijou.[14] With regard to ecclesiastical self-organisation, the main point on the agenda was that of parish councils. The conference decided to avoid reducing the rights of aristocratic patrons and refused the introduction of parish councils.

Even so, the Prussian constitution, introduced by the king in 1848, gave the church greater independence. This was in keeping with the will of the German National Congress meeting in Frankfurt, which stipulated accordingly in its draft of a state constitution. Every religious association, not only the major churches, should be allowed to regulate its own affairs, and no religious association should be given preferential treatment by the state. Although this state constitution was never ratified, the basic idea of greater freedom for the church from the state lived on. Full separation of church and state, however, was not what the established churches wanted to see. The basic idea of greater freedom for the church in relation to the state was also the aim in the revised Prussian constitution of January 1850, even if that freedom was again limited.[15] The recognition of non-established churches was also fundamentally restricted, so that up to 1918 they could only attain the status of a civic association, and not that of an officially recognised religious body (*Religionsgesellschaft*). After the suppression of the revolution, the state sought to control the church more stringently. A new office, the *Evangelischer Oberkirchenrat* (see above), was designed to supply evidence of greater independence for the Protestant church in Prussia, but it had no real significance. The *Evangelischer Oberkirchenrat* answered directly to the king and was thus separate from regular state administration. This council also supervised the synods and the clergy.

The plan for a full synod for all of Prussia, however, had taken care of itself. Self-governance for church congregations was strengthened by a new set of by-laws

---

[13] Besier, "Die Landeskirche und die Revolution von 1848/49".

[14] Meyer, "Monbijou-Konferenz".

[15] Sander, "Die oktroyierte Verfassung".

for the eastern provinces of Prussia. In the west, in Rhineland-Westphalia, congregational self-governance was already in place. Plans for an organisational renewal of the church from the congregations up were connected to this, but they were hardly put into effect. Many pastors and congregations had no interest in self-governance to any significant extent; this only arose in Prussia, Saxony, and Silesia in the formation of parish councils. In the province of Prussia (later the provinces of West and East Prussia) representatives of the parish councils also took part in regional synods. In 1855 they were required to do so. The programme of attaining independence for the church from the state was achieved in the established church of Oldenburg, whose general synod established a new church constitution in 1849. The ecclesiastical self-determination which had been intended by the national constitution was consistently put into practice. As early as 1853, however, the grand count of Oldenburg forced a revision of the church constitution which turned the church's right to self-administration into state sovereignty over the church.

Self-organisation on a National Basis

A major theme throughout the nineteenth century was the construction of national identities. Germany, even after the *Reichsdeputationshauptschluß* of 1803, consisted of multiple small states, and thus also had multiple Protestant state churches. In addition, confessional divisions appeared to be a significant obstacle on the path to unity. Thus it was natural that the question of church unity, whether within Protestantism or even between Protestants and Catholics, was among the tasks facing the Revolution of 1848, regardless of whether the case for the need for unity was implicit or explicitly made. Church self-organisation brought with it particular concerns in this context, especially the removal of boundaries between the Protestant state churches. The increased strength of Catholicism from the 1830s required this, as the *Kulturkampf* was in the making. Dreams of an interconfessional German national church, which accompanied the rise of the *Deutschkatholiken*, must also be seen in this context. In the 1840s, plans for cooperation between the state churches became more concrete. Prussia and Württemberg were the driving forces in this effort, and there was in fact a *Deutsche evangelische Kirchenkonferenz* (German Protestant Church Conference) in Berlin in 1846.[16] Only delegates of the state church administration participated (there were no representatives of the synods, which were only just being established). This can only be described as self-organisation inasmuch as there was a desire to depart from the particularism of the system of separate state churches. The church conference of 1846, however, only presented very modest achievements in this respect.

---

[16] Goeters, "Nationalkirchliche Tendenzen und Landeskirchen".

Another result of the Revolution was the establishment of the *Kirchentage* (church conventions), the first of which was held in September 1848 in Wittenberg.[17] One of the initiators was Moritz von Bethmann Hollweg (1795-1877), who had also been involved in the German Protestant Church Conference in Berlin in 1846. In the spring of 1848, Bethmann Hollweg and others had developed the idea of a conference for all of Germany which would discuss issues of a common creed and church constitution. There were even those who wanted to hold a German general synod. None of that was ever realised. Instead, conservative forces had the majority when further plans were made, and they wanted any such conference to serve as a bulwark against the Revolution. The driving force in this was Philipp Wackernagel (1800-1877) from Wiesbaden, who held a conference of representatives from conservative-revivalist movements near Frankfurt. This prelude was the source of initiatives to hold the planned conference, now referred to as *Kirchentag*, in an anti-revolutionary spirit. The main objective of discussion was to be the founding of a German church confederation in which Lutherans, Reformed, United Churches and Herrnhut Brethren would be included. The church confederation was to reflect the unity of the state churches. The participants were invited personally and had no vote or decision-making powers at all, but could formulate resolutions. When the *Kirchentag* met, it again became clear that the conflicts between Lutherans and United Churches made it impossible to reach consensus. The question of greater independence from the state was not on the agenda. The Lutherans had already had their own meeting in Leipzig at the end of August. The way out of the dilemma of the *Kirchentag* was finally found in a furious speech by Johann Hinrich Wichern on the social question.

A rival to the *Kirchentag* of 1848, which had been dominated by conservative forces, arose in the form of a meeting of representatives of liberal movements, including those from the Protestant Friends. This meeting took place on 26 April 1848 in Koethen and included discussion of a programme aimed at the separation of church and state. As with the model on which the non-established churches were based, each church congregation was to form an independent unit. County, provincial, and national synods were to include two-thirds of laypeople and were to be the highest organs of church leadership at whose head stood a national synod. The second *Kirchentag*, also held in Wittenberg in 1849, was concerned with ecclesiastical self-organisation through councils of elders. The fourth, in 1851 in Elberfeld, discussed the formation of regional synods. At the twelfth *Kirchentag*, in 1862 in Brandenburg, Emil Herrmann (1812-1885), a specialist in ecclesiastical law from Heidelberg, spoke on the foundations for a church constitution which could unify synodal and consistorial elements. It was thanks to Herrmann that self-governance of the churches made progress in Prussia. The *Kirchentage* however remained mere discussion forums. With the founding of the German Empire in 1871, the *Kirchentage* were suspended. The last one took

---

[17] Huber and Huber, eds., *Staat und Kirche*, II, no. 129; Goeters, "Der Wittenberger Kirchentag".

place in 1872. All momentum had been lost, not least because the later meetings had been mainly devoted to internal and theological topics. At the last *Kirchentag*, neither Lutherans nor theological liberals were represented.

The national unity achieved upon the founding of the German Empire constituted a new framework for efforts at church unity. Amid the general euphoria, even confessional differences were left to one side, and attempts were made to place the old idea of the *Kirchentag* on a new foundation. To this purpose a group of dedicated churchmen, including Johann Hinrich Wichern, were invited in the summer of 1871 to a conference to be held later that year. However, most of the Lutherans refused to participate: for them the whole project was merely an attempt to impose the Prussian Union on the rest of Germany. When the meeting began in October, it was unclear what should be on the agenda at all.[18] One important point was, again, the question of moving Lutherans, Reformed, and United Churches closer together, and with it the question of a common basis for the state churches. The result was a fight. Thus the October conference contributed neither to unifying the state churches on a national level, nor to the independence of the churches from the state.

The Eisenach Church Conferences

The *Eisenacher Kirchenkonferenzen* (Eisenach Church Conferences) had been held every two years since 1852 and were more effective than the *Kirchentage*, continuing until 1903.[19] While the *Kirchentage* meetings consisted of interested private individuals, the *Eisenacher Kirchenkonferenzen* were meetings of official representatives of the state churches. Here again the topic was not church self-organisation over against the state, but rather the resolution of questions which concerned all of the state churches.[20] Thus liturgy, church services, and the building of churches were recurring topics. The question of self-organisation was addressed when the roles of councils of elders and synods were being discussed. This at least led to a certain degree of coordination in the development of a church constitution. Besides this, the *Eisenacher Kirchenkonferenzen* supported the work of the *Innere Mission*, which was indeed an important element in self-organisation. In sum, the ability of the church conference to take action was still determined by differences of traditions, creeds, and interests among the state churches, along with misgivings about Prussia gaining dominance.

It was only about thirty years after the founding of the *Kaiserreich* that a national confederation of state churches came into being. The *Eisenacher Kirchenkonferenz* of 1900 resolved to form a commission dedicated to promoting the confederation of state churches and representing that confederation on an imperial level without surrendering any of the state churches' rights. At the conference of 1903, the *Deutscher*

[18] Besier, "Die Oktoberversammlung 1871".
[19] Rogge, "Kirchentage und Eisenacher Konferenzen".
[20] Huber and Huber, eds., *Staat und Kirche*, II, no. 130.

General Synod in Ansbach in 1849, *lithograph*.
[Nürnberg, Landeskirchliches Archiv der Evangelisch-Lutherischen Kirche in Bayern]

Evangelische Kirchenausschuß (German Protestant Church Commission) was founded and took the place of the Eisenach conferences.[21] However, the church commission only had limited powers, so that in effect the state churches still made the decisions. Emperor Wilhelm II supported this undertaking and provided his legal recognition of it in 1905. The church commission saw itself as close to the state and, further, as anti-Catholic. Since the president of the Prussian *Evangelischer Oberkirchenrat* was also the head of the church commission, the church commission had a close connection to the state's church administration. As a representative of Protestant interests on a national level, it also considered itself responsible for Protestant Germans abroad.

---

[21] Sander, "Deutsche Evangelische Kirchenausschuß"; Huber and Huber, eds., *Staat und Kirche*, III, no. 223.

Political Liberalism and Self-organisation of the Churches

In Prussia, the New Era of 1858 led to greater freedom in the self-organisation of Protestant churches.[22] King Friedrich Wilhelm IV had begun to suffer from mental illness and the regency was taken over by the crown prince Wilhelm. He formed a liberal government. Measures taken against the non-established churches were halted, and their members were even allowed to provide religious instruction to their children in the schools. The church by-laws of 1850 were to be binding; if local congregations failed to form councils, the *Evangelischer Oberkirchenrat* was to do so. The motto was basically self-organisation from above. The patrons were to keep their rights, which put another limitation on self-organisation.

In 1861 the holding of regional synods was also required in the province of Prussia, and the same obligation appeared in other provinces very soon afterwards. The initiators of this rule were the *Evangelischer Oberkirchenrat* and the Ministry of Culture. Thus one can only describe this as self-governance in a very limited sense. Since the pastors, who were basically state officials, and the superintendent, who was appointed by the state, formed the majority in the regional synods, the state still had decisive influence. On the other hand, the state administration of the church wanted the *Kreissynoden* (representative bodies on the level of the counties) to be the bases for new provincial synods. In the same year, 1861, Prince Wilhelm was crowned King of Prussia as Wilhelm I, which led to a conservative reorientation on his part. His initial openness to increased independence for the churches disappeared.

Expansion of the Synods

The unification of Germany under an emperor - this time a Protestant one - placed Protestantism in the mainstream. The consequence was a *Kulturkampf* or clash of cultures on the one hand and the attempt to gain more independence for the Protestant churches on the other. Wilhelm I, who was now not only King of Prussia but also Emperor of Germany, pushed for the introduction of synods and parish councils throughout the older provinces of Prussia. In 1873 this was established by law. The basis for self-administration of the churches was applied directly to church congregations. However, the traditional rights of the patrons were maintained, and they received a seat and a vote in the local parish councils for themselves or their representative. One essential task of the local parish council was the religious and moral formation of the congregation. While the local parish councils did not supervise the pastors' work, they were responsible for the finances of the congregation. Nowhere near all congregation members had a vote. Even in the churches, women did not yet have the right to vote. Moreover, voting was connected to a certain degree of economic independence. The

---

[22] Besier, "Die 'Neue Ära'".

regional synods had similar tasks but at a higher level. They supervised the work of the pastors and audited the financial administration in the congregations. At an even higher level was the provincial synod, which, among other things, was responsible for the introduction of new textbooks for religious instruction and new prayer books.

In 1875 there was an extra Prussian general synod which was just as unrepresentative as the one of 1846.[23] The synod was called by the king, who only invited a few liberals among a majority of aristocratic and upper-class representatives. This general synod was rejected by conservative Protestants, and on the liberal side there was a call for greater inclusion of laypeople and non-theologians. Real self-organisation was not possible under such conditions, and instead the internal disunity of Protestantism came to the fore. In this, confessional conflicts between representatives of Lutheranism and the union of Lutherans and Reformed again played a major role.

Plans for a Self-financing Church

The Protestant churches were financially dependent on the state. Because of this, church self-organisation was impossible without greater financial independence. One means of achieving this was church tax, which was only slowly introduced and only partially able to cover the churches' financial needs.[24] Church tax was primarily a tax for the local parishes which served to finance additional expenses e.g. for church buildings. It was expressly intended only for the augmentation of the other church income from their property or investments or donations from aristocratic patrons. In spite of the taxes, the churches still depended on state subventions which were paid on the basis of need and not as a fixed sum. This also applied to the salaries of pastors which were based on a mixed church and state financing system and then regulated in Prussia in 1898 with the introduction of salary scales.

Further plans for greater financial independence of the Protestant churches in Prussia were put forward by the conservative aristocrat Hans von Kleist-Retzow (1814-1892), who was joined by the conservative politician Wilhelm Freiherr von Hammerstein (1838-1904).[25] Both increased their activities in the wake of the *Kulturkampf*, whose result was a secure position for the Catholic Church. The Protestant Church, in the opinion of Kleist-Retzow and Hammerstein, could only be on an equal footing with the Catholic Church if it had a more independent position in relation to the state. When these two men submitted a proposal to the Prussian *Zweite Kammer* (House of Representatives) in 1886 to this end, it failed. Most representatives were apprehensive about giving the Protestant Church too independent a position on the model of the one the Catholic Church already had, and considered state control over the church

---

[23] Rogge, "Die Außerordentliche Generalsynode"; Huber and Huber, eds., *Staat und Kirche*, II, no. 445.

[24] Marré, "Die Kirchenfinanzierung in Deutschland"; Huber and Huber, eds., *Staat und Kirche*, III, no. 24.

[25] Besier, "Die Kleist-Hammersteinschen Anträge".

to be in danger. Nevertheless, Kleist-Retzow and Hammerstein tried to submit their proposal again to the Prussian *Erste Kammer* (House of Lords). There it was accepted. What followed was a controversial public discussion. Both supporters and opponents of the proposed project could be found in the Protestant Church in Prussia. In 1887, the two conservatives put forward another draft for a law intended to make greater independence of the synods from the state and better financial resources for the Protestant Church possible. These efforts came to nothing: the top priority in church politics in Prussia at the time was peace with the Catholic Church and the end of the *Kulturkampf*. The *Evangelischer Oberkirchenrat*, that is, the organ which was dependent on the Prussian state, attempted to find a third way. On the one hand, the church should not be separated from the state, but on the other hand, the church should receive more independence. The *Evangelischer Oberkirchenrat* could refer to resolutions of the general synod of 1891 which had favoured greater independence from the state in a few particular issues. The synodal representative Adolf Stoecker (1835-1909) became an opponent of this compromise. He had a reputation for being an anti-Semite, but was also a leader of the *Innere Mission* in Berlin and speaker of the synodical party Positive Union. So he had his own basis of support. Stoecker produced intense polemics about the state church system.[26]

Even in Prussia, it was clear at the end of the nineteenth century that criticism of the state church system was no longer coming from outside, in particular from social democrats, but also from a large section within the church aiming at a reform of the system. The hobbling of the church by the state appeared to prevent the church from having any real opportunity to have an effect on society. Stoecker and his followers complained that the communion of believers had turned into a community of taxpayers and that the state church system forced all church movements into compromises which damaged the preaching of the gospel. The motto of this group was *freie Volkskirche* ('free people's church'). The ruler of the land, in this case the Prussian king, was not to be head of the church any longer, but rather its patron. Dissatisfaction with the state church system gained strength when the state conceded more freedoms to the Catholic Church in the *Kulturkampf*, but kept the Protestant Church under its control.

Self-organisation in Liberal Protestantism[27]

In 1863, the *Protestantenverein* (Protestant Association) was founded as a meltingpot of liberal Protestantism, that is, of the Protestant educated middle-class.[28] Its establishment was a reaction to the introduction of a new service book and catechisms on the part of the state church administration. Seen from the perspective of church liberals, this was a sign of the dominance of conservative orthodoxy in the church, which

---

[26] Huber and Huber, eds., *Staat und Kirche*, II, no. 221.
[27] Hübinger, *Kulturprotestantismus und Politik*.
[28] Lepp, *Protestantisch-liberaler Aufbruch*, ch. 2.1 ("Grundlagen") and 2.2 ("Die Entwicklung"); Schenkel, *Deutsche Protestantenverein*.

it was necessary to counteract. Many liberal politicians who connected their political reform plans to concerns for the reform of the church were involved in the *Protestantenverein*. Its aims were articulated at the *Protestantentage* (Protestant Conventions). At the first *Protestantentag* in 1865, the association constituted itself formally. The question of church organisation was persistently an important one at these meetings, without which its discussion could not have taken concrete effect. It was expressly stated that reforms in the church were wanted, but not a separation from the state. At exactly the point where liberals were strongest in politics, it was hoped that church reforms could be put through on the same path as political reforms. This group saw the church constitution of Baden of 1861 as an example. It gave parish councils and synods a strong position, but maintained state supervision and the headship of the local patrons.

The *Protestantenverein* was organised throughout Germany and thus a part of the German national movement, but it also had a regional focus. On the regional level, the association organised branches which were independent of each other and could thus develop different programmes. According to the association's leadership, reforms of the church organisation needed to be adapted to the diverse requirements of the individual churches. At the same time, the churches were to be brought into a closer relationship with each other. What was planned was thus not an imperial church, but rather a federation of all state churches. The association was strongest in the southwest of Germany, especially in Baden, where political liberalism was also very strong. The *Protestantenverein* was not a mass movement (in 1908 there were roughly 50,000 members) but the ideas behind it placed it among the associations which most clearly realised Protestant self-organisation. Representatives from the liberal Protestant middle-class came together to organise themselves separately from the structures of the state church. On the other hand, the *Protestantenverein* could not bring itself to pursue the separation of church and state, as its members were too closely connected to the state themselves. The idea, rather, was to reform Protestantism from within and to form a church which was able to enjoy greater independence from the state. Along with this came the idea to make a people's church out of what had been a pastor's church, and thus to strengthen the position of laypeople according to the ideal of the priesthood of all believers. The alienation from the church experienced by many people was seen as a sign of crisis even in liberal circles. However, most leaders within the association were pastors themselves. Self-organisation was characteristic of pastors in this period, and pastors' associations were founded to represent the interests of their members. An important aim of these associations was a greater independence of the pastors from the state church administration. The goal was the introduction of ordained heads of the church, basically of bishops.

The 1865 statutes of the *Protestantenverein* included in their first paragraph a programme for the planned reform of the church. The goal was "renewal of the Protestant Church in the spirit of evangelical freedom and in harmony with the entire cultural development of our time". This was supposed to occur on the basis of the *Gemeindeprinzip* (congregational principle). The church was thus to be organised from the level of the congregations upwards and outwards, and laypeople (non-theologians) were to play a decisive role. Parish councils and synods were, for the *Protestantenverein*, an ambivalent means of self-organisation. On the one hand, they were necessary for the reforms being pursued, but on the other hand it became clear that not the liberals, but rather the conservatives consistently had the majorities. In sum, how exactly the reform of the church should be carried out was controversial among the members of the association and its leaders. In the course of time, it was seen that the association could not push through their reforming aims and did not have support among church members in general.

A concrete blueprint for reform from a liberal perspective was put forward by the pastor Emil Sulze (1832-1914) of Dresden in 1891 with his book *Die evangelische Gemeinde* (The Protestant Congregation). Sulze argued for making the parish congregations more manageable and dividing them into *Gemeindebezirke* (parish districts). A council of laypeople was to have responsibility for the parish districts and the larger parish, which Sulze termed respectively *Presbyterium* (for the parish districts) and *Kirchenvorstand* (for the whole parish). Although the pastor had a key role on this scheme, it was mainly intended to organise the church into more coherent parish structures. In 1887, Martin Rade (1857-1940) founded the journal *Die Christliche Welt* (The Christian World) which intended to be open to a broad spectrum within Protestantism, but primarily represented the views of liberal Protestantism (the German term is *Kulturprotestantismus*). His target group, according to the by-line of his newspaper, consisted of educated people of all classes. Associated with the newspaper was a circle of 'Friends of the Christian World', with 1,415 members in 1913, mostly pastors and theologians.

The *Protestantenverein* and Friends of the Christian World did not form a coalition of interests. The *Protestantenverein* considered the Friends of the Christian World too distant from the church and conforming too closely to contemporary culture. Liberal Protestantism, in the late nineteenth and early twentieth centuries, was under pressure from the church and the state. Liberal pastors were suspected of losing their faith and reprimanded. *Die Christliche Welt* tried to soften such accusations by presenting a modern form of Protestant religiousness. On the other hand, the *Protestantenverein* attracted a great deal of attention when it held the *Weltkongress für freies Christentum und religiösen Fortschritt* (World Congress for Free Christianity and Religious Progress) along with the 'free religious' movement in Berlin in 1910. While the Friends of the Christian World participated, there was controversy within their ranks about whether that participation was appropriate. It was clear that the World Congress provided a platform for those who no longer felt at home in the established churches.

The *Evangelisch-Sozialer Kongress* (Protestant Social Congress) was similarly an organ of liberal Protestantism.[29] It was founded in Berlin in 1890 with strong support

---

[29] Neuser, "Das soziale Experiment des Kaisers"; Greschat, ed., *Vom Konfessionalismus zur Moderne*, no. 102 and no. 109.

Friedrich Naumann, *photograph, c.1900*.
[Potsdam, Friedrich-Naumann-Stiftung]

Adolf von Harnack, *engraving, c.1900*.
[Leuven, K.U.Leuven, Universiteitsbibliotheek]

from Stoecker and was meant to be representative of all movements within the church. This association considered its task to be "the unprejudiced investigation of social conditions among our people", but did not intend to involve itself in "socio-political agitation". One important cause for its founding was the set of initiatives of Emperor Wilhelm II, who, at the time, sought to define himself as a 'social emperor'. The liberal politician Friedrich Naumann (1860-1919) and the social democrat Paul Goehre (1864-1928) were both members of the *Evangelisch-Sozialer Kongress*, and both eventually left the pastorate and the *Kongress* because they found it too conservative. Naumann entered into politics because he felt he could thus better achieve his goal of establishing a cooperation between church-based and political social aid. In 1907 he represented the liberal *Freisinnige Vereinigung* (Association of Liberals) in the Reichstag. In the discussions about the constitution in 1919 he played a major role in redefining the relationship between church and state. The *Evangelisch-Sozialer Kongress* had 1,950 members in 1913. They were organised into regional associations and were a part of the self-organisation of liberal Protestantism which did not go beyond the original goals or harbour ambitions to reform the church.

Theology, taught at the universities of the German states, became a specific source of reform and of self-organisation, too. *Liberale Theologie*, represented above all by Adolf von Harnack (1851-1930), provided an academic foundation on which part of the German middle class could build its ideas of an amalgamation of Protestantism and culture. Other theologians, more inclined to Lutheran confessionalism or to theological conservatism, regarded themselves as the backbone of monarchy and society. Although Protestant theologians, unlike their Catholic colleagues, were not subject to reprimands by their church, they were sometimes accused of a kind of Protestant 'modernism'. When Catholic anti-modernism developed and came to its peak at the end of the nineteenth and at the beginning of the twentieth century, Protestant pastors and theologians were involved in struggles about the Apostolic Creed, namely its clauses on the Virgin Birth and the descent into hell.

The *Innere Mission*

The social question entered the public consciousness gradually at first. It was primarily taken up by revivalist Protestants who saw a connection between the suffering of the workers and unemployed and their alienation from Christianity and the church. This was expressed in the term *Innere Mission*, which appeared in the 1840s. People were to be helped not with their external needs, but rather brought back to the Christian faith. Johann Hinrich Wichern made this his goal and spread the idea throughout Germany in the following years.[30] At the *Kirchentag* of 1848 in Wittenberg he took the opportunity to present his agenda, and this helped his cause when the Central Committee for the *Innere Mission* was founded in 1850 out of the *Kirchentag*-movement. Wichern was head of that committee for many years.

In the time of the *Kaiserreich*, the *Innere Mission* achieved a broad level of activity which ensured public attention. Since the *Kirchentage* were suspended with the founding of the empire, the Central Committee had to be re-organised, as its work had been closely tied to the *Kirchentag*. The Central Committee, which grew by means of voting in new members, became a new organ of the Protestant upper classes in the empire. It included not only Wichern, but also the founder of the Bethel institutions, Friedrich von Bodelschwingh (1831-1910). In 1887 the professor of theology Bernhard Weiss became chairman, and in 1898 the director of the *Reichsversicherungsamt* (Imperial Bureau of Insurance), Otto Gaebel (1837-c.1910), succeeded him. In 1907 the chairman was Friedrich Albert Spiecker (1854-1936), a trustee of the Siemens company. An important member of the Central Committee was Theodor Lohmann (1831-1905). He was an important advisor to the imperial chancellor Otto von Bismarck, but was made to resign in 1884. The reason for his dismissal was that Lohmann wanted the social insurance system planned by Bismarck to be self-organising, since this corresponded to the basic aims of the *Innere Mission*. Bismarck, however, wanted strong state influence.

The *Innere Mission* became influential due to the high degree of dedication on the part of the middle classes. Associations were founded, partly aimed at particular groups. However, these associations did not simply take over the popular association concept of their day, but reconceived it in a Christian spirit. For Wichern, such civil

---

[30] Albert, *Christentum und Handlungsform*, ch. A.I.3 ("Die Vereinskultur") and B.II.4 ("Der Verein").

The association building of the *Innere Mission* in Leipzig, *engraving, c.1880*.
[Leipzig, Diakonie Leipzig]

associations were simply the external form of the priesthood of all believers. The associations were to contribute to building up the kingdom of God, much in accordance with the ideals of the revival movement. Within the church, questions arose about what constituted an appropriate relationship between the associations of the *Innere Mission* and the pastorate and about how to relate to the self-understanding of many pastors. Especially on the side of the Lutherans, Wichern's idea of civil associations was rejected. On the other hand, the boards of the *Innere Mission* did not exactly share Wichern's enthusiasm for the associations, but saw this form of organisation more as a pragmatic issue. Wichern had founded a first *Stadtmission* (city mission) in Hamburg in 1848 on the example of the London City Mission, and further such missions were founded in additional cities, mostly in the time of the *Kaiserreich*. The city missions entered into competition with local churches and pastors, since they were not part of the state church, but rather private institutes financed by boards of trustees. In Berlin, the city mission employed a total of 56 missionaries and 8 parish sisters in 1906. The missionaries' main tasks were to visit workers' homes, many of whom had already broken off their connection to the church, and to hold devotional sessions and Bible studies. The city mission succeeded in strengthening the presence of Christianity and the church in the cities, and, not least, also provided concrete aid. However, it did not achieve any long-term missionary success. The city missionaries were not originally from the working classes, but from the commercial or middle class, and in a strictly socially differentiated society, this presented a major obstacle to communication.

Friedrich Wilhelm Raiffeisen (1818-1888) had come into a close relationship with the *Innere Mission* through friends. Raiffeisen had become familiar with economic want in the countryside while in the Prussian civil service and founded aid associations as a measure to counteract the hardship he observed. The birth of the Raiffeisen movement came with the founding of a loan association in 1854, in which local pastors were also involved. The loan banks were intended to counteract the accumulation of debt which resulted from the activity of private moneylenders, and allow small farmers cheap loans for necessary investments. The Raiffeisen associations were based on mutual obligation, which the founder based on a reading of Acts 2:44. Later, the Raiffeisen associations also concerned themselves with low cost bulk buying of farming equipment.

Since the church saw itself as a factor in social stability, there was hardly any possibility for it to fraternise with the working classes. Pastors themselves often came from pastors' families or from the lower middle class, which, in the nineteenth century, increasingly formed the basis of church congregations. Pastors mainly associated with their colleagues and lost contact with the social life of the middle class.[31] The Protestant established churches had little interest in an organised system of social aid, called *Diakonie*. This was a matter for the *Innere Mission* and its associations. The founding of larger charitable institutions should be seen in this context. Wichern had started collecting abandoned young people in 1834 in Hamburg, and from that had formed not only an institution for the care and education of children and young people, but also a school for men to be trained to care for the children and young people at the institute. At the same time, Theodor Fliedner (1800-1864), along with his wife Friederike (1800-1842), founded a school in Kaiserswerth for the training of lay sisters who shared a common ascetic life. Fliedner's foundation was the example for many others. Similar institutions were founded by Wilhelm Löhe (1808-1872) in the Franconian village Neuendettelsau and by Friedrich von Bodelschwingh in Bethel.

The idea of self-help and self-organisation for the workers was central to the *Innere Mission*. The workers were to come together in cooperatives and associations, for example in buying co-ops or housing associations which were to engage in wage negotiations with employers. Through this, the workers were to become able to own goods and contribute to the maintenance of social and economic order. Political rights were still often dependent on economic status at this time. The workers were to receive financial and non-material support from the higher classes who were also to participate in the workers' associations, a plan which proved illusory. Enthusiasm for this inter-class cooperation was just as lacking on the side of the workers as on that of the middle-class participants.

---

[31] Hölscher, *Geschichte der protestantischen Frömmigkeit*, 273-280.

Large Associations

In 1832, the battle in which the seventeenth-century Swedish king Gustav Adolf II had died was commemorated in Lützen near Leipzig. For Protestants, Gustav Adolf had been the knight in shining armour during the Thirty Years War. Without him, all of Germany would have been re-catholicised. The commemoration was the occasion for the establishment of a foundation to help Protestants living in a situation as minorities, not only in Germany, but also in Europe and around the world. In 1841 an association was founded in Darmstadt with the same purpose. Both branches of this movement combined in 1842 to form the *Evangelischer Verein der Gustav Adolf Stiftung* (Protestant Association of the Gustav Adolf Foundation), located in Leipzig.[32] It was supported by Leipzig's middle class and was thus a part of bourgeois Protestant self-organisation. After this association settled into the cities, it became a major network. The *Gustav Adolf Verein* became organised beyond the boundaries of the Protestant state churches and did not concern itself with inner-protestant divisions. Lutherans, Reformed, and United Churches were all able to be involved. The association was not able to remain free of state influence for long, and did not want to. The Prussian king Friedrich Wilhelm IV became patron of the Prussian branch of the association in 1844. Thus the association actually did become dependent on the state church system and accordingly refused to support dissenters within the church as well as Protestant non-established churches and the German Catholics.

The founding of the *Evangelischer Bund* (Protestant Federation) also had a long-term effect.[33] It occurred after the end of the *Kulturkampf* in 1886, when Protestantism was facing a strengthened and politically influential form of Catholicism.[34] The main goal of the *Evangelischer Bund* was opposition to ultramontanism on the one hand, and materialism and social democracy on the other, together with support of a national form of Protestantism.[35] In 1914 the Protestant Federation had roughly 500,000 members who, like the members of the *Gustav Adolf Verein*, were organised into main, branch, and local units. The *Evangelischer Bund* engaged in intensive public relations and held general meetings which dealt with controversial theological topics. Many men from the state and church leadership were members, such as consistorial councillors, lawyers, and landowners.

The fact that the *Gustav Adolf Verein* saw itself as inner-Protestant and supra-confessional, provoked a reaction from the side of the Lutherans. As a result, the Lutherans founded the *Gotteskastenverein* (literally, Association of the Divine Treasure Chest), a competing association which was intended mainly to support emigrants. This association was a model for many others in Germany which joined together in 1932 to form the *Martin-Luther-Bund* (Martin Luther Federation). The *Gustav Adolf Verein*

---

[32] Kaiser, "Integratives Moment des deutschen Protestantismus"; Beyer, *Geschichte des Gustav-Adolf-Vereins*, 109-127; Fitschen, "Vormärz".
[33] Grote, "Der Evangelische Bund".
[34] Besier, "Beilegung des Kulturkampfs".
[35] Huber and Huber, eds., *Staat und Kirche*, III, no. 219.

was the first Protestant group which provided women with the opportunity to be involved, though without implying support for their wider emancipation. In 1851, the first women's group was founded.

Self-organisation of Protestant Women

Diakonissen (deaconesses) represented a new vocation which had an effect on the way women's issues were dealt with in the church. In contrast to the image suggested by the workers' movement and middle-class efforts at emancipation, the position of women within the church was generally not a matter of debate. Women were seen as objects of paternal activities, primarily in moral terms. Women from the working classes had a very limited degree of enthusiasm for the ascetic ideal, and so the office of parish sister became the domain of the middle class. The *Evangelischer Verband für die weibliche Jugend Deutschlands* (Protestant Alliance for the Female Youth of Germany), founded by the pastor Johannes Burckhardt (1853-1914) in Berlin in 1890, offered an approach to self-organisation for women working as parish sisters. It did not only work for women, but the work itself was organised by women.

In 1899 various women's aid associations joined together to form the *Evangelische Frauenhilfe* (Protestant Women's Aid). In the same year, the *Deutscher Evangelischer Frauenbund* (German Protestant Women's Federation), whose first chairwoman was Paula Mueller-Otfried (1865-1946), was founded. The two groups had a tense relationship with each other, since *Frauenhilfe* was orientated to serving, whereas the *Frauenbund* was dedicated to women's issues in general. The *Frauenbund* was involved in postulating the moral renewal for women that was typical for that time, but also committed to emancipation, supporting women's rights to vote in church and communal elections. In 1908 the women's federation joined the *Bund Deutscher Frauenvereine* (Federation of German Women's Associations) as a middle-class Protestant movement. The *Evangelisch-Sozialer Kongress* went further. At their meetings, women had the right to speak, which was very unusual. In 1894 a Protestant Social Women's Group formed within the *Kongress* under the leadership of Elisabeth Gnauck-Kühne (1850-1917). She was the chief proponent of access to universities for women and had only been able to study economics and politics at the University of Berlin in 1895 on special permission from the Prussian Ministry of Education. In 1895 the *Evangelisch-Sozialer Kongress* had dedicated its annual conference to women's issues. Gnauck-Kühne gave the keynote address, but it stayed well within the framework of the conventional image of women and considered all of those things appropriate as women's professions which could be extrapolated from maternal instincts: home economics, teaching, childcare, paediatric medicine. In these fields women were to take up their specific cultural tasks. However, Gnauck-Kühne advocated employment for women and payment for their social work in the church and in society. With that, she was actually going quite far beyond the limits of the typical Protestant image of women, which took the role of women to be limited to that of housewife and mother. In 1900 however Gnauck-Kühne made a surprise conversion to Catholicism.

The *Gemeinschaftsbewegung*

In the wake of the revival, a new movement which was close to the non-established churches arose at the end of the nineteenth century, namely the *Gemeinschaftsbewegung* (Fellowship Movement).[36] Elias Schrenk (1831-1913) was one of its main proponents. He had been a missionary with the *Basler Missionsgesellschaft* (Basel Missionary Society) and had been travelling through Germany as an itinerant preacher since 1884. Barmen, near Wuppertal, became one of the centres of this evangelisation movement, with a training school for missionaries called the *Johanneum*. With that, theological training had also become a forum for self-organisation. The state theology departments were seen as hotbeds of unbiblical theology. This motivated the founder of the Bethel *Diakonenanstalt* (deacon's institute) Friedrich von Bodelschwingh (1831-1910), to establish a *Theologische Schule* at Bethel in 1905 which was to immunise new pastors against modern liberal theology. The foundation of Bible Schools by promoters of the *Gemeinschaftsbewegung* served the same purpose. The prospective preachers were instructed in mission and evangelisation. Unlike the faculties the Bible Schools opened their doors for women.

The *Gemeinschaftsbewegung*, like the revival movement, tended to join together across regions. Representatives of the *Gemeinschaftsbewegung* met in 1888 in Gnadau near Magdeburg, where there was a settlement of Herrnhut Brethren. The meeting was the birth of the *Gnadauer Verband* (Gnadau Association), which was finally established in 1897 under the name *Deutscher Verband für Evangelische Gemeinschaftspflege und Evangelisation* (German Association for Protestant Fellowship and Evangelisation). The *Gemeinschaftsbewegung* emphasised its connection to the state church, and the motto "in the church, if possible with the church, but not under the church" reaches back to 1919. However, competition between the *Gemeinschaftsbewegung* and the state churches was substantial. The state churches saw the evangelistic preachers as auxiliaries at best who could never have the same status as their own pastors.[37] The *Gemeinschaftsbewegung* concentrated on strengthening their fellowship groups and accordingly sought a strict differentiation from the 'world' and its temptations like theatre, concerts, and parties. It was mainly the middle class that was involved in this movement, and hardly at all the workers.

---

[36] Ohlemacher, "Gemeinschaftschristentum"; Id., ed., *Gemeinschaftsbewegung in Deutschland*, ch. 2.5; Ruhbach, "Die Entstehung der Gemeinschaftsbewegung".

[37] Lange, *Eine Bewegung bricht sich Bahn*, no. 6.

Klaus Fitschen

Freikirchen

The real breakthrough for the *Freikirchen* or free churches, as well as for the free religious movement, only came about in Germany after 1918. Previously, state control was strict, and the organisation of alternative religious forms was only possible within a tight framework.[38] Only with the founding of the empire in 1871 could private associations with a religious purpose be officially registered by the state. However, these groups continued to be viewed with suspicion as sects by both the church and the state, since *Freikirchen*, from the point of view of the Protestant state churches, represented significant competition, and from the point of view of state officials, had potential for fomenting unrest. Many Protestants who joined *Freikirchen* remained members of their local state church to avoid raising suspicions of deviance. On the other hand, the *Freikirchen* had far more sympathisers than they had members.

The first *Freikirche* known and tolerated in Germany was that of the Herrnhut Brethren (Moravians) established in Saxony in the early eighteenth century. Their founder, Nikolaus von Zinzendorf (1700-1760), had tried to avoid giving the impression that he wished to found a church, but this proved unavoidable. The Brethren were very mobile because of their itinerant preachers and were often in contact with revivalist groups. Another movement which had been tolerated in certain regions in Germany went back to the time of the Reformation, namely that of the Mennonites. Other influences came from England and the United States, as well as Switzerland, especially from Geneva. Methodists and Baptists, later also Seventh Day Adventists and Jehovah's Witnesses came from these countries, strengthening the call for freedom from any state church system. For the state officials, the home countries of these groups also signalled political, democratic tendencies, which increased their monitoring of the *Freikirchen*. Not only political, but also religious dissenters were often left with no choice but to emigrate. Some of them came back, and had in the meantime become acquainted with the possibilities of confessional pluralism in the United States where free or 'non-established' churches were allowed. Besides these external impulses, there were also autonomous *Freikirchen* in Germany, for example the German Catholics, Old Lutherans, and others.

Transnational and transatlantic connections provided an important source of encouragement for free church activities in Germany. These connections did not only come from emigrants, those who stayed abroad as well as those who returned home, but also from networks which were established in the second half of the nineteenth century. The first of these was the Evangelical Alliance founded in London in 1846.[39] Its founders wanted a union with a distinct anti-Catholic orientation, bringing together different Protestant confessions. About 800 delegates took part in the founding meeting, including many from the United States, coming from the most diverse branches of Protestantism. There were eleven participants from Germany present. In 1851, a

---

[38] Heinrichs, *Freikirchen*; Voigt, *Freikirchen in Deutschland*.

[39] Greschat, *Vom Konfessionalismus zur Moderne*, no. 79.

branch of the Evangelical Alliance was founded in Germany. King Friedrich Wilhelm IV supported the work of the Alliance, since he expected it to motivate Protestant religiosity. Thus a meeting of the Evangelical Alliance could be held in Berlin in 1857. This was a unique event for its time due to its internationalism. Exactly this internationalism caused conservative church groups to criticise the king. Agreement about fellowship in prayer put the Evangelical Alliance in a position beyond questions of creed, which included each and every congregation and individual Christian. The invisible fellowship of the churches was supposed to be made visible.

Another network was the international students' movement, which was home to later fathers of ecumenism like John Mott (1865-1955). The *Allgemeine christliche Studentenkonferenz* (General Christian Students Conference) was founded in 1890 in Niesky, one of the centres of the Herrnhut Brethren in Saxony. In 1895 the *Deutsche Christliche Studenten-Vereinigung* (German Christian Students' Union), which also had a women's branch from 1905, was founded. The students' movement had the same roots as the YMCA, which had been organised in Germany from 1883 as the *Christlicher Verein Junger Männer*, not only in church congregations, but also beyond them.

The members of these groups mainly came from the state churches and not the free or non-established ones. The forms of self-organisation, along with the international basis, had come from the non-established churches. With the turn of the twentieth century, these impulses were assimilated to those of the youth movement, which before the First World War aimed at opposing everything old and traditional. Within Protestantism there were also forms of organisation typical of their generation, like the *Jünglingsvereine* (youth associations), which had more than 100,000 members in 1900. The student Bible Study Groups (the *Bibelkränzchen* or *Bibelkreise*) were also part of the Christian youth movement, but these only had about 3,000 members in 1907. In 1894 the *Jugendbund für entschiedenes Christentum* (Youth Union for Committed Christianity) was founded, and its members (about 4,580 in 1907) were pledged to a convinced Christian lifestyle. The Protestant workers' associations, however, had much less success than their Catholic equivalents. In 1900, they had about 100,000 members.

The first Baptist churches in Germany were founded in Hamburg in 1834. By 1848 there were 25 of them in Germany. These received support from England and the USA based on the missionary ideals of the movement. In 1849 the Baptist churches in Germany and Denmark joined together. The mission was carried out mainly by itinerant preachers and the distribution of Bibles and tracts. King Friedrich Wilhelm IV tolerated the Baptists in Prussia and pronounced toleration for all 'sects' in 1852. In 1890 the Baptists had 30,000 members. The Baptist churches had a high degree of self-organisation. This was also the case with the Methodists. Methodism had appeared in Germany in 1830 in various branches. It was recognised officially by the state in Bremen and Württemberg. In 1890 the Methodists had about 10,000 members.

Apart from the typical *Freikirchen*, more charismatic movements were also arising. These included the *Heiligungsbewegung* or Holiness Movement, which appeared in Germany in 1872. Especially the Pentecostal Movement, with its emphasis on the immediate experience of the effects of the Holy Spirit, attracted attention. Pentecostalism fell on fertile soil provided by the fellowship and salvation movements. The immediacy of the spiritual experience which was first manifested in Kassel in 1907 led to ecstatic episodes, of which the officials did not approve. Even the fellowship and salvation movement and the Pietists were sceptical of Pentecostalism. The *Gemeinschaftsbewegung*, in cooperation with the German branch of the Evangelical Alliance and the non-established churches, in 1909 published the *Berliner Erklärung* (Berlin Statement), which condemned the charismatic experiences of Pentecostalism and the salvation movement as ambivalent if not demonic. The Pentecostal Movement took on a certain reserve after that. In Mühlheim there were two Pentecostal conferences in 1909, emphasising speaking in tongues as their main characteristic, and founding the *Mühlheimer Verband* (Mühlheim Union) for the Pentecostal congregations.

New Opportunities?

With the end of the First World War, the sovereignty of the state over the church was no more. The German monarchs resigned. With that, the Protestant state churches were headless and had to organise themselves.[40] At this point, hopes of stronger self-organisation were pointedly expressed by the local congregations. The *Volkskirche* (people's church) became an ideal to express this. In the end, however, the old powers, set on centrally led state churches, won back dominance again. Civil servants of the previously state-run church administration preferred reorganisation. The synods, which were to be voted in to put in place a church constitution and determine new heads for the state churches, were no longer dependent on a prince or king, but on the church administrative offices. The revolution in Germany in November 1918 disconcerted many representatives of the church. Most wanted nothing to do with the new republic, and certainly did not want to hear anything about democracy. The opportunities which the church could have had under these changed circumstances were not made use of. In 1933 it seemed that new opportunities for the church had appeared. Only when people noticed that the National-Socialist state intended to exploit the Protestant Church for its own purposes did opposition from within the church become noticeable. The opposition was able to continue with a tried and true means of self-organisation, namely the instrument of the synods. The synod of Barmen in 1934 was in line with the movement which, a century before, had led to the Rhenish-Westphalian church by-laws of 1835.

---

[40] Besier, "Die neue preußische Kirchenverfassung".

Bibliography

Catholic Germany

Achleitner, Wilhelm. *Gott im Krieg: die Theologie der österreichischen Bischöfe in den Hirtenbriefen zum Ersten Weltkrieg*. Vienna, 1997.

Arbeitskreis für kirchliche Zeitgeschichte (AKKZG), Münster. "Katholiken zwischen Tradition und Moderne. Das katholische Milieu als Forschungsaufgabe". *Westfälische Forschungen*, 43 (1993), 588-654.

Arbeitskreis für kirchliche Zeitgeschichte (AKKZG), Münster. "Konfession und Cleavages im 19. Jahrhundert. Ein Erklärungsmodell zur regionalen Entstehung des katholischen Milieus in Deutschland". *Historisches Jahrbuch*, 120 (2000), 357-395.

Arnold, Claus. *Katholizismus als Kulturmacht: der Freiburger Theologe Joseph Sauer (1872-1949) und das Erbe des Franz Xaver Kraus*. Veröffentlichungen der Kommission für Zeitgeschichte B/86. Paderborn, 1999.

Arnold, Claus. "Bistumsjubiläen und Identitätsstiftung im 20. Jahrhundert am Beispiel der Diözesen Rottenburg-Stuttgart und Limburg". *Römische Quartalschrift*, 100 (2005), 313-332.

Arnold, Claus. "Konfessionalismus und katholische kirchenhistorische Forschung in Deutschland (1900-1965)" in: Massimo Faggioli and Alberto Melloni, eds. *Religious Studies in the 20th Century. A Survey on Disciplines, Cultures and Questions. International Colloquium Assisi 2003*. Christianity and History 2. Münster, 2006, 251-271.

Arnold, Claus. *Kleine Geschichte des Modernismus*. Freiburg i. Br., 2007.

Arnold, Claus. "Wimpfen und das Bistum Mainz im 19. und 20. Jahrhundert". *Archiv für mittelrheinische Kirchengeschichte*, 59 (2007), 367-381.

Bachem, Karl. *Vorgeschichte, Geschichte und Politik der deutschen Zentrumspartei. Zugleich ein Beitrag zur Geschichte der katholischen Bewegung sowie zur allgemeinen Geschichte des neueren und neuesten Deutschland 1815-1914*. Vol. 1. Aalen, 1967.

Baumeister, Martin. *Parität und katholische Inferiorität. Untersuchungen zur Stellung des Katholizismus im Deutschen Kaiserreich*. Politik- und Kommunikationswissenschaftliche Veröffentlichungen der Görres-Gesellschaft 3. Paderborn, 1987.

Bischof, Franz Xaver. *Das Ende des Bistums Konstanz. Hochstift und Bistum Konstanz im Spannungsfeld von Säkularisation und Suppression (1802/03-1821/27)*. Münchener Kirchenhistorische Studien 1. Stuttgart-Berlin-Cologne, 1989.

Bischof, Franz Xaver. *Theologie und Geschichte. Ignaz von Döllinger (1799-1890) in der zweiten Hälfte seines Lebens. Ein Beitrag zu seiner Biographie*. Münchener Kirchenhistorische Studien 9. Stuttgart-Berlin-Cologne, 1997.

Blaschke, Olaf. *Katholizismus und Antisemitismus im Deutschen Kaiserreich*. Kritische Studien zur Geschichtswissenschaft 122. Göttingen, 1997.

Blaschke, Olaf, ed. *Konfessionen im Konflikt. Deutschland zwischen 1800 und 1970: ein zweites konfessionelles Zeitalter*. Göttingen, 2002.

Blaschke, Olaf and Kuhlemann, Frank-Michael, eds. *Religion im Kaiserreich. Milieus - Mentalitäten - Krisen*. Religiöse Kulturen der Moderne 2. Gütersloh, 1996.

Brack, Rudolf. *Deutscher Episkopat und Gewerkschaftsstreit 1900-1914*. Bonner Beiträge zur Kirchengeschichte 9. Cologne, 1976.

Brandt, Hans-Jürgen. *Eine katholische Universität in Deutschland? Das Ringen der Katholiken in Deutschland um eine Universitätsbildung im 19. Jahrhundert*. Bonner Beiträge zur Kirchengeschichte 12. Cologne, 1981.

Bucher, Rainer. *Hitlers Theologie*. Würzburg, 2008.

Burkard, Dominik. *Staatskirche - Papstkirche - Bischofskirche. Die 'Frankfurter Konferenzen' und die Neuordnung der Kirche in Deutschland nach der Säkularisation*. Römische Quartalschrift, Supplementheft 53. Rome-Freiburg-Vienna, 2000.

Burkard, Dominik. "Volksmissionen und Jugendbünde. Eine kritische Analyse und die Diskussion um ein katholisches Milieu in der Diözese Rottenburg" in: Hubert Wolf and Jörg Seiler, eds. *Das Katholische Sonntagsblatt (1850-2000). Württembergischer Katholizismus im Spiegel der Bistumspresse*. Ostfildern, 2001, 109-189.

Burkard, Dominik. "Zum Wandel der Domkapitel von adeligen Korporationen zum Mitarbeiterstab der Bischöfe". *Römische Quartalschrift*, 99 (2004), 134-162.

Burkard, Dominik. "Presse und Publizistik" in: Erwin Gatz, ed. *Geschichte des kirchlichen Lebens in den deutschsprachigen Ländern seit dem Ende des 18. Jahrhunderts*. 8: *Laien in der Kirche*. Freiburg, 2008, 559-602.

Busemann, Jan Dirk. "'Haec pugna verum ipsam religionem tangit'. Römische Indexkongregation und Deutscher Literaturstreit" in: Hubert Wolf and Judith Schepers, eds. *"In wilder zügelloser Jagd nach Neuem". 100 Jahre Modernismus und Antimodernismus in der katholischen Kirche*. Römische Inquisition und Indexkongregation 12. Paderborn, 2009, 289-310.

Damberg, Wilhelm. *Moderne und Milieu. 1802-1998*. Geschichte des Bistums Münster 5. Münster, 1998.

De Maeyer, Jan; Leplae, Sofie and Schmiedl, Joachim, eds. *Religious Institutes in Western Europe in the 19th and 20th Centuries: Historiography, Research and Legal Position*. KADOC Studies on Religion, Culture and Society 2. Leuven, 2004.

Denzler, Georg and Grasmück, Ernst L., eds. *Geschichtlichkeit und Glaube. Gedenkschrift zum 100. Todestag Ignaz von Döllingers*. Munich, 1990.

Dowe, Christopher. *Auch Bildungsbürger. Katholische Studierende und Akademiker im Kaiserreich*. Kritische Studien zur Geschichtswissenschaft 171. Göttingen, 2006.

Ebertz, Michael. "'Ein Haus voll Glorie, schauet (...)'. Modernisierungsprozesse der römisch-katholischen Kirche im 19. Jahrhundert" in: Wolfgang Schieder, ed. *Religion und Gesellschaft im 19. Jahrhundert*. Stuttgart, 1993, 62-85.

Fitschen, Klaus. *Der Katholizismus von 1648 bis 1870*. Kirchengeschichte in Einzeldarstellungen III/8. Leipzig, 1997.

Fitschen, Klaus. *Was ist Freiheit? Liberale und demokratische Potentiale im Katholizismus 1789-1848*. Forum Theologische Literaturzeitung. Leipzig, 2001.

Fleckenstein, Gisela and Schmiedl, Joachim, eds. *Ultramontanismus: Tendenzen der Forschung*. Paderborn, 2005.

Fuchs, Stephan. *"Vom Segen des Krieges". Katholische Gebildete im Ersten Weltkrieg. Eine Studie zur Kriegsdeutung im akademischen Katholizismus*. Contubernium 61. Stuttgart, 2004.

Garhammer, Erich. *Seminaridee und Klerusbildung bei Karl August Graf von Reisach. Eine pastoralgeschichtliche Studie zum Ultramontanismus des 19. Jahrhunderts*. Münchener Kirchenhistorische Studien 5. Stuttgart-Berlin-Cologne, 1990.

Gatz, Erwin, ed. *Akten der Fuldaer Bischofskonferenz 1871-1919*. Veröffentlichungen der Kommission für Zeitgeschichte. Reihe A: Quellen 22, 27, 39. Mainz, 1977-1985, 3 vols.

Gatz, Erwin, ed. *Die Bischöfe der deutschsprachigen Länder 1785/1803 bis 1945. Ein biographisches Lexikon*. Berlin, 1983.

Gatz, Erwin, ed. *Die Bistümer und ihre Pfarreien*. Geschichte des kirchlichen Lebens in den deutschsprachigen Ländern seit dem Ende des 18. Jahrhunderts 1. Freiburg, 1991.

Bibliography

Gatz, Erwin, ed. *Kirche und Muttersprache: Auslandsseelsorge, nichtdeutschsprachige Volksgruppen*. Geschichte des kirchlichen Lebens in den deutschsprachigen Ländern seit dem Ende des 18. Jahrhunderts 2. Freiburg, 1992.

Gatz, Erwin, ed. *Katholiken in der Minderheit: Diaspora, ökumenische Bewegung, Missionsgedanke*. Geschichte des kirchlichen Lebens in den deutschsprachigen Ländern seit dem Ende des 18. Jahrhunderts 3. Freiburg, 1994.

Gatz, Erwin, ed. *Der Diözesanklerus*. Geschichte des kirchlichen Lebens in den deutschsprachigen Ländern seit dem Ende des 18. Jahrhunderts 4. Freiburg, 1995.

Gatz, Erwin, ed. *Caritas und soziale Dienste*. Geschichte des kirchlichen Lebens in den deutschsprachigen Ländern seit dem Ende des 18. Jahrhunderts 5. Freiburg, 1997.

Gatz, Erwin, ed. *Die Kirchenfinanzen*. Geschichte des kirchlichen Lebens in den deutschsprachigen Ländern seit dem Ende des 18. Jahrhunderts 6. Freiburg, 2000.

Gatz, Erwin, ed. *Die Bistümer des Heiligen Römischen Reiches von ihren Anfängen bis zur Säkularisation*. Freiburg i. Br., 2004.

Gatz, Erwin, ed. *Die Bistümer der deutschsprachigen Länder von der Säkularisation bis zur Gegenwart*. Freiburg i. Br., 2006.

Gatz, Erwin, ed. *Klöster und Ordensgemeinschaften*. Geschichte des kirchlichen Lebens in den deutschsprachigen Ländern seit dem Ende des 18. Jahrhunderts 7. Freiburg, 2006.

Gatz, Erwin, ed. *Laien in der Kirche*. Geschichte des kirchlichen Lebens in den deutschsprachigen Ländern seit dem Ende des 18. Jahrhunderts 8. Freiburg, 2008.

Geschichtsverein der Diözese Rottenburg-Stuttgart, ed. *Kulturkampf und Kulturkämpfe. Staat, Gesellschaft, Kirche im 19. Jahrhundert*. Rottenburger Jahrbuch für Kirchengeschichte 15. Ostfildern, 1996.

Geschichtsverein der Diözese Rottenburg-Stuttgart, ed. *Die Revolution von 1848 - Geburtsstunde des deutschen Katholizismus?* Rottenburger Jahrbuch für Kirchengeschichte 19. Ostfildern, 2000.

Geschichtsverein der Diözese Rottenburg-Stuttgart, ed. *Integration oder Gegengesellschaft? Der deutsche Katholizismus um 1900*. Rottenburger Jahrbuch für Kirchengeschichte 21. Ostfildern, 2002.

Geschichtsverein der Diözese Rottenburg-Stuttgart, ed. *Christentum und Krieg in der Moderne*. Rottenburger Jahrbuch für Kirchengeschichte 25. Ostfildern, 2006.

Hammerstein, Notker. *Aufklärung und katholisches Reich. Untersuchungen zur Universitätsreform und Politik katholischer Territorien des Heiligen Römischen Reiches deutscher Nation im 18. Jahrhundert*. Berlin, 1977.

Graf, Friedrich Wilhelm and Renz, Horst, eds. *Umstrittene Moderne. Die Zukunft der Neuzeit im Urteil der Epoche Ernst Troeltschs*. Troeltsch-Studien 4. Gütersloh, 1987.

Haupt, Heinz-Gerhard and Langewiesche, Dieter, eds. *Nation und Religion in der deutschen Geschichte*. Frankfurt am Main, 2001.

Hausberger, Karl. *Herman Schell (1850-1906). Ein Theologenschicksal im Bannkreis der Modernismuskrise*. Quellen und Studien zur neueren Theologiegeschichte 3. Regensburg, 1999.

Haustein, Jörg. *Liberal-katholische Publizistik im späten Kaiserreich. "Das Neue Jahrhundert" und die Krausgesellschaft*. Forschungen zur Kirchen- und Dogmengeschichte 80. Göttingen, 2001.

Heitz, Claudius. *Volksmission und badischer Katholizismus im 19. Jahrhundert*. Forschungen zur oberrheinischen Landesgeschichte 50. Freiburg, 2005.

Himmelein, Volker and Rudolf, Hans U., eds. *Alte Klöster, neue Herren. Die Säkularisation im deutschen Südwesten 1803. Große Landesausstellung Baden-Württemberg 2003*. Ostfildern, 2003, 2 vols.

Holzapfel, Christoph. "Krieg als 'heilsame Kreuzes- und Leidensschule'. Die religiöse Deutung der Weltkriege". *Rottenburger Jahrbuch für Kirchengeschichte*, 25 (2006), 97-126.

Holzem, Andreas. *Kirchenreform und Sektenstiftung. Deutschkatholiken, Reformkatholiken und Ultramontane am Oberrhein 1844-1866*. Veröffentlichungen der Kommission für Zeitgeschichte, Reihe B: Forschungen 65. Paderborn etc., 1994.

Holzem, Andreas. *Weltversuchung und Heilsgewißheit. Kirchengeschichte im Katholizismus des 19. Jahrhunderts*. Münsteraner Theologische Abhandlungen 35. Altenberge, 1995.

Holzem, Andreas. *Religion und Lebensformen. Katholische Konfessionalisierung im Sendgericht des Fürstbistums Münster 1570-1800*. Paderborn, 2000.

Holzem, Andreas. "Das katholische Milieu und das Problem der Integration. Kaiserreich, Kultur und Konfession um 1900". *Rottenburger Jahrbuch für Kirchengeschichte*, 21 (2002), 13-39.

Holzem, Andreas and Weber, Ines, eds. *Ehe - Familie - Verwandtschaft: Vergesellschaftung in Religion und sozialer Lebenswelt*. Paderborn, 2008.

Horstmann, Johannes. *Katholizismus und moderne Welt. Katholikentage, Wirtschaft, Wissenschaft - 1848 bis 1914*. Abhandlungen zur Sozialethik 1. Munich, 1976.

Hürten, Heinz. *Kurze Geschichte des deutschen Katholizismus: 1800-1960*. Mainz, 1986.

Hürten, Heinz. "Karl Muths 'Hochland' in der Vorkriegszeit - oder der Preis der Integration" in: Martin Huber and Gerhard Lauer, eds. *Bildung und Konfession. Politik, Religion und literarische Identitätsbildung 1850-1918*. Studien und Texte zur Sozialgeschichte der Literatur 59. Tübingen, 1996, 133-146.

Hürten, Heinz. *Akten deutscher Bischöfe über die Lage der Kirche 1918-1933*. Veröffentlichungen der Kommission für Zeitgeschichte. Reihe A: Quellen 51. Paderborn, 2007, 2 vols.

Jürgensmeier, Friedhelm, ed. *Handbuch der Mainzer Kirchengeschichte*. 3: *Neuzeit und Moderne*. Würzburg, 2002, 2 vols.

Kany, Roland. "A Century of Catholic Theology Reflected in Three Editions of the Lexikon für Theologie und Kirche". *Journal of Religious & Theological Information*, 7 (2006), 9-27.

Klöcker, Michael. *Katholikentage im Erzbistum Köln 1919/20. Analysen und Dokumente mit besonderer Berücksichtigung des Kreises Jülich*. Forum Jülicher Geschichte 25. Jülich, 2002.

Klueting, Harm, ed. *Katholische Aufklärung: Aufklärung im katholischen Deutschland*. Hamburg, 1993.

Köster, Norbert. *Der Fall Hirscher: ein "Spätaufklärer" im Konflikt mit Rom? Römische Inquisition und Indexkongregation* 8. Paderborn, 2007.

Krieg, Robert A. *Karl Adam. Catholicism in German Culture*. Notre Dame, 1992.

Krieg, Robert A. *Romano Guardini. A Precursor of Vatican II*. Notre Dame, 1997.

Krumeich, Gerd. "'Gott mit uns'? Der Erste Weltkrieg als Religionskrieg" in: Gerd Krumeich and Hartmut Lehmann, eds. *"Gott mit uns". Nation, Religion und Gewalt im 19. und frühen 20. Jahrhundert*. Göttingen, 2000, 273-283.

Kustermann, Abraham Peter. "Romantik: II. Theologiegeschichtlich". *Lexikon für Theologie und Kirche*. Vol. 8. Freiburg i. Br., 1999³, 1270-1273.

Landersdorfer, Anton. "'Hie Staatsschule, dort Kirchenschule' - Der Streit um die Klerusausbildung an staatlichen Universitätsfakultäten oder kirchlichen Seminaren um die letzte Jahrhundertwende" in: Peter Neuner and Manfred Weitlauff, eds. *Theologie an der Universität. Zum 525. Stiftungsfest der Ludwig-Maximilians-Universität München*. Special issue *Münchener Theologische Zeitschrift*, 48 (1997) 3-4. St. Ottilien, 1997, 313-330.

Lehmann, Hartmut, ed. *Säkularisierung, Dechristianisierung, Rechristianisierung im neuzeitlichen Europa*. Göttingen, 1997.

Leitgöb, Martin. *Vom Seelenhirten zum Wegführer. Sondierungen zum bischöflichen Amtsverständnis im 19. und 20. Jahrhundert. Die Antrittshirtenbriefe der Germanikerbischöfe (1837-1962)*. Römische Quartalschrift für christliche Altertumskunde und Kirchengeschichte, Supplementheft 56. Rome-Freiburg-Vienna, 2004.

Liedhegener, Antonius. *Christentum und Urbanisierung. Katholiken und Protestanten in Münster und Bochum 1830-1933*. Veröffentlichungen der Kommission für Zeitgeschichte. Reihe B: Forschungen 77. Paderborn, 1997.

Lill, Rudolf. "Der Bischof zwischen Säkularisation und Kulturkampf (1803-1885)" in: Peter Berglar and Odilo Engels, eds. *Der Bischof in seiner Zeit. Bischofstypus und Bischofsideal im Spiegel der Kölner Kirche. Festgabe für Joseph Kardinal Höffner*. Cologne, 1986, 349-396.

Lill, Rudolf, ed. *Der Kulturkampf*. Beiträge zur Katholizismusforschung. Reihe A: Quellentexte zur Geschichte des Katholizismus 10. Paderborn, 1997.

Loth, Wilfried. *Katholiken im Kaiserreich. Der politische Katholizismus in der Krise des wilhelminischen Deutschlands*. Beiträge zur Geschichte des Parlamentarismus und der politischen Parteien 75. Düsseldorf, 1984.

Maclear, J.F., ed. *Church and State in the Modern Age. A Documentary History*. Oxford, 1995.

Mayeur, Jean-Marie et al., ed. *Die Geschichte des Christentums*. Vols. 10-13. Freiburg i. Br., 1992-2002.

Meiwes, Relinde. *"Arbeiterinnen des Herrn". Katholische Frauenkongregationen im 19. Jahrhundert*. Geschichte und Geschlechter 30. Frankfurt-New York, 2000.

Merlio, Gilbert. "Carl Muth et la revue 'Hochland'. Entre catholicisme culturel et catholicisme politique" in: Michel Grunewald and Uwe Puschner, eds. *Le milieu intellectuel catholique en Allemagne, sa presse et ses résaux (1871-1963). Das katholische Intellektuellenmilieu in Deutschland, seine Presse und sein Netzwerk (1871-1963)*. Bern, 2006, 191-208.

Müller, Karl. *Joseph Schmidlin (1876-1944). Papsthistoriker und Begründer der katholischen Missionswissenschaft*. Studia Instituti Missiologici SVD 47. Nettetal, 1989.

Müller, Wolfgang. *Fünfhundert Jahre theologische Promotion an der Universität Freiburg i. Br*. Beiträge zur Freiburger Wissenschafts- und Universitätsgeschichte 19. Freiburg i. Br., 1957.

Nipperdey, Thomas. *Religion im Umbruch. Deutschland 1870-1918*. Munich, 1988.

Nowak, Kurt. *Geschichte des Christentums in Deutschland. Religion, Politik und Gesellschaft vom Ende der Aufklärung bis zur Mitte des 20. Jahrhunderts*. Munich, 1995.

Obermann, Heiko A. et al. eds. *Kirchen- und Theologiegeschichte in Quellen. 4: Vom Konfessionalismus zur Moderne. 5: Das Zeitalter der Weltkriege und Revolutionen*. Neukirchen-Vluyn, 1999.

Osinski, Jutta. *Katholizismus und deutsche Literatur im 19. Jahrhundert*. Paderborn, 1993.

Pahud de Mortanges, Elke. *Philosophie und kirchliche Autorität. Der Fall Jakob Frohschammer vor der römischen Indexkongregation (1855-1864)*. Römische Inquisition und Indexkongregation 4. Paderborn etc., 2005.

Raffelt, Albert. "Die Erneuerung der katholischen Theologie" in: Jean-Marie Mayeur and Kurt Meier, eds. *Erster und Zweiter Weltkrieg. Demokratien und totalitäre Systeme (1914-1958)*. Die Geschichte des Christentums 12. Freiburg i. Br., 1992, 216-237.

Rak, Christian. *Krieg, Nation und Konfession. Die Erfahrung des deutsch-französischen Krieges von 1870/71*. Veröffentlichungen der Kommission für Zeitgeschichte. Reihe B: Forschungen 97. Paderborn, 2004.

Rödel, Walter Gerd and Schwerdtfeger, Regina, eds. *Zerfall und Wiederbeginn. Vom Erzbistum zum Bistum Mainz (1792/97-1830). Ein Vergleich. Festschrift für Friedhelm Jürgensmeier*. Beiträge zur Mainzer Kirchengeschichte 7. Würzburg, 2002.

Ruster, Thomas. *Die verlorene Nützlichkeit der Religion. Katholizismus und Moderne in der Weimarer Republik*. Paderborn, 1994.

Scharfenecker, Uwe. *Die Katholisch-Theologische Fakultät Gießen (1830-1859). Ereignisse, Strukturen, Personen*. Veröffentlichungen der Kommission für Zeitgeschichte. Reihe B: Forschungen 81. Paderborn, 1998.

Schatz, Klaus. *Geschichte des Bistums Limburg*. Mainz, 1983.

Schatz, Klaus. *Zwischen Säkularisation und Zweitem Vatikanum. Der Weg des deutschen Katholizismus im 19. und 20. Jahrhundert*. Frankfurt am Main, 1986.

Schepers, Judith. "Widerspruch und Wissenschaft. Die ungleichen Brüder Wieland im Visier kirchlicher Zensur (1909-1911)". *Rottenburger Jahrbuch für Kirchengeschichte*, 25 (2006), 271-290.

Scheidgen, Hermann-Josef. *Die Deutsche Bischöfe im Ersten Weltkrieg. Die Mitglieder der Fuldaer Bischofskonferenz und ihre Ordinariate 1914-1918*. Kölner Beiträge zur Kirchengeschichte 18. Cologne, 1991.

Schreiner, Klaus. "'Helm ab zum Ave Maria'. Kriegstheologie und Kriegsfrömmigkeit im Ersten Weltkrieg". *Rottenburger Jahrbuch für Kirchengeschichte*, 25 (2006), 65-98.

Schmidt, Susanna. *"Handlanger der Vergänglichkeit". Zur Literatur des katholischen Milieus 1800-1950*. Paderborn, 1994.

Schneider, Bernhard. "Wallfahrt, Ultramontanismus und Politik. Zu Vorgeschichte und Verlauf der Trierer Hl.-Rock-Wallfahrt von 1844" in: Erich Aretz et al., eds. *Der Heilige Rock zu Trier. Studien zur Geschichte und Verehrung der Tunika Christi*. Trier, 1995, 237-280.

Schneider, Bernhard. "Entwicklungstendenzen rheinischer Frömmigkeits- und Kirchengeschichte in der ersten Hälfte des 19. Jahrhunderts". *Archiv für mittelrheinische Kirchengeschichte*, 48 (1996), 157-195.

Schneider, Bernhard. "'Katholische Aufklärung': Zum Werden und Wert eines Forschungsbegriffs". *Revue d'Histoire Ecclésiastique*, 93 (1998), 354-397.

Schneider, Bernhard. *Katholiken auf die Barrikaden? Europäische Revolutionen und deutsche katholische Presse 1815-1848*. Veröffentlichungen der Kommission für Zeitgeschichte. Reihe B: Forschungen 84. Paderborn, 1998.

Schneider, Bernhard and Persch, Martin, eds. *Auf dem Weg in die Moderne 1802-1880*. Geschichte des Bistums Trier 4. Trier, 2000.

Schneider, Bernhard and Persch, Martin, eds. *Beharrung und Erneuerung 1881-1981*. Geschichte des Bistums Trier 5. Trier, 2004.

Schwedt, Herman H. *Das römische Urteil über Georg Hermes (1775-1831). Ein Beitrag zur Geschichte der Inquisition im 19. Jahrhundert*. Römische Quartalschrift für christliche Altertumskunde und Kirchengeschichte: Supplementheft 37. Rome, 1980.

Schwedt, Herman H. "Die katholischen Abgeordneten der Paulskirche und Frankfurt". *Archiv für mittelrheinische Kirchengeschichte*, 34 (1982), 143-166.

Schwedt, Herman H. "Die Verurteilung der Werke Anton Günthers". *Zeitschrift für Kirchengeschichte*, 101 (1990), 301-343.

Schwedt, Herman H. "Vom ultramontanen zum liberalen Döllinger" in: Georg Denzler and Ernst L. Grasmück, eds. *Geschichtlichkeit und Glaube. Gedenkschrift zum 100. Todestag Ignaz von Döllingers*. Munich, 1990, 107-167.

Smith, Helmut Walser. *German Nationalism and Religious Conflict. Culture, Ideology, Politics, 1870-1918*. Princeton, 1995.

Smolinsky, Heribert, ed. *Die Geschichte der Erzdiözese Freiburg*. 1: *Von der Gründung bis 1918*. Freiburg, 2008.

Smolinsky, Heribert. "Synoden - Antizölibatsbewegung - Deutschkatholizismus - Das Erste Vatikanische Konzil und der Altkatholizismus" in: Heribert Smolinsky, ed. *Geschichte der Erzdiözese Freiburg*. 1: *Von der Gründung bis 1918*. Freiburg, 2008, 211-234.

Stambolis, Barbara. "Nationalisierung trotz Ultramontanisierung oder: 'Alles für Deutschland. Deutschland aber für Christus'. Mentalitätsleitende Wertorientierung deutscher Katholiken im 19. und 20. Jahrhundert". *Historische Zeitschrift*, 269 (1999), 57-98.

Weber, Christoph. *Aufklärung und Orthodoxie am Mittelrhein 1820-1850*. Beiträge zur Katholizismusforschung. Reihe B: Abhandlungen. Paderborn, 1973.

Weichlein, Siegfried. "Religion und Nation: Bonifatius als politischer Heiliger im 19. und 20. Jahrhundert". *Schweizerische Zeitschrift für Religions- und Kulturgeschichte*, 100 (2006), 45-58.

Weiß, Otto. *Die Redemptoristen in Bayern (1790-1909). Ein Beitrag zur Geschichte des Ultramontanismus*. St. Ottilien, 1983.

Weiß, Otto. *Der Modernismus in Deutschland. Ein Beitrag zur Theologiegeschichte*. Regensburg, 1995.

Weiß, Otto. *Kulturen - Mentalitäten - Mythen. Zur Theologie- und Kulturgeschichte des 19. und 20. Jahrhunderts*. Paderborn, 2004.

Weiß, Otto. *Begegnungen mit Klemens Maria Hofbauer (1751-1820)*. Regensburg, 2009.

Weitlauff, Manfred. "'Modernismus litterarius'. Der 'Katholische Literaturstreit', die Zeitschrift 'Hochland' und die Enzyklika 'Pascendi dominici gregis' Pius' X. vom 8. September 1907". *Beiträge zur altbayerischen Kirchengeschichte*, 37 (1988), 97-175.

Wolf, Hubert. *Ketzer oder Kirchenlehrer? Der Tübinger Theologe Johannes von Kuhn (1806-1887) in den kirchenpolitischen Auseinandersetzungen seiner Zeit*. Mainz, 1992.

Wolf, Hubert. "Generalvikar oder Domdekan? Zum Streit um monarchische und kollegiale Diözesanleitung im Bistum Limburg" in: Josef Hainz et al., eds. *"Den Armen eine frohe Botschaft". Festschrift für Bischof Franz Kamphaus zum 65. Geburtstag*. Frankfurt, 1997, 251-265.

Wolf, Hubert. "Der Historiker ist kein Prophet. Zur theologischen (Selbst-) Marginalisierung der katholischen deutschen Kirchengeschichtsschreibung zwischen 1870 und 1960" in: Hubert Wolf and Claus Arnold, eds. *Die katholisch-theologischen Disziplinen in Deutschland. Ihre Geschichte, ihr Zeitbezug.* Programm und Wirkungsgeschichte des II. Vatikanums 3. Paderborn, 1999, 71-93.

Wolf, Hubert, ed. *Johann Michael Sailer: Das postume Inquisitionsverfahren*. Römische Inquisition und Indexkongregation 2. Paderborn, 2002.

Wolf, Hubert, ed. *Ökumenische Kirchengeschichte. 3: Von der Französischen Revolution bis 1989*. Darmstadt, 2007.

Wolf, Hubert and Arnold, Claus, eds. *Die katholisch-theologischen Disziplinen in Deutschland. Ihre Geschichte, ihr Zeitbezug*. Programm und Wirkungsgeschichte des II. Vatikanums 3. Paderborn, 1999.

Wolf, Hubert and Seiler, Jörg, eds. *Das Katholische Sonntagsblatt (1850-2000). Württembergischer Katholizismus im Spiegel der Bistumspresse*. Ostfildern, 2001.

Wolf, Hubert and Unterburger, Klaus, eds. *Eugenio Pacelli. Die Lage der Kirche in Deutschland 1929*. Veröffentlichungen der Kommission für Zeitgeschichte. Reihe A: Quellen 50. Paderborn, 2006.

Zimmermann, Wolfgang and Priesching, Nicole, eds, *Württembergisches Klosterbuch. Klöster, Stifte und Ordensgemeinschaften von den Anfängen bis in die Gegenwart*. Ostfildern, 2003.

Protestant Germany

Albert, Jürgen. *Christentum und Handlungsform bei Johann Hinrich Wichern (1808-1881). Studien zum sozialen Protestantismus*. Heidelberg, 1997.

Benrath, Gustav Adolf. "Die Erweckung innerhalb der deutschen Landeskirchen 1815-1888. Ein Überblick" in: Gustav Adolf Benrath and Ulrich Gäbler, eds. *Geschichte des Pietismus. 3. Der Pietismus im neunzehnten und zwanzigsten Jahrhundert*. Göttingen, 2000, 150-202.

Besier, Gerhard. "Die Landeskirche und die Revolution von 1848/49" in: Gerhard Goeters and Rudolf Mau, eds. *Die Geschichte der Evangelischen Kirche der Union. 1. Die Anfänge der Union unter landesherrlichem Kirchenregiment*. Leipzig, 1992, 366-391.

Besier, Gerhard. "Die 'Neue Ära' und die Einleitung eines kirchlichen Verfassungsneubaus (1858-1862)" in: Joachim Rogge and Gerhard Ruhbach, eds. *Die Geschichte der Evangelischen Kirche der Union. 2: Die Verselbständigung der Kirche unter dem königlichen Summepiskopat*. Leipzig, 1994, 109-119.

Besier, Gerhard. "Die Oktoberversammlung 1871 und die nationalkirchliche Einheit" in: Joachim Rogge and Gerhard Ruhbach, eds. *Die Geschichte der Evangelischen Kirche der Union. 2: Die Verselbständigung der Kirche unter dem königlichen Summepiskopat*. Leipzig, 1994, 181-196.

Besier, Gerhard. "Die Beilegung des Kulturkampfs und die Gründung des 'Evangelischen Bundes' (1878-1886)" in: Joachim Rogge and Gerhard Ruhbach, eds. *Die Geschichte der Evangelischen Kirche der Union. 2: Die Verselbständigung der Kirche unter dem königlichen Summepiskopat*. Leipzig, 1994, 247-257.

Besier, Gerhard. "Die Kleist-Hammersteinschen Anträge auf größere Selbständigkeit der evangelischen Kirche (1886/1887)" in: Joachim Rogge and Gerhard Ruhbach, eds. *Die Geschichte der Evangelischen Kirche der Union. 2: Die Verselbständigung der Kirche unter dem königlichen Summepiskopat*. Leipzig, 1994, 284-296.

Besier, Gerhard. "Die neue preußische Kirchenverfassung und die Bildung des Deutschen Evangelischen Kirchenbundes" in: Gerhard Besier and Eckhard Lessing, eds. *Die Geschichte der Evangelischen Kirche der Union. 3. Trennung von Staat und Kirche. Kirchlich-politische Krisen. Erneuerung kirchlicher Gemeinschaft (1918-1992)*. Leipzig, 1999, 76-117.

Besier, Gerhard and Lessing, Eckhard, eds. *Die Geschichte der Evangelischen Kirche der Union. 3. Trennung von Staat und Kirche. Kirchlich-politische Krisen. Erneuerung kirchlicher Gemeinschaft (1918-1992)*. Leipzig, 1999.

Beyer, Hermann Wolfgang. *Die Geschichte des Gustav-Adolf-Vereins in ihren kirchen- und geistesgeschichtlichen Zusammenhängen*. Göttingen, 1932.

Brederlow, Jörn. *"Lichtfreunde" und "Freie Gemeinden". Religiöser Protest und Freiheitsbewegung im Vormärz und in der Revolution von 1848/49*. Munich, 1976.

Fitschen, Klaus. "Vormärz, 'Los von Rom' und Erster Weltkrieg. Der Gustav-Adolf-Verein im 19. und frühen 20. Jahrhundert" in: *Diasporaarbeit im Wandel der Zeit. Festschrift anlässlich des 175. Gründungsjubiläums des Gustav-Adolf-Werks e.V. - Diasporawerk der Evangelischen Kirche in Deutschland*. Leipzig, 2007, 34-47.

Gäbler, Ulrich. "Erweckung - Historische Einordnung und theologische Charakterisierung" in: Ulrich Gäbler, ed. *"Auferstehungszeit". Erweckungsprediger des 19. Jahrhunderts. Sechs Porträts*. Munich, 1991, 161-178.

Bibliography

Geck, Albrecht. "Die Synoden und ihre Sistierung in der Reaktionszeit (1817-1850)" in: Gerhard Goeters and Rudolf Mau, eds. *Die Geschichte der Evangelischen Kirche der Union*. 1: *Die Anfänge der Union unter landesherrlichem Kirchenregiment*. Leipzig, 1992, 125-133.

Goeters, J.F. Gerhard. "Bekenntnis und Staatskirchenrecht: Das Wöllnersche Edikt (1788) und das Allgemeine Preußische Landrecht (1794)" in: Gerhard Goeters and Rudolf Mau, eds. *Die Geschichte der Evangelischen Kirche der Union*. 1: *Die Anfänge der Union unter landesherrlichem Kirchenregiment*. Leipzig, 1992, 46-54.

Goeters, J.F. Gerhard. "Die Reorganisation der staatlichen und kirchlichen Verwaltung in den Stein-Hardenbergschen Reformen" in: Gerhard Goeters and Rudolf Mau, eds. *Die Geschichte der Evangelischen Kirche der Union*. 1: *Die Anfänge der Union unter landesherrlichem Kirchenregiment*. Leipzig, 1992, 54-58.

Goeters, J.F. Gerhard. "Die kirchliche Reformdiskussion" in: Gerhard Goeters and Rudolf Mau, eds. *Die Geschichte der Evangelischen Kirche der Union*. 1: *Die Anfänge der Union unter landesherrlichem Kirchenregiment*. Leipzig, 1992, 83-87.

Goeters, J.F. Gerhard. "Nationalkirchliche Tendenzen und Landeskirchen. Gustav-Adolf-Verein und Berliner Kirchenkonferenz (1846)" in: Gerhard Goeters and Rudolf Mau, eds. *Die Geschichte der Evangelischen Kirche der Union*. 1: *Die Anfänge der Union unter landesherrlichem Kirchenregiment*. Leipzig, 1992, 332-341.

Goeters, J.F. Gerhard. "Der Wittenberger Kirchentag und die Innere Mission (1848/49)" in: Gerhard Goeters and Rudolf Mau, eds. *Die Geschichte der Evangelischen Kirche der Union*. 1: *Die Anfänge der Union unter landesherrlichem Kirchenregiment*. Leipzig, 1992, 391-401.

Goeters, Gerhard and Mau, Rudolf, eds. *Die Geschichte der Evangelischen Kirche der Union*. 1. *Die Anfänge der Union unter landesherrlichem Kirchenregiment*. Leipzig, 1992.

Greschat, Martin, ed. *Vom Konfessionalismus zur Moderne*. Neukirchen, 1997.

Grote, Heiner. "Der Evangelische Bund zur Wahrung der deutsch-protestantischen Interessen (1886-1918)" in: Walter Fleischmann-Bisten and Heiner Grote, eds. *Protestanten auf dem Wege. Geschichte des Evangelischen Bundes*. Göttingen, 1986, 9-56.

Heinrichs, Wolfgang E. *Freikirchen - eine moderne Kirchenform*. Giessen, 1989.

Hölscher, Lucian. *Geschichte der protestantischen Frömmigkeit in Deutschland*. Munich, 2005.

Huber, Ernst Rudolf and Huber, Wolfgang, eds. *Staat und Kirche im 19. und 20. Jahrhundert*. 1. *Staat und Kirche vom Ausgang des alten Reichs bis zum Vorabend der bürgerlichen Revolution*. 2: *Staat und Kirche im Zeitalter des Hochkonstitutionalismus und des Kulturkampfs 1848-1890*. 3. *Staat und Kirche von der Beilegung des Kulturkampfs bis zum Ende des Ersten Weltkriegs*. 4. *Staat und Kirche in der Zeit der Weimarer Republik*. Berlin, 1973-1988.

Hübinger, Gangolf. *Kulturprotestantismus und Politik. Zum Verhältnis von Liberalismus und Protestantismus im wilhelminischen Deutschland*. Tübingen, 1994.

Kaiser, Jochen Christoph. "Integratives Moment des deutschen Protestantismus. Die Entstehung des Gustav-Adolf-Vereins (GAW) im Kontext von Sozial- und Kirchengeschichte" in: *Diasporaarbeit im Wandel der Zeit. Festschrift anlässlich des 175. Gründungsjubiläums des Gustav-Adolf-Werks e.V. - Diasporawerk der Evangelischen Kirche in Deutschland*. Leipzig, 2007, 11-31.

Lange, Dieter. *Eine Bewegung bricht sich Bahn. Die deutschen Gemeinschaften im ausgehenden 19. und beginnenden 20. Jahrhundert und ihre Stellung zu Kirche, Theologie und Pfingstbewegung*. Berlin, 1979.

Lepp, Claudia. *Protestantisch-liberaler Aufbruch in die Moderne. Der deutsche Protestantenverein in der Zeit der Reichsgründung und des Kulturkampfes*. Gütersloh, 1996.

Marré, Heiner. "Die Kirchenfinanzierung in Deutschland vom Ausgang des 18. Jahrhunderts bis zum Ende des Zweiten Weltkriegs". *Zeitschrift der Savigny-Stiftung für Rechtsgeschichte. Kanonistische Abteilung*, 85 (1999), 448-464.

Meyer, Dietrich. "Monbijou-Konferenz (1856) und Evangelische Allianz (1857)" in: Joachim Rogge and Gerhard Ruhbach, eds. *Die Geschichte der Evangelischen Kirche der Union. 2: Die Verselbständigung der Kirche unter dem königlichen Summepiskopat*. Leipzig, 1994, 97-109.

Neuser, Wilhelm H. "Die Entstehung der Rheinisch-Westfälischen Kirchenordnung" in: Gerhard Goeters and Rudolf Mau, eds. *Die Geschichte der Evangelischen Kirche der Union. 1. Die Anfänge der Union unter landesherrlichem Kirchenregiment*. Leipzig, 1992, 241-256.

Neuser, Wilhelm H. "Landeskirchliche Reform-, Bekenntnis- und Verfassungsfragen. Die Provinzialsynoden und die Berliner Generalsynode von 1846" in: Gerhard Goeters and Rudolf Mau, eds. *Die Geschichte der Evangelischen Kirche der Union. 1. Die Anfänge der Union unter landesherrlichem Kirchenregiment*. Leipzig, 1992, 342-366.

Neuser, Wilhelm H. "Die Revision der Rheinisch-Westfälischen Kirchenordnung" in: Joachim Rogge and Gerhard Ruhbach, eds. *Die Geschichte der Evangelischen Kirche der Union. 2: Die Verselbständigung der Kirche unter dem königlichen Summepiskopat*. Leipzig, 1994, 78-97.

Neuser, Wilhelm H. "Das soziale Experiment des Kaisers und der Kirche. Der Evangelisch-soziale Kongreß" in: Joachim Rogge and Gerhard Ruhbach, eds. *Die Geschichte der Evangelischen Kirche der Union. 2: Die Verselbständigung der Kirche unter dem königlichen Summepiskopat*. Leipzig, 1994, 307-318.

Nixdorf, Wolfgang. "Die lutherische Separation. Union und Bekenntnis (1834)" in: Gerhard Goeters and Rudolf Mau, eds. *Die Geschichte der Evangelischen Kirche der Union. 1. Die Anfänge der Union unter landesherrlichem Kirchenregiment*. Leipzig, 1992, 220-240.

Nowak, Kurt. *Schleiermacher. Leben, Werk und Wirkung*. Göttingen, 2000.

Obst, Helmut. "Lichtfreunde, Deutschkatholiken und Katholisch-apostolische Gemeinden" in: Gerhard Goeters and Rudolf Mau, eds. *Die Geschichte der Evangelischen Kirche der Union. 1. Die Anfänge der Union unter landesherrlichem Kirchenregiment*. Leipzig, 1992, 317-332.

Ohlemacher, Jörg, ed. *Die Gemeinschaftsbewegung in Deutschland. Quellen zu ihrer Geschichte 1887-1914*. Gütersloh, 1977.

Ohlemacher, Jörg. "Gemeinschaftschristentum in Deutschland im 19. und 20. Jahrhundert" in: Gustav Adolf Benrath and Ulrich Gäbler, eds. *Geschichte des Pietismus. 3. Der Pietismus im neunzehnten und zwanzigsten Jahrhundert*. Göttingen, 2000, 393-426.

Roensch, Manfred and Klän, Werner, eds. *Quellen zur Entstehung und Entwicklung selbständiger evangelisch-lutherischer Kirchen in Deutschland*. Frankfurt am Main, 1987.

Rogge, Joachim. "Kirchentage und Eisenacher Konferenzen" in: Joachim Rogge and Gerhard Ruhbach, eds. *Die Geschichte der Evangelischen Kirche der Union. 2: Die Verselbständigung der Kirche unter dem königlichen Summepiskopat*. Leipzig, 1994, 42-55.

Rogge, Joachim. "Die Außerordentliche Generalsynode von 1875 und die Generalsynodalordnung von 1876. Fortschritt und Grenzen kirchlicher Selbstregierung" in: Joachim Rogge and Gerhard Ruhbach, eds. *Die Geschichte der Evangelischen Kirche der Union. 2: Die Verselbständigung der Kirche unter dem königlichen Summepiskopat*. Leipzig, 1994, 225-233.

Rogge, Joachim and Ruhbach, Gerhard, eds. *Die Geschichte der Evangelischen Kirche der Union*. 2: *Die Verselbständigung der Kirche unter dem königlichen Summepiskopat*. Leipzig, 1994.

Ruhbach, Gerhard. "Die Erweckungsbewegung und ihre kirchliche Formation" in: Gerhard Goeters and Rudolf Mau, eds. *Die Geschichte der Evangelischen Kirche der Union*. 1. *Die Anfänge der Union unter landesherrlichem Kirchenregiment*. Leipzig, 1992, 159-174.

Ruhbach, Gerhard. "Die Entstehung der Gemeinschaftsbewegung (1888)" in: Joachim Rogge and Gerhard Ruhbach, eds. *Die Geschichte der Evangelischen Kirche der Union*. 2: *Die Verselbständigung der Kirche unter dem königlichen Summepiskopat*. Leipzig, 1994, 296-307.

Sander, Hartmut. "Die oktroyierte Verfassung und die Errichtung des Evangelischen Oberkirchenrats (1850)" in: Gerhard Goeters and Rudolf Mau, eds. *Die Geschichte der Evangelischen Kirche der Union*. 1. *Die Anfänge der Union unter landesherrlichem Kirchenregiment*. Leipzig, 1992, 402-418.

Sander, Hartmut. "Der Deutsche Evangelische Kirchenausschuß (1903)" in: Joachim Rogge and Gerhard Ruhbach, eds. *Die Geschichte der Evangelischen Kirche der Union*. 2: *Die Verselbständigung der Kirche unter dem königlichen Summepiskopat*. Leipzig, 1994, 355-373.

Schenkel, Daniel. *Der Deutsche Protestantenverein*. <http://germanhistorydocs.ghi-dc.org/pdf/deu/10_R_Schenkel_Deutsche%20Protestantenverein.pdf> (29 June 2010).

Voigt, Karl Heinz. *Freikirchen in Deutschland (19. und 20. Jahrhundert)*. Leipzig, 2004.

THE NORDIC COUNTRIES

The Nordic countries included in this study experienced some alterations of political alliance during the period, with Norway being first part of a composite Danish state, then briefly independent after the Treaty of Kiel in 1814, when it adopted a very liberal constitution, and finally part of a union with Sweden until 1905. Though the situations were not identical, each had a Lutheran established church with particularly close links to the state so that the clergy were effectively civil servants, though in Denmark a secular civil service gradually took over local responsibilities from the clergy from 1841. Like the other countries in the study all were affected by Pietism and other varieties of religious renewal but all were generally successful in containing these differing opinions within the established church until the Svenska missionsförbundet *was formed in 1878. In this section we will deal first with Denmark, then Sweden and finally Norway.*

Church, State and Reform in Denmark

Jes Fabricius Møller

The Church

Remarkably little happened to the fundamental structure of the Danish church[1] between 1780 and 1920. The church carried out crucial reforms only towards the end of the period, in response to extensive social change. Around 1780 the Danish church was not an independent organisation; in fact, it was barely an organisation at all since it functioned virtually as part of the absolutist Danish state. For example, the Danish church had no synod. The bishop of Sealand, who resided in Copenhagen, acted as *primus inter pares* whenever the church had to be represented externally, but did so only to a limited extent. Because the absolutist state defined itself as a Christian state, and thus as a defender of the true faith, it is impossible in this period to distinguish precisely between state and church.[2] The king of Denmark was the head of the church. Hence the minister was a public servant. In the nineteenth-century kingdom of Denmark the right to appoint a parson (*jus vocandi*) belonged in principle to the king, although in the duchies of Schleswig and Holstein a local patron or parish sometimes possessed it. In some cases, local authorities, typically the local lord of the manor, exerted a significant measure of influence through the right to propose a candidate for the post.

From its formation in the early twelfth century until the Local Government Reform (*Kommunalreformen*) of 1970 the parish remained the fundamental administrative unit not just of the church, but of Danish society. Following a minor reorgani-

---

[1] The best introductions to Danish ecclesiastical history of the long nineteenth century are Koch, *Den danske kirkes historie*, and Lindhardt, *Den danske kirkes historie*.

[2] Severinsen, *Folkekirkens Ejendoms-Historie*, 110.

sation of the church structure in 1806, the kingdom was divided into eight dioceses; the duchies each had one diocese called a *Generalsuperintendentur*. A minister could serve several parishes in a so-called *pastorat*, a benefice. The kingdom possessed 1,008 benefices and 1,758 parishes, Schleswig 209 benefices and 227 parishes, and Holstein 137 benefices and 139 parishes. According to the census of 1801-1803, the kingdom of Denmark had a population of 925,680, Schleswig 276,339, and Holstein 602,087.[3] These figures can only give an idea of the size of an average parish, but a minister was expected to know every parishioner personally.

The Minister

Apart from attending to clerical duties, church services and religious ceremonies, the minister performed civil duties on behalf of the state, except for law enforcement. One essential duty was registering the population by entering births (christenings), marriages, and deaths (funerals) into the church register. The minister also fulfilled the essential task of taking the census, necessary for taxation purposes and the military draft. On behalf of the government he supervised poor relief, medical issues such as smallpox vaccination and midwifery, and the levy of troops. The minister furthermore read official announcements from the pulpit, and reported to the central authorities on matters ranging from historical relics to population figures. He not only confirmed the young people but also watched over their further prospects in life. Confirmation had been compulsory since 1736 and without a certificate of confirmation youths were barred from apprenticeships, jobs and marriage.

Studies indicate that literacy was high in rural areas as early as the seventeenth century.[4] Reading material consisted mainly of devotional literature. Not surprisingly, then, the high levels of literacy in the rural population was mainly thanks to the church. Similarly, teaching at school was based on the catechism. The local teacher was typically also the parish clerk (*degn*), while tithes were used in part to pay for the schools. Later, after primary education had been regulated by central law in 1814, the minister took on the influential role of school superintendent. Some ministers even established schools for the education of teachers, the so-called *præstegårdsseminarier* (vicarage seminaries). Thus there existed a tradition of decentralised teacher training outside the universities. The minister would normally be the only university graduate in the parish. Since the Reformation, it had been the main task of the University of Copenhagen, the only university in the kingdom of Denmark, to educate future clergymen. The German speaking ministers of the duchies were also educated at the important faculty of theology at the University of Kiel. The minister often regarded himself

---

[3] Bergsøe, *Den danske Stats Statistik*, I, 446 and IV, 59. Lauenborg, which between 1815 and 1864 was ruled by the king of Denmark, comprised 28 parishes and 31,996 people.

[4] Appel, "Literacy in Seventeenth Century Denmark".

as more than just a religious teacher and preacher. Some ministers acted as philanthropists and contributed to educating peasants, for example by lending them books. In the decades around 1800 it had become a regular trend among ministers to publish historical-topographical sketches of their parishes.

As a state church (the term was introduced only in the 1830s), the church was a centralised organisation, while on the local level the churches were fully incorporated into the community. The parsonage house was the official residence of a state official but also a farm. As such it had a social and economic function in the parish community. At the end of the eighteenth century Denmark was by European standards not very urbanised. About 80% of the population lived in rural areas, where agricultural production was predominant. While bishops had been employed and paid directly by the Crown since the Reformation, the minister was not salaried by the king. Instead, the minister drew his income from the land belonging to the parsonage house; in the kingdom the tithe, a tax on agricultural output, also contributed to his earnings. A tenth of the harvest had to be set apart for the church; this was then divided into equal parts, for respectively the king as head of the church, the maintenance of church buildings, and the minister. In order to settle the national debt, around 1700 the Crown had sold most of its rights to the tithe to local patrons, so that the administration of church funds in practice remained decentralised. In addition, the minister derived additional benefits from perquisites. The church was paid in kind, that is in agricultural products, but the payments were increasingly converted into cash. In social and economic terms the minister was part of the local community. His income mainly derived from his own farming and tithes, and it was important for him to be well integrated into the local community. Typically not of local stock, the minister could expect to experience nothing but trouble and disputes if he remained a stranger to local customs and habits. On the other hand, since he was also a state representative, a clergyman and a university graduate, the minister stood above the other inhabitants of the parish.

Reforms

From the 1770s onwards, Danish farming underwent comprehensive reforms, resulting in the disintegration of the old village community to which the parsonage house belonged. In this process, in which the minister typically played a central role, the foundation was laid for the economic and cultural autonomy of the rural population. In due course this led to the cooperative movement and the rise of a culturally and politically independent class of citizens in non-urban areas. Before the reforms, farmers were typically tenants and the land was jointly cultivated by the village inhabitants. The reforms involved land redistribution, so that each farmer had a lot separate from that of his neighbour, both enabling and forcing him to make his own decisions as to what he wanted to cultivate. In the next generations most farmers became freeholders. This was the Danish version of the transition from the pre-modern subsistence economy to the modern market economy, or what is usually called the transformation of peasants into farmers. The reforms have gone down in history as an emancipation of the peasants. However, they were just as much about centralising taxation, drafting young men and enforcing the law. Structurally, they undermined the power of the local landed elite.

Reforms in the domain of political administration gradually undermined the central role of the minister as the local state official. In 1841, an administrative reform introduced local civil administration or local government in administrative units typically coterminous with the existing benefices, now called *Sognekommune* (parish-municipality). They were governed by a parish council, with members drawn from among the greatest landowners. The minister was a member *ex officio*. The council took over responsibility for the schools, poor relief, and local roads. In time the elections for the parish council became more democratic; after 1867 the minister was no longer *ex-officio* a member of the council. He did, however, remain responsible for the supervision of the school. With the professionalisation of medical practice, trained physicians and surgeons took over the supervision of public health, slowly undermining the role of the minister as the primary government official for health issues in the rural areas. As early as 1850 there were 500 doctors in the kingdom, 20% of whom were public employees.[5] The revolution of 1848-1849 and the introduction of the constitutional monarchy had relatively little influence on the position of the church. It remained a state church, headed not by the king but by the *Kultusminister* or Minister of Religious Affairs, who was also responsible for education.

The financial structure of the church remained unaltered until the end of the nineteenth century. Due to urbanisation and a growing money economy, even less of the church income was received in kind. However, the source of church income remained unchanged. After the introduction of *parlamentarisme* (the system whereby the government falls if it does not have the support of parliament) in 1901 and the rise to power of the liberal farmers' party *Venstre*, a range of reforms were implemented during the next twenty years. In 1903, an act introduced democratically elected church councils (not to be confused with the local government's parish councils). The minister was *ex officio* a member of the church council. Another act passed in 1903, the Commutation Act (*Tiendeafløsningsloven*), regulated the abolition of tithes. The yearly payment of tithes was commuted into a lump sum equivalent to 25 times the annual amount. Progressively implemented during the early decades of the twentieth century, the reforms resulted in semi-autonomous local churches. The church council was in charge of the church building and employed the staff, with the exception of the minister who remained an employee of the Ministry of Ecclesiastical Affairs. In 1913 an act standardised the ministers' salaries and pensions in order to match salaries of other public servants. To finance this, the income derived from such things as duties was transformed into a church tax based on regular income, which was supplemented by direct state subsidies.

---

[5] Bergsøe, *Den danske Stats Statistik*, IV, 92.

Finally, in 1919, a law on the expropriation of vicarage land holdings was approved. The interests accruing from the capital formed by the commutation of tithes and the expropriation of land was expected to compensate the church for the loss of income. Unfortunately, inflation and mismanagement reduced the capital considerably, and by the middle of the twentieth century the church was left with no significant assets except for a large and steady income through church taxes supplemented by state subsidies. The reforms of 1903-1919 adjusted church finances to fit a modern money economy based on earned income, while at the same time it bound the church even more firmly to the state.[6] The minister's legal position as an employee began to resemble that of a government official, in spite of the fact that the minister now performed only one civic act: the registration of births, marriages and deaths. The church still holds this responsibility in Denmark today, with the exception of the northern parts of Schleswig (*Sønderjylland*), which were ceded by Germany to Denmark in 1920.

The Revivalists

Pietism came to Denmark in the first decades of the eighteenth century, under the sponsorship of Frederik IV, who drew ecclesiastics from Halle to his court. Zinzendorf visited Copenhagen in 1731 and a Moravian Society (*Herrnhutisk Societet* or *Brødremenigheden*) was founded in 1739. In 1773, the Moravians obtained permission to found a colony called Christiansfeld in northern Schleswig.[7] The pietism that emerged towards the end of the eighteenth century was influenced by Moravian emissaries as well as the Norwegian preacher, Hans Nielsen Hauge. The majority of Danish revivalists were as committed to the Lutheran-Evangelical confession as was the Danish state church. In spite of sharp disagreements, these never led to the establishment of an independent church of any significance. During the nineteenth century Anglo-American Christian movements grew in importance, although they were never as significant as in Sweden.[8] Thus the British and Foreign Bible Society helped the clergyman Bone Falck Rønne (1764-1833) to found a Danish parallel organisation in 1814, *Det danske Bibelselskab*.

Characteristic of the revivalist movements that arose in Denmark in the first decades of the nineteenth century was an emphasis on the freedom of lay people to interpret the Bible according to the literal reading common to traditional Lutheranism. True belief, it was thought, was derived not primarily through study, but involved heart-felt experience and personal expressions of sincerity and piety. The lay revivalists drew the attention of the authorities, since their self-confidence undermined the minister's statutory monopoly on preaching. The revivalists also insisted that religious confessions were beyond the government's mandate. A decree from 1741 (the *Konventikelplakaten*) had made it illegal to hold revival meetings in the absence of a minister

---

[6] Møller, "Folkekirkens økonomi og staten".
[7] The Moravians did intensive missionary work in Greenland.
[8] On Anglo-American influence in general see Olesen, *De frigjorte og trællefolket*.

or without his permission. Revival meetings challenged the state church unless the minister himself led them or took part in them. However, it was not uncommon for the minister more or less openly to support or encourage revival meetings.

The revivalists perceived themselves as a minority of holy people who opposed the 'world'. They were willing to give up all worldly benefits for the sake of their faith. Niels Johansen, a weaver, wrote in a pamphlet published in 1837 "that the Kingdom of Christ is not of this world, the community of the holy in this World is looked down upon and can no longer be found in churches or schools, but all holy people who love the Lord Jesus and live devoutly in the World will be persecuted by kings, princes, bishops, ministers and teachers and by everything in this world that is high and mighty".[9] The pamphlet cost him a fine and four years of silence under censorship. In the 1830s and 1840s the absolutist state rarely imposed severe punishments in matters of conscience, restricting itself to meting out short imprisonments and fines. Niels Johansen was required to pay a fine of 150 *rigsbankdaler*, the equivalent of three live cattle. Fortunately for him, Queen Caroline Amalie, known for her persistent support of the revivalists, was willing to pay it.[10]

Revivalism tried to realise the Lutheran vision of the direct relationship between man and God by empowering the individual. Faith was taken out of its institutional context and individualised, and in this sense revivalism could be seen as a modern phenomenon.[11] On the other hand, the revivalists were sectarian. Their confession of faith meant exclusion from established social contexts and the formation of strong social ties that severely restricted individualisation. Nevertheless, even in this sense they were modern, being communities of choice rather than of tradition. The revivalist challenge to the church's monopoly of faith caused the church to direct its attention towards dogmatics and the question of Christian faith as a matter of personal conviction, leading to an emphasis on the role of the clergyman as a theologian and a preacher. It may be argued that the church was significantly more focused on theology and piety at the end of the nineteenth century than at the beginning.[12] Attempts to suppress revivalist movements failed. About 1850 they had branched out into two main movements, Inner Mission and Grundtvigianism.

Indre Mission

Founded in 1853, the *indre mission* (Inner or Home Mission) began as a loose association of different societies. During the 1860s the organisation was improved under Vilhelm Beck (1812-1901), chairman from 1881 until his death. While Beck was strongly influenced by Kierkegaard, it cannot be said that *indre mission* stood in the same rela-

---

[9] Johansen, *Herrens Ord i de sidste Verdens Dage*, 3.
[10] Bricka, ed., *Dansk Biografisk Leksikon*, XII, 47.
[11] Sanders, *Bondevækkelse og sekularisering*; Eriksen, "Drunken Danes and Sober Swedes?".
[12] See the discussion of the rise of 'New-Style Religion' in Bayly, *The Birth of the Modern World*, 330.

A. Ancher, Mission meeting at Fyrbakken in Skagen, *oil on canvas, 1903*.
[Skagen, Skagens Museum]

tionship to Kierkegaard as the Grundtvigians did to Grundtvig. *Indre mission* developed into an organisation governed from above, absorbing most branches of Lutheran revivalism but ceasing to be a laypeople's movement. It attached great importance to personal conversion and confessions of faith and supported the literal interpretation of Scripture common to traditional Lutheranism. Its adherents stressed the mortification of the flesh and the renunciation of worldly pleasures. It has been claimed that *indre mission* appealed especially to poor smallholders and fishermen, motivated by the expectation that what they were not able to have in this life they would obtain after death. However, whether a parish was marked by *indre mission* or Grundtvigianism largely depended not on wealth or poverty but on the presence of a charismatic minister or lay preacher who had gained the respect of the local population.

Supporters of *indre mission* were determined to stay within the framework of the official church. They attended the Sunday morning service and actively sought influence in the church. They also built chapel-like meeting houses, where they gathered for informal services that included personal confessions, prayers, and the singing of hymns. In 1919 there were *indre mission* 'chapels' (*Missionshuse*) in nearly a third of all the parishes in the kingdom.[13]

---

[13] Thestrup, *Nærbutik og næringslovs-omgåelse*, 343.

Although *indre mission* was against disestablishment, members of the association remained sectarian in the sense that they kept to themselves socially and culturally. They were not as active in civil life or in politics as the Grundtvigians. The distinction between the two movements is reflected even in name giving. Followers of *indre mission* often gave their children biblical names such as Martha, Maria, Simon, Peder, Jakob and Johannes, while the Grundtvigians revived Old Norse names such as Gunhild, Ingeborg, Thyra, Rolf and Hagbard. The people behind the rise of agricultural cooperatives in the 1880s typically belonged to Grundtvigian circles. Independent evangelical cooperative dairies also sprang up, responding to the wish of some members to stop production on the Sabbath. In the first decades of the twentieth century, approximately 100 of the country's 1,400 dairies respected the Sunday rest (*søndagshvilende*).[14]

The *indre mission* culminated in the first decades of the twentieth century. Although we have no exact knowledge of the actual size of the organisation, the circulation of the major bulletin for members suggests that 50,000 households were affiliated to *indre mission*.[15] *Indre mission* was active in philanthropy and youth work in urban areas. It all but dominated religious life in Copenhagen. About 1920 approximately four out of ten members of the parochial church councils in Copenhagen belonged to the *indre mission*, while only one out of ten was Grundtvigian. On a national level the two movements were equally represented in parochial church councils, each occupying almost one fourth of the available positions. Before 1920, the remaining positions on the councils were held by poorly organised groups, often of a conservative nature. From the mid-1920s, social democrats were also represented.

After the church had undergone democratic reforms through the Parochial Church Councils Act (*Menighedsrådsloven*) of 1903 and the Election of Bishops Act (*Lov om udpegning af biskopper*) of 1922, *indre mission* actively sought to influence the appointment of ministers and bishops. For most of the twentieth century, *indre mission* was successful, often allying itself with the social democrats. In the 1930s as many as six out of nine bishops were associated with *indre mission*.

Grundtvigianism

While *indre mission* was a mainstream Lutheran revivalist movement that fitted into a broader Northern European pattern, Grundtvigianism was more uniquely Danish. In his personal spiritual and intellectual development, Nikolaj Frederik Severin Grundtvig (1783-1872) went through several phases. After having successively been an orthodox Lutheran and a literary Romantic, he made a so-called 'unique' or 'marvellous discovery' in 1825. This amounted to a way of perceiving the church historically, which brought him into direct confrontation with Lutheran literalism. Grundtvig himself had carried out extensive historical studies, and it was clear to him that the

---

[14] Haue, "Mejerikrigen".

[15] Møller, *Grundtvigianisme i det 20. århundrede*, 104.

Bible was a historical document, a narrative handed down through generations rather than the pure word of God. The scriptures, he believed, are "obscure and indefinable; they can be interpreted by scholars only with a certain amount of probability, and used for anything whatsoever". He therefore sought "the rock in the sea of interpretations".[16] He hit on the idea that there was a source of teaching older and more original than the gospels. This he called "the living Word", which Jesus had spoken to the very first congregation (the apostles) and which had since been handed down intact through the history of the church as the Lord's Prayer, the words of institution at the Eucharist, and the Apostles' Creed. Again and again the living Word had been repeated in history at the 'bath' (the christening font) and at the 'table' (the altar).

From this insight grew a whole new perception of the church. The Danish church historian Hal Koch put it as follows: "[Grundtvigian] Christianity is neither right belief, as orthodoxy and rationalism tended to maintain; nor the correct moral attitude, which was in essence the pietist (evangelical) and rationalist view; nor right experience or feeling, as pietism believed; but on the contrary, godly actions. Man becomes Christian through God's creative action in baptism and Christian life is nourished through God's creative action in the Eucharist."[17]

Grundtvigian 'fundamentalism of the font' is sometimes opposed to the 'fundamentalism of the written word' as a characteristic of *indre mission*. Nor did the Grundtvigians attach importance to personal conversion as a turning point in the life of the Christian. Because the Grundtvigian perception is historical, Christianity is not something a person converts to, but rather something he realises that he is already part of, a wholeness into which he is incorporated through baptism. Grundtvig was regarded, by himself as well as by others, as a rebel against the rationalism of academic theologians, whom he regarded as a 'new exegetical papacy'. His works were read in revivalist circles, from which he recruited some of his first supporters. Grundtvig gained a significant following. The *Grundtvigianere* (Grundtvigians), as they are called, were never as tightly organised as the *indre mission*, nor did they adhere to specific political or theological views. Until about 1840 Grundtvigianism was a marginal phenomenon, comparable to other revivalist movements. When Grundtvig became part of the nationalist movement, however, he gained a great deal of popularity. He combined the concept of the living word with the notion that national languages had a special significance. Since the mother tongue in his view was the primary medium by which the word of God was disseminated, the Christian confession was bound indissolubly to nationhood.

Grundtvig's philosophy was inspired by German Idealism, but his political thoughts were influenced by British liberalism with which he came into contact during three visits to England between 1829 and 1831. Grundtvig became an ardent spokesman for freedom of religion, disestablishment, and the separation of church and school;

---

[16] Thyssen, "Grundtvig's Ideas on the Church and the People", 231-232.

[17] Koch, *Danmarks kirke gennem tiderne*, 139.

and he opposed compulsory baptism and confirmation (both were abolished in 1849). As an active politician from 1848 onwards, Grundtvig voiced liberal political views. Although his own role as a politician remained insubstantial, many of his followers helped organise the liberal opposition. Their constituency consisted of socially active farmers who from the 1880s launched the cooperative movement. The latter became the backbone of a strong agricultural sector known for its export of butter, eggs and bacon, especially to the British market.

After the defeat in the 1864 war against Prussia and Austria, private schools for children (*friskoler*) and people's high schools for young people (*folkehøjskoler*) sprouted up all over the country, reflecting Grundtvig's thoughts on the nation, education, and the church. Founded by private initiative to educate young people in rural areas, the schools opposed the established educational system which in the Grundtvigian view was based on 'the dead languages' of Latin and Greek. Grundtvigianism gained ever more adherents among the church clergy. This sometimes led to local conflicts. Unlike *indre mission*, the Grundtvigians in some places established semi-independent churches with ministers of their own choice (*Frimenigheder* or free congregations and *Valgmenigheder* or elected congregations), largely adopting the confession and liturgy of the state church. These new churches were, however, fully independent financially. In 1911 there were 28 such churches with a membership of approximately 10,000 households. The large majority of Grundtvigians stayed within the state church but no exact figures are available as to how many precisely.

Søren Kierkegaard

Søren Kierkegaard (1813-1855) grew up in a home influenced by old-fashioned pietism. His father brought him to meetings of the Moravian Society. Whereas Grundtvig gained a following through his ideas about the connections between history, language and people, Kierkegaard consistently remained an individualist. He shunned the crowd and the masses, and cared for neither nationalism nor democracy. One of the difficulties in reading Kierkegaard is his play with genres and identities. He wrote sophisticated philosophical tracts under several different pseudonyms for the cultured Copenhagen reader, who was usually perfectly aware of their authorship. He also published, under his own name, so-called edifying discourses (*Opbyggelige Taler*): simple, pious sermons rooted in his childhood Christian faith.[18] A substantial part of his work is concerned with a critique of the idea of *Bildung* (*Dannelse* in Danish), German philosophy of history and Hegelianism. He attacked the well-known writer and poet Hans Christian Andersen, and his *Bildungsroman Kun en Spillemand* (Only a Fiddler, 1837). Another object of Kierkegaard's ridicule was Grundtvig's historical and philosophical vision of church and nation.

---

[18] Garff, *Søren Kierkegaard*.

L. Janssen, Sören Kierkegaard at his high desk, *oil on canvas, 1902*.
[Hillerød, Det Nationalhistoriske Museum på Frederiksborg Slot]

Kierkegaard wrestled with a problem characteristic of his time: whether or not man is born with an identity. He believed that human identity had to be gained, but discarded the idea that it was the result of an evolutionary development, whether personally through *Bildung* or historically in a civilisation process. Man could achieve identity only through a momentary leap of faith. He could not hope to "catch up with himself", as Kierkegaard put it, through education or historical experience, since no single generation was privileged over another. The common fisherman who had personally known Jesus stood in a similar relation to him as Christ, the son of God, as did the educated man in Copenhagen in the 1840s. Kierkegaard's views conflicted with those of the established church. In the words of Kierkegaard's biographer Joakim Garff: "The critique of the clergy, which Kierkegaard begins to express more systematically by the mid-1840s and increasingly so till his death in 1855, is especially due to the clergy's neglect of the distance between humanistic and Christian ideas of identity. Instead, they allowed *Bildung* parasitically to suck out the Christian identity, which consequently fades away, quietly and unheeded."[19]

Kierkegaard's critical writings culminated in the so-called ecclesiastical controversy of 1854-1855. In a eulogy on Jakob Peter Mynster (1775-1854), his predecessor as bishop of Sealand, Hans Lassen Martensen (1808-1884) had employed the term 'martyr'. Kierkegaard launched an attack in which he used both Martensen and Mynster as whipping boys in a critique of the established church, which he denounced as an institution of comfort and conformity rather than martyrdom. Kierkegaard died in 1855 without bringing the controversy to a conclusion. He did not have many immediate followers. His fervour was of some significance to the conservative branch of the revival movement, and his philosophy had deeply influenced individual thinkers such as Georg Brandes (on whom more below). But he did not contribute broadly to opinion-forming. Even his own brother, Peter Christian Kierkegaard (1805-1888), was a Grundtvigian who ended up as a bishop in the state church.

State and Nation

The end of the eighteenth century brought what in Danish history are known as 'the flourishing days of overseas trade'. Since 1720 Denmark had stayed out of the major military conflicts. Still a significant naval power, it protected a thriving trade that generated great wealth among merchants, who consolidated their status by buying land. By the beginning of the nineteenth century approximately half of the larger estates in Denmark were owned by non-nobles. Social status was determined by talent as well as birth. There were opportunities for upward social mobility, for example by becoming a merchant or obtaining a degree in law, medicine or theology.

The typical minister, himself appointed and patronised by the king, around 1780 regarded society as a well-organised hierarchy with the monarch at the top. All subjects were the king's dependents or clients, whose devotion to the sovereign gradually took on emotional forms (the term used in Danish history-writing is 'sentimental patriotism').[20] A minister from Holstein, Heinrich Harries (1762-1802), in 1797 expressed his devotion to his king and country in a poem, written in German. The first stanza reads: "Oh, Denmark, what causes my cheek and breast to glow on hearing your name?

---

[19] Garff, "Dannelse, identitetsdannelse og dannelseskritik", 129.

[20] Lyngby, *Den sentimentale patriotisme*.

Ah! It is the pride of being Danish! It is the love for you, my fatherland!"[21] This strongly felt connection between church and state and especially church and nation was maintained throughout the nineteenth century. Martensen, the bishop of Sealand, regarded the nation as part of God's order and a natural foundation of the state. In his view, it was therefore a duty of the state to protect the church: "The Protestant State, in so far as it still retains its Christian character, and has not sunk to the level of a liberal and rationalist state that upholds mere humaneness (*Humanitätsstaat*), generally expresses its specific character by protecting and supporting the national church of its own confession, and by promoting the Christianity of the people, maintaining Christian customs and usages."[22]

The idea that nation and church formed a unity, while the state protected both, was popular in the established church. Grundtvigians were more in favour of disestablishment and allied themselves with the liberal opposition. Attempts at disestablishment came to nothing, and ultimately the Grundtvigians made their peace with the established church without ever falling in love with it.

Minorities

Nineteenth-century Denmark went through a marked demographic transition as a result of a high birth rate, a low death rate, and relatively little emigration. The population increased by approximately 160%, mostly in urban areas, and mostly in the second half of the century. Copenhagen grew from approximately 150,000 around 1850 to 500,000 at the end of the century. The 1901 census of the Danish population shows a remarkably homogenous population with respect to religious affiliation. Practically all 2.5 million citizens of the kingdom were members of the established church. They were divided into three main groups: mainstream Lutherans, *indre mission* and Grundtvigians. Minorities comprised only about 1.3% of the population (around 33,000 people), mostly affiliated to churches of Anglo-American origin. [See table on the next page.]

A Calvinist church had been founded in Copenhagen as early as the seventeenth century. Its members were initially Huguenots who were sometimes able to occupy high positions in Danish society. The first Baptist church was founded in 1839, at a time when child baptism was compulsory. Conservatives like Bishop Mynster tried to prevent Baptists from gaining a foothold in Danish society, but not every church dignitary was as eager as he to enforce the law. Ideas concerning the freedom of religion were gaining popularity even within the church, especially among Grundtvigians like P.C. Kierkegaard. Following the inclusion of a guarantee for religious freedom in the Danish constitution of 1849, Mormons from the USA made Denmark a mission field.

---

[21] "O Dania! was glüht bey deinem Namen/ Mir Wang' und Busen durch?/ Ha! es ist Dänenstolz! es ist die Liebe/ Zu dir, mein Vaterland!". Harries, *Gedichte*, 13.

[22] Martensen, *Christian Ethics, Special Part*, 102.

Religious affiliation in Denmark in 1901 (excluding the state church)

Baptists	5,501
Roman Catholics	5,373
Methodists	3,895
Irvingites	3,812
Jews	3,476
Other protestant societies	3,260
Reformists	1,112
Adventists	764
Mormons	717
Anglicans	176
Greek Orthodox	106
Quakers	66
Unitarians	62
Misc. Christian societies	208
Other religious societies	873[23]
No religious community	3,628

Despite opposition and even direct persecution the Mormons were quite successful, partly because they were able to convert many Baptists. According to an estimate based on the Mormon church's own statistics, between 1850 and 1904 there were 46,500 converts in the whole of Scandinavia, about half of them Danish. Approximately 16,800 Danish Mormons emigrated to America during the same period.[24]

Less controversial than the Baptist and Mormon churches were the Methodist church, founded in 1858 by C. Willerup (1815-1886), and the Catholic Apostolic Church (the Irvingites), founded in 1861. Their members often maintained an affiliation with the established church. Christian philanthropy in the cities was pioneered especially by the Methodists (and after 1887 the Salvation Army). Other minor groups included the Adventists, who came to Denmark in 1877, the Pentecostal Movement, which founded its first church in 1908, and the Unitarians, who seceded from the established church in 1908. The Danish branch of the YMCA (*Kristelig Forening for Unge Mænd*) was founded in 1878 and the YWCA (*Kristelig Forening for Unge Kvinder*) in 1889. Both served as *indre mission* youth organisations. The Anglican Church had had a small congregation in Elsinore before 1800 and in 1887 established its own church in Copenhagen.

Before 1849, the Church of Denmark was openly anti-Catholic, while Catholic church services, missionary work or anything else that smacked of 'papism' were offi-

---

[23] This category consisted of Norwegian and especially Swedish immigrants, most of whom settled in Copenhagen.

[24] Calculations by William Mulder in Hvidt, *Flugten til Amerika*, 280-300.

cially forbidden. Only in the free town of Fredericia and in the Austrian legation chapel in Copenhagen had Catholics been free to celebrate Mass. The Catholic Church, which at first came under the direct jurisdiction of the bishop of Osnabrück, became an apostolic prefecture in 1868, an apostolic vicariate in 1892, and finally an ordinary diocese in 1953.

In an 1897 report from the Danish mission field to the *Sacra Congregatio de Propaganda Fide* in Rome, the Catholic bishop Johannes von Euch (1834-1922) expressed himself in optimistic terms about the future of the Catholic Church in Denmark, because there were more than 200 conversions a year. According to von Euch, this was especially due to the ecumenical nature of the *secta Grundtvigianismi* (an ironic comment because Grundtvig regarded himself as an ardent Lutheran).[25] The growth of the Catholic Church was certainly considerable. According to official statistics, in 1890 there were 3,647 Roman Catholics in Denmark; by 1921 there were 22,137.[26] These figures do not take into account the seasonal migrant workers who typically came from Poland or Germany, so that the total number of Catholics was probably larger.

Rationalism, Atheism, Anticlericalism

Rationalism, as an appeal to reason rather than faith, is known mostly through its opponents, who exaggerated its effects. In the 1790s, several 'rationalist' authors openly and harshly criticised both church and Christianity, a critique almost completely silenced by the restriction of press freedom in 1799. Furthermore, there are some examples of rationalist ministers who wanted to change the church into an institution that restricted its teachings to matters concerning morality. Presumably only a minority of the clergy and the population were affected by such 'Enlightened' ideas. Many ministers were active advocates for the improvement of farming. One often repeated but not verified anecdote concerns a minister who instead of preaching the gospel on Sunday gave a talk on potato growing.[27]

As elsewhere, historical-philological studies were of great importance since they undermined the traditional understanding of the Bible. Frederik Münter (1761-1830), bishop of Sealand, carried out critical studies, which exposed him to the criticism of revivalists. By contrast, Mynster, who succeeded Münter as bishop, was the most popular preacher in Copenhagen. He was a declared critic of rationalism, partly because like many others of his generation he had been influenced by Kant in his youth, partly because he upheld absolutist political principles. As a conservative, he distrusted human reason.[28]

Hegelianism began to manifest itself in Denmark in the 1830s as a new way of looking at education and history. The Hegelian view on religion was provocatively

---

[25] Werner, "Grundtvig", 92.
[26] Statistique du Danemark, *Annuaire Statistique* 1901, 14 and 1925, 13.
[27] Bregnsbo, "Præster under pres".
[28] Huntington, "Conservatism as an Ideology".

C. Hansen, Jakob Peter Mynster, *oil on canvas, s.d.*
[Roskilde, Cathedral]

P.S. Krøyer, Hans Lassen Martensen, *oil on canvas, s.d.*
[Roskilde, Cathedral]

phrased in 1833 by the most influential writer and critic of its time, Johan Ludvig Heiberg (1791-1860): "There is no point in trying to conceal or embellish the truth: we must admit to ourselves that religion in our day is mostly a matter for the uneducated while for the educated world it is a thing of the past, the bygone."[29]

The passage is characteristic of the Hegelian understanding of secularisation as part of a historical development. From this perspective, the historical development of Christianity mirrors the events of Easter. Thus the present can be likened to Easter Sunday: God has died but Christianity is resurrected in the guise of philosophy.

Martensen was one of the most influential theologians of his time. A Hegelian, he suggested that there is a fundamental compatibility between philosophy and ethics on one hand and Christianity on the other. Like Heiberg he saw himself as belonging to a philosophical avant-garde, a privileged generation who experienced what no earlier generation had done, a resurrection of Christianity. Both mankind and Christianity have matured in the course of a historical process. Martensen points out "that Christianity in eighteen centuries has shown itself to possess the peculiar power of recovering life when apparently it was almost defunct, a peculiarity entirely absent in mythology, which when once dead can never be restored, but remains for ever in the realm of shadows; that Christianity has a phoenix-like nature, arising anew from the grave

---

[29] Heiberg, *Prosaiske Skrifter*, I, 385; Stewart, *A History of Hegelianism in Golden Age Denmark*, I, 404-413.

after every historical death; and along with the resurrection of Christianity in our days, although many do not believe in this resurrection, the true conception of humanity has also arisen from the grave, in the living, indissoluble union of morality and religion."[30]

The history of Christianity is presented here both in terms of the myth of the Phoenix and as a historical retelling of Easter, according to which Christianity dies only in order to be resurrected in philosophy. It was an attempt to combine the inevitability of secularisation as a historical phase with the idea that the church is an indispensable element in human history.

Although Martensen was decidedly conservative, Hegelianism developed into the liberal theology that arose in the first decades of the twentieth century. Among others Adolf von Harnack exerted some influence on Danish theology. Liberal theology provoked opposition, especially from the *indre mission*. Interestingly, twentieth-century liberal theology did not differ all that much from Martensen's theology. The reason why Martensen had not stirred up as much controversy was perhaps that the opposition - i.e. those who adhered to a literalist understanding of the Bible in the *indre mission* - was still weak. By the First World War, however, *indre mission* had positioned itself well within the established church. It now took the opportunity to 'purify the temple', for example by attempting to get rid of liberal clergymen. A famous case brought by the conservative clergy against the liberal minister Niels Arboe Rasmussen (1866-1944), failed to have him dismissed; in the end he resigned of his own accord.

Georg Brandes (1842-1927) also was targeted by Bishop Martensen's anti-Semitism and anti-liberalism. Brandes, who united nineteenth-century French naturalism, the English utilitarianism of Stuart Mill and Nietzsche's German nihilism, came from a Jewish family; but he was also an avowed atheist, and thus the logical target of criticism. Around 1870 it was still difficult for non-Christians, especially Jews, to become professors at the University of Copenhagen, so that Brandes had to settle for a life as an independent intellectual. Brandes inspired intellectuals, writers and artists all over Scandinavia, including August Strindberg and Henrik Ibsen. Though few in number and elitist in outlook, they successfully articulated (together with the first socialists) a set of modernist ideas (realism, utilitarianism, naturalism) as an alternative, non-religious *Weltanschauung*. Called *Kulturradikalisme* in Danish, the movement was controversial.[31]

The crematorium movement is often associated with Brandes and regarded as leftist, naturalist and atheist. Established as an association (*Foreningen for Ligbrænding*) in 1881, it took pains not to antagonise the church, focusing instead on hygiene and stressing its non-confessional character.[32]

Edvard Brandes (1847-1931), Georg's brother, became a member of the *Folketing* (the second chamber of parliament) for the Liberal Party in 1880. He was the first to

---

[30] Martensen, *Christian Ethics*, 18.
[31] Sørensen, "Nogle Reflektioner om Nationalisocialismen", 359.
[32] Møller, "Brændes eller begraves?".

refuse to swear on the Bible when appointed, which created a sensation. As a result, the parliament in practice stopped insisting that members take the oath. In the 1870s, a professor of mathematics who insisted that all faculties work according to the same scientific standards caused a dispute at the university between the sciences and the Faculty of Theology. The conflict was resolved but led to some self-reflection. The Faculty of Theology pointed out that the historical-philological method characteristic of the Harnack historical school guaranteed the academic nature of theological training. While theology remained a university discipline, the necessity for professors of all faculties to sign the Augsburg confession was silently abolished at this time.[33]

The conflict at the university reflected frictions that had been building up between church and science, particularly Darwinism. Often described in terms of martial metaphors, the reception of Darwinism among Danish theologians was actually quite peaceful. Theologians accepted modern science with the exception of some literalists, whose general response was resignation rather than protest. Some Grundtvigians and most liberal theologians tended to accept science as a valid explanation for the nature of life.[34]

Conclusion

In 1920, Danes who did not belong to any religious community at all amounted to 12,400, as opposed to approximately 3,600 around 1900. This was a substantial but hardly alarming increase. The church stood on firm ground. Owing to comprehensive financial reforms in the first decades of the twentieth century, the church was successfully brought from an agricultural to an industrial economy. The challenge from the relatively strong revivalist movements during the nineteenth century had caused neither disestablishment nor schism. The wish to disestablish the church expressed among others by Grundtvig, especially during the transition from absolutist rule to constitutional monarchy in 1848-1849, was not fulfilled. The freedom of religion according to the new constitution of 1849 resulted in missionary initiatives by both the Catholic Church and Anglo-American church societies. However, only the Mormons came close to being a success. The bond between church and state remained strong and became even stronger during the reforms of the first decades of the twentieth century. At the same time a democratisation of the church via the elected parochial church councils inspired by Grundtvig counterbalanced state centralisation, so that ultimately competence and authority were diffusely distributed in the church. The church had also tapped into the strong nationalist movement. It defined itself as an essential part of the Danish nation, thereby strengthening even further the ties between church and state.

---

[33] Grane and Hørby, eds., *Københavns Universitet*, 361 ff.

[34] Møller, "Teologiske reaktioner på darwinismen i Danmark".

Self-Reform and Swedish Christianity

Erik Sidenvall

More than in many other European nations the concept of religious homogeneity had become a tangible reality in Sweden.[1] In 1780, at a time when a limited religious liberty had manifested itself in many regions, church and nationhood were still intertwined at every level, from the national Diet to the rural household. In such a context the issue of the 'self-reform' of the church poses particular problems. When the church was made visible at every level of society, and comprised virtually every individual, what could be the meaning of self-reform? Or, perhaps better, what was not self-reform? What actions, that had a bearing on the Christian life of the nation, could not be considered as measures bent on making the church better suited to its divine calling? Such a line of reasoning rests on what I would like to call a *maximalist* definition of self-reform; self-reform could then be undertaken, in the end, by every baptised man or woman (it can indeed be argued that the extension of arenas where lay influence could be felt was one of the central features when we consider self-reform during this period). The problems inherent in such an approach are obvious, but it also has certain indisputable merits. It draws our attention to groups of agents that might otherwise have been left below the scholarly horizon. Furthermore, by using the maximalist definition we may avoid a certain a-historical teleology when looking at church reform - in other words, we need to include measures undertaken by groups of people that in the long-run led to the formation of schismatic bodies in our concept of self-reform. It is those very mistakes that are so easily made when instead we attempt to define self-reform in a *minimalist* way. In the standard version this approach targets the clergy (or even certain leading

---

[1] This chapter is built on the recent multi-volume history of Swedish Christianity, see Bexell, *Folkväckelsens och kyrkoförnyelsens tid*; Jarlert, *Romantikens och liberalismens tid*; Lenhammar, *Individualismens och upplysningens tid*.

clerics, i.e. the episcopacy) as the principal originators of change; sometimes they are accompanied by a choice selection of top laymen. Such a definition is easily put into operation within a scholarly study, but the objection that it imposes too rigid restrictions on our present subject carries much weight.

I will here operate with a concept of self-reform that approaches the maximalist definition. In this chapter I will paint the contours of an extensive reform process that virtually transformed church life in Sweden between 1780 and 1920. Four interlocking aspects of reform have here been singled out for scrutiny: the reform of the laity, the reform of church life, the reform of church workers and the reform of church theology. Under these headings the most important facets of self-reform in Sweden can be captured. A diverse group of people can be found as the originators of this process; to be sure we find several members of the clergy and other elite groups, but we will also find many a humble male or female Christian enthusiast. It remains one of the paradoxes of Swedish church history that, even though I argue that we can speak of extensive self-reform during the 140 years here under consideration, we must be aware of the fact that, seen from another perspective, reform was only in its infancy. Save a few periods around the year 1810 and 1860 the legal framework within which the church operated underwent very few changes. Indeed, change of church life as initiated from above remained limited in scope. Since most of these alterations have been dealt with in Volume I of the present series, and since my own maximalist definition of self-reform implies a 'from below' perspective, I will mostly leave these shifts aside.

Reform of the Laity

The cornerstone of ecclesiastical self-reform during the long nineteenth century was the new ideal of the layman that had begun to appear in the late 1700s. Whereas the laity in Lutheran orthodox teaching were assigned a series of essential roles within the church, their position was still circumscribed; in the affairs of the church the clergy were generally held to be the ones responsible for managing the affairs of the church. The relatively passive role of the laity under the *ancien régime* was now gradually exchanged for a more activist one; since the layman was now expected, by the reform-minded, to assume responsibility in religious matters it was also essential that the standard and the manners to be found among the laity were elevated. These two aspects, which interlock with other fundamental shifts within Swedish society such as the emergence of a representative democracy, the appearance of the middle class and the reorganisation of the national economy, were omnipresent during the period here under consideration. Its shapes and expressions differed from time to time but the rationale remained the same - the laity were to assume new responsibilities and were to behave accordingly.

Unsurprisingly, the first exponents of the new ideal were to be found among leading members of society. Count Rosenblad (1758-1847), for example, was one of the principal movers behind several of the religious societies that came to life during the

Matthias Rosenblad, *lithograph*, c.1830.
[Leuven, K.U.Leuven, Centrale bibliotheek: 2A5327]

first decades of the nineteenth century. He was a sober, controlled and serious character who took life seriously and was not afraid to assume responsibility in religious matters when clerical leadership stumbled. As one of the leaders of the *Svenska bibelsällskapet* (Swedish Bible Society, 1815), the *Evangeliska sällskapet* (Evangelical Society, 1808) and the *Svenska missionsällskapet* (Swedish Missionary Society, 1835) he was to be of much significance for the future. On the boards of these bodies he was joined by other members of the aristocracy and of the gentry, but also by representatives of a new middle class that emerged during these decades. Indeed, such bodies can be seen as the first signs of a conscious attempt on the part of the bourgeoisie to assume responsibility within society. The ideals espoused by such bodies came later to underpin the religious vision of the middle class.[2]

During this early period, before the impact of industrialisation and urbanisation, it was mostly the rural population (it should be noted that 90% of the population lived in the countryside in 1810) that was singled out as the object of reform. In years to come the call to elevate the customs, manners and morals of the rural population was frequently heard. It was not only their behaviour in church that was increasingly regarded as a problem, but also many other aspects of traditional rural life. To a new generation rising to power, rural life seemed hopelessly flawed, riddled with irrationality and a hereditary backwardness. The new ethical agenda, within which also was included temperance and Bible reading, was to a considerable extent shared by the nascent Swedish bourgeoisie. As several scholars have remarked, such ideals were later used to justify bourgeois hegemony; they represented a class of people with the 'right' values for the present age whose task it was to elevate their still un-enlightened brothers and sisters. This was a category of people bent on reform and not afraid of assuming the responsibility of uplifting the people at large.

But the ideals of the reformed laity were not only to be found in the religious societies that now began to emerge. The new church books that appeared during the first decades of the nineteenth century also carried the seeds of a new social order. Whereas the old, Lutheran orthodox teaching of the church had emphasised human depravity and the redemption that is in Christ, the new books tended to place greater stress on ethical teaching. Terms like 'virtue', 'diligence' and 'thrift' can be used to summarise the new gospel but also to paint the contours of a new society. The explanation of the seventh commandment in the Catechism of 1810 read as follows: "work promotes health and prosperity, it hinders sin, helps us to resist evil desires, it gives comfort and spiritual strength under distress".[3] Quite surprisingly, the attempt at social reconstruction, or even social disciplining, was most strongly felt within the reforms of the church hymnody that also occurred at this time. The aesthetic ideals of the early nineteenth-century bourgeoisie clashed heavily with the way in which hymn singing and liturgical chanting was conducted in most parishes. To those who struggled for purity and simplicity, popular practice tended to be associated with ugliness, unruliness and disorder. Johann Christian Friedrich Haeffner (1759-1833), the principal reformer of church music during this period, wrote: "Quite often it appears as if the organ player and the singing congregation were engaged in battle, both trying to surpass the other in wild screams and loud noises; the chanting priest, instead of seeking reconciliation, contributes frequently to the clamour."[4]

---

[2] A classic study of these associations is Jansson, *Adertonhundratalets associationer*.

[3] "arbete befordrar hälsa och välstånd, hindrar många tillfällen till synd, hjälper oss att emotstå onda begärelser, bidrager till tröst och sinnesstyrka under motgången". As quoted in Jarlert, *Romantikens och liberalismens tid*, 40.

[4] "Ofta synes det, som låge Kantorn och den sjungande församlingen i strid med varandra, båda strävande att överträffa varandra i vilda skrän och stojande larm; och den mässande prästen, i stället för att stifta försoning, ökar icke sällan oredan." As quoted in Jarlert, *Romantikens och liberalismens tid*, 32.

It is difficult to guess how successful the middle-class 'reform program' might have been if their ideals and ambitions had not coincided with those of a new rural elite that was rising to power at about this time. As the urban middle class emerged in Sweden, rural life became increasingly stratified. The new 'class' of relatively well-to-do freehold farmers that emerged after the year 1830 saw itself (in a markedly paternalistic way) as the natural stewards of rural life. They defined themselves *vis-à-vis* their inferior brothers and sisters by advocating the reform of traditional rural life and by imitating the behaviour of the urban elites. Even though the new ideals did not go uncontested by the mostly reactionary pietistic revivals, they too built on ideals of a reformed laity - an assembly of believers who behaved in an orderly way and actively struggled to deepen their piety.

It was an integral part of the logic of reform that those people whose lives had been transformed by the new ideals should also struggle to bring others into the fold. The successes of the reform program entailed a growth in the number of active agents trying to convince their brothers and sisters of the ultimate truth of the new ideals. Seen in a longer perspective, it was an expansion in terms of numbers but also in terms of groups. In future years, people further down the social ladder were to be found among the agents of change; even more importantly the ideal of the new laity meant that women increasingly came to assume active roles in religious matters. It can even be argued that these ideals were essential for the expansion of women's roles that can be observed during the latter half of the nineteenth century.

The ideal of a reformed, responsible and active laity was taken one step further by the low-church, evangelical phalanx which became increasingly vocal after 1830. Within these circles 'the converted' became a new and ideal image of what it was to be a layman. Being a converted Christian meant subscribing to certain devotional standards, a prescribed code of conduct and a new standard of lay behaviour. For these people, conversion included not only a new relationship with God, but also a call to lay Christian activism. Groups of converted members of the *Svenska kyrkan* (Church of Sweden) thus created a plethora of groups and activities - Sunday schools, tract societies, temperance societies and missionary auxiliaries - aimed at extending the evangelical spirit and the ethical uplift of the populace at large. After the repeal of the Conventicle Act in 1858 lay-led prayer-meetings (initially intended as supplement to the ordinary Sunday service) became a standard feature among these groups (see further comments below). It may even be argued that the emergence of the lay preacher, the tract distributor and the Bible woman, all of whom were found within these groups, meant the arrival of a new, semi-professional, kind of lay worker (see below). Much of this evangelical enthusiasm lived in a state of constant tension with the ecclesiastical establishment; yet, it was only after the formation of the *Svenska missionsförbundet* (the Swedish Mission Covenant) in 1878 that we can speak of a serious schismatic move away from the *Svenska kyrkan* within evangelical circles. Even though they first emerged as a 'party' within the church, their new concept of church life was to be of much importance for the future even among those who cannot rightly be labelled 'evangelical'.

Erik Sidenvall

Reform of Church Life

At the end of the eighteenth century religious activity in Sweden was severely circumscribed. The Conventicle Act of 1723 and the Statute of Religion of 1735 made it a virtual impossibility to make additions to officially endorsed parish religion. Yet, the eighteenth century had also witnessed the arrival of a kind of Protestantism radically different in nature. The Moravian impact on the religious life of Sweden dates back to the first decades of the eighteenth century; the teaching of this 'pietist' German group spread above all in the southern provinces and had a considerable influence among the upper strata of society. Although not uncontested, Moravian piety was incorporated into the framework provided by the Lutheran church. The news of Moravian missions was spread above all through the dissemination of the *Gemein-Nachrichten* produced at Herrnhut. This 'publication' was quite well known, at least among members of the Swedish clergy, before its decline in popularity during the first decades of the nineteenth century. Moravianism was in some ways the forerunner of the new kind of religious organisations that came to life during the nineteenth century. First, it operated with a conception of community (national or international) that went beyond the framework provided by the age-old parish grid. Secondly, as a loosely organised body, it communicated with its sympathisers in a manner that was markedly 'modern'. The *Gemein-Nachrichten* can be seen as an early attempt to create a shared sense of identity within a diverse community.

The religious societies that emerged during the first decades of the nineteenth century developed these traits one step further (it should be noted that several of the key figures in these bodies were connected with Moravian circles). However, for the future, it was the *Svenska missionssällskapet* that most effectively disseminated new organisational ideals.[5] What in particular came to characterise this agency was the way in which local adherents were organised; from the 1830s and onwards local auxiliaries began to emerge, later recognised by the central board, in order to boost participation. In the year 1846 the *Svenska missionssällskapet* had 27 affiliated bodies. Even though these associations in most cases lived under the auspices of the recognised parochial organisation, they nevertheless represented a powerful new way to organise religious life within the church. A majority became strongholds of an evangelical piety and through this network of like-minded people a new vision of revitalised Christianity came to life for large groups of people. As the century progressed it became evident that these organisations concerned themselves with much more than raising the cause of missions, both foreign and domestic. During the 1850s, the mission halls became the hot-houses of a popular revivalist Christianity. Even though these assemblies of people declared their principled attachment and support of Lutheranism (which was, of course, the only possibility), fears that these groups would drift into schism grew,

---

[5] For the SMS, see Sundkler, *Svenska missionssällskapet*.

especially as it now had become evident that the state was increasingly less inclined to uphold the monopoly of the *Svenska kyrkan*. In order to prevent this from happening, and to provide local revivalist groups with a more firm organisational structure, both regional and national organisations were created. The most important of these was the *Evangeliska fosterlands-stiftelsen* (Swedish Evangelical Mission, 1858). In the 1860s an alternative church structure existed alongside, and within, the official Church of Sweden. At the national level, the evangelical revival was still a nebulous phenomenon held loosely together by associating local societies to national and/or regional organisations. Even though early evangelical religiosity was seldom directly opposed to traditional parochial life, it nevertheless represented a radical departure. Because it was organised through voluntary associations it operated with a completely different rationale from that of the traditional, geographically defined, church parish.

Not all churchmen found it necessary to engage in such a manifest drive to go beyond, and perhaps even to undermine, the traditional church structure when they wanted to revive national religion. Emerging from the 1840s and onwards, the women's societies, most of which shared the missionary enthusiasm of the *Svenska missionssällskapet* were organised locally as parochial bodies[6]; the Sunday schools that began to appear a few years later were arranged in a similar way.[7] During the latter half of the nineteenth century there was a conscious effort on the part of leading ecclesiastics and certain groups of laymen to rely on the traditional diocesan/parochial network when they wanted to instil new life into the established church. It remains one of the paradoxes of the age that even those who struggled to revive the parishes were forced to rely on a voluntary organisation to reach their goal. Without doubt the explanation of this phenomenon lies in the rigidity of church governance. The legal framework within which the church operated regulated what the church could do, even at parish level, and virtually all attempts at exploring a possible extension of parochial work had to go all the way to government offices in Stockholm. This led to an inflexibility which made the church ill-prepared to deal with the radical changes that transformed Sweden towards the end of the nineteenth century. For many an ardent reformer what remained was to found some kind of voluntary organisation. This was true in particular for those who struggled to revive the church's charitable work as well as those who struggled for church extension in increasingly crowded cities.

Towards the end of the period here under consideration we can observe a clear tendency to create voluntary organisations within the existing structure. 'Voluntary parochial work', as opposed to parochial work as defined by the law, was the motto of the day. The two forms began to merge. At the local level a host of minor activities and societies came to life; often the progenitors of such bodies drew direct inspiration from the modes of operation so successfully launched within the international evangeli-

---

[6] For women's societies, see Wejryd, *Svenska kyrkans syföreningar*.

[7] For the early development of Sunday schools and Christian youth societies, see Fjellander, *Korset och ringen*, ch. 2.

Erik Sidenvall

Parish hall in Hedemora, *postcard, c.1920*.
[Private collection]

cal movement. After the end of the Great War the members of many Swedish parishes (most, albeit not exclusively, city parishes) would find a range of activities to engage in. To the women's society were added youth groups, laymen's groups and groups aimed at social outreach. In many cases this renewed, and often vigorously active parish life, took physical shape in *församlingshem* or *församlingshus* (parish halls), which since the final years of the nineteenth century had begun to appear in many Swedish cities.

A similar range of activities can be observed at a diocesan level during the first decades of the twentieth century. To the diocesan edifice, formally organised as chapter and bishop, was added a range of voluntary organisations, sometimes understood as an extension of the voluntary work that was done in the parishes. In this form the diocese emerged as a regional body often rivalling free-church organisations on the district level. Among the most important of the diocesan activities thus created should be mentioned the diocesan conferences, pioneered within the diocese of Kalmar in 1906, which provided a forum for the loyal and committed laity to meet the clergy in discussions. There was also a tendency to use the diocese as a platform for measures to tie the laity more firmly to the church. To belong to a diocese was to be a part of a larger communion with its own unique history, its own traditions and its own ambitions. In the face of nascent free churches and an often agnostic socialism, the diocese became much more than a mere department of the state church apparatus - it was something to be proud of. In the atmosphere of late-nineteenth-century Romanticism, each diocese was to espouse a certain 'spirit'. In most dioceses members of the clergy began serial publications, such as diocesan yearbooks and gazettes, in order to further such sentiment. In some cases these publications have survived into the late twentieth century - a fact that in itself bears witness to the considerable impact such measures had on generations of churchmen.[8]

Reform of Church Workers

With respect to the formal education of the clergy, the most significant steps of reform were taken during the first half of the nineteenth century. Before 1831 most members of the clergy had received their formal education at the *gymnasium* (diocesan college) and received their academic credentials after having been duly examined by bishop and chapter. The successful young candidates were thus ordained to serve the diocese within which they were born (*jus indignatus*). In 1831 educational demands were heightened. The universities were given the role of providing mandatory intellectual training to the future clergy. Instead of the examination overseen by the diocesan authorities, each candidate was to gain a degree conferred by the university. We may easily come to the conclusion that, by such measures, the church was denied the right to train its own clergy; however, it should be borne in mind that the theological faculties, which were primarily responsible for clerical education, were closely allied to the church, with professors combining their academic posts with various high-ranking positions at the cathedrals of Lund and Uppsala. Simultaneously, a new pastoral examination was created, to be confirmed by the chapters, and mandatory for those seeking their own benefices.

In other words, early-nineteenth-century Sweden witnessed a rather extensive re-professionalisation of the clergy. Seen from a purely academic perspective, the demands placed on the clergy of the *Svenska kyrkan* were similar to those placed on other civil servants. Compared to these measures the reforms in clerical education that occurred during the early twentieth century, which included the creation of seminaries for the practical training of future clergymen, remained much more limited in scope. If the extensive early-nineteenth-century academic reforms tied the clergy to the nascent 'class' of civil servants, most clergymen still remained tied to the agricultural economy. Even though there were indications that members of the bourgeoisie were increasingly drawn to the clerical profession during the period under consideration, the average cleric was still firmly rooted in the social fabric of the countryside.[9] For many generations the best way forward for the intellectually gifted farmer's son was to join the clergy. Furthermore, though formalised during the 1830s, the stipend of the clergy was

---

[8] For the 'diocesan revival' in Sweden, see Aldén, *Stiftskyrkans förnyelse*.

[9] For the social background of the clergy, see Carlsson, *Svensk ståndscirkulation*, 99-101.

still based on the tithe offerings of their parishioners. A majority of the clergy also gained an income from the farmland that was attached to the vicarage; this meant that many a cleric combined his priestly duties with those of an agricultural householder. In reality, there was little that separated the minister from the parishioners on the countryside - he was a farmer among farmers. This grounding in a rural way of life was gradually diminished during the nineteenth century, but it is not until the first decade of the twentieth century that we can safely say that the ties that bound the clergy to the rural economy were definitely loosened.

More notable reforms occurred when we take a closer look at the expansion, and indeed the creation of new categories, of Christian workers. Already during the 1840s many prominent voices within the church pointed out that the church, once again, needed to take another look at its responsibility to cater to the needs of the poor and the destitute. With a parochial system increasingly under stress due to overpopulation in many rural areas and beginning urbanisation, the church needed a new vision for its task of assisting those in need. Though the call was not unanimously heard, some of these voices also spoke about the need for a new kind of Christian worker whose task it was to meet the needs of a changing society. In 1849 the *Sällskapet till beredande av en diakonissanstalt i Stockholm* (Society in Aid of Forming a Deaconess Institute in Stockholm) was formed. Inspired by the recently launched deaconess training college in Kaiserwerth in Germany, but also the Catholic Sisters of Mercy, it began training its first Christian aid workers in 1851. In 1855 the two first deaconesses were initiated in Stockholm. The operation expanded rapidly. Aided by wealthy benefactors, the Deaconess Institute was to admit nearly 900 students before the year 1900; 255 of these were initiated as deaconesses. In addition to being a large-scale training institute for women, it was to launch a hospital and various nursing and rescue homes. In many ways the Deaconess Institute represented a significant departure; its students not only formed a new, and much needed, category of Christian workers (though due to the rigidity of the ecclesiastical system, few of them would be formally employed by the church), but they also brought a new sense of up-to-date professionalism to the church's task to aid those in need. Moreover, the deaconesses were the first nurses in Sweden, thereby granting respectability to female work outside the home. Christian aid work was thus to form a significant arena for those women who struggled for a recognised public position.

The ecclesiastical position of the deaconesses remained ambivalent for more than a century, occupying a relatively undefined border region between the clergy and the laity. It was not until 2000 that they were formally recognised as ordained. The nineteenth century witnessed a virtual explosion of other categories of Christian workers. As indicated above, to a large extent the national evangelical revival depended on lay forces to spread its message. Tract distributors, lay preachers and Bible women spread the message of conversion to numerous localities in Sweden. In contrast to the deaconesses who were firmly rooted within the respectable classes, these workers were in general to be found in much lower social strata. It was the farmhands, the artisans and the shop assistants that were prone to pick up such forms of Christian work. They were formally recognised by such agencies as the *Evangeliska fosterlands-stiftelsen* or regional tract societies; for their upkeep they depended on the charity of the faithful. Within many circles these lay workers were much despised and the source of much ridicule; even evangelical-minded elites remained undecided as to their existence. On the one hand, their work was necessary for the spiritual renewal of the *Svenska kyrkan*; on the other, they were a source of much concern, doctrinally as well as socially. Within circles affiliated to the *Evangeliska fosterlands-stiftelsen* measures were taken to educate these, more or less proletarian, church workers. In 1862 a tract distributor class was begun at Grythyttan in central Sweden; similar courses were later given at the missionary training college of the *Evangeliska fosterlands-stiftelsen*, Johannelund, outside Uppsala. The students were taught general subjects, the Bible and the Lutheran creed. In spite of such obvious attempts to tie these forces more firmly to the church, with the gradual radicalisation of a large part of the evangelical revival and the hardening opposition from the ecclesiastical establishment, many of these lay preachers found the *Svenska kyrkan* too narrow an ecclesiastical habitat. Towards the end of the nineteenth century many of them were instrumental in forming seceding congregations.

A desire to educate the laity to take a more active role in the church's mission became manifest during the first decades of the twentieth century. With the growth of popular socialism and a fiercely anti-establishment free-church movement, the need to include the faithful laity in the church's struggles against these foes was more strongly felt. A new cadre of laypeople, together with numerous reform-minded clergy connected with the *Ungkyrkorörelsen* (Young Church Movement, see below), were instrumental in bringing this reorientation about. The newly erected parish halls were utilised to mobilise and to educate the laity in the traditions of the church and the challenges of the modern world. To some extent, therefore, this should be understood as a movement among grass-root adherents, but as such it needed organisational backing. In addition to volunteer diocesan organisations, the *Svenska kyrkans diakonistyrelse* (Church of Sweden Diaconal Board, 1908) was created with the aim of supporting various kinds of volunteer parish-work that now mushroomed. Among its many responsibilities was included the task of providing the parishes with up-to-date educational material, publications aimed at lay consumption and a selection of choice lecturers to be used at various parish events. Many of those enlivened by this new drive to include the laity in the defence of the church found a home in yet another national organisation, the *Kyrkobröderna* (Church Brotherhood), initiated after the end of the Great War. When we move further on into the 1920s the mobilising efforts on the part of the church were further developed with the inauguration of the *Lekmannaskolan* (Laymen's School) at Sigtuna in 1922. For the future this institution was to be of much significance as a centre for educating the laity as responsible members of the *Svenska kyrkan* - a church that was not only the state church but also *folkyrkan*, 'the church of the people'.

Erik Sidenvall

Reform of Church Theology

Those who struggled to reform the *Svenska kyrkan* during the first years of the 1800s carried with them the beginning of a new theology. It was a system of new doctrinal ideals, still in its infancy, which was to cause much concern in years to come. The Lutheran teaching of old had been built on the collective nature of the church - the *ecclesia*; the new voices placed the individual Christian at the centre. The unity of the religious collective was seen as of less importance than the spiritual condition of individual men and women. By many later exponents, albeit not by all, conversion was seen as the event that marked the entrance into a new spiritual state; it was these people, and not the populace at large, that formed the basis of the true church. Thereby a rift, at least in theory, tore asunder the social fabric that had hitherto been understood to be the natural foundation of the church. This division became manifest in the various societies and unions to which many born-again Christians flocked; indeed, in the latter half of the nineteenth century they were increasingly understood as expressions of the true church - voluntary associations of converted Christians. As may be expected, hand in hand with this ecclesiological re-orientation came a decidedly 'lower' view of the clergy. Whereas the Lutheran establishment had held a relatively 'high' view of the clergy as being a people set apart, by virtue of their ordination, as the preachers of divine truth and as guardians of the sacraments, their position in the new church that was beginning to emerge was far from self-evident. As we have seen, the new organisations tended to encourage lay leadership. Among the more radical voices, especially those that found their position within the national church increasingly troublesome, the criticism of the clergy was far-reaching. With a fundamental commitment to the idea that the laity had to be born-again, this was to be demanded also of the clergy; ordination alone was not enough for those that were to assume a position of leadership in the church. To the separatist voices that grew increasingly powerful among the low-church phalanx of the church after 1860, the ministry of those clerics who did not share in the low-church religion of experience was seen as of little consequence. It was much better to hear a born-again lay preacher than a state church minister with little interest in evangelical spirituality. Even though Sweden was not unaffected by the controversies that arose in the wake of advanced Biblical scholarship, theological liberalism and agnostic natural science, it was the complex of theological notions outlined above that was to dictate the theological agenda well beyond the year 1920.

The claims of increasingly vocal modernisers of church theology were forcefully resisted by groups of conservative sentiment. In some regions the new individualistic ethos was met with vigorous resistance on the part of 'old church', i.e. pietistic revivalist, followers. Even though they had much in common with low-church activists, they stuck tenaciously to the ordinances of the church as the visible means of divine grace. A somewhat different theological riposte came from a group of markedly high-churchmen attached to the theological faculty of Lund University. They all rose to high office within the church during the latter half of the nineteenth century, but when they launched their theological programme during the 1850s they spoke as academics through their mouthpiece, *Swensk Kyrkotidning* (Swedish Church Times, 1855). Infused with the spirit of German Romanticism they understood the church as an evolving organism gradually taking shape over time. Against the individualism of the evangelicals they put forward a collective, historically given, social order - the family, the state and the church. Consequently, it was not the faith of the individual that constituted the church; rather, the reverse was true. To be dependent on individual men and women for the extension and endurance of the church was deemed to be a violation of divine ordinances; it was the sacraments, a duly ordained ministry and the visible church that together created the fountainhead of Christian life.[10]

By the 1870s the low-church party within the church had became increasingly divided. Those who had struggled to foster a movement of loyal churchmen found their task increasingly difficult. The separatist forces found a congenial expression in the teaching of Paul Petter Waldenström (1838-1917), a high school lecturer and an ordained minister. Ecclesiology was now, once again, the issue at stake. Waldenström, like many others in the international evangelical milieu, resorted to the notion of 'the New Testament church polity'. Waldenström took low-church teaching one step further. The true church, as an assembly of converted believers, should have the power to create their own ordinances with the New Testament as their foundation. They were the true church and not the ecclesiastical establishment. Loyalty to the church organisation became a conscience question: how could they, as Christians, remain loyal to an un-Christian organisation? How could they have communion with the ungodly? The conflict with the *Svenska kyrkan* grew in intensity and 1878 the *Svenska missionsförbundet* came to life as an umbrella organisation for those expressing such radical sentiment. A large segment of the low-church party joined the SMC. As a national organisation it grew rapidly; by 1895 the *Svenska missionsförbundet* had no fewer than 74,595 members (out of a population of approximately 4,800,000).

Around 1900 the principal supporters of the Church of Sweden were profoundly anxious about the church's future. As we have seen, the schism that had occurred with the evangelical revival at the formation of the *Svenska missionsförbundet*, and the growth of other free-church denominations threatened the church from one side; from the other side the danger arose from a manifestly hostile, and rapidly expanding, social democracy which drew most of its support from an urban proletariat with little knowledge of Christianity. The main theological response to these threats came from those who had attempted to breathe life into the traditional church structure by voluntary parish work. These were people who, like those espousing a Lutheran high-church ecclesiology, were sacramental in their orientation, valued the church, respected its ordinances, took pleasure in its history and saw it as the visible means of channelling God's love to the Swedish people. But unlike many traditional ecclesiastics, they voiced their support (at least in principle) for the contemporary call for religious liberty and

---

[10] Nineteenth-century Swedish high-church theology has been given a thorough treatment in Wallgren, *Individen och samfundet*.

struggled to come to grips with radical thought. Against the individualism and dangerous modernism of both the free churches and the socialists, they upheld the parish as a centre of solidarity, social responsibility and spiritual life. The most well-known manifestation of this sentiment is found within the, so-called, *Ungkyrkorörelsen*, which originated among students at Uppsala University before 1910. Resorting to a method successfully tried out among the student missionary volunteers in the United States during the 1880s, the movement spread its message through 'crusades'. Pairs of students toured the parishes with an aim to instil new life and to meet the enemies of the church face-to-face. At the end of our period the agenda of the *Ungkyrkorörelsen*, which was founded on a traditional ecclesiology (albeit brought to new life by youthful vigour and up-to-date rhetoric), represented the most powerful theological answer to the contemporary challenges facing the *Svenska kyrkan*.[11]

Conclusion

This chapter has painted a picture of an extensive, albeit somewhat diffuse, self-reform of Swedish Christianity. In some ways it was a response to the new conditions under which the church lived during an era when many old certainties were called into question. Urbanisation and industrialisation, as well as the demands of a more liberal state, meant that some of these reforms were in response to stimuli coming from outside. But the church was not just a passive agent without initiatives of its own. This chapter has also argued that several of these changes grew out of a reinterpretation of the Christian tradition which evolved into a new vision of society, the church and, indeed, of mankind.

To what extent was this reform 'movement' successful in altering the shape of Swedish Christianity? On the one hand, it was a failure. Some of its ideals failed to get a more general acceptance beyond being mere notions of party. Indeed, the split that occurred within the national evangelical revival in 1878 bears witness to the conflicts that existed between these groups and principal organs of the church, but also to essential divisions within the low-church camp. Self-reform could actually be too far-reaching for the church organisation. On the other hand, when we reach our terminal point in 1920 it is obvious that the new vision of lay responsibility, of new forms of parish work and the need for an expanded Christian workforce had in fact become commonplaces widely accepted within the church at large. In spite of the immobility and the conservatism of the state church, vital components in its credo had in fact undergone significant change.

---

[11] The standard treatment of the *Ungkyrkorörelsen* is still Tergel, *Ungkyrkomännen, arbetarfrågan och nationalismen*.

The Limits of Ecclesiastical Reform in Norway

Øyvind Norderval, Dag Thorkildsen & Hallgeir Elstad

From the Reformation to the time of the Napoleonic Wars, Norway was a part of the composite Danish state which included Iceland, the Faeroe Islands and the duchy of Schleswig-Holstein. The church was organised as a state church with a Lutheran confession. Since the sixteenth century, the government of the church had been an integrated part of the government of the state. This church order was strengthened during the age of absolutism (from 1660). For this reason religious confession and church order were an important part of legislation. The church not only had a religious, but also a political aim. Until the nineteenth century, Lutheran religion gave legitimacy to the authorities, and confession marked the identity of state and people.[1]

Around 1780 both Pietism and Enlightenment influenced the church. Pietism from Halle had been introduced around 1700 and found adherents among the upper class. It gained admittance at the royal court as well, and the Danish king sponsored the sending of pietistic missionaries to India. Various pieces of legislation which were of great importance for religious life were passed during the reign of Christian VI (1730-1746). In 1736 confirmation as an act of confession was introduced and made compulsory. Elementary education for all was established three years later. The later bishop of Bergen, Erik Pontoppidan (1698-1764), produced an 'explanation' of Luther's Minor Catechism, for the instruction of confirmands. Pontoppidan's book clearly had a pietistic colour. It came to be used as reader in elementary schools, and thus had a great impact on most people's understanding of Christianity.

---

[1] Introductions to Norwegian church history of the period under consideration are Aarflot, *Norsk kirkehistorie*, II; Wisløff, *Norsk kirkehistorie*, III; and Molland, *Norges kirkehistorie i det 19. århundre*. An introduction in English is Molland, *Church Life in Norway*; also Hope, *German and Scandinavian Protestantism*.

The Enlightenment emerged in the second part of the eighteenth century and reached a climax shortly after 1800. In Norway Enlightenment ideas gained support mainly from the elite, especially the bishops. The clergy as a whole displayed greater variety. Probably most of them were orthodox or pietistic, some were supranaturalists in their teaching, and a small number could be regarded as outright rationalists. Many pastors demonstrated broad scientific interests and engaged in the improvement of people's education. The pastoral ideal of the time was the pastor as *folkelærer* or 'folk teacher'. The minister in rural areas commonly took care of many 'worldly' matters. But he was also the only religious 'specialist' in his parish, so that the parish people went to him for both worldly and religious advice. He thus represented both church and king.

During the nineteenth century, population growth posed a challenge to the church. The Norwegian population grew from 900,000 in 1815 to 1,800,000 in 1875 and to 2,200,000 in 1900. Some 800,000 people emigrated to the USA between 1825 and 1920. Mobility increased, as did the rate of urbanisation. The number of people living in towns rose from 440,000 in 1875 to 1,200,000 in 1920, from about 25 to 45% of the total population.[2] While the Norwegian population during the nineteenth century increased by 150%, the number of pastors rose by only 80%. Certain suburban districts lacked both pastor and church. The number of people served by a pastor increased, and many pastors complained that they had too much to do. The government tried to meet the situation by building churches and increasing the number of pastors and parishes. The existing ecclesiastical structures were, however, unable to cope with the population growth.

Nation Building

Following the Treaty of Kiel in January 1814, Denmark was reduced to a small independent nation. In spring 1814 a Norwegian constitutional assembly formulated the most liberal constitution in Europe. After a short war against Sweden, a new union between Norway and Sweden was established until 1905. The liberal constitution of 1814 marked a starting point for Norwegian nation building, and the constitution itself became an important symbol of the Norwegian nation state. The second article declared that the Lutheran religion should remain the official religion of the state. Furthermore Jesuits, monastic orders and Jews were not permitted to enter Norway. Another symbol of the nation was the University of Christiania (Oslo), founded in 1811. An important goal of university education was to produce civil servants to administer the state, and among these the clergy were the most important group. Through the local ministers the authorities reached all parts of the nation. The first teachers of theology were Svend Borchmann Hersleb (1784-1836) and Stener Johannes Stenersen (1789-1835), who had

---

[2] Danielsen et al., *Norway*.

studied at the University of Copenhagen. They represented a 'theology of repristination', i.e. they fell back on the more orthodox theology that had preceded the rise of Enlightenment rationalism. Hersleb was a friend of N.F.S. Grundtvig (1783-1872) from the time both had lived in the College of Walchendorph in Copenhagen as students. In 1816 Hersleb helped establish *Det norske bibelselskap* (Norwegian Bible Society) and from 1833 he supervised the practical theological training in Christiania. Although 1814 represented a political and cultural break, the degree of continuity should not be underestimated. For example, Pietistic religiousness continued through new forms of revivalism.

Revivalism

At the end of the eighteenth century, an important shift took place within Protestant piety and practice as a result of pietistic revivalist movements among lay Christians. The laity demanded freedom from the religious tutelage of the state. As a system absolutism represented both political and religious conformity and indoctrination, the formative cultural signals coming from the top of the social hierarchy. The collapse of absolutism meant that this situation was turned upside down. Change was initiated from below through demands for political and religious freedom. Important and influential cultural currents arose, as is shown by the popularisation and democratisation of cultural initiatives. This was a marked development away from the seventeenth and eighteenth centuries. Within the absolute Danish-Norwegian monarchy pietism had been an affair of the state. The clergy had introduced religious ideals from above. They were officers of the Crown and thus controlled religious life. This control was carried out through a royal ordinance - the so-called *Konventikkelplakaten* (Act of Conventicles) of 1741 - that prohibited private religious assemblies without the consent and surveillance of the local minister.

At the beginning of the nineteenth century several revivalist movements emerged in which a free and independent laity demanded the right to assemble and preach. The established church was criticised for imposing spiritual constraints, and for its apparent lack of Christian commitment. The pietist revivalism from below was to have an enormous influence on the further development of Christian life in nineteenth and twentieth-century Norway.[3]

---

[3] Thorkildsen, "Vekkelse og modernisering i Norden på 1800-tallet".

The Hauge Movement

Revivalism was introduced in Norway by the farmer Hans Nielsen Hauge (1771-1824). Hauge had a religious breakthrough following an ecstatic experience in 1796. He started wandering about as a preacher and spiritual adviser, attending gatherings of the pious in private homes (conventicles) and writing edifying books and tracts. He travelled, mostly by foot, throughout Norway during the next eight years. In his preaching and vast number of publications, Hauge opposed a spiritually stagnant church, headed by a state clergy who in his view lacked the earnestness brought on by a conversion experience. In his first published pamphlet, *Reflections on the Poverty of the World*, he reprimanded the enlightened clergy for their superficial preaching and for not living by sound moral standards: "You recognise it in their words and acts: their sermons and prayers are worldly, and they are concerned about how to become happy. They believe that they can enter heaven asleep. [...] Some also expect honour and reverence from their listeners. Further they partake in games and voluptuousness."[4] Hauge's conception of Christendom was concentrated around law and penance with an emphasis on repentance and a new life in obedience.

Another remarkable feature of Hauge's understanding of Christian life is that he combined a puritan ethos with Enlightenment ideas on the need for public education, agricultural reforms and practical skills. His ethics of vocation emphasised the Christian's need to manage and multiply God's material gifts in piety and modesty. Hauge for his part tried to fulfil this way of life. After obtaining a trading license in Bergen in 1801, he set up a comprehensive network of business and industry around the country. He helped many of his followers to establish and run enterprises such as printing offices, textile factories, timber mills, paper mills and salt works. On his trips around the country he combined preaching and trade, and his target group were the members of his own social class, the farmers. The combination of preaching and business explains the strong opposition against Hauge and his movement from the clergy, the officials and the merchant elite alike. Hauge was arrested many times before the Chancellery in Copenhagen jailed him permanently in 1804. He was charged with breaching the Act of Conventicles, with vagrancy and with economic irregularities. The allegations indicate that the Hauge movement was regarded as a political threat to the old hierarchical society. He not only defied the religious hegemony of the clergy through his lay preaching, but also opened up the way for the advancement of farmers across time-honoured social boundaries and subverted the power apparatus of the officials. Hauge remained in prison for more than four years before the authorities issued charges against him. However, he was released from prison in 1811, before the case came to trial. By that time his health had been ruined. When the case finally came up for trial in 1813, the charges had been reduced to breaching the Act of Conventicles and offending public

---

[4] Ording, ed., *Hans Nielsen Hauges skrifter*, I, 84.

A. Tidemand, Haugianerne (The Haugeans), *oil on canvas, 1852.*
[Oslo, Nasjonalgalleriet]

officials. Hauge was sentenced to two years in prison, but following his appeal in 1814 the sentence was reduced to a fine.

Hauge spent the last ten years of his life as a farmer outside the capital, Christiania. He no longer travelled but kept in touch with a large network of supporters around the country, maintaining contact through letters and receiving guests at his farm. Hauge continued to advise financial entrepreneurs within the movement. He managed to recover financially and enjoyed respect among many of the officials and the social elite in Christiania. His only son studied theology and was ordained. At his death in 1824, it was clear that his opposition to the hierarchical society had been successful.[5]

Haugianism was a conventicle movement which regularly organised private meetings for edification, but at the same time it underlined its commitment towards the established church. This explains the special relationship between lay movements and the Church of Norway, where revivalists understood themselves as *ecclesiolae* in

---

[5] Norderval, "Ikke som hiine elendige Tullemutter eller Sammenløb".

Ecclesia. Hauge himself had realised that his crusade for the religious freedom of lay people could lead to separatism, both within the established church and within the movement itself. He understood that a confessional and denominational line had to be maintained. In a testament to his 'friends', written three years before his death, he wisely emphasised precisely this: "Therefore, it is my last will, that you in the future just as in the past, in unity keep to the religion of our state, so that you receive from the public teachers all that their public offices provide. Then you will go to church, and you will receive the sacraments. They shall officiate at weddings, likewise at graveside ceremonies, and at everything else that belongs to good order."[6]

The Laestadius Movement

The Laestadius movement was one of the most important cultural imports from Sweden to northern Norway in the late 1800s. It was one of the most influential and formative cultural impulses in this part of the country, not only with regard to Christian faith and life, but also to culture, politics and business. The originator of the movement, Lars Levi Laestadius (1800-1861), was a remarkably gifted minister who combined academic and intellectual interests with the revivalist's simple call for repentance. Partly of Sámi descent, he was born in Jäkkvik in Swedish Lapland. He studied botany and theology at Uppsala between 1820 and 1822. After obtaining his theological degree, Laestadius worked for a few years as a minister in Arjeplog and a missionary in Pite Lapp district. He was appointed minister of Karesuando in 1825, a post he held until he moved to the congregation of Pajala in 1849.

In his early years Laestadius adopted fundamental pietistic beliefs. He had a spiritual breakthrough in 1844. He afterwards claimed that his sermons were 'heightened in colour', which possibly refers to his straightforward way of preaching in Sámi and Finnish, using metaphors which people recognised. A revival started in Karesuando the following year. One of the characteristic features of this new group of free laypeople was their ecstatic behaviour, which in Finnish is called *liikutukset*. The crying, singing, groaning, and jumping during the service often led to conflicts with the local minister.

In the beginning the revival took place among the predominantly Sámi population in Karesuando and its surroundings. The social conditions in the district were miserable. Laestadius drew a harsh picture of the situation. According to Laestadius, alcohol was the root cause of poverty and the first step towards social and moral degeneration. Alcoholism led to lack of responsibility, to poverty, and ultimately to violence. He also criticised extramarital relations that resulted in children growing up in unsafe conditions and denounced the theft of reindeer. These themes run like a thread through his sermons and his theological writings in general. They represent the

---

[6] Ording, ed., *Hans Nielsen Hauges skrifter*, VIII, 243-244.

essence of his preaching of repentance. Laestadius did not glorify poverty by denying that the poor were responsible for their own situation. On the contrary, he believed that only repentance could release them from their misery. On the other hand, he did censure the general lack of solidarity with the socially deprived. People in the higher echelons of society lived superficial lives, governed by 'the devil of honour', as bad role models for the poor, whom they also exploited.

Laestadius' preaching was successful. Many members of the Sámi population repented, joined the movement and changed their life style. Alcoholism declined, as did thefts and promiscuity. Laestadius' understanding of the bad social situation among the Sámi population was religiously motivated. At the same time, he opposed revolution and political liberalism. He considered political radicalism to be a sign of apocalyptic tendencies in Europe. The church with its insipid rationalist theology had little to offer. Only revivalism was able to change the situation and secure society. Political radicalism led irrevocably to social disorder.

Against this background the development of Laestadianism in Norway is highly interesting. As early as the late 1840s the Laestadius movement was spreading from Karesuando to northern Norway via the Sámi districts: to Kautokeino in western Finnmark, Lyngen in northern Troms and Ibestad in southern Troms. Kautokeino was Laestadianism's first Norwegian stronghold. This Sámi village was the neighbouring parish to Karesuando in Sweden, where Laestadius was a minister until 1849. Laestadius had come into contact with the Kautokeino Sámis through their frequent visits to Karesuando. He realised that they were in need of guidance and for this reason he sent a delegation to Kautokeino in the autumn of 1847. Preachers from Karesuando arrived the following year, but thereafter contact was lost, and the revival evolved without any direct spiritual guidance from Laestadius. Sámis in Kautokeino assumed beliefs that cannot in any way be attributed to Laestadius, namely the possibility to be free from sin through identification with Christ and God, and the direct guidance of the Holy Ghost. The Kautokeino revivals involved ecstatic visions and raptures. The revivalists emphasised their religious independence. They criticised the established church and interfered in the Sunday services. They also castigated the local minister and other civil servants for their unwillingness to repent.

The developments at Kautokeino illustrate the latent danger within the revivalist movement, and such situations could easily get out of control. This happened in the famous Kautokeino uprising that took place in the morning of 8 November 1852, when a group of Sámis attacked and killed the local sheriff and the merchant. They beat up the newly appointed minister and his servants and set fire to the merchant's house. They were allegedly motivated by their wish to preach repentance to the unbelievers and to punish them. The two leaders of the revolt were executed, while other participants in the riot were given heavy prison sentences. The tragedy has been diagnosed in different ways. The Supreme Court maintained that the uprising ought to be viewed in the light of contemporary revolutionary currents, and that the frictions involved class

E. Lasalle, Lars Levi Laestadius, *lithograph, c.1860.*
[Tromsø, University of Tromsø]

Gisle Johnson, *photograph, c.1880.*
[Oslo, University of Oslo, Library]

distinctions. Consequently, it was necessary to set a warning example through severe punishment in order to prevent the destruction of civilised society.[7]

However, there is no evidence that the Sámis in Kautokeino had been in contact with revolutionary groups. The revolt has been explained as an acute ethnic protest against both the way Norwegian culture was forced upon the Sámi people and the bad social and economic conditions in which they lived. As representatives of the Norwegian social elite, the sheriff, the merchant and the minister naturally became the victims. However, the causal relations are probably more complex. The Kautokeino uprising is the only example within Laestadianism of a religiously motivated revolt. Laestadius dissociated himself from the events. The Kautokeino revolt had important consequences for the further expansion and development of the Laestadian movement in the north. In the 1850s the movement made no further progress in that part of the country. Its renaissance came in the 1860s through Finnish immigrants and Norwegian settlers. The Sámis in Kautokeino and elsewhere in Finnmark did not return to Laestadianism until after the First World War. For a long time the clergy looked upon the movement with scepticism but relations improved towards the end of the nineteenth century, not least because the clergy and the Laestadians made a common front against rival independent congregations.[8]

As revivalist movements, Hauganism and Laestadianism show striking similarities, but also differences. Both claimed religious freedom for the laity, criticising the established church and its clergy. This reflects a modern opposition towards the

---

[7] Zorgdrager, *De rettferdiges strid*.

[8] Norderval, "Fra revolusjon til reaksjon?".

old hierarchical society. On the other hand, whereas Haugianism caught on among farmers capable of advancing socially, Laestadianism originally was mostly an ethnic phenomenon among the poor Sámi population who lacked the possibility of social advancement. At an early stage women were allowed to preach within both the Haugian and Laestadian movements, but this came to an end relatively soon. Both movements, and especially Laestadianism, increasingly adopted an attitude antithetical to modern culture.

The Johnsonian Revival

Both the Laestadian and Haugian movements began as informal networks. In the 1850s Haugianism entered its organised phase through the home or inner mission (*indremisjonen*). Professor Gisle Johnson (1822-1894) at the Faculty of Theology became its leading figure. He not only educated church ministers, but was also a preacher and a church strategist. During the cholera epidemic in Christiania in the early 1850s he began to hold devotional meetings, which led to a revival. Because of Johnson's influence it has been called 'the Johnsonian revival'. Johnson managed to create a strategic alliance between the Faculty of Theology, the clergy and the lay people. The Johnsonian revival dominated Norwegian church life in the second part of the nineteenth century.

Theologically, Johnson combined strict Lutheran orthodoxy with pietism. In his academic lectures he developed his own theological system, in which he united academic theology and the revivalist demand for repentance. The Johnsonian revival clearly put its mark on the clergy. A new generation of theologians arose. Partially this was connected with a shift in the recruitment of students at the Faculty of Theology. The clergy had mainly been recruited from the upper class. Ministers' sons had tended to study theology in order to become ministers like their fathers. During the nineteenth century the number of ministers' sons among the student population declined, while the number of farmers' sons, especially from the Hauge movement, increased. Some of these students had taken part in local revivals, and they aspired to a career as ministers in the established church. At the Faculty of Theology they found that Johnson's combination of Lutheran orthodoxy and pietism corresponded to their own views. Through Johnsonian theology, the revival gained an academic flavour. This may explain why many of the students left the Faculty of Theology as Johnsonian theologians. In the 1850s these pastors began to replace the older generation educated by Hersleb and Stenersen.[9] The new pastors advocated the same religious ideals as the revivalists. They distinguished sharply between believers and non-believers. In their opinion non-believers were 'unworthy' to take part in communion. This attitude led to a massive decline in the number of communicants, one of the most profound changes in religious life in Norway during the nineteenth century.[10]

---

[9] Elstad, *"en Kraft og et Salt i Menigheden"*.   [10] Sandvik, *Det store nattverdfallet*.

In the 1850s the first local home mission associations were founded. The *dissenterloven* (Dissenters Law) of 1845 had made it possible to cancel membership of the national Lutheran church in order to join a 'free' denomination. Gisle Johnson, who feared separation, engaged in integrating revivalism into the home mission. The first home mission association had been established in 1853. Two years later, in 1855, Johnson founded the *Foreningen for den indre Mission i Christiania* (Christiania Home Mission). The German Johann Heinrich Wichern's (1808-1881) Hamburg-based *Innere Mission* was taken as a model. Wichern combined evangelisation with social work among the poor. In Norway, however, evangelisation became especially important, more so than social work.

In 1868 a national society for home mission was founded, the *Lutherstiftelsen* (Luther Foundation). Gisle Johnson was its chairman until 1891. The Foundation's objective was primarily to disseminate the gospel through the printed word. Its publications were to be circulated by tract distributors called *bibelbud* (Bible messengers), who were expected also to converse with individuals and lead family devotions. A central question was, however, how far these distributors could go in preaching. The Luther Foundation did not authorise anyone to preach, but did encourage lay preaching in practice. Very soon the Bible messengers appeared as preachers. After 1842, lay preaching was no longer considered illegal according to the civil law. However, the question arose whether it was ecclesiastically legitimate. Johnson, who advocated a strictly orthodox Lutheranism, legitimated this activity by what he called the *nødsprinsippet* or 'emergency principle', which justified a deviation from Article 14 of the Augsburg Confession. According to that article public preaching was reserved for those 'called in the correct manner' (*rite vocatus*). As Johnson saw it, this principally meant the ordained pastors. However, Johnson argued that the extraordinary 'spiritual need' in church and society made an exception from this principle necessary. The population was growing rapidly. The clergy could not cope with the demands made on them, and there was also a lack of churches. Parts of the population especially in the cities, were gradually losing touch with the church. So, in order to reach the population, the strategy was to encourage lay preaching. In 1891 the Luther Foundation became *Det Norske Lutherske Indremisjonsselskap* (Norwegian Lutheran Home Mission Society). The organisation now no longer based its programme on the 'emergency principle'. Sending out lay preachers was considered to be its normal task.[11]

The Johnsonian revival opposed Grundtvigianism. One important reason for this was the revival's antagonism towards modern culture. As Gisle Johnson put it, the "basic delusion" of Grundtvigianism was its "failure to view man's sinfulness in all its depth".[12]

---

[11] Rudvin, *Indremisjonsselskapets historie*.

[12] Thorkildsen, "Da kirken oppdaget folket", 104.

Wilhelm Andreas Wexels, *photograph, c.1860*.
[Oslo, University of Oslo, Library]

I. Falander, Ole Vig, *engraving, c.1880*.
[Trondheim, NTNU, Universitetsbiblioteket]

Norwegian Grundtvigianism

The Danish Grundtvigian revival also made an impact on Norway. The Norwegian followers of Grundtvig in the first half of the century did not, however, belong to a popular national movement. The leading theologian among them was Wilhelm Andreas Wexels (1797-1866). He was born in Copenhagen, but got his theological education in Christiania. He spoke proper Danish his whole life and considered Danish to be the cultural language in Norway. He became catechist and later chaplain at the Cathedral of Christiania. As a theologian he strongly opposed rationalism and became an ardent follower of Grundtvig. When Grundtvig made his one and only visit to Norway during the Pan-Scandinavian student meeting in 1851, he stayed at Wexels' home.

During the 1850s, Norwegian Grundtvigianism became a national movement promoting educational reform as a part of a programme of nation building. It also began to be associated with liberal politics. An important Grundtvigian during this decade was the teacher and educator Ole Vig (1824-1857). He became the first editor of a periodical, *Folkevennen* (Peoples' Friend), founded by the *Folkeopplysningsselskapet* (Norwegian Society for Enlightenment). After the death of Ole Vig, Eilert Sundt (1817-1875) replaced him as editor. Educated as a theologian, Sundt was a follower of the theologian, author and poet Henrik Wergeland (1808-1845) as well as Grundtvig. He is also regarded as the founder of sociological studies in Norway, even becoming a member of the first organised labour movement, whose founder and leader was Marcus Thrane (1817-1890). This movement (*thranittene*) stood for political reforms and more democracy.

The labour movement was a symptom of the tensions inherent in a new type of society burdened with growing urban poverty. When the followers of Thrane attempted to found a labour society at Enerhaugen, a suburb of Christiania, the local chaplain Honoratius Halling (1819-1886), managed to take over the initiative. He began his own group, which was to lay the foundation for the home mission movement. Since 1848 Halling had published a periodical called *For Fattig og Riig* (For Poor and Rich) with 30,000 subscribers, it was as large as the labour movement at its peak. Later the periodical became the mouthpiece of the home mission movement.

The young Grundtvigians linked nation and religion. They thought that nationality was an expression of the character of the people, and that Christianity must be national in order to appeal to the common man. Like Grundtvig they claimed that the spirit of the Creator manifests itself in the spirit of the people. For this reason, the nation as a whole and not only the people of God had a particular value. An expression of this link between nation and religion is found in the Norwegian national anthem: "Ja, vi elsker dette landet" ("Yes, we love this country"). It was written around 1860 by the second national poet or *scald*, Bjørnstjerne Bjørnson (1832-1910), when Grundtvig's influence on him was especially strong. The anthem claims that God himself has given the Norwegian people its rights and freedom, and that he has protected it against enemies.[13]

Missionary Work

A remarkable feature of religious life in nineteenth-century Norway regards foreign missionary work. This was not a source of conflict. Both Grundtvigans and the revivalists supported it. In 1826 Moravians founded the first local missionary association in Stavanger on the west coast. But soon the followers of Hauge too engaged in foreign mission. Local missionary associations were established from the 1830s onwards. In 1842 *Det norske misjonsselskap* (Norwegian Missionary Society) was founded in Stavanger. Its first missionaries engaged in missionary work in Southern Africa (Zululand); later the organisation operated particularly in Madagascar.[14]

Women played an important role in the missionary movement. Missionary associations for women were founded, the first one by Gustava Kielland (1800-1889), a minister's wife, in 1840. In fact these associations were the first public arena for women in Norway and played an important role in the process of liberation of women in society.[15] The missionary associations greatly increased in number during the second part of the nineteenth century, from c.250 in 1850 to as many as 900 in 1890. Most of these were missionary associations for women. In 1904, women obtained the right to vote in the Norwegian Missionary Society.

---

[13] Thorkildsen, *Grundtvigianisme og nasjonalisme i Norge i det 19. århundre*.
[14] Jørgensen, *I tro og tjeneste*.

[15] Predelli, *Issues of Gender, Race, and Class in the Norwegian Missionary Society*.

The Culture Crisis 1870-1900

The integration of revivalism into the church in the 1850s had disastrous consequences for the church, because it was the opposition to modern culture that won out. Both clergy and laity were totally unprepared for, and unable to cope with, the liberal ideas and positivistic ideals of science introduced in Norway during the 1870s. A purely immanent understanding of nature brought the dogmas of the church into sharp relief. This resulted not only in criticism of the church and Christianity, but often also in direct hostility.

The first serious challenge was Charles Darwin's theory of evolution. Evolutionism rapidly became the dominant outlook in the disciplines of botany, zoology, history and philosophy. For some, Darwin's theory of evolution became a view of life that was contrasted to Christian belief. The historical-critical approach to the Bible began to influence intellectuals, as did the comparative history of religion. The distance between the church and secular intellectual life was abysmal. The introduction of positivism and evolutionism at the University of Christiania in the 1870s led to a confrontation between a Christian monoculture and academic freedom. Under vigorous protests from conservative Christians, positivists and Darwinists were appointed professors at the university.

Positivistic ideas and church criticism were disseminated mainly through liberal newspapers. Influential fictional authors like Bjørnstjerne Bjørnson (1832-1910), Henrik Ibsen (1828-1906), Arne Garborg (1851-1924) and Alexander Kielland (1849-1906) likewise criticised the church for teaching a bigoted dogmatism and a double standard of morality. A typical example is Ibsen's drama *Et dukkehjem* (A Doll's House, 1879) where the character Nora leaves her husband and children in order to seek self-realisation. Most painful for the church was Bjørnstjerne Bjørnson's break with Christian belief in 1877. Through dramas, pamphlets, articles and lectures he declared the Christian faith to be incompatible with a scientific outlook. A few years earlier he had been known as a Grundtvigian Christian. The poet Arne Garborg went through a similar development.

Even more striking was the attack from the so-called *Kristianiabohemen* ('Kristiania bohemia'), a group of radical artists. They promoted free love, rejected marriage and criticised the church's defence of bourgeois morality, which in their view upheld prostitution and the oppression of women. Most Christian apologists adopted a stance which totally rejected the new ideas. One of the few exceptions was the professor of systematic theology at the University of Kristiania, Fredrik Petersen (1839-1903), who developed a mild 'repristination theology', which saw seventeenth-century Lutheran orthodoxy as normative - the first sign of a theological shift in Norway. In a lecture held in 1880, "How should the church meet modern unbelief?", he maintained that the church had to satisfy the modern desire for knowledge and prosperity. He wished to reconcile science with the Christian belief in miracles and prayer. He was also in favour of the use of historical criticism in biblical studies. Conservative Christians lodged fierce protests against Petersen's attempt at dialogue. A more consistent theological attempt to approach modern culture emerged with a new generation of theologians in the 1890s, after liberal theology had been introduced at the Faculty of Theology at the University of Kristiania. But this reinforced tensions between modern culture and conservative forces within the church.[16]

Modern Theology and the Break-up of Union with Sweden

The main challenge for the Church of Norway at the end of the nineteenth century, as we have seen, was how to cope with modern society and culture. The official theology and church life had become separated from the national and democratic movement, and the church had withdrawn from the political arena. The only minister elected a Member of Parliament in 1903 came from the newly established radical Labour Party. But a greater challenge came from so-called 'liberal theology', a dispute that merged with older tensions between revivalist lay organisations and the official state church.

Modernist theology had made little headway in Norway before the 1880s and 1890s. Around the turn of the century tensions increased, reaching a first peak with the vacancy for a professor of systematic theology, following the death of Frederik Petersen. Johannes Ording (1869-1929) was considered the only qualified applicant, but Sigurd Odland (1857-1937), who was professor of New Testament theology, accused him of a non-Lutheran view of the sacraments. For this reason the chair was kept vacant, causing a political crisis, which threatened to split the conservative coalition government. At the same time, there was a serious national crisis in connection with the union with Sweden. For this reason the vacancy was put on hold till the union crisis was solved.

After the break-up of the union in 1905, the conflict around the professorship in theology still had to be dealt with. Once again Johannes Ording was considered the best qualified applicant by a committee of experts. He was appointed by a new coalition government, with Christian Michelsen (1857-1925) from the liberal left as prime minister. The minister of ecclesiastical affairs, Christoffer Knudsen (1843-1915), resigned in protest, as did Sigurd Odland. Together they campaigned for a private theological high school. It was opened in 1908 as *Det teologiske Menighetsfakultet* and became the centre of a countercultural theological conservatism.[17]

This theological and ecclesiastical conflict again came to a head in 1920, when a meeting was organised in the Mission House in Calmeyer Street in Kristiania. No fewer than 950 delegates took part, while 1,700 tickets were sold to an audience in the gallery. The meeting attacked Ording's appointment, and decided that there would be no voluntary cooperation between theologians faithful to the Bible and liberal theologians critical of the ecclesiastical traditions. This division decided the course of Norwegian church life for decades. Ironically, the first to suffer from this ban was the conservative bishop Bernt Støylen (1858-1937). In 1923 he officiated at the installation

---

[16] Molland, "Den moderne ånds gjennombrudd og kirkens møte med den"; Hagemann, *Det moderne gjennombrudd*; Seip, *Nasjonen bygges*.

[17] Thorkildsen, *Kirkestrid og unionsoppløsning*.

of Jens Gleditsch (1860-1931) as bishop of Nidaros (Trondheim), although Gleditsch was accused of being a liberal theologian.

Ecclesiastical Reforms

Owing to the conflicts over theology, several churchmen and theologians advocated the separation of state and church. The Church of Norway was a state church in which ordinary church members had no voice. After 1814 the *Stortinget* (Norwegian Parliament) had been the legislative body that decided on issues regarding the external framework of the church. Internal church matters, such as the appointment of ministers and the regulation of worship, were taken care of by the Crown (i.e. the government after 1884). Mainly as a result of increasing religious pluralism within church and society, efforts were made to pursue ecclesiastical reform. In the 1840s the clergy had discussed the relationship between state and church. Plans were developed for reorganising the church in order to gain a more independent position with regard to the civil authorities. The idea was that a church with greater freedom in internal matters would be in a better position to cope with the external challenges posed by the growing religious pluralism. "The state cannot be the church", a parish pastor wrote in the 1840s. "The state rules the church with an iron hand", he continued.[18] After the 1850s, the lay movement also engaged in the debate. An ecclesiastical reform movement arose.

However, it was not possible to reach agreement concerning a church order. Within the reform movement two opposing branches developed. One, based on the west coast in the radical revivalist areas, advocated the representation of church people from below through parish councils. The other group, which had strong ties to the official church, demanded reforms from the top, starting with a synod for the whole church. Another point of controversy concerned the question whether all adult members of the church or only confessing Christian believers should have the right to elect parish councils.

In 1859 the Norwegian government appointed a reform committee, which presented several proposals during the 1860s. In 1869 a majority in parliament voted for the introduction of parish councils. The king, however, refused to sanction the law. In 1887 the Parliament voted against parish councils. Later the Parliament also voted against instituting a church synod. In the end, the nineteenth century did not bring any reforms to ecclesiastical structures, except for one. In 1873 parish meetings were instituted, mainly with the task of deciding on hymn books and liturgy.

During the nineteenth century it had been impossible to reach an agreement concerning church order. In 1906, however, the issue was put on the agenda once again in connection with the appointment of Johannes Ording as professor in theology. Absa-

---

[18] *Morgenbladet*, 300 (1840).

lon Taranger (1858-1930), a professor of the history of law, advocated the idea of a *fri folkekirke* or 'free folk church', implying that the church should have no ties to the state at all. It was in the context of this renewed debate that the Norwegian parliament appointed a commission, known as the *Kirkekommissionen av 1908* (Church Commission of 1908), to elaborate on questions concerning the relationship between state and church. A majority in the commission wanted to keep the state church, while a minority supported the 'free folk church'. However, Taranger's idea proved to have very little support among local civil councils, school authorities, and church meetings.

Finally, a reform did come about, within the boundaries of the state church. In 1920, parish councils were instituted. These councils decided on local ecclesiastical matters such as church services and the use of church buildings. They also participated in the process of appointing ministers in their parishes and had the right to vote for bishops in their dioceses. All adult members of the church were entitled to take part in the election of parish councils.[19]

Conclusion

Between 1780 and 1920 Norway experienced profound social, political and cultural changes. In 1780 the Danish-Norwegian union was still intact. Absolutism had been the form of government of the Danish-Norwegian monarchy since 1660. The Norwegian church did not in fact exist as an independent institution. Religion was an affair of the state. The minister was a public servant.

In 1814 Denmark had to give up its rights to Norway. That year Norway wrote its constitution, the most liberal in Europe at the time. However, Norway was forced into a union with Sweden until 1905. During the nineteenth century Norway developed into a democratic national state. Its society went through a modernisation process of industrialisation, urbanisation and democratisation. The democratisation of the state also led to a democratisation of the religious life. Religious freedom was gradually introduced. Still the official Lutheran state church kept a strong position throughout the period. From the time of Hans Nielsen Hauge onwards revivalism clearly influenced the church. The revivalist movement did not break with the official church, but was integrated within it.

The advent of 'modern culture' towards the end of the century led to a cultural conflict. Mainly the church rejected the new ideas as anti-religious. This strategy caused a division between church and society. Despite the modernisation of Norwegian society, very little actually happened to the fundamental structure of the church. But reforms were debated. Around 1850 an ecclesiastical reform movement arose. The main question of the time concerned church order. However, it was not possible to reach any agreement on how the church should be organised. In fact, institutional reform was not introduced until 1920, when parish councils were created.

---

[19] Ellingsen, *Kirkelig visjon - politisk drakamp*.

Bibliography

Denmark

Appel, Charlotte. "Literacy in Seventeenth Century Denmark" in: Pernille Hermann, ed. *Literacy in Medieval and Early Modern Scandinavian Culture*. The Viking Collection 16. Odense, 2005, 323-346.

Bayly, C.A. *The Birth of the Modern World 1780-1914*. Oxford, 2004.

Bergsøe, A.F. *Den danske Stats Statistik*. Copenhagen, 1844-1853, 4 vols.

Bregnsbo, Michael. "Præster under pres. Den danske statskirkegejstligheds reaktioner på udfordringen fra Oplysningen i 1790'erne". *Den jyske Historiker*, 105 (2004), 94-108.

Bricka, Carl Frederik, ed. *Dansk Biografisk Leksikon*. Copenhagen, 1887-1905, 19 vols.

Bugge, K.E. *Grundtvig og slavesagen*. Aarhus, 2003.

Eriksen, Sidsel. "Drunken Danes and Sober Swedes?" in: Bo Stråth, ed. *Language and the Construction of Class Identities*. Gothenburg, 1990, 55-94.

Garff, Joakim. *Søren Kierkegaard - A Biography*. Princeton, 2005.

Garff, Joakim. "Dannelse, identitetsdannelse og dannelseskritik" in: Joakim Garff, ed. *At komme til sig selv*. Copenhagen, 2008, 120-146.

Glædemark, H.J.H. *Kirkeforfatningsspørgsmaalet i Danmark indtil 1874*. Copenhagen, 1948.

Grane, Leif and Hørby, Kaj, eds. *Københavns Universitet 1479-1979*. Vol. 2. Copenhagen, 1979-2005.

Harries, Heinrich. *Gedichte. Erster Theil*. Altona, 1804.

Haue, Harry. "Mejerikrigen". *Fortid og Nutid*, 1978, 359-390.

Heiberg, Johan Ludvig. *Prosaiske Skrifter*. Vol. 1. Copenhagen, 1861.

Huntington, Samuel. "Conservatism as an Ideology". *The American Political Science Review*, 51 (1957) 2, 454-473.

Hvidt, Kristian. *Flugten til Amerika*. Aarhus, 1971.

Johansen, Niels. *Herrens Ord i de sidste Verdens Dage*. Odense, 1837.

Koch, Hal. *Den danske Kirkes Historie*. Vol. 6. Copenhagen, 1954.

Koch, Hal. *Danmarks kirke gennem tiderne*. Copenhagen, 1960.

Lausten, Martin Schwartz. *Frie jøder?* Copenhagen, 2005.

Lindhardt, P.G. *Den danske Kirkes Historie*. Vol. 7. Copenhagen, 1958.

Lyngby, Thomas. *Den sentimentale patriotisme*. Copenhagen, 2001.

Martensen, Hans Lassen. *Christian Ethics*. Transl. C. Spence. Edinburgh, 1873.

Martensen, Hans Lassen. *Christian Ethics. Special Part. Second Division: Social Ethics*. Transl. Sophia Taylor. Edinburgh, 1882.

Møller, Anna Sommer. "Brændes eller begraves?". *Fortid og Nutid*, (2007) 2, 83-102.

Møller, Jes Fabricius. "Teologiske reaktioner på darwinismen i Danmark 1860-1900". *Historisk Tidsskrift*, 100 (2000) 1, 69-92.

Møller, Jes Fabricius. *Biologismer*. Thesis PhD. Copenhagen, 2003.

Møller, Jes Fabricius. *Grundtvigianisme i det 20. århundrede*. Copenhagen, 2005.

Møller, Jes Fabricius. "Folkekirkens økonomi og staten". *Dansk Kirketidende*, 158 (2006) 10, 162-167.

Olesen, Elith. *De frigjorte og trællefolket: amerikansk-engelsk indflydelse på dansk kirkeliv omkring år 1900*. Copenhagen, 1996.

Sanders, Hanne. *Bondevækkelse og sekularisering. En protestantisk folkelig kultur i Danmark og Sverige 1820-1850*. Stockholm, 1995.

Severinsen. P. *Folkekirkens Ejendoms-Historie*. Copenhagen, 1920.

Smith, Peter Scharff. *Moralske hospitaler*. Copenhagen, 2003.

Sørensen, Arne. "Nogle Reflektioner om Nationalisocialismen". *Gads Danske Magasin*, 30 (1936), 358-367.

Statistique du Danemark. Annuaire Statistique. Copenhagen, 1901 and 1925.

Stewart, Jon. *A History of Hegelianism in Golden Age Denmark*. Vol. 1. Copenhagen, 2007.
Thestrup, Poul. *Nærbutik og næringslovsomgåelse*. Odense, 1986.
Thing, Morten. *De russiske jøder i København 1882-1943*. Copenhagen, 2008.
Thyssen, Anders Pontoppidan. "Grundtvig's Ideas on the Church and the People 1825-47" in: Christian Thodberg and A. Pontoppidan Thyssen, eds. *N.F.S. Grundtvig*. Copenhagen, 1983, 226-294.
Werner, Yvonne Maria. "Grundtvig - en kyrkofader för danska katolska konvertiter runt 1900?" in: Hanne Sanders, ed. *Grundtvig - nyckeln till det danska?* Göteborg, 2003, 91-125.
<www.folketinget.dk/pdf/constitution.pdf> (1 January 2009).

Sweden

Aldén, Lars. *Stiftskyrkans förnyelse: framväxten av stiftsmöten och stiftsråd i Svenska kyrkan till omkr 1920*. Lund, 1989.
Bexell, Oloph. *Folkväckelsens och kyrkoförnyelsens tid*. Sveriges kyrkohistoria 7. Stockholm, 2003.
Carlsson, Sten. *Svensk ståndscirkulation 1680-1950*. Uppsala, 1950.
Fjellander, Sture. *Korset och ringen: Det kyrkliga ungdomsarbetets organisationshistoria 1905-1945*. Stockholm, 1972.
Jansson, Torkel. *Adertonhundratalets associationer. Forskning och problem kring ett sprängfullt tomrum eller sammanslutningsprinciper och föreningsformer mellan två samhällsformationer c:a 1800-1870*. Uppsala, 1985.
Jarlert, Anders. *Romantikens och liberalismens tid*. Sveriges kyrkohistoria 6. Stockholm, 2000.
Lenhammar, Harry. *Individualismens och upplysningens tid*. Sveriges kyrkohistoria 5. Stockholm, 2000.
Sidebäck, Göran. *Kampen om barnets själ: barn och ungdomsorganisationer för fostran och normbildning 1850-1980*. Stockholm, 1992.
Sundkler, Bengt. *Svenska missionssällskapet 1835-1876*. Uppsala, 1937.
Tergel, Alf. *Ungkyrkomännen, arbetarfrågan och nationalismen 1901-1911*. Stockholm, 1969.
Wallgren, Erik. *Individen och samfundet. Bidrag till kännedomen om samfundstänkandet i Swensk Kyrkotidning*. Lund, 1959.
Wejryd, Cecilia. *Svenska kyrkans syföreningar 1844-2003*. Stockholm, 2005.

Norway

Aarflot, Andreas. *Norsk kirkehistorie*. Vol. 2. Oslo, 1967.
Danielsen, Rolf et al. *Norway. A History from the Vikings to our own Times*. Oslo, 1995.
Ellingsen, Terje. *Kirkelig visjon - politisk drakamp. Fra reformarbeidet i Den norske kirke*. Stavanger, 1973.
Elstad, Hallgeir. *"en Kraft og et Salt i Menigheden". Ein studie av dei såkalla "johnsonske prestane" i siste halvpart av 1800-talet i Noreg*. Oslo, 2000.
Hagemann, Gro. *Det moderne gjennombrudd 1870-1905*. Aschehougs norgeshistorie 9. Oslo, 2005.
Hope, Nicholas. *German and Scandinavian Protestantism 1700-1918*. Oxford, 1995.
Jørgensen, Torstein. *I tro og tjeneste. Det norske misjonsselskap 1842-1992*. Stavanger, 1992.
Molland, Einar. "Den moderne ånds gjennombrudd og kirkens møte med den" in E. Molland, *Norges kirkehistorie i det 19. århundre*. Oslo, 1979, vol. I, 312-347.
Molland, Einar. *Church Life in Norway 1800-1950*. Westport, 1978.
Molland, Einar. *Norges kirkehistorie i det 19. århundre*. Oslo, 1979, 2 vols.
Norderval, Øyvind. "Ikke som hiine elendige Tullemutter eller Sammenløb. Om Hans Nielsen Hauges siste år: Resignasjon eller ny strategi?". *Historisk Tidsskrift*, 78 (1999), 496-524.

Bibliography

Norderval, Øyvind. "Fra revolusjon til reaksjon? Læstadianisme og vekkelse" in: R. Jensen et al, eds. *Kirke, protestantisme og samfunn. Festskrift til professor dr. Ingun Montgomery*. Oslo, 2006, 123-138.

Ording, H., ed. *Hans Nielsen Hauges skrifter*. Vols. 1 and 8. Oslo, 1947-1954.

Predelli, Line Nyhagen. *Issues of Gender, Race, and Class in the Norwegian Missionary Society in Nineteenth-Century Norway and Madagascar*. Oslo, 2003.

Rudvin, Ola. *Indremisjonsselskapets historie*. Oslo, 1967-1970, 2 vols.

Sandvik, Bjørn. *Det store nattverdfallet. En undersøkelse av avsperring og tilhørighet i norsk kirkeliv*. Trondheim, 1998.

Seip, Anne Lise. *Nasjonen bygges, 1830-1870*. Aschehougs Norges Historie 8. Oslo, 1997.

Thorkildsen, Dag. *Kirkestrid og unionsoppløsning. Tre studier om forholdet mellom religion, kultur og politikk i Norge ved århundreskiftet*. Oslo, 1989.

Thorkildsen, Dag. "Da kirken oppdaget folket" in: S. Aa. Christoffersen and T. Wyller, eds. *Arv og utfordring. Menneske og samfunn i den kristne moraltradisjon*. Oslo, 1995, 90-110.

Thorkildsen, Dag. *Grundtvigianisme og nasjonalisme i Norge i det 19. århundre*. KULTs skriftserie 70. Oslo, 1996.

Thorkildsen, Dag. "Vekkelse og modernisering i Norden på 1800-tallet". *Historisk Tidsskrift*, 77 (1998), 160-180.

Thorkildsen, Dag. "Scandinavia: Lutheranism and National Identity" in: *The Cambridge History of Christianity*. Vol. 8. Cambridge, 2006, 342-358.

Wisløff, Carl Fredrik. *Norsk kirkehistorie*. Oslo, 1971, 3 vols.

Zorgdrager, Nellejet. *De rettferdiges strid. Kautokeino 1852. Samisk motstand mot norsk kolonialisme*. Oslo, 1997.

Index

Adam, Karl 184
Agar, Charles 32
Allaer, Canon 121
Altenstein, Karl Freiherr von 162
Andersen, Hans Christian 238
Aristotle 60
Arnold, Matthew 56
Avis, Paul 91

Bachem, family 172
Barberi, Dominic 80
Barton, John 91
Baumgartner, Alexander 173
Baur, Ferdinand Christian 146
Bautz, Joseph 176
Bavinck, Herman 141
Beck, Vilhelm 12, 234
Benson, E.W. 88-89, 91
Benson, R.M. 71
Berg, Franz 160
Best, Geoffrey 67
Bethmann Hollweg, Moritz von 197
Bismarck, Otto von 172, 174, 206
Bjørnson, Bjørnstjerne 272-273
Blomfield, C.J. 35, 45
Blum, Peter Joseph 167, 174
Blum, Robert 167
Bodelschwingh, Friedrich von 206, 208, 211
Booth, William 73
Brandes, Edvard 245
Brandes, Georg 240, 245
Breidbach zu Bürresheim, Emmerich Joseph von 160
Brilioth, Yngve 54-55
Broderick, Charles 32
Brohée, Abel 122
Brown, Callum 68
Brown, David 91
Brown, Kenneth 78
Brugier, Gustav 173
Buchberger, Michael 179
Burckhardt, Johannes 201
Burgess, Thomas 22, 33
Burkitt, F.C. 91

Burns, Arthur 67-69
Busken Huet, Conrad 143, 146, 150
Butler, Joseph 57, 60, 65

Calvin, John 83
Cardijn, Joseph 118, 122
Carlyle, Aelred 71
Caroline Amalie, Queen 234
Cauchi, Alfred 120
Chalmers, Thomas 15, 42-44, 71, 82
Chantepie de la Saussaye, Daniël 147
Cheyne, A.C. 83
Cheyne, T.K. 91
Christian VI 261
Clercq, Willem de 136
Cock, Hendrik de 15, 129-130
Colenso, John William 88-90, 92
Colmar, Joseph Ludwig 165
Costa, Isaac da 136
Crolly, William 48, 74
Cullen, Paul 74

Daens, Adolf 117
Daly, Robert 41
Daneo, Paul Francis 80
Darwin, Charles 90, 146, 151, 273
Davidson, Samuel 92-93
De Beauffort, Ernest 105
De Broglie, Maurice 104
De Brome, Adam 61
Delahaye, Hippolyte 120
De Lamennais, Félicité 104-105, 108
De Mean, François-Antoine 105
De Mérode, Henri 105
Denison, George Anthony 91
Denzinger, Heinrich 170
De Smedt, Charles 120
Diepenbrock, Melchior von 164, 167
Dill, Samuel 41
Disraeli, Benjamin 83
Dölger, Franz Joseph 177
Döllinger, Ignaz von 167-171, 176
Doyle, James Warren 48, 74
Driver, S.R. 91

Ducpétiaux, Eduard 112

Easton, David 84
Ehrhard, Albert 176
Erasmus, Desiderius 133
Euch, Johannes von 243
Eyre, Charles 74

Faber, Frederick William 81
Falk, Johannes 191
Farnham, Lord 41
Febronius > Hontheim
Finke, Heinrich 179
Fliedner, Friederike 208
Fliedner, Theodor 208
Frederik IV 233
Frederik VI 22
Friedrich Wilhelm III 189, 193
Friedrich Wilhelm IV 189-190, 192-195, 200, 209, 213
Frohschammer, Jakob 164
Froude, Richard Hurrell 53, 58, 62
Funk, Franz Xaver 179
Fürstenberg, Franz von 160

Gaebel, Otto 206
Gallitzin, Amalie von 165
Gansfort, Wessel 133
Garbett, James 66
Garborg, Arne 273
Garff, Joakim 240
Geissel, Johannes von 168-169
Gentili, Luigi 80
Gladstone, William, 83
Gleditsch, Jens 275
Gnauck-Kühne, Elisabeth 210-211
Goehre, Paul 205
Goethe, Johann Wolfgang von 177
Goffiné, Leonhard 172
Gore, Charles 71, 90-91
Gorham, George 87
Görres, Joseph 23, 165
Gorringe, Tim 91
Green, Simon 68
Gregory XVI 106
Groen van Prinsteren, Guillaume 136, 147
Grote, Geert 133

Grundtvig, Nikolai Frederik Severin 11, 15, 19, 23-25, 132, 235-238, 243, 246, 263, 271-272
Guardini, Romano 184
Gunning, Johannes Hermanus Jr. 147
Günther, Anton 164
Gustav Adolf II 209

Haeffner, Johann Christian Friedrich 250
Haffner, Leopold 177
Halling, Honoratius 272
Hammerstein, Wilhelm von 201-202
Hardy, Daniel 91
Harnack, Adolf von 178, 183, 205, 245-246
Harries, Heinrich 240
Harris, Howell 37
Harrison, Benjamin 59
Hauge, Hans Nielsen 15-16, 233, 264-266, 269, 272, 276
Hawkins, Edward 64
Hebblethwaite, Brian 91
Hefele, Carl Joseph von 171, 176
Hegel, Georg Wilhelm Friedrich 146
Heiberg, Johan Ludvig 244
Hergenröther, Joseph 170
Herling, Georg von 179
Hermes, Georg 164
Herrmann, Emil 197
Hersleb, Svend Borchmann 262-263, 269
Heusde, Philip Willem van 132-133
Hinclifff, Peter 91
Hirscher, Johann Baptist 167
Hitze, Franz 180
Hoedemaker, Philip Jacob 142, 147
Hoekstra, S. 147
Hofbauer, Clemens Maria 165
Hofstede de Groot, Petrus 133
Holl, Karl 183
Hommer, Joseph von 163
Hontheim, Johann Nikolaus von 159
Horsley, Samuel 33-34
Hort, F.J.A. 87-90
Hügel, Friedrich von 94
Hugenholtz, Peter Herman 143, 151
Hugenholtz, Philip Reinhard 143
Huxley, Thomas 90

Ibsen, Henrik 245, 273
Innes, Joanna 68

Isenbiehl, Johann Lorenz 160

Jarrett, Thomas 90
Jebb, John 55
Johansen, Niels 15, 234
Johnson, Gisle 15, 25, 268-270
Joseph II 101-102, 107, 159-160

Kant, Immanuel 241
Kasper, Katharina 170
Kasper, Walter 179
Kaye, John 35
Keble, John 35, 53, 56-57, 61, 65
Keller, Michael 182-183
Kelly, Herbert 71
Keppler, Paul Wilhelm von 177, 184
Kersten, G.H. 141
Ketteler, Wilhelm Emmanuel von 167, 169, 171, 174
Kielland, Gustava 272-273
Kierkegaard, Peter Christian 240-241
Kierkegaard, Søren 23, 234-235, 238-240
Kilham, Alexander 38
Kirkpatrick, A.F. 91
Kleist-Retzow, Hans von 201-202
Knöpfler, Alois 178
Knox, Alexander 55
Knox, John 83
Knudsen, Christoffer 274
Koch, Hal 237
Kolping, Adolf 169
Kopp, Georg von 180-181
Korum, Michael Felix 177, 181
Kraus, Franz Xaver 176-178
Kuenen, Abraham 146
Kuenzer, Vincenz 167
Kuhn, Johannes Evangelist von 164, 170-171, 176
Kuyper, Abraham 139-142, 147-148, 152

Ladeuze, Paulin 120
Laestadius, Lars Levi 14-15, 266-267, 269
Langlois, Claude 170
Law, William 57
Leclerq, Jacques 114
Leo XIII 118, 120, 145, 148
Liddon, H.P. 91
Liebermann, Bruno Franz Leopold 165

Liefde, Jan de 151
Lightfoot, J.B. 87-91
Lippert, Peter 182
Livingstone, James C. 68
Löhe, Wilhelm 208
Lohmann, Theodor 206
Loisy, Alfred 176
Louth, Andrew 91
Ludwig I 170
Luther, Martin 174, 177
Lyttleton, Arthur 91

Macaulay, Zachary 39
Macdonald, John, 42
MacHale, John 74
Magee, William 41
Majendie, H.W. 33
Majunke, Paul 172
Malou, Jean-Baptiste 108
Mann, Horace 68
Manning, Henry Edward 74, 81, 87
Mansel, Henry 90
Mant, Richard 32
Maria Theresa 160
Marsh, P.T. 68
Martensen, Hans Lassen 240-241, 244-245
Maximilian Franz of Austria 159
McGrath, Alister 91
Mercier, Désiré 119-122
Merkle, Sebastian 177, 183
Meysenburg, Malwida von 194
Michelsen, Christian 274
Middleton, Thomas 52
Mill, John Stuart 245
Milner, John 47-48
Mivart, St. George Jackson 25, 94
Möhler, Johann Adam 165
Monk, J.H. 25
More, Hannah 39
Morgan, Robert 91
Mott, John 213
Moylan, Francis 48, 74
Mozley, J.B. 91
Mozley, Thomas 60
Muddiman, John 91
Mueller-Otfried, Paula 210
Muller, Max 90
Mumm, Susan 71

Munter, Frederik 243
Murray, Daniel 48, 74
Muth, Carl 177
Mynster, Jacob Peter 240-241, 243-244

Napoleon 102-104, 162
Naumann, Friedrich 205
Newman, John Henry 53, 55-56, 60-64, 81, 94
Nicholls, David 91
Nietzsche, Friedrich 245
Nörber, Thomas 180

O'Beirne, Thomas Lewis 32
O'Brien, James 41
Odland, Sigurd 274
Opzoomer, Cornelis Willem 146
Ording, Johannes 274
Ozanam, Antoine Frédéric 169

Pacelli, Eugenio 184
Paget, Francis 91
Paley, William 64-65
Pattison, Mark 55
Petersen, Fredrik 273-274
Phillipps de Lisle, Ambrose 80
Phillpotts, Henry 87
Pierson, Allard 143
Pius VII 103
Pius IX 74, 111, 113, 165, 168, 171
Pius X 146, 178, 181, 183
Pontoppidan, Erik 21, 261
Poppe, Edouard 118
Pottier, Antoine 117
Pusey, Edward Bouverie 53, 64-65, 91

Rade, Martin 204
Rahner, Karl 179
Raiffeisen, Friedrich Wilhelm 208
Rasmussen, Niels Arboe 245
Rautenstrauch, Franz Stephan 160
Reisach, Karl August von 168, 171
Renan, Ernest 146
Ritschl, Albrecht 92
Roe, Peter 41
Rønne, Bone Falck 233
Rosenblad, Matthias 248-249
Rowell, Geoffrey 91
Rowland, Daniel 37

Ryder, Henry 41

Sacconi, Carlo 168
Sage ten Broek, Joachim George le 135
Sailer, Johann Michael 24, 160, 164-165
Sanday, William 91
Sauer, Joseph 178
Scheibel, Johann Gottfried 192
Schell, Herman 25, 176-177
Scherr, Gregor von 171
Schiller, Friedrich von 177
Schleiermacher, Friedrich 23, 146-147, 186-187
Schmidlin, Joseph 178
Schnitzer, Joseph 177
Scholten, Joannes Henricus 139, 146-147
Schott, Anselm 183
Schrenk, Elias 211
Scott, Walter 56
Seabury, Samuel 51
Simeon, Charles, 39, 45
Sintenis, Wilhelm Franz 194
Smith, William Robertson 88, 92-93
Spahn, Martin 183
Spencer, George 80
Spiecker, Friedrich Albert 206
Spiegel, Ferdinand August von 164
Spinoza, Baruch 151
Stahl, Friedrich Julius 192
Stanley, A.P. 63
Stattler, Benedikt 160
Stenersen, Stener Johannes 262, 269
Stephen, James 39
Sterckx, Engelbert 105, 112
Stoecker, Adolf 174, 202, 205
Stolz, Alban 172
Støylen, Bernt 274
Strauss, David Friedrich 146,
Strindberg, August 245
Stuart, William 32
Stubs, William 66
Sulze, Emil 204
Sumner, Charles 41
Sumner, John Bird 41
Sundt, Eilert 271
Swedenborg, Emanuel 193
Sykes, Stephen 91

Tait, Archibald Campbell 90

Index

Talbot, E.S. 91
Taranger, Absalon 275-276
Teignmouth, Lord 39
Temple, Frederick 91
Thompson, David 88-89
Thornton, Henry 39
Thrane, Marcus 271-272
Tiele, Cornelis Petrus 143
Tillich, Paul 148
Tillmann, Fritz 178
Tits, Arnold 108
Trench, William 41
Triest, Petrus Jozef 104
Troy, John Thomas 48, 74
Tyrell, George 25, 94

Ubaghs, Gerard Casimir 108
Uhlich, Leberecht 194

Van Bommel, Cornelis 105
Van Hoonacker, Albin 120
Van Mildart, William 45
Vaughan, Bernard 74
Venn, John 39
Veralby, O. 123
Ver Huell, Alexander 123-124, 129
Victoria 78
Vig, Ole 271
Vinet, Alexandre 147
Visscher, Hugo 142

Wade, John 68
Wackernagel, Philipp 197
Waldenström, Paul Petter 15, 259
Warburton, William 64
Ward, Keith 91
Ward, W.G. 93
Warren, John 33
Weber, Friedrich Wilhelm 173
Weiss, Bernhard 206
Welsh, David 44, 82
Wergeland, Henrik 271
Werner, Gustav 192
Werthmann, Lorenz 180
Wesley, Charles 37-38
Wesley, John 15, 37-38
Wessenberg, Ignaz Heinrich von 21, 160-162
Westcott, B.F. 87-91

Wexels, Wilhelm Andreas 15, 271
Whitefield, George 37
Wichern, Johann Hinrich 15, 191-192, 197-198, 206-208, 270
Wieland, Franz 178
Wilberforce, William 15, 39-40, 87
Wiles, Maurice 91
Wilhelm I 200
Wilhelm II 174, 199, 205
Willem of Orange 151
Willem I 101, 131, 135
Willem II 135
Willerup, C. 242
Williams, Isaac 61
Williams, Rowan 91
Williams, Trevor 91
Wilson, Daniel 54
Windhorst, Ludwig 173
Wiseman, Nicholas 74-75, 79-80
Wislicenus, Gustav Adolf 194
Wolff, Christian 160
Wood, Charles 60
Wood, Samuel Francis 60
Wordsworth, William 56

Yorke, James 34

Zinzendorf, Nikolaus von 212, 233
Zöllner, Johann Friedrich 21
Zwijsen, Joannes 144

'Northern Europe' c.1870.
[Concerning the definition of 'Northern Europe':
see volume I, 7-10.]

Authors

Claus Arnold, professor of church history, Goethe-University Frankfurt/Main. Research interests: modernist crisis, ecclesiastical censure (sixteenth-twentieth centuries), Roman Curia, German Catholicism (nineteenth-twentieth centuries).

Jan Art, professor of modern history at Ghent University. Research interests: religious and cultural history (nineteenth century).

Jan De Maeyer, professor of church history at the K.U.Leuven and director of KADOC. Research interests: religion, culture and society in Belgium/Western Europe (nineteenth-twentieth centuries).

Ward De Pril, research fellow of the History of Church and Theology Research Unit (K.U. Leuven). Research interests: history of the Louvain Faculty of Theology, theological reform and renewal (c. 1900-1950).

Hallgeir Elstad, professor of Norwegian church history at the University of Oslo. Research interests: modern church history (nineteenth-twentieth centuries).

Joris van Eijnatten, professor of cultural history at Utrecht University. Research interests: religious history, history of ideas and history of media and communication in Europe in the (early) modern period.

Klaus Fitschen, professor of church history at the University of Leipzig. Research interests: history of Christianity (nineteenth-twentieth centuries).

Leo Kenis, professor in the history of church and theology at the K.U.Leuven. Research interests: history of church and theology (nineteenth-twentieth centuries).

Frances Knight, associate professor at the department of Theology and Religious Studies (University of Nottingham). Research interests: church history in nineteenth-century England and Wales, nineteenth-century Christianity in a European and global perspective.

Peter Nockles, librarian and curator of the Methodist Church Archives and Research Centre and research fellow in Religions & Theology (University of Manchester). Research interests: British religious history (eighteenth-nineteenth centuries).

Jes Fabricius Møller, professor of history at the SAXO-institute (University of Copenhagen). Research interests: Danish cultural history (nineteenth-twentieth centuries).

Øyvind Norderval, professor of church history at the University of Oslo. Research interests: church history, science and religion.

Erik Sidenvall, professor of church history at the University of Lund. Research interests: religious conversions, Christian missions and religion and social change in Sweden and Britain (nineteenth-twentieth centuries).

Dag Thorkildsen, professor of theology at the University of Oslo. Research interests: national and religious identity in Scandinavia, Norwegian Protestantism.

Nigel Yates, late professor of ecclesiastical history at the University of Wales, Lampeter. Research interests: church architecture and liturgical arrangements, Anglican ritualism, and church-state relations in Britain, Ireland and Europe in the post-Reformation period.

Paula Yates, lecturer in modern church history at the University of Wales Trinity St David (formerly University of Wales, Lampeter). Research interests: religion and politics, religion and education, interdenominational relations in Britain (eighteenth-nineteenth centuries).

Colophon

Final editing
Beatrice Van Eeghem (UPL)
Luc Vints (KADOC)

Copy editing
Lieve Claes (KADOC)

Lay-out
Alexis Vermeylen (KADOC)

Printing and binding
Lannoo Printers, Tielt (Belgium)

KADOC
Documentation and Research Centre for Religion, Culture and Society
Vlamingenstraat 39
B - 3000 Leuven
http://kadoc.kuleuven.be

Leuven University Press
Minderbroedersstraat 4
B - 3000 Leuven
http://upers.kuleuven.be